# THE ROMAN POETS

OF THE

# AUGUSTAN AGE

# THE ROMAN POETS

## OF THE

# AUGUSTAN AGE

## VIRGIL

BY

W. Y. SELLAR, M.A., LL.D. *William Young 1825-1890*

**THIRD** EDITION

BIBLO and TANNEN
NEW YORK
1965

First published 1908



Reprinted 1965, with the permission of
Oxford University Press by
Biblo and Tannen Booksellers and Publishers, Inc.
63 Fourth Avenue          New York, N.Y. 10003

Library of Congress Catalog Card Number: 65-23489

*Printed in U.S.A. by*
NOBLE OFFSET PRINTERS, INC.
NEW YORK 3, N. Y.

TO

# E. L. LUSHINGTON, Esq., D.C.L., LL.D., etc.,

### LATE PROFESSOR OF GREEK IN THE UNIVERSITY OF GLASGOW.

My dear Lushington,

Any old pupil of yours, in finishing a work either of classical scholarship or illustrative of ancient literature, must feel that he owes to you, probably more than to any one else, the impulse which directed him to these studies. It is with this feeling that I should wish to associate your name with this volume. Many of your former pupils can confirm my recollection that one of the happiest influences of our youth was the admiration excited by the union, in your teaching, of perfect scholarship with a true and generous appreciation of all that is excellent in literature. The intimate friendship of many subsequent years has afforded me, along with much else of still higher value, ample opportunities for verifying these early impressions.

Ever affectionately yours,

W. Y. SELLAR.

# PREFACE TO THE FIRST EDITION

---

This volume has been written in continuation of one which appeared some years ago on the Roman Poets of the Republic. I hope in a short time to bring out a new edition of that work, enlarged and corrected, and afterwards to add another volume which will treat of Horace and the Elegiac Poets. I have reserved for this later volume the examination of the minor poems which have been attributed to Virgil, most of which belong to the Augustan Age.

Besides the special acknowledgments of ideas or information derived from various sources, which are made in notes at the foot of the page where an occasion for them arises, I have to make a general acknowledgment of the assistance I have received in my studies of the Augustan literature from the earlier volumes of Dr. Merivale's 'History of the Romans under the Empire,' from the 'History of Roman Literature' by W. S. Teuffel, from M. Sainte-Beuve's 'Étude sur Virgile,' and from the Introductions and Notes to Professor Conington's edition of Virgil, and Mr. Munro's edition of Lucretius. In the account given of the Alexandrian literature in Chapter I, I have availed myself of the chapters treating of that subject in Helbig's 'Campanische Wandmalerei'; in treating of the estimation in which Virgil was held under the Roman Empire, I have taken several references from the work by Sr. Comparetti, 'Virgilio nel Medio Evo'; and in examining the order in which the Eclogues were composed, I have adopted the opinions expressed in Ribbeck's Prolegomena. I have also derived some suggestions from the notes in the edition of Virgil by M. E. Benoist, and from the work of M. G. Boissier, 'La Religion Romaine d'Auguste aux Antonins.' As the greater part of this volume was written before the appearance of Dr. Kennedy's Virgil, I have not been able to make so much use of his notes as I should have wished: I have, however, profited by them to correct or to illustrate statements made before I had seen his work, and, in revising the Virgilian quotations for the press, I have followed his text.

I did not read Mr. Nettleship's valuable and original 'Suggestions Introductory to the Study of the Aeneid' until I had finished writing all I had to say about that poem. I have drawn attention in the text or in notes at the foot of the page to some places in which I modified what I had originally written after reading his 'Suggestions,' to others in which my own opinions are confirmed by his, and to one or two points of divergence in our views.

Since the third chapter was printed off, I have received what seems a confirmation of the opinion expressed there as to the probable situation of Virgil's early home, from a friend who recently visited the district, where I suppose it to have been. He writes of the country which he passed through—'The result of my observations perfectly confirms what you had already supposed. The country south of the Lago di Garda for a distance of at least twenty miles is of a gently undulating character, and is intersected by long ranges of hills which gradually sink down towards the lake and the Mincio. The loftiest of these hills may perhaps reach a height of 1000 feet above the lake-level, but that is a point on which I cannot say anything certain.'

EDINBURGH, *Nov.* 1876.

# PREFACE TO THE SECOND EDITION

———

The only material change which I have made in this edition is that I have added translations of the passages quoted, for the convenience of any readers, who, without much knowledge of Latin, may yet wish to learn something about Latin literature. In the translations from Virgil, I have sometimes made use of expressions which I found in Conington's prose Translation and in Mr. Papillon's recently published edition of Virgil. I have also availed myself of Sir Theodore Martin's Translation of the Odes of Horace. In correcting or supplementing some statements made in the first edition, I have occasionally profited by remarks made in criticisms on that edition which appeared shortly after its publication.

EDINBURGH, *March*, 1883.

# CONTENTS

## CHAPTER I.

### GENERAL INTRODUCTION.

## CHAPTER II.

### VIRGIL'S PLACE IN ROMAN LITERATURE.

# CONTENTS

# CHAPTER III.

## LIFE AND PERSONAL CHARACTERISTICS OF VIRGIL.

# CONTENTS

# CHAPTER IV.

## THE ECLOGUES.

# CONTENTS

## CHAPTER V.

### MOTIVES, FORM, SUBSTANCE, AND SOURCES OF THE GEORGICS.

# CONTENTS

## CHAPTER VI.

### STRUCTURE AND COMPOSITION OF THE POEM IN RELATION TO THE POEM OF LUCRETIUS.

# CONTENTS

## CHAPTER VII.

### THE GEORGICS A POEM REPRESENTATIVE OF ITALY 261-279

## CHAPTER VIII.

### THE ROMAN EPIC BEFORE THE TIME OF VIRGIL . 280-294

## CHAPTER IX.

### FORM AND SUBJECT OF THE AENEID.

# CONTENTS

## CHAPTER X.

### THE AENEID AS THE EPIC OF THE ROMAN EMPIRE.

## CHAPTER XI.

### THE AENEID AS AN EPIC POEM OF HUMAN LIFE.

# CONTENTS

# THE ROMAN POETS OF THE
# AUGUSTAN AGE

——◆——

## CHAPTER I.

### GENERAL INTRODUCTION.

### I.

THE Augustan Age, regarded as a critical epoch in the history of the world, extends from the date of the battle of Actium, when Octavianus became undisputed master of the world, to his death in the year 14 A.D. But the age known by that name as a great epoch in the history of literature begins some years earlier, and ends with the death of Livy and Ovid in the third year of the following reign. Of the poets belonging to that age whose writings have reached modern times—Virgil, Horace, Tibullus, Propertius, and Ovid—all were born, and some had reached manhood, before the final overthrow of the Republic at the battle of Philippi. The earlier poems of Virgil and Horace belong to the period between that date and the establishment of the Empire. The age of the Augustan poets may accordingly be regarded as extending from about the death of Julius Caesar in 44 B.C. to the death of Ovid 17 A.D.

The whole of this period was one of great literary activity, especially in the department of poetry. Besides the writers just mentioned, several others were recognised by their contemporaries as poets of high excellence, though there is no reason to doubt that the works which have reached our time were the

most distinguished by original genius and finished execution.
These works, though differing much in spirit and character as
well as in value, have some common characteristics which mark
them off from the literature of the Republic.  It seems remarkable, if we consider the short interval which divides the Ciceronian from the Augustan Age, and the enthusiasm with which
poetry was cultivated by the younger generation in the years
immediately preceding the battle of Pharsalia, that so few of the
poets eminent in that generation lived on into the new era.  The
insignificant name of Helvius Cinna is almost the only poetic
link between the age of Catullus and the age of Virgil [1].  Perhaps, also, the Quintilius whose death Horace laments in the
twenty-fourth Ode of Book I. may be the Varus of the tenth poem
of Catullus.  The more famous name of Asinius Pollio also
connects the two eras; but in Catullus he is spoken of, not as
a poet, but simply as 'a youth of wit and graceful accomplishments [2],' and in his later career he was more distinguished as a
soldier, statesman, and orator than as a poet [3].  It is remarked
by Mr. Munro that there are indications that the new generation
of poets would have come into painful collision with those of
the preceding generation had their lives been prolonged [4].  This
spirit of hostility appears in the somewhat contemptuous notice
of Calvus and Catullus in the Satires of Horace :—

Quos neque pulcher
Hermogenes unquam legit, neque simius iste
Nil praeter Calvum et doctus cantare Catullum [5]

But it is rather in their political feelings and relations, and in
the views of life arising out of these, than in the principles and
practice of their art, that the new poets are separated from, and

---

[1] Eclog. ix. 35.

[2]      'Leporum
Disertus puer ac facetiarum.'  Catullus xii. 8.

[3] The name of Trebatius also, though one associated with law rather
than literature, may be added as a connecting link between the friends of
Cicero and of Horace.

[4] Munro's Lucretius, Introduction to Notes, ii. page 305.

[5] 'These writers your fine Hermogenes never reads, nor that ape, whose
whole art is to repeat the songs of Calvus and Catullus.'  Hor. Sat. i. 10.
17–19.

antagonistic to, the old.   Had Calvus and Catullus survived the
extinction of liberty, it would have been impossible for them to
have adopted the tone of the poets of the following age.   By
birth, position, and all their associations and sympathies, they
belonged to the Senatorian party.   If they could have yielded
an outward submission to the ascendency of Julius Caesar and
Augustus, they never could have become sincerely reconciled to
the new order of things, nor could they have employed their
art to promote the ideas of the Empire.   On the other hand,
L. Varius, the oldest among the poets of the new era, seems
first to have become famous by a poem on the death of Julius
Caesar.   Virgil, in the poem placed first in order among his
acknowledged works, speaks of Octavianus in language which no
poet of the preceding generation could have applied to a living
contemporary: 'O Meliboeus, it was a God that gave to me
this life of ease.'   In the Georgics, planned, and, for the
most part, composed before the establishment of the monarchy,
the person of Caesar is introduced, not only as the centre of
power in the world, but as an object of religious veneration;
and the national and ethical teaching of that poem is entirely in
harmony with the objects of his policy.   And, although Horace
in the Satires and Epodes, composed between the years 40 and
30 B.C., is so far true to the cause of his youth as to abstain
from any direct declaration of adherence to the winning side,
yet he attributes to his adviser Trebatius the counsel 'to celebrate the exploits of the invincible Caesar[1];'   and his whole
relation to Maecenas is one of the most characteristic marks of
the position in which the new literature stood to the State and
to its leading men.

Yet, while separated from the literature of the Republic in
many of its ideas, and in the personal and political feelings on
which it is founded, the poetry of the Augustan Age is, in form
and execution, the mature development of the efforts of the
previous centuries.   Much of its literary inspiration is derived
from the age immediately preceding it, and from still older

---

[1] Hor. Sat. ii. 1. 11.

native sources. The thought of Lucretius acted upon the mind of Virgil through the force both of sympathy and antagonism, as a strong original nature acts upon one which is at once receptive of influence and possessed of firm convictions of its own. The national sentiment of Ennius and the censorious spirit of Lucilius reappeared in new forms in the Augustan poetry; while the more humane and social feelings, and the enjoyment of beauty in Nature and art, fostered by Greek studies, as well as the taste for less elevated pleasures, stimulated by the life of a luxurious capital, are elements which the poetry of the early Empire has in common with that of the last years of the Republic.

But the poetry of the new era has also certain marked characteristics, the result not so much of antecedent as of concomitant circumstances, which proclaim its affinity with great literary epochs of other nations rather than with any period of the national literature. By Voltaire the Augustan Age at Rome is ranked with the Age of Pericles at Athens, that of Lorenzo de Medici at Florence, and that of Louis XIV. in France, as one of four epochs in which arts and letters attained their highest perfection. The affinity between the Augustan Age and those of Pericles and Lorenzo is more superficial than real. They were all indeed periods in which the cultivation of the arts to the highest degree of perfection was fostered by the enlightened patronage of the eminent men who have given their name to their eras. But the position of Augustus, as an absolute ruler, acted more directly and potently, as a modifying and restraining power, on the thoughts and feelings expressed in his age, than that of the leading men of a republic; and the unique position of Rome as the mistress and lawgiver of the civilised world gives to the literature of the Augustan Age an imperial character and interest, which the national literature of no other city or country, even though superior in other respects, can possess. Those who regard all Latin poetry as exotic and imitative have, with some plausi-bility, attempted to establish a parallel between the Alexandrine

poetry of the third century B.C. and that of the Augustan Age.
Nor can it be denied that the relation of the Augustan poets
to the Emperor was somewhat parallel to that of the scholars
and poets of Alexandria to the Ptolemies.  The Alexandrine
science and literature were also important factors in Roman
culture; and the most eminent poets both of the Augustan Age
and of that immediately preceding it, with the exception of
Horace and Lucretius, acknowledged, in the form as well as
the materials of their art, the influence of this latest development of Greek poetry.  The nature and amount of the debt
incurred to the learned school of Alexandria will be considered
later, and it will be seen that it does not seriously affect the
originality of the best Roman writers.  The age of Queen
Anne and of the first George, again, has been called the
Augustan Age of English literature.  The parallel between the
two eras consists in the relation which poets and writers held
to men eminent in the State, and also in the finished execution
and moderation of tone common to both.  The writers of
England in our Augustan Age had the advantage over those
of Rome in the freedom with which they could express their
thoughts; but, even with this advantage, and with the still
greater advantage that the English race, in the long course of
its literary annals, has given proof of a richer poetical faculty
than any other race except the Hellenic, the blindest national
partiality would scarcely claim as general and as durable an
interest for any poetical work of that era as that claimed for
the Georgics and Aeneid of Virgil and for the Odes and
Epistles of Horace.

On the whole the closest parallel, in respect not so much of
the substance and form of composition as of the circumstances
and conditions affecting the lives and tastes of poets and men
of letters, is to be sought in the age of Louis XIV. of France.
The position and the policy of Augustus and of Louis XIV.
were alike in some important features.  As absolute rulers, the
one over a great empire, the other over the most powerful and
enlightened nation then existing, they each played the most

prominent part in history during more than half a century. They were each animated by a strong passion for national and personal glory, and encouraged art and literature, not merely as a source of refined pleasure congenial to their own tastes, but as the chief ornament of their reigns, and as important instruments of their policy.

And not only the political but the purely literary conditions of the two epochs were in some respects parallel. They were both times, not of growth, but of maturity; not so much of the spontaneous inspiration of genius, as of systematic effort directed in accordance with the principles of art and the careful study of ancient models. In each time circumstances and mutual sympathies brought men of letters into close and familiar contact both with one another and with men of affairs and of social eminence. And, while the relation of patronage to literature is not in any circumstances favourable to original invention, and though, except under most advantageous conditions, its tendency is to produce a tameness of spirit, or even an insincerity of tone, yet it has its compensating advantages. It imparts to literature the tone of the world—of the world not only of social eminence, but of practical experience and conversance with great affairs. The good taste, judgment, and moderation of tone which have enabled the Augustan literature to stand successfully the criticism of nineteen centuries, as well as its deficiency in the highest creative power, when compared with such eras as the Homeric Age, the Age of Pericles, and the Elizabethan Age in England, mark the limits of the good influence which this relation between the great in worldly station and the great in genius can exercise on literature.

A further parallel might be drawn between the material conditions of the Augustan Age and those of the Age of Louis XIV. The aspect which the world they lived in presented to the writers of the two eras was that of a rich, luxurious, pleasure-loving city, the capital of a great empire or kingdom. And this aspect of the world acts upon the susceptible nature of the poet with both an attractive and a repellent force. He may feel the spell of outward pomp and magnificence and the attractions of pleasure; or he may be driven back on his own thought, and into communion with Nature, and to an ideal longing for simpler and purer conditions.

But, instead of tracing these resemblances further, it is more important to observe that, though the outward influences acting upon the poets of the two eras were in many respects parallel, yet in form and substance the poetry of the Augustan Age is quite different from that of the Age of Louis XIV. However striking the parallel between any two periods of history may at first sight appear, the points of difference between them must be much more numerous than those of agreement: and, though outward conditions have a modifying influence upon national temperament and individual genius, yet these last are much the most important factors in the creative literature of any age. The genius of ancient Italy was, in point of imaginative susceptibility, very different from that of modern France; and, though his countrymen recognise in Racine a moral affinity with Virgil, yet the works these poets have left to the world are as different as they well can be, in form, purpose, and character. The conditions indicated in the comparison between the two periods are to be studied as modifying, not as productive, influences. The forms which the highest spiritual life in an age or an individual assumes, the power of free and happy development which it obtains, or the limitations to which it has to submit, can, to a very considerable extent, be explained by reference, in the case of nations, to the political, social, and material circumstances of the age, and, in the case of the individual, to his early life and environment, his education and personal fortunes. But the quality and intensity of that spiritual force which manifests itself from time to time in the world, giving a new impulse to thought, a new direction to feeling, and a new delight to life, are not to be explained by any combination of circumstances. Yet, just as it is desirable to realise all that can be known of the life and fortunes of an individual poet before endeavouring to extract from his various works the secret of his power and charm, so it is desirable, before entering on a separate study of the various books which constitute the literature of any age, to take a general survey of the most important conditions affecting the lives, thoughts, and art of all who lived and wrote in that age. In the Augustan Age these conditions may be classified under four heads: (1) the political circumstances of the Empire and the state of moral and religious feeling resulting from them; (2) the social relation of men of letters to men eminent in the State; (3) the wealth, luxury, and outward splendour which met the eye and gratified the senses, in the great city itself, and in the villas scattered over the shores and inland scenes of central Italy; (4) the intellectual culture inherited from the preceding age and modified by the tastes and conditions of the new generation. These will be reviewed as conditions acting on the imagination, and forming the intellectual atmosphere in the midst of which the productions of poetical genius expanded into various shapes and dimensions of beauty and stateliness.

## II.

The battle of Actium marked the end of a century of revolution, civil disturbances and wars, of confiscations of property, proscriptions and massacres, such as no civilised state had ever witnessed before. The triumph of Augustus secured internal peace and order for a century. The whole world was, as Tacitus says[1], exhausted, and gladly consented to the establishment of the Empire in the interests of peace. The generation to which Virgil, Horace, Tibullus, and Propertius belonged had passed through one of the worst crises of this long period of suffering. The victors of Philippi, so far from following the example of clemency set to them by the great victor of Pharsalia, had emulated the worst excesses of the times of Marius and Sulla[2]. The poets whose works record the various

---

[1] Ann. i. 1; Hist. i. 1.
[2] Cf. Juv. ii. 28: In tabulam Sullae si dicant discipuli tres.

phases of feeling through which that age passed had in their
own person experienced the consequences of the general
insecurity.  Virgil, in addition to the loss of his paternal farm,
had incurred imminent danger from the violence of the soldier
to whom his land had been allotted.  The language of Horace
indicates that his life had been more than once in jeopardy—
at the rout of Philippi, and in his subsequent wanderings by
land and sea [1]—till he found himself a needy adventurer, 'hu-
milem decisis pennis,' again at Rome.  Tibullus lost the
greater part of the estates which his ancestors had enjoyed for
generations [2].  A similar calamity befell Propertius [3].  Their own
experience must thus have deepened the horror of prolonged
war and bloodshed natural to men of humane and unwarlike
temper, as they all were; for Horace, who alone among them
took part in the civil war, describes himself, a few years later,
as 'weak and unfit for war [4],' and Tibullus pleads his effeminacy and timidity as a justification of a life devoted to indolent
enjoyment [5].  The works of that age, composed between the
dates of the battles of Philippi and Actium, express the deep
longing of the world for rest: those written later express the
deep thankfulness for its attainment.  In Virgil the recoil from
the cruel and violent passions of the time in which his early
manhood was cast draws forth his tender compassion for all
human suffering, and creates in his imagination the ideal of
a life of peace—'far from the clash of arms,' the vision of a
place of rest after toil and danger—'where the fates hold out
to us peaceful dwelling-places;' just as the recoil from the
political anarchy of his own age and from the cruel memories
of the Marian times deepens the sense of human misery in
Lucretius, and forces on his mind the ideal refuge from the

[1] Od. iii. 4. 28.
[2] Cf. Eleg. i. 41–42:—
> Non ego divitias patrum fructusque requiro
> Quos tulit antiquo condita messis avo.
[3] Cf. v. 1. 129–130:—
> Nam tua cum multi versarent rura iuvenci
> Abstulit excultas pertica tristis opes.
[4] 'Imbellis et firmus parum.'  Ep. i. 16.          [5] Eleg. i. 1; i. 10.

storms of life in 'the high and serene temples well bulwarked
by the learning of the wise.'   In Horace the feeling of insecurity arising out of his early experience confirms the lessons
of Epicurean wisdom, and teaches him not to expect too much
from life, but to enjoy thankfully whatever good the passing
hour brought to him.   In all of them the sense of the real
miseries from which the world had escaped, and of the real
blessings which it enjoyed after the battle of Actium, induces
an acquiescence in the extinction of liberty and in the establishment of a form of government which had been for centuries most repugnant to Roman sentiment.

Another influence reconciling men to the great political
change which took place in that era was the restored sense of
national union.   With whatever feelings Octavianus may have
been regarded in the early years of the Triumvirate, after the
final departure of Antony from Rome he was looked upon both
as the main pillar of order and as the champion of the national
cause, the true representative of Italy, of the 'Senatus Popu-
lusque Romanus' against the motley hosts of the East, arrayed
under the standards of Antony and his Egyptian queen :—

> Hinc Augustus agens Italos in proelia Caesar
> Cum Patribus Populoque, Penatibus et magnis Dis.
> \*       \*       \*       \*       \*       \*
> Hinc ope barbarica variisque Antonius armis,
> Victor ab Aurorae populis et litore rubro,
> Aegyptum viresque Orientis et ultima secum
> Bactra vehit, sequiturque, nefas, Aegyptia coniunx [1].

With the Romans in the later age of the Republic the
feeling of the glory and greatness, the ancient and unbroken
tradition, of their State was a more active sentiment than the
love of political liberty.   The care for the 'Respublica Romana'

---

[1] 'On the one side Augustus leading the Italians into battle with the
Senate and people, the Penates and the great Gods—on the other Antonius
with a barbaric and motley host, advancing in triumph from the peoples of the
dawn and the shore of the Red Sea, bears with him Egypt, and the might of
the East, and furthest Bactria, and following in his train,—sin accursed!
—an Egyptian bride.'   Aen. viii. 678 *et seq.*

as a free commonwealth was in the last century of its existence
confined to the leaders of the Senatorian aristocracy; the pride
in the 'Imperium Romanum' was a feeling in which all classes
could share, and which could especially unite to Rome the
people of Italy, who had been admitted too late into citizenship,
and were separated by too great a distance from the capital, to
make the exercise of the political franchise an object of value in
their eyes. They probably felt themselves more truly in the
position of equal citizenship after the establishment of the
monarchy than before it. This feeling of the pride of empire
asserts itself much more strongly in the poets of the Augustan
Age than in the writers of the preceding generation. It is
scarcely, if at all, apparent in Lucretius and Catullus. It is
only in the idealising oratory of Cicero, who, with all his
devoted attachment to the forms of the constitution and the
traditions of political freedom, still had a strong sympathy with
the imperial spirit of Rome, that we find the expression of the
same kind of sentiment which suggested to Virgil such lines as

> Tu regere imperio populos, Romane, memento[1],

and inspired the national Odes of Horace.

The majesty of the State, moreover, impressed the imagination more immediately and more deeply when it was visibly and
permanently embodied in a single person than when the
administration of affairs and the government of the Provinces
were distributed for a brief tenure of office among many competitors. By enabling them to realise the unity and vast extent
of their dominion, Augustus reconciled the prouder spirits of
his countrymen to his rule, as by restoring peace, order, and
material prosperity he enlisted their interests in his favour. At
the same time the success of his arms over the still unsubdued
tribes of the West, and of his diplomacy in wiping out the
stain left on the Roman standards by the disastrous campaign
of Crassus, continued to gratify the passion for military glory,
without endangering the security and prosperity of Italy.

---

[1] 'Be it thine, O Roman, to govern the nations with thy imperial rule.'

The national sentiment of Rome was further gratified by the maintenance of the old forms of the constitution, by the revival of ancient usages and ceremonies, and by the creation of a new interest in the early traditions of the city, and in the 'manners and men of the olden time[1].' In his brief summary of the glories of the Augustan Age, Horace specifies this return to the ancient ways, 'by which the Latin name and the might of Italy grew great,' as one of the best results of Caesar's administration. The revolution effected in the first century before our era, so far from seeking, as other revolutions have done, abruptly to sever the connexion between the old and the new, strove to re-establish the continuity of national existence. The Augustan Age impressed itself on the minds of those living under it as an era not of destruction but of restoration. Though in the early part of his career Augustus availed himself of the revolutionary passions of his time to overthrow the Senatorian oligarchy, yet he sought to establish his own power on the conservative instincts of society, and especially on the religious traditions intimately connected with these instincts[2]. The powerful hold which these instincts and the feeling of the vital relation subsisting between the past and the present had on the Roman nature was the secret of the great stability of the Republic and Empire. We shall find how largely this sentiment enters into the poetry of the age, how it is especially the animating principle of the great national Epic, as it was of the national commemorative poem of Ennius.

But the age witnessed a restoration of the past, not only in its action on the imagination, but in a more direct influence on opinion and conduct. Horace says of it, in the same passage as that referred to above,—'It put a curb on licence violating all the rules of order, and caused ancient sins to disappear.' The licence of the previous age in speculation, as

---

[1] 'Moribus antiquis stat res Romana virisque.' Ennius.

[2] In the Ancyraean inscription we find the following passage (Bergk's reading): 'Legibus novis latis multa revocavi exempla maiorum exolescentia iam ex nostra civitate,' etc.

in life, had provoked a moral and religious reaction. The idea
of a return to a simpler and better life, and of a revived faith
in the gods and in the forms and ceremonies of religion,
existed at least as an aspiration, if it did not bear much fruit in
action. This ideal aspiration finds its expression not only in
the two great poems of Virgil, whose whole nature was in
thorough harmony with it, who may be regarded almost as the
prophet of a new and purer religion, but in many of the Odes
of the sceptical disciple of Aristippus. It was part of the policy
of Augustus, whether from sincere conviction or as an instrument of social and political regeneration, to revive religion
and morality. Among the great acts of his reign commemorated by himself he especially mentions the building and
restoration of the temples[1]. The ' Julian laws' aimed also
at a social and moral restoration. There is no ground for
attributing any hypocrisy to Augustus, as a legislator, or to
Horace, as his panegyrist, though neither the life of the
Emperor nor that of the poet showed a strict conformity with
the object of these laws. Yet, if it failed to re-establish the
ancient faith in the minds of the educated classes and to restore
a primitive austerity of life, this revival affected the best literature of the time by the influence which it exercised on the
deeper and more serious feeling of Virgil and the manlier
sympathies of Horace, and by imposing at least some restraint
on Tibullus, Propertius, and Ovid in the record of their
pleasures[2].

---

[1] Cf. Ancyraean inscription: 'Templum Apollinis in Palatio cum
porticibus, aedem Divi Iulii, Lupercal,' etc. (where we notice the
recognition of the divinity of Julius Caesar, along with the old Olympian
and national gods, Apollo, Jupiter Tonans and Feretrius, Quirinus,
the Lares and Penates, and with the deified abstractions Libertas and
Juventas).

[2] A similar influence is attributed by M. Sainte-Beuve to Louis XIV.
After speaking of the freedom and licence of French literature under the
patronage of Fouquet, he adds, ' Le jeune roi vint, et il amena, il suscita
avec lui sa jeune littérature; il mit le correctif à l'ancienne, et, sauf des
infractions brillantes, il imprima à l'ensemble des productions de son temps
un caractère de solidité, et finalement de moralité, qui est aussi celui qui
règne dans ses propres écrits, et dans l'habitude de sa pensée.'

The poets with whom our enquiry is concerned, and especially the two most illustrious of their number, thoroughly represent, as they helped to call forth, the spirit in which the Roman world passed through the great change from the Republic to the Empire. They give expression to the weariness and longing for rest, to the revival of Roman and Italian feeling, to the pride of empire, the charm of ancient memories and associations, the aspiration after a better life and a firmer faith. But, further, the expression of these feelings is made subordinate to the personal glory of Augustus, who stands out as the central and commanding figure in all their representations. He is celebrated as the restorer of the golden Saturnian age[1]; the closer of the gateway of Janus[2]; the leader of the men and the gods of Italy against the swarms of the East and her monstrous divinities[3]; the 'father of his country[4];' the ruler destined to extend the empire, on which ' the sun never set,' ' beyond the Garamantians and Indians[5];' the descendant and true representative of the mythical author of the Roman State[6]; the man in whom the great destiny of Rome and the great labours of all her sons were summed up and fulfilled[7]; the conqueror who raised three hundred shrines to the gods of Italy[8]; the legislator who by his life and his laws had reformed the corrupt manners of the State[9]. The sense of gratitude for the rest and prosperity enjoyed under Augustus, the admiration for the real power of intellect and character which made him the most successful ruler that the world has ever seen, the confidence in the unbroken good fortune which marked all his earlier career, may account, without the necessity of attributing any unworthy motive, for the eulogies bestowed upon him as a ruler and organiser of empire. But the language of admiration goes beyond these into a region in which modern sympathies can

---

[1] Aen. vi. 795.
[2] Hor. Od. iv. 15. 9.
[3] Aen. viii. 678 *et seq.*
[4] Hor. Od. i. 2. 50.
[5] Aen. i. 287; vi. 796; Hor. Od. iv. 15. 15.
[6] Aen. i. 288.
[7] Georg. ii. 170.
[8] Aen. viii. 716.
[9] Hor. Od. iv. 5. 20; Ep. ii. 1. 2.

with difficulty follow it.   Modern criticism may partially explain, but it cannot enable us to enter with sympathy into that peculiar phase of the latter days of Paganism which first appears in the literature and the historical monuments of the Augustan Age as the Deification of the Emperors.   In the pages of Tacitus the worship of the Emperor appears as an established ' cultus,' as the symbol and the instrument of Roman domination over foreign nations [1].   The cities of Spain vie with the cities of the Asiatic Greeks in their desire to raise temples in honour of the living Emperor.   Tacitus seems to regard it as even something discreditable in Tiberius that he disclaims divine attributes [2]. The origin of this ' cultus,' as it first established itself in the Greek cities of Asia, may be referred to a survival of the old Greek hero-worship, which led even in the Republican times to the offering of divine honours to Roman Proconsuls and to the excess of the monarchical sentiment among Asiatics, which had led to the worship of the successors of Alexander, and had prompted Alexander himself to claim a divine origin.   This foreign vein of feeling united with a native vein,—the strong Roman faith in a secret invisible power watching over the destiny of the State, and revered as ' Fortuna Urbis.'   This secret invisible divinity became as it were incarnate in the person of the supreme ruler of the world, wielding the whole power, representing the whole majesty of Rome.

The feeling with which the contemporary poets attribute to Augustus a divine function in the world, and anticipate for him a place and high office among the gods after death, is something different from this literal adoration of a living man as invested with the full power and attributes of Deity.   But it is difficult to find any rational explanation of the tone adopted by them in such passages as Georg. i. 24–42, or Horace, Ode iii. 3. 11–12. There is, however, a striking coincidence in the manner in which Virgil and Horace suggest the blending of the mortal

[1] ' Ad hoc templum divo Claudio constitutum quasi arx aeternae domi-nationis aspiciebatur.' Tac. Ann. xiv. 31.
[2] Tac. Ann. iv. 38.

with the immortal, which seems to imply a common source of
inspiration.   Horace asserts the divinity of Augustus by claiming for him qualities and services equal to, or greater than,
those which raised Castor, Pollux, Hercules, Bacchus, and
Romulus to the dwelling-place of the gods [1].   Virgil, in one of
the cardinal passages of the Aeneid, in which the action is
projected into his own age, claims, for the restorer of order
then, a vaster range of beneficent influence than that over
which the civilising labours and conquests of Bacchus and
Hercules had extended [2].   In another passage Horace speaks
of the Roman as worshipping the ' numen' of Caesar along
with the Lares, 'even as Greece keeps Castor and mighty
Hercules in memory [3].'   In all these passages the idea implied
is that, as great services to the human race have in other times
raised mortals from earth to heaven, so it shall be with Augustus
after the beneficent labours of his life are over [4].   Probably
the earliest suggestion of the idea in its manifestation at Rome
came from the consecration of Julius Caesar after his death.
The ' Iulium Sidus'—'the star beneath which the harvest-
fields should be glad with corn'—is appealed to both by
Virgil and Horace as a witness of the mortal become immortal.
As the office of the deified Julius is to answer the prayers of
the husbandman, such too will be the office of Augustus; and
it is in this relation that he is invoked in the first Georgic
among the deities whose function it is to watch over the fields.
Both poets recall also the divine origin of the Emperor,—
' Augustus Caesar, of the race of heaven,'—as the descendant
of Venus.   Both too dwell on the especial protection of which
he was the object.   The divine care which had watched over
Rome from its origin was now centred on him as the supreme
head of the State, the heir and adopted son of the great Julius.

---

[1] Od. iii. 3. 9, etc. ; Ep. ii. 1. 5.
[2] Aen. vi. 801.                                    [3] Od. iv. 5.
[4] These comparisons may be more naturally referred to Roman ' Euhemerism,' than to the survival of the spirit of hero-worship, which, although
still active in Greece, was a mode of feeling alien to the Roman
imagination.

But, although we cannot ascribe to Virgil and Horace the ignorant superstition which raised temples to the living Emperor in the cities of Asia and in the various provinces of the Empire, it is difficult to extract from their language any germ of sincere conviction. And yet to condemn them of a base servility and hypocrisy would be to judge them altogether from a modern point of view. At such a time as the Augustan Age the minds of men were very variously affected by the different modes of religious belief, national and foreign, philosophical and artistic, which had been inherited from the past[1]. It must have been difficult for any one to be altogether unmoved by the innumerable symbols of religion visible around him, suggestive of a constant and immediate action of a supernatural power on all human, and especially all national, concerns : and it must have been equally difficult for any one trained in Greek philosophy to accept literally the incongruous fables of mythology, or to attach a definite personality to the imaginary beings of which it was composed. Horace and Virgil appear to stand at opposite extremes of incredulity and faith. Horace, in his Odes, accepts the beings of the Greek mythology as materials for his art, while, by his silence on the subject in his Satires and Epistles, he clearly implies that this acceptance formed no part of his real convictions. To Virgil, on the other hand, the gods of mythology appear to have a real existence, as manifestations of the divine energy, revealed in the religious traditions which connect the actual world of experience with a supernatural origin. So too Horace, in his Odes, treats the blending of the divine with the human elements in Augustus artistically or symbolically—represents him as drinking nectar between Pollux and Hercules, or as inspired with wisdom by the Muses in a Pierian cave—in much the same spirit as the great painters of the Renaissance introduced in their pictures living popes or patrons of art into the company of the most sacred personages. Virgil, to whose mind, in all things affecting either the State or the individual, the invisible world of faith

[1] Cp. infra, chap. vi.

appears very near the actual world of experience, seems sincerely to believe in the delegation of supernatural power and
authority on the Emperor, and in the favour of Heaven watching
over him. The divine energy diffused through all living things
might appear to be united with the human elements in Augustus
as it was in no other man, so that while still on earth he might
be thought of, if not as a 'praesens divus,' yet as acting
'praesenti numine,' as the representative and vicegerent of
omnipotence [1].

Some further light is thrown on this subject by considering
the manifestation of this same spirit in other forms of the art
of that age. The famous statue of the Emperor, found recently in the ruins of a villa of the Empress Livia, and at present seen among the statues of the *Braccio Nuovo* in the
Vatican, has been critically examined by an eminent German
scholar, as furnishing the best commentary on the language
of the Augustan poets. In this statue the Emperor appears
as blending the attributes of a Roman imperator with those
of a Greek hero or demigod [2]. Beside him a Cupid, symbolical
of the Julian descent from Venus, appears riding on a dolphin.
The breast-plate represents, among other protecting deities,
those whom Horace addresses in the Carmen Saeculare, Phoebus and Diana, and the Sun and Earth-goddess. In the centre
there is a figure of Mars attended by the wolf, receiving back
the standards from the Parthian; on either side are seen two
figures, representative of races recently conquered, probably the
Celtiberians and the tribes of the Alps. From the coincidence
of its symbolism it may be inferred that the statue was produced at the same time as the Carmen Saeculare was composed. Its object is to impress on the minds of men the image

---

[1] The belief in the divinity of the genius attending on each individual,
and also the custom of raising altars to some abstract quality in an individual, such as the 'Clemency of Caesar,' help also to explain this
supposed union of the god and man in the person of the Emperor. The
language of Virgil in Eclogue IV. also throws light on the ideas possible
as to the union of the divine with human nature.

[2] This is indicated by the bare feet.

of Augustus as at once a great earthly conqueror and a being
of divine descent and possessed of more than mortal attributes:
the especial object of care to the supreme God of Heaven; to
Apollo, whom, since the victory of Actium, he claimed as his
tutelary divinity; to the Earth-goddess, the giver of fruitfulness
and prosperity; to Mars, the second divine ancestor of the
Roman race, in whose honour the famous temple, of which the
ruins are yet visible, had been raised after the battle of Philippi.
The statue is of Greek workmanship; the Greek divinities are
presented in the forms familiar to Greek art; but the idea is
purely Roman, and born of the immediate circumstances of
the age.

Other extant works of art illustrate the divine functions and
attributes claimed for Augustus. In one cameo he is seen
throned beside the goddess Roma, with the sceptre and lituus,
symbolical of his secular and spiritual function, and the eagle
of Jupiter at his side. In others both the Emperor himself and
various members of his family are represented under the form
of gods, goddesses, and demigods. Thus, in one in which the
figure of Aeneas is introduced, the young C. Caesar (Caligula)
appears as Cupid, and in another Germanicus and Agrippina
are represented as Triptolemus and Ceres [1]. But still more
important, as attesting not the idealising fancies of contemporary Greeks, but the native feeling with which the house of
Caesar came to be regarded even in the early years of the
Empire, is the one great extant monument of that age, a monument of Roman inspiration and Roman workmanship, the Pantheon, raised by Agrippa in honour of the deities connected
with the Julian race.

The prominence given to this representation of Augustus
in the poetry and in the art of his age is probably to be explained by his own character and policy. He was animated

---

[1] The substance of these remarks is taken from the late O. Jahn's
'Höfische Kunst und Poesie unter Augustus,' published in his 'Populäre
Aufsätze.' The account of the cameos is given solely on his authority.
Several ideas on the whole subject of the deification of the Emperors are
derived from the same source.

in no ordinary degree by that love of fame and distinction
which very powerfully influenced the greatest Roman con-
querors and statesmen, orators and poets. The disdain of
such distinctions and the dislike of public spectacles are mentioned, in contrast to the tastes of his predecessor, among the
causes of the unpopularity of Tiberius. The enumeration in
the Ancyraean inscription of the honours and titles bestowed
on him, recorded with 'imperial brevity' and dictated by a
proud self-esteem, attests the strength of this ruling passion
in the latter years of the life of Augustus. The direct pressure
which he brought to bear on the most eminent poets of the time
to celebrate his wars is sufficiently indicated in many passages
in the Odes and familiar writings of Horace. Belonging by
descent to the comparatively obscure families of the Octavii
and Atii, Augustus attached peculiar importance to the glories
of the Julian line, which he inherited through his great-uncle
and adoptive father. Even Julius Caesar, notwithstanding his
Epicurean disregard of the religious ideas of his age, had encouraged the belief in his divine descent, as marking him out
for the special favours of fortune. There was moreover in
Augustus, in contradistinction to Julius Caesar, a strong vein
of religious or superstitious sentiment. His personal courage
has been questioned, probably with injustice, but he appears to
have been in a marked degree liable to supernatural terrors [1].
As happens not unfrequently with men who have been invari-
ably successful in great and hazardous enterprises, along with
a strong reliance in the resources of his own mind, he seems to
have had faith in a supernatural guidance and assistance attending him. His politic understanding appreciated the use of such
a belief to secure a divine sanction for his rule, which rested
substantially on military force. He availed himself of the
enthusiasm and willing services of the poets of the age, who
regarded him as at once the saviour of the State and their own
benefactor, to impress this idea of himself on the imagination
of the cultivated classes, and at the same time to glorify the

---

[1] Sueton. De Vita Caesarum, ii. 90 *et seq.*

actual successes of his reign, to further his policy of national regeneration, and to make men feel the security of a divinely-appointed government, along with the pride of belonging to a powerful imperial State.

## III.

The political revolution which transformed the Republic into the Empire, and the state of public feeling, which, arising spontaneously, yet received direction from the will and policy of Augustus, thus appear to be the most important conditions determining the character of the Augustan literature, and distinguishing it from that of the previous age. Poetic art was employed as it had never been in any former time as an instrument of government. If anything could have made the new order of things acceptable to the best representatives of the old Republican traditions, the purity and elevation imparted to the idea of the Empire in the verse of Virgil must have had this effect. The poetical imagination, susceptible as it is in the highest degree of emotions produced by the spectacle of ancient or powerful government or of a people nobly asserting its freedom, has little prophetic insight into the working of political causes. Nor need it be regarded as a sign of weakness or time-serving in the poets of the Augustan Age that they did not foresee the gloom and oppression which were destined to follow so soon after the prosperous dawn of the Roman Empire.

The establishment of the Empire affected the new poetry also by the personal relations which it established between the leaders of society and the leaders of literature. The early Republican poets were for the most part strangers to Rome, men of comparatively humble position, who by their merit gained the friendship of some of the great families, but who at the same time depended for their success on popular favour. The poets of the last days of the Republic were themselves members of the great families, or men intimately associated with them; and they wrote to please themselves and their equals. What remains of their poetry has thus all the independence of the older Republican literature, with the refinement of a literature addressed to a polished society. The poets of the Augustan Age were men born in the country districts or provincial towns of Italy, and the two most illustrious of their number were of humble origin: yet they lived after their early youth in familiar intercourse with the foremost men of their time; they owed their fortunes and position in life to the favour of these men, and thus could not help sharing, and to some extent reproducing, their tastes and tone in their writings.

Among the names of the patrons of literature that of Maecenas has become proverbial, but perhaps even more important than his patronage was that exercised by the Emperor himself. Not only was he a man of great natural gifts, but he had received a most elaborate education. He was a powerful and accomplished orator, and a practised writer [1]. As was not unusual with men who had received a thorough rhetorical training, he attempted the composition of a tragedy, and had the sense to treat his failure with good-natured humour [2]. He made other attempts in verse, and composed several works in prose, chiefly turning on the history of his own times. He showed in his composition an especial regard for purity and correctness of style. Suetonius tells us that he allowed no composition to be written on himself 'except in a serious spirit and by the best writers.' Horace testifies to this fastidiousness in the line,—

Cui male si palpere, recalcitret undique tutus [3].

[1] 'Eloquentiam studiaque liberalia ab aetate prima et cupide et laboriosissime exercuit.' Sueton. ii. 84.
'Augusto prompta ac profluens, quaeque deceret principem, eloquentia fuit.' Tac. Ann. xiii. 3.
[2] 'Aiacem tragoediam scripserat, eandemque, quod sibi displicuisset, deleverat. Postea L. Varius tragoediarum scriptor interrogabat eum, quid ageret Aiax suus. Et ille, "in spongium," inquit, "incubuit."' Macrob. ii. 4. 2.          [3] Sat. ii. 1. 20.

Suetonius testifies further to his liberal patronage of genius; 'ingenia saeculi sui omnibus modis fovit;' a statement confirmed by Horace's account of his liberality to Virgil and Varius,—

Dilecti tibi Vergilius Variusque poetae[1].

We are told also that in literary works he especially regarded 'the inculcation of precepts and the exhibition of examples of a useful tendency for the state and for private life,' which may partly account for the didactic and practical aim which the higher poetry of the age set before itself. He corresponded in terms of intimacy with Virgil, and made repeated advances, which were at first somewhat coldly received, to Horace, with the wish to number him among his familiar friends. But there was another side to the temper of Augustus, which those admitted to his favour did well not to forget. If he could be a liberal patron and genial companion, he could also be a hard and pitiless master. Literature, like everything else, had to be at his command, obedient to his will, and in harmony with his policy. The fate of Gallus, that of Iulus Antonius, and that of Ovid, prove that neither brilliant genius nor past favours and familiarity could procure indulgence for whatever thwarted his purpose or offended his dignity.

The relation between Maecenas and the members of his literary circle was one of more intimacy and unreserve. This circle included among its members Virgil and Varius, Horace and Propertius. The great works with which the name of Maecenas is inseparably associated,—the Georgics of Virgil, the first three books of the Odes of Horace, and the first book of his Epistles,—entitle him to be honoured as among the most enlightened and fortunate of all the patrons of literature. Virgil addresses him in language not only of loyal admiration, but of acknowledgment for the encouragement and guidance which he owed to him: and that such an influence may have been really exercised by the inferior over the superior mind is shown

---

[1] Ep. ii. 1. 248.

by the testimony given by Goethe of the stimulus which his
genius derived from the encouragement of the Duke of Wei-
mar[1].   Horace writes of Maecenas in the language not only of
admiration and gratitude, but of warm and disinterested affection ; and the favour shown to Propertius, a poet of a very
opposite type, shows that his appreciation of genius was not
limited by a narrow partisanship.   His character seems to have
left very different impressions on the minds of his contemporaries, according as they knew him intimately or merely from
the outside.   It is a proof of his capacity and his loyalty[2] that
he was the one man thoroughly trusted by Augustus in all affairs
of state, as Agrippa was in war : and that his qualities of heart
were no less admirable appears not only from the poetical
eulogies in the Georgics, the Elegies of Propertius, and the
Odes of Horace, but also from the more natural tribute to
his worth as a man and his sincerity as a friend contained
in Horace's Satires and Epistles.   On the world outside his
own immediate circle he produced the impression of an
effeminate devotion to pleasure.   His love of pleasure and
his shrinking from death seem to be confirmed by the testimony of Horace :—

Cur me querelis, etc.

The sketch of him by Velleius Paterculus presents the view of his
character suggested by the contrast between his ability as a statesman and the apparent indolence of his private life: 'A man, who,
while in all critical emergencies displaying sleepless vigilance,
foresight, and capacity for action, yet, during intervals of re-
laxation, was in his indolent self-indulgence almost more effeminate than a woman[3].'   It is remarkable that Tacitus ascribes
a similar character to the man in whom, after the death of

---

[1] Essays Literary and Theological, by R. H. Hutton.
[2] Cf. Propert. El. iv. 9. 34 :—
Maecenatis erunt vera tropaea fides.
Do. ii. 1. 36 :—
Et sumta et posita pace fidele caput.
[3] Velleius ii. 88.

Maecenas, Augustus most confided—Sallustius Crispus[1]. Perhaps the position of Maecenas, as the trusted confidant of a jealous and imperious master, required him to begin his career by playing a part which afterwards became habitual to him. Among the traits of his character indicated by Horace are knowledge of men, reticence, and indifference to the outward distinctions of birth and rank. Whatever ambition he had was to exercise real power as the minister of Augustus, not to enjoy official titles. He certainly used his position to direct the genius both of Virgil and Horace to public objects. There is no reason to doubt the fact noticed in the Life of Virgil, that he influenced him in the choice of the subject of the Georgics with the view to revive the chief among the ancient arts, 'by which the Latin name and the strength of Italy had grown great.' But it was with Horace that he shared all his public interests and private feelings, and it is not a very hazardous conjecture to presume that many of the Odes and familiar writings of the latter poet reflect the tastes and sentiments of Maecenas, perhaps give back the very style and manner of his conversation. The alternation observable in the Odes of Horace between an apparent devotion to the lighter themes of lyrical poetry and the serious interest in great affairs, the irony disclaiming all lofty and austere pretension, the Epicurean taste for simplicity combined with the Epicurean love of pleasure, the indifference to outward state, and the urbanity and knowledge of the world, more conspicuous in Horace than in any other ancient poet, are suggestive of habitual contact with the worldly wisdom, the real power disguised under an appearance of carelessness, the refined enjoyment of life, the genial social nature, which were not only a great power in the State, a great charm in the life of a by-gone age, but have

---

[1] Tac. Ann. iii. 30: 'Ille quamquam prompto ad capessendos honores aditu, Maecenatem aemulatus sine dignitate senatoria multos triumphalium consulariumque potentia anteiit, diversus a veterum instituto per cultum et munditias, copiaque et affluentia luxu propior: suberat tamen vigor animi ingentibus negotiis par, eo acrior quo somnum et inertiam magis ostentabat.'

through their action on the literature of the time become a permanent and beneficent influence on human culture.

Other names of men eminent among the 'lights and leaders' of the time are also intimately connected with its literature. The earliest patron by whom Virgil's genius was recognised was not Maecenas but Asinius Pollio, who in his early youth had lived in the gay circle of Catullus ; who, as the lieutenant of Antony, had governed the province of Cisalpine Gaul; who had filled the office of Consul, commanded an army, and obtained a triumph; who is mentioned by Horace in one of his early Satires as among the few critics whose appreciation he valued; who in later life obtained great distinction as an orator; to whose talent as a writer of tragedy both Virgil and Horace bear witness; who undertook the composition of a work the loss of which is one of the most irreparable gaps in historical records—a contemporary History of the Civil Wars 'ex Metello consule;'—and who performed the important service to literature of being the first to establish a public library at Rome, and the more questionable service of instituting the practice of public recitations.

M. Valerius Messala, the next in importance among the patrons of letters, unlike Maecenas and Pollio, who, though of old provincial families, were 'novi homines' at Rome, was a representative of one of the oldest and most illustrious patrician houses. He had held high command in the Republican army at Philippi, and was distinguished as an orator, an author, and patron of literature. He became the centre of a literary circle the most brilliant member of which was Tibullus; which, though living in friendly relations with the circle of Maecenas, did not share with it the enthusiasm for the new *régime.* Men like Pollio and Messala are important as elements contributing to the general taste and culture of the age, but not as determining the political or ethical character stamped upon the literature.

No direct literary influence was exercised by Agrippa, who is described by the elder Pliny as 'A man, whose manners more nearly approached rustic plainness than refinement of taste;' but his military and naval successes, and still more the great works of utility and beauty erected under his superintendence, contributed to the same end as the poetry of Virgil and Horace, that of perpetuating the spell of the name of Caesar upon the imagination of the world.

Cornelius Gallus, like Pollio, was eminent both in action and in poetry, but his brilliant and erratic career was cut short too soon to enable him to obtain a foremost place either among poets or among literary patrons. Yet an undying interest attaches to his name from the evidence afforded in the Eclogues of his being the first and apparently the only one who inspired in Virgil that affection, partly of the heart, partly of the imagination, which fascinates and attaches the finer nature of the poet to the stronger or bolder nature of one in whom it recognises some ideal of heroism, combined with the qualities which unite men in friendship with one another. It is of Gallus alone that Virgil writes in such a strain as this :—

> Gallo cuius amor tantum mihi crescit in horas
> Quantum vere novo viridis se subicit alnus [1];

and it is to Gallus that he assigns the pre-eminence in his own especial province of poetry,—as he represents the shepherd-poet Linus presenting him with the reeds which the Muses had of old given to 'the sage of Ascra [2].'

The Odes of Horace, addressed to men of high official station and ancient family, such as Sestius, Munatius Plancus, Sallustius Crispus, Aelius Lamia, Manlius Torquatus, still further illustrate the close connexion between the great world and the world of letters. His later Epistles, many of which are addressed to young men of rank devoting themselves to literary studies and pursuits, attest the continuance of the same tendency as time went on. And in the following generation Ovid and

---

[1] 'Gallus for whom my love grows from hour to hour even as the green alder-tree shoots up in the early spring.'

[2] Eclog. vi. 70, etc.

his contemporaries enjoyed the favour and friendship of the sons of these men and of other illustrious patrons.   Juvenal, in the Satire in which he complains of the absence of a liberal patronage in his own age, unites the names of Fabius and Cotta Messalinus (son of Messala), whose protection and encouragement Ovid had enjoyed, with that of Maecenas [1].   The chief cause of this close bond of union between social rank and literary genius was the fact that the men who in a former age would, from their birth and education, have had a great political career before them, were now debarred from the highest sphere of active life ; while they were not yet, what they became under the systematic corruption of the later Caesars, too enervated and demoralised to continue susceptible of the nobler kinds of intellectual pleasure.

Probably in no other aristocratic or courtly society has there been so large a number of men possessing the ability and knowledge, the accomplishments and leisure, required for the appreciative enjoyment of a literature based on so fine and elaborate a culture.   There are some circumstances which made the patronage of the earlier half of the Augustan Age more favourable to letters than that of other periods in which the same influence has been exercised.  The chief literary patrons then were men who had played a prominent part in a revolutionary era,—men indeed of ancient birth or hereditary distinction, yet owing their pre-eminence to their talent, energy, and aptitude for the time, and thus open to new influences, and free from the prejudices of an old-established nobility.   They had the culture and careful education of an aristocratic class, combined with the liberal tendencies of revolutionary leaders. The distance which in the preceding age would have kept apart men born into a high social and political position from men of genius of humble origin was easily passed in a time immediately succeeding that in which the great C. Julius had practically proclaimed the doctrine of ' an open career to every

---

[1] Sat. vii. 93, 94.

kind of merit.' Among the liberal traits in the character of
Maecenas, as painted by Horace, the indifference to distinctions
of birth is specially marked :—

> Cum referre negas quali sit quisque parente
> Natus, dum ingenuus[1].

The new men at the court of Augustus were naturally attracted
to the new men in literature, sprung from quite a different class
from that to which Lucretius, Catullus, or Calvus belonged, and
yet, in respect of education, refinement, and even early associations, in no respect their inferiors.

Another bond of union between them was that they were
nearly all of the same age, born with one or two exceptions
between the years 70 B.C., and 60 B.C., and that several of
them had studied under the same masters. The distinguished men of the Ciceronian Age had passed away, with
the exception of one or two, such as Varro and Atticus, living
in retirement, and consoling themselves with their farms and
libraries for the changes they had witnessed. The leaders in
action, as in literature, were all young men, beginning their
career together in an altered world, the characters and destinies of which they were called upon to mould. One by
one they dropped away, most of them before passing the
period of middle life, leaving the Emperor almost the sole
survivor among a younger generation who had grown up
under the new order of things, and, while acquiescing in it
as complacently, sharing neither in the energy nor in the
enthusiasm of the early years (from about 27 B.C. to about
10 B.C.) during which the Empire left its greatest and happiest
impression.

This relation of men of letters to the leaders of society under
the Empire could not but exercise a strong influence both for
good and evil on the literature of the age. Such a society,—
able, versed in affairs, accomplished, fond of pleasure,—whatever

---

[1] 'When you say it makes no matter what a man's father was, provided
he is of free-birth.' Sat. i. 6. 7–8.

else it may be,· is sure to be characterised by good sense, a
strong feeling of order and dignity, an acute perception of
propriety in conduct and manners, an urbanity of tone
restraining all arrogant self-assertion and violent animosity of
feeling.    Such a society is the determined enemy of all
pedantry, eccentricity, and exaggeration, of all austerity or
indecorum, of one-sided enthusiasm or devotion to a single
idea.    The 'aurea mediocritas' in feeling, conduct, thought,
and enjoyment is the ideal which it sets before itself.    Horace,
except in his highest and most thoughtful moods, is the true
representative of such a society; but its indirect influence may
be noted also in the moderation, the invariable propriety and
dignity, both of thought and language in Virgil, and in the
tones of refinement with which Propertius and Ovid record
the experience and preach the philosophy of pleasure.    Yet
literature probably lost as much from the limitation of sympathy
imposed upon it as it gained from this acquired dignity and
urbanity of tone.    The Roman poets of this era, even while
expressing national sentiments and ideas, were not like Homer,
Pindar, or Sophocles, who, while putting a sufficiently high
value on distinctions of birth and fortune, and on the personal
qualities accompanying these distinctions, are yet, in a sense in
which the poets of the Augustan Age are not, the poets of a
whole people.    Horace introduces that series of his Odes which
most breathes a national spirit by disclaiming all sympathy with
the 'profanum vulgus.'    He looks upon it as one of the
privileges of genius, 'to scorn an ill-natured public.'    He did
not wish his Satires to be thumbed by the multitude or by men
of the class of Hermogenes Tigellius.    He cared only for the
appreciation of men belonging to the class in which all culture
and regard for the traditions of Rome were now centred.    The
urban populace, as represented in literature, appears only as a
rabble,—and this is still more the case in the days of Juvenal,—
which had to be kept in order, fed,· amused, and tended, like
some dangerous wild beast.    The middle class, absorbed in
money-making and commercial adventure, supplies to Horace

the representatives of the misers and parvenus whom he painted in his Satires for the amusement of his aristocratic readers. The tone of Virgil is equally anti-popular. The view of society which he delights to present is that of a paternal ruler giving laws to his people and caring for their welfare. His repugnance to the influence of the 'popularis aura' on government is indicated in such passages as the famous simile near the beginning of the Aeneid,

> Ac veluti magno in populo cum saepe coorta est
> Seditio, saevitque animis ignobile vulgus[1],

and in his representation of 'the good King Ancus' as he is called by Ennius and Lucretius, among the unborn descendants of Aeneas, as

> iactantior Ancus
> Nunc quoque iam nimium gaudens popularibus auris[2].

The encouragement and appreciation of the leaders of society involved on the part of the poets a position of deference or dependence; the relation between them had thus its limiting as well as its corrective effects; it tended to make literature tamer in spirit and thought, perhaps also less original in invention and more bounded in its range of human interest.

## IV.

The great wealth and luxury of Rome, during the latter years of the Republic and the early years of the Empire, exercised also an influence on the life, the imagination, and the thoughts of the poets living in those times. Through commerce and conquest Rome had entered into the possession of the long accumulated wealth of the world, and, as generally happens in eras of advanced civilisation, the

---

[1] 'And as when often in a mighty multitude discord has arisen and the base rabble storms with passion.'

[2] 'Ancus, unduly vain, even already delighting too much in the veering wind of the people's favour.'

enjoyment of these was very unequally distributed. Nothing appears more remarkable in the social life of the latter days of the Republic than the great riches possessed and expended by a few individuals, such as Crassus, Hortensius, and the Luculli. One proof of the immense accumulation of money at that time is the large price which, as we learn from Cicero's letters, was paid for the houses of the leading men among the nobility. The number of villas possessed by Cicero himself, the son of a provincial Eques, and debarred by stringent laws (though probably they were evaded) from turning his pre-eminence as an advocate to profit, and the sums spent by him in their adornment, suggest to us to what an extent the soil of Italy, the works of Greek art, and the natural and artificial products of the East, were at the disposal of the ruling aristocracy of Rome. Still more is this thought forced on us when we think of Proconsuls and Propraetors who came home glutted with the spoils of their provinces, which they squandered in the coarsest luxury. The change to the Empire, though it put a considerable check on this kind of plunder, did little to distribute wealth more generally, or to limit luxurious living. The appropriation during the Civil Wars of the sacred treasures long accumulated in the temples of the gods[1], and the great stimulus given to commerce by the establishment of peace, added largely to the wealth available at Rome for purposes of munificence, of ostentation, or indulgence. But the largest share in the disposal of the wealth of the world had passed from the representatives of the old governing class to the ruling powers of the new Empire, and this change was decidedly for the public advantage. Augustus and his ministers possessed the old Greek virtue of μεγαλοπρέπεια, and understood that immense wealth could be better expended on great public objects than on beautifying their villas and fish-ponds, or giving a more dangerous variety to their entertainments. The policy of Augustus in restoring and building the temples of the gods had an artistic as well as a religious purpose. He wished

[1] Cp. Merivale's Roman Empire.

to make his countrymen proud of the outward beauty of Rome,
as Pericles had made the Athenians proud of the beauty of
Athens.

The most enduring result of this munificence, more enduring
even than the noble ruins of temples and theatres—the visible
monuments preserved from that age—is the finished art of the
verse of Virgil and Horace.   By the liberality of the Emperor,
Virgil was able to devote to the composition of his two great
works nearly twenty years of 'unhasting and unresting' labour
in the beautiful scenery of Campania.   The wealth and lands
at the disposal of Maecenas enabled Horace to change the
wearisome routine and enervating pleasures of Rome for hours
of happy inspiration among the Sabine Hills or in the cool
mountain air of Praeneste, amid the gardens and streams of
Tibur or by the bright shores of Baiae [1].   To the liberality of
their patrons these poets owed not only the leisure and freedom
from the ordinary cares of life [2], which allowed them to give
all their thought and the unimpaired freshness of their genius
to their art, but the opportunity of enjoying under the most
favourable circumstances that source of happiness and inspiration which has given its most distinctive charm to their poetry—
the beauty of Italian Nature.   It is only in their appreciation
of the living beauty of the world for its own sake (and apart
from divine or human associations) that the great Roman poets
possess an interest beyond that of the poets of any other age
or country, with the exception of the English poets of the
present century.   Nowhere is the familiar charm of a well-
loved spot suggested in truer and more graceful words than
these :—

[1]      Vester, Camenae, vester in arduos
        Tollor Sabinos; seu mihi frigidum
            Praeneste, seu Tibur supinum,
                Seu liquidae placuere Baiae.   Od. iii. 4. 21-24.
[2] Cf. the lines of Juvenal, vii. 66-68, in especial reference to Virgil :—

        Magnae mentis opus nec de lodice paranda
        Attonitae, currus et equos, faciesque Deorum
        Aspicere, et qualis Rutulum confundat Erinnys, etc.

> Te flagrantis atrox hora Caniculae
> Nescit tangere ; tu frigus amabile
> Fessis vomere tauris
> Praebes, et pecori vago, etc.[1]

Nor can any lines express better a real love for the actual beauty of familiar scenes combined with an imaginative longing for the ideal beauty consecrated by old poetic associations, —like to that which in modern times has often driven our Northern poets and artists across the Alps,—than the

> Rura mihi et rigui placeant in vallibus amnes;
> Flumina amem silvasque inglorius. O ubi campi
> Spercheosque, et virginibus bacchata Lacaenis
> Taygeta, etc.[2]

of the Georgics.

The literature of the Augustan Age has often been compared with that of England in the first half of the eighteenth century. In so far as each literature is the literature of town life, in so far as it has a moral and didactic purpose, the comparison holds good. The Satires and Epistles of Horace present a parallel both to the poetical Satires of Pope, which in outward form are imitated from them, and still more to the prose Essays of the Spectator. They resemble those Essays in their union of humour and seriousness, in the use they make of character-painting, anecdote, and moral reflection, in the justice and at the same time the limitation of their criticism both on life and literature, in the colloquial ease combined with the studied propriety of their style. But while Horace, in addition to his powers as a moralist and painter of character, ranks high among those poets who enable us to feel the secret and the charm of Nature, latent in particular places, the only period

---

[1]      ' 'Gainst flaming Sirius' fury thou
           Art proof, and grateful cool dost yield
        To oxen wearied with the plough,
           And flocks that range afield.'   Martin.

[2] ' May my delight be in the fields and the flowing streams in the dales ; unknown to fame may I love the rivers and the woods. O to be, where are the plains, and the Spercheos, and the heights, roamed over in their revels by Laconian maidens, the heights of Taygetus.'

of English literature from which this power is absent is that of which Addison and Pope are among the chief representatives. A similar superiority in this respect may be claimed for the Augustan poetry over that of the Age of Louis XIV. As was said before, French criticism points to Racine as a genius with a certain moral affinity to Virgil; but it equally acknowledges his inferiority as the interpreter of Nature. 'C'est cet amour,' says M. Sainte-Beuve, 'cette pratique de la nature champêtre qui a un peu manqué à notre Racine, dont le goût et le talent de peindre ont été presque uniquement tournés du côté de la nature morale.'

The ease of their circumstances and the fact that they owed this ease to others ('Deus nobis haec otia fecit') have impressed themselves in other ways on the character of the Augustan poetry. The spirit of that poetry is certainly tamer than that of other great literary epochs. Even the enjoyment of Nature is a passive rather than an active enjoyment derived from adventurous or contemplative energy. There is no suggestion, as there is in Homer and in many modern poets, of vivid contact with the sterner forces of Nature. The sense of discomfort as well as of danger was then, as it has been till the present century, sufficient to repress the imaginative love of the sea or of mountain scenery[1]. Horace expresses a shrinking from the dangers of the sea, nor is there in Virgil any trace of that enjoyment of perilous adventure which is one of the great sources of delight in the Odyssey.

The profuse expenditure and luxury of the age called forth in its poets a spirit of reaction to a simpler and more primitive ideal, as they did in the French literature of the latter part of the eighteenth century. By contrast with the unreal enjoyment of luxury and the ennui occasioned by it, which Lucretius had satirised in the previous generation, a stronger sense of the

---

[1] Cf. Virg. Georg. ii. 470: 'Mollesque sub arbore somni.'
   Hor. Ep. i. 14. 35: 'Prope rivum somnus in herba.'
   Virg. Eclog. ii. 40: 'Nec tuta mihi valle reperti.'
   Hor. Ep. i. 11. 10: 'Neptunum procul e terra spectare furentem.'

purer sources of human enjoyment, of friendly and intellectual society, of family affection, of the beauty of Nature, of the simpler tastes of the country, was awakened even in those who in their actual lives did not realise all these sources of happiness.   But in Horace this feeling of contrast does not express itself in the tones of vehement antagonism which appear a century later in Juvenal.   Luxury and profuse expenditure are indeed repugnant to his taste, and they suggest to him, as they do to Virgil, the purer enjoyment of simple living.   There is no doctrine which Horace preaches more constantly in all his works, or with more apparent sincerity, than that of being independent of fortune, and of the greater happiness enjoyed in the mean station in life between great wealth and poverty. Yet, while preaching the same doctrine, he does not express it in terms of such deep and earnest conviction as the

> Divitiae grandes homini sunt vivere parce
> Aequo animo [1]

of Lucretius.   In at least the earlier part of his poetic career he had had his share of the luxurious living and the other pleasures of Roman life.   Experience had satisfied him that the 'slight repast, and sleep on the grass by a river's side [2],' contributed more to his happiness in later life than drinking Falernian from midday; and as years went on, it gave him more pleasure to recall the memory of his old loves in song than to involve himself in new engagements.   The Horatian maxims in favour of simplicity have this recommendation, that they are the result of experience in both ways of living. The luxurious life of the capital seems at no time to have possessed charms for Virgil or Tibullus.   Though the latter was a man of refinement, and not averse to pleasure, yet he has a feeling similar to that of Rousseau in favour of an ideal of rudeness and simplicity as compared with the pomp and profusion of life in Rome.   The more active and energetic

---

[1] 'It is great riches for a man to live sparingly with a contented mind.'
[2] Ep. i. 14. 34-35.

temperament of Propertius and of Ovid induced them to
participate with less restraint in the pleasures of the city,
and they appealed to congenial tastes among their contemporaries in the choice of the topics treated in their poems.

## V.

The conditions hitherto considered enable us to appreciate
the prominence given to national and imperial ideas in the
literature of the Augustan Age, and also to understand the chief
differences in tone and spirit between that literature and the
literature of the Ciceronian Age. Along with these marked
differences, obvious points of agreement are also observable.
The cultivated men of each time had the same refined enjoyment in Nature, art, literature, and social life. And in turning
to the intellectual conditions affecting literary form and style,
the later period will be seen to be still more closely connected
with the earlier. The golden age of Latin poetry, commencing
in the years preceding the overthrow of the Republic, reaches
its maturity in the earlier part of the reign of Augustus, and
then begins to decline, till under Tiberius the last poetic voice
is silenced. Though Latin prose-literature had yet to be
enriched by some of its greatest and most original works, yet
neither the glory of the Empire, the charm of the Italian life,
nor the vivifying ideas and creations of Greek genius were ever
again able to revive the genuine poetical inspiration which
ancient Italy once, and once only, enjoyed in abundant
measure.

The half-century from about 60 B.C. to about 10 B.C. was, at
once, one of those rare and germinative epochs in the history
of the world, in which a powerful intellectual movement coincides with, influences, and is influenced by a great movement
and change in human affairs; and it was at the same time
a period of a rich and elaborate culture, in which the inheritance
of Greek genius, art, and knowledge came for the first time into
the full possession of the Romans. The earlier half of this

period was more distinguished by original force of mind, the latter half by more complete and perfect culture. The age of Cicero was one of great energy in the chief provinces of human activity—in war and politics, in oratory, poetry, and philosophy. There is no intellectual quality so characteristic of his own oratory, of the poetry of Lucretius, of the military and political genius of Julius Caesar, as the ' vivida vis,'—the energy, at once rapid and enduring in its action, as of a great elemental force. Among their contemporaries, though there was no man of high political capacity, yet there was a many-sided intellectual activity manifesting itself in the forum and senate-house, in social intercourse and correspondence, and in varied literary and philosophical discourse. As a result of this novel activity of mind, the Latin language developed then for the first time all its resources as a powerful organ of literature, inferior indeed to the language of Greece in the days of its purity, but much superior as the instrument of poetry and oratory, history and philosophy, to that language in its decay[1]. The writers of the Augustan Age received this language from their predecessors, in its most sensitive period of growth, while able to present to the mind in unimpaired freshness the immediate impressions from outward things and from the inner world of consciousness, but still capable of more delicate and varied combinations to fit it to become the perfectly harmonious organ of sustained poetical emotion. This further development was given to it by the Augustan poets, but not without some loss of native force and purity of idiom. They too felt the influence of the strong intellectual movement of the preceding age. But it came upon their minds with a less novel and vehement impulse. They are greater in execution than in creative design. They are more concerned with the results than with the processes of thought. Virgil may have been as assiduous a student of philosophy as Lucretius, but he does not feel the same need of consistency of view and firmness of speculative conviction; he

---

[1] Compare Munro's Lucretius, p. 306 (third edition).

shares with Lucretius the strong passion for poetry ('dulces
ante omnia Musae'), but neither he nor Horace, though each
recognises the supreme claims of philosophy, shows the passion
for enquiry which induced Lucretius

> Noctes vigilare serenas,
> Quaerentem dictis quibus et quo carmine demum
> Clara tuae possim praepandere lumina menti,
> Res quibus occultas penitus convisere possis [1];

so that even in his dreams he describes himself as ever busy
with the search after and exposition of truth,—

> Nos agere hoc autem et naturam quaerere rerum
> Semper et inventam patriis exponere chartis [2].

The master-pieces of the Augustan literature were not the
products of that vivid and rapidly-working creative energy which
marked the Ciceronian Age.   There never was an age in which
great writers trained themselves so carefully for their office,
strove so much to conform to recognised principles of art,
reflected so much on the plan and purpose of their compositions, or used more patient industry in bringing their conceptions to maturity.   The maxim 'nonum prematur in annum'
illustrates the spirit in which the great artists of that age
worked.   The cultivated appreciation of Greek art and poetry—
the essential condition of the creative impulse of Italy—then
reached its highest point, produced its supreme effect in a
national Roman literature of similar perfection of workmanship,
and, after that, rapidly declined and passed away from the
Roman world as a source of literary inspiration, leaving
however the educating influence of this new literature in its
place.   The Greek language had indeed been studied at Rome
for nearly two centuries before the Ciceronian Age.   The
earliest Roman writers—Naevius, Ennius, Pacuvius, etc.—had

---

[1] 'To be sleepless through the calm nights, searching by what words
and verse I may succeed in holding a bright light before your mind, by
which you may be able to see thoroughly things hidden from view.'

[2] 'While I seem ever to be plying this task, to be searching into the
nature of things, and revealing it, when discovered, in writings in my native
speech.'

used the epic and dramatic poetry of Greece as a kind of quarry for their own rude workmanship.    The age of Laelius had imbibed much of the humanity and wisdom of Greek speculation.    But it was not till the age of Cicero and Catullus that the long process of education and the largely increased intercourse between the two nations had raised the Roman mind to a full sense and enjoyment of artistic excellence, as revealed both to the eye and to the mind.    The men of that age, in the midst of all their active pursuits, were moved by this foreign influence as the men of the Renaissance were moved by the recovery of classical literature.    In the case of some among them the passion for accumulating books and works of art became the absorbing interest in their lives.    Though in some of the orators and men of letters, e. g. Memmius, as we learn from Cicero, their Greek tastes fostered an affected indifference to their own nationality, yet on the best minds, such as those of Cicero himself, Lucretius, and Catullus, this intimate contact with Greek genius acted with a vivifying power by calling forth the native genius of Italy.    It was the peculiarity of the Roman mind to be capable of receiving deep and lasting impressions from other nations with whom it came in contact, without sacrifice of the strong individuality of its own character.    What Columella says of the Italian soil, 'that it is most responsive to the care bestowed on it, since, through the energy of its cultivators, it has learned to yield the products of nearly the whole world[1],' might be said with equal truth of the Italian mind.    This adaptability to foreign influences, without loss of native genius and character, enabled Rome to exercise spiritual supremacy over the world for more than a thousand years after the loss of her temporal supremacy.    In the age of Cicero and the following age this adaptability to another form of spiritual influence gave to Rome a great national literature.

Virgil, Horace, and their immediate contemporaries devoted themselves to Greek studies with even more ardour than their

[1] iii. 8.

immediate predecessors.   Education and preparation for a
career in literature was a more elaborate process than it had
ever been before, perhaps we might add, than it has ever been
since.   Virgil was still an unknown student, carefully preparing
himself for the labour of his life almost till he reached the age
at which Catullus died.   Horace at the age of twenty-three was,
to use his own words, still ' seeking for the truth among the
groves of Academus.'   The taste for literary leisure was greatly
developed among the educated classes by the suppression of all
active political life; while at the same time the establishment of
public libraries made the access to books more easy and general.
Women equally with men made themselves familiar with at
least the lighter fancies of the learned Greeks.   There are none
of his Odes into which Horace is so fond of introducing his
mythological allusions as those in which some real or fictitious
heroine, Galatea or Asterie, Lyde or Phyllis, is addressed.   The
poems of Propertius which celebrate his love for Cynthia could
only be appreciated by the possessors of much recondite
learning.

Though the greatest poets of the Augustan Age drew much
of their inspiration from the purer sources of Greek genius,
especially from Homer and the early lyric poets, yet the period
of Greek literature which was most familiar to the Romans of
the Augustan Age was the Alexandrian.   It was nearest to
them in point of time; it was most congenial to the taste of
the learned Greeks who now gathered from the widely-scattered
centres of Greek culture to Rome, as they had formerly done to
Alexandria; it was of all the forms of Greek literature the most
cosmopolitan, or rather the least national, in spirit, and thus
most easily adopted by another race; it was moreover, like
that of the Augustan Age, the literature of a courtly circle enjoying the favour and contributing to the glory of a royal
patron.   The earliest imitators of this poetry were Catullus
and the other poets contemporary with him, such as Calvus,
Caecilius, Cinna, and Varro Atacinus, the author of the epic
poem of Jason.   In the Augustan Age Gallus had not only

obtained distinction as the author of original elegies in the style of the amatory poetry of Alexandria, but had translated a poem of Euphorion of Chalcis[1], whom Cicero holds up as the type of effeminacy in literature in contrast with the manliness of Ennius[2]. Tibullus to a certain extent, but still more Propertius and Ovid, followed in the same line. From the Alexandrine poets they derived the form and many of the materials of their art. Virgil, while familiar with the whole range of Greek poetry and pressing it all into his service, has used the Alexandrians more freely than any other Greek writers, with the exception of Homer. Horace is most independent of them; there are no direct traces of their works in any of his writings. The Greek authors to whom he acknowledges his debt are the early Lyrists and Iambic writers, the poets of the New Comedy, the philosophic writers of the later schools which arose out of the teaching of Socrates, and especially Aristippus. Yet even in him the influence of the Alexandrine tone is apparent, especially in his treatment of the subjects taken from the Greek mythology.

This poetry of Alexandria, or rather this poetry of the Greek race in its latter days, was, to a much greater extent, the artificial product of culture and knowledge than the manifestation of original feeling or intellectual power. The very language in which it was written was artificial, far removed, not only in phraseology but in dialectical forms, from the language of common life. Poetry was pursued as the recreation of scholars and men of science; its chief aim was to satisfy a dilettante curiosity :—

Cetera quae vacuas tenuissent carmine mentes, etc.[3]

The writers of this school whose names are most familiarly known are Callimachus, one of the Battiadae of Cyrene, Euphorion of Chalcis, Philetas of Cos, Aratus of Soli, Hermesianax

[1] Virg. Eclog. vi. 72; x. 50.  [2] Tusc. Disp. iii. 19.
[3] 'All other themes which might have charmed the idle mind in song,' etc.

and Nicander of Colophon, Apollonius of Rhodes[1], Lycophron of Chalcis, Eratosthenes of Cyrene, from whom Virgil takes a passage about geographical science, Zenodotus of Ephesus, a grammarian,—names suggestive of the widely-diffused culture of the Hellenic race, and at the same time indicative of the absence of any great centre of national life such as Athens had been in former times. To these are sometimes added the more interesting names of Theocritus of Syracuse, and of the idyllic poets Moschus of Syracuse and Bion of Smyrna, although they are more associated with the fresh woods and pastures of Sicily and Southern Italy. The chief materials used by the Alexandrine writers in their poetry were the tales and fancies of the old mythology and the results of natural science; the modes of human feeling to which they mainly gave expression were the passion of love and the sensibility to the beauty of Nature.

Nothing attests more forcibly the original power and richness of faculty which shaped the primitive fancies of the Greek mythology into legend, poetry, and art, than the perennial vitality with which this mythology has reappeared under many forms, satisfying many different wants of the human mind, at various epochs, from the time of its birth even down to the present day. In the contrasts often drawn between the classical and the romantic imagination, it is sometimes forgotten that this Greek mythology was richer in romantic personages, situations, and incidents, than the mythology or early legends of any other race. In the nobler eras of Greek literature, after the creative impulse ceased out of which the mythology and its natural accompaniment epic poetry had arisen, the legends and personages of gods and heroes supplied to the lyrical poets an ideal background by connexion with which they glorified the passions and interests of their own time: to the tragic poets of Athens they supplied beings of heroic stature, situations of transcendent import, by means of which

---

[1] Born at Alexandria, but afterwards settled at Rhodes. He ultimately returned to Alexandria.

they were enabled to give body and shape to the deepest
thoughts on human destiny. The Alexandrians, and those
Greek writers who came long after them, such as Quintus
Calaber and Nonnus, did not seek to impart any recondite
meaning to the legends which they revived, but rather to divest
them of any sacred or ethical associations, and to present them
to their readers simply as bright and marvellous tales of passion
and adventure. They endeavoured, either in the form of continuous epics or in the more appropriate form of 'epyllia' or
epic idyls, to enable their readers to escape in fancy from the
dull uniformity of their own time into a world of action in the
bright morning of the national life. They sought especially
to satisfy two impulses of the Greek nature which still survived
out of the more powerful energies which had given birth to art
and poetry,—the childlike curiosity (Ἕλληνες ἀεὶ παῖδες) which
delights in hearing a story told, and the artistic passion to make
present to the eye or the fancy distinct pictures and images of
beauty and symmetry.

The later development of the Greek intellect was however
more critical and scientific than creative. Science, learning,
and criticism were especially encouraged and cultivated at
Alexandria. The impulse given by Aristotle to natural observation and enquiry, and the large intercourse with the East
which followed on the conquests of Alexander and the establishment of the kingdoms of his successors, led to a great in-
crease of knowledge, or, in the absence of definite knowledge,
of curiosity and speculation. The spirit of enquiry no longer,
as in the days of the older philosophers, endeavoured to solve
the whole problem of the universe, but to observe and system-
atise the phenomena of the special sciences. Natural history,
botany, and medicine were studied zealously and successfully;
the subjects of astronomy and meteorology excited equal interest, though the want of the appliances necessary for these
studies made them more barren in results. A great advance
was made in the knowledge of remote places of the earth and
of their various products. The novelty of these enquiries, and

of the knowledge resulting from them, stimulated curiosity and the imaginative emotion which accompanies it ; and the enthusiasm of science combining with the enthusiasm of literary criticism gave birth to a new kind of didactic poetry, which aimed at expounding the phenomena of Nature in the epic diction of Homer. Among the best-known authors of this didactic poetry are Aratus, Callimachus, and Nicander,—the last described as being a poet, a grammarian, and a physician, a combination characteristic of the spirit in which both science and literature were cultivated. These writers supplied materials which Virgil used in the Georgics, and in the special examination of that poem it will be seen that he adopted other characteristics of the Alexandrine learning. The description by Ovid of the poem of Aemilius Macer in the lines

> Saepe suas volucres legit mihi grandior aevo,
> Quaeque necet serpens, quae iuvet herba, Macer[1],

indicates the character not only of that poem, but also of the Alexandrine models on which it was founded.

The poetry of Alexandria touched most on the realities of human life in its treatment of the passion of love and the enjoyment of the beauty of Nature. These are, in unadventurous times and in eras of advanced civilisation, the main motives of the imaginative literature which seeks its interest in the actual life of the present. Callimachus and Euphorion are mentioned as the models followed by Gallus, Propertius, and Tibullus[2]. They, as well as their Roman followers, seem largely to have illustrated their own feelings and experience by recondite allusions to the innumerable heroines of ancient mythology. The passion of Medea for Jason is the motive which gives its chief human interest to the Argonautics of Apollonius, as the passion of Dido for Aeneas, suggested by it, gives the chief purely human interest to the Aeneid. But the

---

[1] 'Often did Macer, now advanced in years, read to me his poem on birds, and of the serpent whose sting is deadly, and of the herb that heals.' Trist. iv. 10. 43–44.
[2] Sueton. De Viris Illustribus.

most powerful delineation of this kind in any writer of that
period, recalling in its intensity the 'burning passion set to the
lyre by the Aeolian maiden,' is the monologue of Simaetha in
the second Idyl of Theocritus, of which Virgil has produced
but a faint echo in his

Ducite ab urbe domum, mea carmina, ducite Daphnim[1].

The love of Nature, though not then for the first time
awakened,—for there are clear indications of the powerful
influence of this sentiment, though in subordination to human
interests, in the earlier epic, lyric, and dramatic poetry,—came
then prominently forward as an element of refined pleasure in
life, and as an inspiring influence both to poets and painters.
The cause of the growth of this sentiment has been sought[2]
partly in the rise of great cities, such as Antioch, Seleucia,
Alexandria, which by debarring men from that free familiar
contact with the forms, movement, and life of Nature enjoyed
by the older Greeks, created an imaginative longing for a
return to this communion as to a lost paradise.   The longing
to escape from the heat and confinement of a great southern
city to the fresh sights and free air of woods and mountains
must have been often felt by poets and artists who had exchanged their homes on the shores and the islands of the
Aegean for the dusty streets of Alexandria.   Probably the
Metamorphoses of Ovid convey as good an idea as anything in
Latin literature of the various influences active in the Alexandrine poetry; and the kind of scene which he takes most
delight in painting in that poem is that of a cool and clear
stream hidden in the thick shade of woods and haunted
by the Nymphs.   The taste for gardens within great cities,
first developed at this time and afterwards carried to an extreme
pitch of luxury in the early Roman Empire[3], further illustrates

---

[1] 'Lead him home from the city, my strain, lead Daphnis home.'
[2] Woermann, Ueber den landschaftlichen Natursinn der Griechen und
Römer; Helbig, Campanische Wandmalerei.
[3] Cf. 'Senecae praedivitis hortos.'   Juv.   'Pariterque hortis inhians, quos
ille a Lucullo coeptos insigni magnificentia extollebat.'   Tac. Ann. xi. 1.

the need felt for this kind of refreshment from objects of natural beauty.

Other causes have been suggested for the growth of this sentiment, as, for instance, the decay of the polytheistic fancies, which, by regarding each natural object as identified with some spiritual being, made it less an object of affection and curiosity for its own sake. The sudden growth of this sentiment in ancient times in an age of great luxury and culture is analogous to the great development and expansion of the feeling under similar circumstances in the latter part of the eighteenth century. In both cases the sentiment arose from the desire to escape from the tedium of an artificial life. The love of Nature is not, as we might naturally expect it to be, a feeling much experienced by those who live in constant contact and conflict with its sterner forces, as by husbandmen, herdsmen, and hunters ; nor is it developed consciously in primitive times or among unsophisticated races. It is the accompaniment of leisure, culture, and refinement of life. Some races are more susceptible of this feeling than others; and perhaps the Greek with his lively social temper, and the tendency of his imagination to reduce all beautiful objects to a human shape, was less capable of the disinterested delight in the sights and sounds of the outward world than the Italian. It was apparently among Siculians, the kindred of the people of Latium, and not among men living in the mountains of Arcadia or Thessaly, that Theocritus found the personages of his rustic idyl. Whether it was from the greater susceptibility of their national temperament, or from the fact that they lived in the later times of the world, to which the sentiment was more congenial, the Roman poets of the Augustan Age and of that immediately preceding it are the truest exponents of the love of Nature in ancient times; though it may be that, without the originating impulse given by the Greek mind in the Alexandrian period, and perpetuated by educated Greeks living in Southern Italy, this love of natural beauty might never have been consciously realised by them as a source of poetic inspiration.

The pursuit of literature in the Alexandrian Age was accompanied with great activity in the other arts, especially in sculpture and painting. These last continued to be carried on by Greeks in Italy after Rome had succeeded to Alexandria as the centre of human culture. Sculpture and carving on wood, works of art in bronze, and the graving on gems continued to perpetuate an aesthetic half-belief in the Olympian deities and in the other creations of the Greek theology. Painting seems to have treated the same kind of subjects and to have aimed at satisfying the same class of feelings as the poetry of the Alexandrian time. Many of its subjects it seems to have drawn directly from the works of poets[1]. The paintings recovered from Pompeii, which may be presumed to have continued the traditions of a somewhat earlier art, illustrate the same tastes which were gratified by the poetical treatment of mythological subjects, of landscape, and of the passion of love. The knowledge acquired by science seems also to have been pressed into this service by the artist. The frequent representations of wild animals originated in the same kind of interest which animated Nicander to the composition of the Θηριακά[2]. Realistic reproductions from common life seem also to have been frequently executed by ancient, as by modern, painters. If, as is not improbable, the 'Moretum' and the 'Copa' are translations or imitations of Greek originals, they exemplify still further the close connexion between the art of the poet and of the painter among the Alexandrian dilettanti.

The various kinds of art which bring human forms and scenes from outward nature before the eye, and especially the art of the painter, must accordingly be taken into account as means of making the creations of Greek fancy and the objects of Greek sentiment vividly present to the Roman imagination. They not only acted immediately on the mind of the poet by

---

[1] The substance of these remarks is derived from Helbig's Campanische Wandmalerei.

[2] Cf. Plautus, Pseudolus, i. 2. 14:—

Neque Alexandrina beluata conchuliata tapetia.

suggesting to him directly subjects for his art and supplying
frequent illustrations for the treatment of native subjects, but
they helped to interpret to cultivated minds his allusions to or
reproductions from the poets of former times. The whole
learning, fancy, and sentiment of the Alexandrians seem to
have been absorbed and made their own by the Augustan
poets. Virgil and Horace, indeed, formed their ideal of art
from the works of a greater time. Their studies of Greek
familiarised their minds with what was most perfect in form,
noblest in thought, feeling, and expression in the older poets.
Yet in so far as Roman poetry is a reproduction of Greek
poetry, it is the mind of the Alexandrian rather than of the
old Ionian, Aeolian, or Athenian Greek that lives again in the
Augustan literature. Probably this has been in favour of the
Roman writers. With their highly susceptible and cultivated
appreciation of excellence, their originality might have been
altogether overpowered by an exclusive study of the nobler and
severer models. In receiving the instruction of contemporary
Greeks, based to a great extent on the Alexandrine learning,
and in reproducing the materials, manner, and diction of
Alexandrine poets, they must have become conscious of the
greater freshness and vigour of their own genius, of the more
vital force of their own language, of their grander national life,
of the privilege of being Romans, and of the blessing of
breathing Italian air. Whatever was most worthy to survive
in the spirit which animated the refined industry of the Alexandrian Age has been preserved in greater beauty and vitality
in Virgil, Propertius, and Ovid, combined with the ideas,
feelings, passions, and experience of a new and more vigorous
race.

One other circumstance has yet to be taken into account as
affecting the culture and taste of the age, viz. the number of
poets who lived at the time and the relations which subsisted
between them. Those whose works have been preserved are
only a few out of a larger circle who worked each in his own
province of art, and listened to and criticised the works of their

friends. Of the poets belonging to this circle whose works
have not reached us, Varius, the older contemporary and life-
long friend of Virgil, first acquired distinction as a writer of
that kind of epic peculiar to Rome which treated of contemporary subjects and was dedicated to the personal glory of
some great man. This kind of poem had probably originated
with the ' Scipio' of Ennius, but it had been especially cultivated in the age of Cicero. Varius performed the office from
which Virgil and Horace shrank, that, namely, of telling in
verse the contemporary history of his own time, glorifying
in one poem the memory of Julius Caesar, in another celebrating the wars of Augustus. Afterwards he resigned to
Virgil the honours of epic poetry, and entered into rivalry
with Pollio as the author of tragedy. His drama of Thyestes
was represented at the Games celebrated after the battle of
Actium, and for this drama he is said to have received a
million sesterces[1]. This play is praised both by Quintilian and
Tacitus in the dialogue De Oratoribus. Quintilian says of it,
' it may be compared with any work of the Greeks:' but the
drama is the branch of literature in which the judgment of a
Latin critic is of least value. The Thyestes, like the Medea of
Ovid, was probably a play of that rhetorical kind which was
cultivated under the Empire, and which never got possession of
the stage as the older tragedies of Attius and Pacuvius did.
Cornelius Gallus has been already mentioned among the men
of public eminence who cultivated poetry. He was a follower
of the Alexandrians, and is mentioned by Propertius and Ovid
as their own precursor in elegiac poetry. Aemilius Macer, a
native of Verona, nearly of the same age as Virgil, and supposed to be shadowed forth as the Mopsus of the fifth Eclogue,
was the author of a didactic poem called Ornithogonia, written
in imitation of the Alexandrine Nicander. Valgius Rufus and
Aristius Fuscus, mentioned by Horace as among the friendly
critics by whom he wished his Satires to be approved, and to

---

[1] Scholium quoted by W. S. Teuffel in his account of L. Varius.

whom he addresses some of his Odes and Epistles, are also known as authors. In his later life Horace maintained friendly relations and correspondence with the younger men, such as Iulus Antonius, Florus, etc., who united a taste for poetry with the pursuits of young men of rank. And among the pleasures which Ovid recalls in the dreary days of his exile, none seem to have been more prized by him than the familiar relations in which he had lived with the older poets and with those of his own standing[1]. The Alexandrine influence is visible in the kinds of poetry chiefly cultivated by these writers, especially in the didactic poem, the artificial epic, and the erotic elegy. We hear also of epic or narrative poems on contemporary subjects, of one or two dramatic writers, and also of writers in verse on grammatical and rhetorical subjects[2].

There is no feature in the social life of the Augustan Age so pleasant to contemplate as the brotherly friendship, free apparently from the jealousies of individuals and the petty passions of literary coteries, in which the most eminent poets and men of letters lived with one another. The only exception to the general state of good feeling of which there is any indication is an apparent coolness between Horace and Propertius. The latter poet neither mentions nor alludes to his illustrious contemporary, though both were friends of Maecenas and of Virgil; and Horace, though he does not mention Propertius by name, as he does Tibullus and most of the other distinguished poets of the time, probably alludes to him in a passage which was not intended to be complimentary[3]. But in general what Plato says of the souls engaged in the pursuit and contemplation of intellectual beauty—'Envy stands aloof from the divine company'—was true of the 'divine company' of poets

---

[1] Tristia, iv. 10. 41, etc.
[2] W. S. Teuffel.
[3]     Discedo Alcaeus puncto illius: ille meo quis?
    Quis nisi Callimachus? Si plus adposcere visus,
    Fit Mimnermus, et optivo cognomine crescit. Ep. ii. 2. 99.
Propertius may have been dead at the time when these lines were published; but we may remember that the famous lines on 'Atticus' did not see the light till after the death of Addison.

in the Age of Augustus. And the sincere and appreciative
interest which they took in one another was not only a source
of great happiness in their lives, but was able to fulfil the
function of an enlightened and generous criticism. Poets were
in the habit of reading their works to their friends before sub-
mitting them to the public. It is characteristic of the modesty
of Virgil and of his unceasing aim at perfection that he was in
the habit of reading to his friends chiefly those passages in his
works of which he was himself distrustful. The fastidious
taste of Horace sometimes rebelled against the importunity of
those who desired to hear him read his own compositions.
Yet the well-known testimony   Ovid proves that he was not
averse to gratify an appreciative listener :—

> Et tenuit nostras numerosus Horatius aures,
> Dum ferit Ausonia carmina culta lyra[1].

The appreciation and criticism of cultivated friends, themselves authors as well as critics, must have stimulated and
corrected the taste of the poets of the age. The genius which
is most purely original in its activity, and which communicates
an altogether novel impulse to the world, relies absolutely on
itself, and may be little stimulated by sympathy or affected by
criticism. Of such a type Lucretius in ancient and Wordsworth in modern times are probably the best examples, though
Dante and Milton seem to approach nearer to it than to the
type of those whose genius is equally great in receiving from,
as in giving to, the world—the type of genius of Homer,
Sophocles, Shakspeare, and Goethe. The great qualities of
writers of the first type are force, independence, boldness of
invention and speculation, absolute sincerity. They are at the
same time liable to the defects of incompleteness, one-sided-
ness, disregard of the true proportion of things. Their works
do not produce the impression of that all-pervading, perfectly-
balanced sanity of genius, which the Greeks meant when they

---

[1] 'And the musical voice of Horace charmed my ears, while he makes
his polished song resound on the Ausonian lyre.'

applied the word σοφοί to their poets, and which makes the
great men of the second type not only powerful movers but
also the wisest teachers of the world.  The best poetry of the
Augustan Age, if wanting in the highest mode of creative
energy, is eminently free from the defects which sometimes
result from the intenser form of imagination; it is in a remarkable degree pervaded and controlled by this sanity of
genius.  This excellence of the Augustan literature may be
partly, as was said before, attributed to the familiar intercourse which men of letters enjoyed with men of action and
large social influence; partly, and probably to a greater degree, to the cultivated and generous criticism which men of
genius and fine accomplishment imparted to and received from
one another.

Outside of this friendly circle of men eminent in letters and
social position there were other literary and critical coteries
hostile to them, who seem to have chosen the merits of the old
writers as the battle-ground on which they engaged the new
school of poetry and criticism.  These critical coteries Horace
treats, as Catullus treats his 'vile poets, pests of the age,' and
as Pope treated Dennis and the other poetasters of his time.
He was evidently sensitive to the envy excited by his genius
and by the favour of Maecenas, and in his later years it
afforded him pleasure to be less exposed than he had been to
carping criticism :—

> Romae principis urbium
> Dignatur soboles inter amabiles
> Vatum ponere me choros,
> Et iam dente minus mordeor invido[1].

But with the final establishment of his reputation his fastidiousness suffered more from the pedantry and importunities of
admirers and imitators :—

[1] Od. iv. 3. 13. 16 :—
> 'At Rome, of all earth's cities queen,
>   Men deign to rank me in the noble press
> Of bards beloved of man : and now, I ween,
>   Doth envy's rancorous tooth assail me less.'  Martin.

O imitatores, servum pecus, ut mihi saepe
Bilem, saepe iocum vestri movere tumultus[1].

Even the 'mitis sapientia' of Virgil has condescended to
immortalise the names of Bavius and Maevius, as Pope has
immortalised the heroes of the Dunciad. The often quoted
line of Horace,—

Scribimus indocti doctique poemata passim[2],

marks the beginning of that 'cacoethes scribendi' which continued to prevail till the days of Juvenal as a symptom of the
'strenua inertia' of life under the Empire.


## VI.

The almost exclusive devotion to poetry on the part of the
meanest as well as the greatest writers of the Augustan Age
seems to demand some explanation. The natural genius of
Rome was more adapted to oratory, history, and didactic exposition than to any of the great forms of poetry. In the previous generation prose literature had reached the highest degree
of perfection. The style of Cicero is one of the most admirable
and effective vehicles for the varied purposes of passionate
invective or persuasive oratory, of familiar correspondence, and
of popularising the results of ethical, political, and religious
reflection. In Caesar and Sallust the record of great events
in the national life had at last found a power of clear, terse,
and chastened diction, superior as a vehicle of simple narrative
to the style of the two great historians of later times, if not so
rich and varied in colouring and in poetical and reflective suggestion. Of the prose literature of the Augustan Age we
possess only one great monument, the extant parts of 'the

[1] Ep. i. 19. 19-20.
     'O servile crew! how oft your antics mean
       Have moved my laughter, oh,. how oft my spleen.'  Martin.
[2] Ep. ii. 1. 117.
     ''Tis writing, writing now is all the rage.'  Martin.

colossal master-work of Livy;' and that was the product of the later and least brilliant period of this epoch.

The cause of the sudden and permanent decline of Roman oratory was the extinction of political life.   Public speech could no longer be, as it had been for nearly two centuries, a great power in the commonwealth.   Under the vigilant and judicious administration of Augustus there was not scope even for that kind of oratory which flourished under his successors, and became a very formidable weapon in the hands of the 'delatores,' —that, namely, which is employed in the prosecution and defence of men charged with grave offences against the State. Neither was there scope or inclination for philosophical or historical composition.   Such freedom of enquiry as Cicero allowed himself in his treatises De Legibus and De Republica would scarcely have been tolerated under the monarchy;  and the world was in no mood for any severe strain of thought or any questioning of the first principles of things.   The new era desired ease, an escape from care and the perplexities of thought, as well as peace and material well-being.   The spirit of the age was announced in the pastoral strain, which celebrated its commencement in the apotheosis of Julius Caesar, 'amat bonus otia Daphnis.'   Nor would it have been possible for any one to have composed or at least to have published a candid history of the times; and it may have been the discovery of this impossibility that induced Asinius Pollio to leave his work unfinished.   It would indeed have been a gain for all time had a Roman Thucydides recorded the 'movement in the State' from the Consulship of Metellus till the battle of Actium with the accuracy and impartiality, the graphic condensation, the sober dignity, the sensitive perception of the varying phases of passion and character in states and individuals, the philosophical discernment of great political principles destined to act in the same way 'so long as the nature of man remains the same,' and the deep tragic pathos which make, even at the present day, the record of 'the twenty-seven years' war of the Peloponnesians and Athenians' the most

vividly interesting and permanently instructive historical work
which the world possesses.　But even had the genius of Rome
been capable of producing a Thucydides, the circumstances
of the time would have reduced him to silence.　Tacitus regards the establishment of the Empire as equally fatal to the
genius of the historian, as it was to the genius of the orator :—
'Postquam bellatum apud Actium atque omnem potentiam ad
unum conferri pacis interfuit, magna illa ingenia cessere.　Simul
veritas pluribus modis infracta, primum inscitia rei publicae ut
alienae, mox libidine assentandi [1].'

On the other hand, many circumstances contributed to give
a great stimulus to poetical literature in its most trivial and
transitory as well as its noblest and most enduring manifestations.　It is remarked by a recent French writer [2], that poetry
is the last form of literature to wither under a despotism.　But
it suffers from it most irretrievably in the end.　The poetic
imagination is able to deceive itself by turning away from what
is painful and repulsive in the world, and by appearing to extract the element of good, of vivid life, or impressive grandeur
out of things evil and fatal in their ultimate effects.　Thus it is
able to glorify the pomp and state of imperialism, just as it is
able to glorify the charm to the senses or the attraction to the
social nature afforded by the life of passion and pleasure.　But,
in the long run, the decay in the higher energies arising either
from the loss of liberty or the loss of self-control is more fatal
to the nobler forms of art and poetry than to any other products of intelligence.

Again, the mechanical difficulties of the art had been to a
great extent overcome in the previous age.　The discovery of
the new and rich ore of the Latin language, revealed and
wrought into shapes of massive beauty and delicate grace by

---

[1] 'After the result of the campaign of Actium, when the interests of
peace demanded that supreme power should be conferred on one man,
those great geniuses disappeared.　Truth too suffered in many ways, at
first from ignorance of public life, as a matter with which men had no
concern, and soon from the spirit of adulation.' Hist. i. 1.

[2] E. Quinet.

Lucretius and Catullus, awakened and kept alive in the great writers of this age the desire to perfect the work commenced by their predecessors, and to develope all the majesty, beauty, and harmony of which their native speech was capable. The education in grammar, rhetoric, and Greek literature, which in the later years of the Republic had trained men for the contests of public life, prepared them to recognise and appreciate the perfection of style and of rhythm which was now for the first time attained. But the attainment of this perfection was a stumblingblock to writers of an inferior order, and to all the poets who came afterwards. The Augustan poets left to their successors, what they had not themselves received, the fatal legacy of an established poetical diction. The resources of the language for the highest purposes of poetry seem to have been exhausted by the supreme effort of this epoch. The golden perfection of the Augustan style gave place to the forced rhetoric and the sensational extravagance of the Neronian age and to the soberer but tamer imitations of the Flavian era.

In its inner inspiration, as well as its outward expression, the Augustan poetry was the maturest development of the national mind. The inspiring influences of Latin poetry were the idea of Rome, the appreciation of Greek art, the genial Italian life. We have seen how the first establishment of the Empire gave to the national idea a temporary importance and prominence which it had not had since Ennius first awoke his countrymen to the consciousness of their destiny. It was only in the Augustan Age, or during the few years preceding it, that the taste of the Romans was sufficiently educated to appreciate the perfect art of the Greeks. The whole of Italy was now for the first time united in one nation. A new generation had been born and grown to manhood since the Social War. The pride in Rome and the love of the whole land might now be felt by all men born between the Alps and the Straits of Sicily. The districts far removed from the capital, ' by the sounding Aufidus' or 'the slow-winding Mincius,' still kept alive the traditions of a severer morality and the habits of a simpler and happier life[1]. They were still able to nourish the susceptible mind of childhood with poetic fancies[2]. In the following generation the idea of the empire was one no longer of inspiring novelty, but rather of a dull oppression. The taste for Greek literature had lost its freshness and quickening power. The natural enjoyment of life, the susceptibility to beauty in art and nature, the love of simplicity, were no longer possible to minds enervated and hearts deadened by the unrelieved monotony of luxurious living.

[1] Traditum ab antiquis morem.   Hor. Sat. i. 4. 117.
[2] Me fabulosae Vulture in Apulo, etc.   Hor. Od. iii. 4. 9.

# CHAPTER II.

## VIRGIL'S PLACE IN ROMAN LITERATURE.

VIRGIL is the earliest in time and much the most important
in rank among the extant poets of the Augustan Age. It is
only in comparatively recent times that any question has arisen
as to the high position due to him among the great poets of all
ages. His pre-eminence not only above all those of his own
country, but above all other poets with the exception of Homer,
was unquestioned in the ancient Roman world. His countrymen
claimed for him a rank on a level with, sometimes even above,
that of the great father of European literature. And this
estimate of his genius became traditional, and was confirmed
by the general voice of modern criticism. For eighteen
centuries, wherever any germ of literary taste survived in
Europe, his poems were the principal medium through which
the heroic age of Greece as well as the ancient life of Rome
and Italy was apprehended. No writer has, on the whole,
entered so largely and profoundly into the education of three
out of the four chief representatives of European culture—the
Italians, the French, and the English—at various stages of their
intellectual development. The history of the progress of taste
might be largely illustrated by reference to the place which the
works of Virgil have held, in the teaching of youth and among
the refined pleasures of manhood, between the age of Dante
and the early part of the present century.

Since that time, however, an undoubted reaction has set in
against the prestige once enjoyed by Latin poetry. And from
this reaction Virgil has been the chief sufferer. The peculiar

gifts, social and intellectual, of Horace have continued to secure for him many friends in every country and in every generation. The spirit of Lucretius is perhaps more in unison with the spirit of the present than with that of any previous age, owing to changes both in imaginative feeling and in speculative curiosity and belief through which the world is now passing. The sincerity and unstudied grace of Catullus are immediately recognised by all who read his works. But in regard to Virgil, if former centuries assigned him too high a place, the criticism of the present century, in Germany at least, and for a certain time in England, has been much less favourable. French criticism has indeed remained undeviatingly loyal, and regards him as the poet, not of Rome only, but of all those nations which are the direct inheritors of the Latin civilisation [1]. And in England, at the present time, the estimate of his genius, expressed both by writers of acknowledged reputation and in the current criticism of the day, is much more favourable than it was some thirty years ago.

It would be neither desirable nor possible to enter on a critical examination of the value of a writer, who has been so much admired through so long a time, without taking some account of the prestige attaching to his name. It may be of use therefore to bring together some of the more familiar evidences of his reputation and influence in former times, to show the existence of a temporary reaction of opinion and to assign causes for it, and to indicate the grounds on which his pre-eminence as the culminating point in Latin literature and his high position among the poets of the world appear to rest.

## I.

It was as a great epic poet, the poet of national glory and heroic action, that he was most esteemed in former times.

---

[1] ‘ Virgile depuis l'heure où il parut a été le poëte de la Latinité tout entière.’   Sainte-Beuve.

The Aeneid may not have been regarded as more perfect in execution than the Eclogues and Georgics, but it was regarded as a work of higher inspiration.   The criticism which Virgil by implication applies to his earlier works, in the use of such expressions as 'ludere quae vellem,' 'carmina qui lusi pastorum,' ' in tenui labor [1],' etc., as compared with the high ambition with which he first indicates his purpose of composing an epic poem in celebration of the glory of Augustus—

> Temptanda via est qua me quoque possim
> Tollere humo, victorque virum volitare per ora [2]—

coincides with the view which the ancients took of the relative value of the poetry of external nature and of heroic action. The contemporaries and successors of Virgil did not share in the sense of some failure in the treatment of his subject which is attributed to Virgil himself; and hence they ranked him as the equal of Homer in the largest and most important province of poetry.   And as this comparison was the source of excessive honour in the past, it has been the cause of the depreciation to which he has been exposed in the present century.

The great reputation enjoyed by the Aeneid dates from the first appearance of the poem.   The earliest indication of the admiration which it was destined to excite appears in the tones of expectation and enthusiasm with which Propertius predicts the appearance of a work greater than the Iliad:—

> Cedite Romani scriptores, cedite Graii:
> Nescio quid maius nascitur Iliade [3].

The immediate effect produced by the poem may be traced in the frequent allusions to the story of Aeneas in the fourth

---

[1] 'To sing, at my own will, my idle songs,' 'who sang the idle songs of shepherds,' 'my task is on a lowly theme.'

[2] 'I must strive to find a way by which I may raise myself too above the ground, and speed to and fro triumphant through the mouths of men.'

[3] 'Give place, all ye Roman writers, give place, ye Greeks: some work, I know not what, is coming to the birth, greater than the Iliad.'   Eleg. iii. 32. 64–65.

book of the Odes of Horace. The continuance of this
influence is unmistakeable in Ovid, and there are also many
traces of Virgilian expression in the prose style of Livy [1]. The
author of the dialogue 'De Oratoribus' testifies to the favour
which the poet enjoyed, even before the publication of his epic,
both with the Emperor and with the whole people, who 'on
hearing some of his verses recited in the theatre rose in a body
and greeted him, as he happened to be present at the spectacle,
with the same marks of respect which they showed to the
Emperor himself [2].' He would thus appear, even in his lifetime,
to have thoroughly 'touched the national fibre [3],' and to have
gained that place in the admiration of his countrymen which he
never afterwards lost. By the poets who came after him his
memory was cherished with the veneration men feel for a great
master, united to the affection which they feel for a departed
friend. Lucan indeed rather enters into rivalry with him than
follows in his footsteps; nor can there be any surer way of
learning to appreciate the peculiar greatness of Virgil's manner
than by reading passages of the Aeneid alongside of passages of the Pharsalia. The new poets under the Flavian
dynasty, Valerius Flaccus, Silius Italicus, and Statius, though
they failed to apprehend the secret of its success, made the
Aeneid their model, in the arrangement of their materials, in
their diction, and in the structure of their verse. Statius, in
bidding farewell to his Thebaid, uses these words of acknow-
ledgement :—

> Vive, precor, nec tu divinam Aeneida tempta,
> Sed longe sequere et vestigia semper adora [4];

and Silius, having occasion to mention Mantua, celebrates
it as—

---

[1] Cf. Wölflin in the Philologus, xxvi, quoted by Comparetti.

[2] Tac. De Oratoribus, ch. xiii.

[3] 'Si Virgile faisait aux Romains cette illusion d'avoir égalé ou surpassé
Homère, c'est qu'il avait touché fortement la fibre Romaine.' Sainte-
Beuve.

[4] 'Live then, I pray, yet rival not the divine Aeneid, but follow it from
afar, and ever reverence its track.' Thebaid xii. 816.

Mantua, Musarum domus, atque ad sidera cantu
Evecta Aonio, et Smyrnaeis aemula plectris[1].

Martial, among many other tributes of admiration[2] scattered over his poems, says of Virgil that he could have surpassed Horace in lyric, Varius in tragic poetry, had he chosen to enter into rivalry with them[3]. The younger Pliny[4], speaking of the number of books, statues, and busts possessed by Silius, adds these words: 'of Virgil principally whose birthday he kept with more solemnity than his own, especially at Naples, where he used to visit his monument as if it were a temple.' But the greatest proof of Virgil's influence on the later literature of Rome is seen in many traces of imitation of his style in the language of the historian Tacitus, the one great literary genius born under the Empire. So great a master of expression would not have incurred this debt except to one whom he regarded as entitled above all others to stamp the speech of Rome with an imperial impress. In Juvenal there are many references and allusions to familiar passages in the Aeneid[5]: and it appears from him that the works of Virgil and Horace had in his time become what they have since continued to be, the common school-books of all who obtained a liberal education. It is one of the hardships of the schoolmaster's life, described in his seventh Satire, to have to listen by lamplight to the 'crambe repetita' of the daily lesson,—

Quum totus decolor esset
Flaccus et haereret nigro fuligo Maroni[6].

After the end of the first century A.D., even the imitative poets of Rome become rare; but the pre-eminence still enjoyed by

---

[1] 'Mantua, home of the Muses, raised to the stars by Aonian song, and rival of the music of Smyrna.'   Silius, Punic. viii. 595.
[2] E.g. iv. 14. 14; xii. 4. 1; xiv. 186; v. 10. 7; viii. 56, etc.
[3] viii. 18. 5-9.
[4] Ep. iii. 7.
[5] E.g. i. 162; iii. 199; v. 45, 138; vi. 434, etc.; vii. 66, 226, 236, etc.
[6] 'When the whole Horace had lost its natural colour, and the soot was sticking to the blackened Virgil.'   vii. 226.

Virgil is attested by the number of commentaries written on his works, the most famous of them being the still extant commentary of Servius, belonging to the latter part of the fourth century. The fortune of Virgil has in this respect been similar to that of his great countryman Dante. From the time of his death till the extinction of ancient classical culture, there was a regular succession of rhetoricians and grammarians who lectured and wrote treatises on his various poems. Among those who preceded Servius, the most famous names are those of Asconius Pedianus, Annaeus Cornutus, the friend of Persius, and Valerius Probus, in the first century A.D. These commentators supplied materials to Suetonius for the life on which that of Aelius Donatus, which is still extant, is founded. The frequent quotations from Virgil in the desultory criticism of Aulus Gellius and the systematic discussions in the Saturnalia of Macrobius attest the minute study of his poems in the interval between the second and the fifth centuries. Similar testimony to his continued influence is afforded by the early Christian writers, especially by Augustine. And though there may be traced in them a struggle between the pleasure which they derived from his poetry and the alienation of their sympathies owing to his paganism, yet it is probable that the favour shown to him and to Cicero during the first strong reaction from everything associated with the beauty of the older religion, was due as much to the pure and humane spirit of their teaching as to the fascination of their style : nor perhaps was this teaching inoperative in moulding the thought and giving form to the religious imagination of the Latin Church. The number and excellence of the MSS. of Virgil, the most famous of which date from the fourth and fifth centuries, confirm the impression of the continued favour which his works enjoyed before and subsequently to the overthrow of the Roman rule in the West. Wherever learning flourished during the darkest period of this later time, the poems of Virgil were held in special esteem. Thus we read in connexion with the literary studies of Bede : 'Virgil cast over him the same spell which he cast over Dante: verses from the Aeneid break his narratives of martyrdoms, and the disciple ventures on the track of the great master in a little eclogue descriptive of the approach of spring[1].' His works were taught in the Church schools: and the feeling with which he was regarded by the more tolerant minds of the mediaeval Church appears in a mass sung in honour of St. Paul at the end of the fifteenth century:—

> Ad Maronis mausoleum
> Ductus fudit super eum
>   Piae rorem lacrimae;
> Quem te inquit reddidissem
> Si te vivum inuenissem
>   Poetarum maxime[2]!

The traditional veneration attaching to his name, among the classes too ignorant to know anything of his works, survived during the middle ages in the fancies which ascribed to him the powers of a magician or beneficent genius, appearing in many forms and at various times and places widely separated from one another.

With the first revival of learning and letters in different countries, the old pre-eminence of Virgil again asserts itself. In England 'the earliest classical revival' (to quote again the words of Mr. Green) 'restored Cicero and Virgil to the list of monastic studies, and left its stamp on the pedantic style, the profuse classical quotations of writers like William of Malmesbury or John of Salisbury.' One of the earliest works in Scottish literature is the translation of the Aeneid by Gawain Douglas. It is characteristic of the rudimentary state of learning at the time when this translation appeared that the Sibyl is represented as a nun, who directs Aeneas to tell his beads[3]. But the greatest testimony to the persistence of Virgil's fame and influence in the western world is the homage which the genius of Dante pays to the shade of his great

---

[1] Green's History of the English People, p. 37.
[2] Quoted by Comparetti; and also in Bähr's Römische Literatur.
[3] Works of Gavin Douglas, Bishop of Dunkeld, by John Small, M.A., vol. i. p. cxlv.

countryman. 'May the long zeal avail me and the great love
that made me search thy volume. Thou art my master and my
author. Thou art he from whom I took the good style that did
me honour[1].' The feeling with which Dante gives himself up
to the guidance of Virgil through all the mystery of the lower
realms is like that under which Ennius evokes the shade of
Homer from the 'halls of Acheron' to interpret to him the
secrets of creation. Dante combines the reverence for a great
master, which seems to be more natural to the genius of Italy
than to that of other nations, with a high self-confidence and
a bold and original invention. Lucretius expresses a similar
enthusiasm for Homer, Ennius, Empedocles, and Epicurus;
and by Virgil the same feeling is, though not directly expressed,
yet profoundly felt towards Homer and Lucretius. And in all
these cases the admiration of their predecessors is an incentive,
not to imitative reproduction, but to new creation. It was as
the poet of 'that Italy for which Camilla the virgin, Euryalus,
and Turnus and Nisus died of wounds' that the poet of
mediaeval Florence paid homage to the ancient poet of Mantua.
The admiration of Dante, like that of Tacitus, is the more
corroborative of the spell exercised over the Italian mind by the
art and style of Virgil from the difference in the type of genius
and character which these poets severally represent. The
influence of Virgil was exercised, with a power more over-
mastering and injurious to their originality, upon the later
poets and scholars of Italy with whom the Renaissance begins.
The progress of modern poetry was for a long time accompanied—and it would be difficult to say whether it was thereby
more obstructed or advanced—by a new undergrowth of Latin
poetry, for the higher forms of which Virgil served as the
principal model. Petrarch attached more importance to his
epic poem of 'Africa,' written in imitation of the rhythm and
style of the Aeneid, than to his Sonnets. The influence of
Virgil on the later Renaissance in Italy is abundantly proved in

---

[1] Carlyle's Translation of the Inferno.

the works of poëts, scholars, and men of letters in that age. Ninety editions of his works are said to have been published before the year 1500[1]. From Italy this influence passed to France and England, and was felt, not by scholars and critics only, but by the great poets and essayists, the orators and statesmen of the seventeenth and eighteenth centuries. It was discussed as an open question whether the Iliad or the Aeneid was the greater epic poem : and it was then necessary for the admirers of the Greek rather than of the Latin poet to assume an apologetic tone[2]. Scaliger ranked Virgil above Homer and Theocritus. His prestige was greatest during the century of French ascendency in modern literature, that, namely, between the age of Milton and that of Lessing. The chief critical law-giver in that century was Voltaire, and no great critic has ever expressed a livelier admiration of any poem than he has of the Aeneid. It is to him we owe the saying, ' Homère a fait Virgile, dit-on; si cela est, c'est sans doute son plus bel ouvrage[3].' He claims elsewhere for the second, fourth, and sixth books of the Aeneid a great superiority over the works of all Greek poets[4]. He says also that the Aeneid is the finest monument remaining from antiquity. As Spenser was called the 'poet's poet,' so Virgil might be called the orator's poet. Even by a rhetorician of the second century the question was discussed whether Virgil 'was more a poet or an orator[5].' Bossuet is said to have known his works by heart[6]. In the great era of English oratory, no author seems to have been so familiarly known or was so often quoted. We read in a recent sketch of the life of Burke[7], 'Most writers have constantly beside them some favourite classical author, from whom they

---

[1] Mr. Small, in his account of the writings of Bishop Gavin Douglas, says, ' The works of Virgil passed through ninety editions before the year 1500.'

[2] See Conington's Introduction to the Aeneid.

[3] Appendix to the Henriade.

[4] Dict. Philos., art. Epopée.

[5] Quoted by Comparetti.

[6] Sainte-Beuve, ' Causeries du Lundi.'

[7] By Mr. Payne, in the Clarendon Press Series.

endeavour to take their prevailing tone. . . . Burke, according to Butler, always had a ragged Delphin Virgil not far from his elbow.' A vestige of the attraction which his words had for an older school of English politicians may be traced in the survival of Virgilian quotation in some of the parliamentary warfare of recent times. The important place which Virgil has filled in the teaching of our public schools—the great nurses of our classic statesmen—has perhaps not been without some influence in shaping our national history [1]. It would be no exaggeration to say that the poems of Virgil, and especially the Aeneid, have contributed more than any other works of art in modern times, not only to stamp the impression of ancient Rome on the imagination, but to educate the sensibility to generous emotion as well as to literary beauty. There is probably no author, even at the present day, of whom some knowledge may be with more certainty assumed among cultivated people of every nation.

## II.

This unbroken ascendency of eighteen centuries, which might almost be described in the words applied by Lucretius to the ascendency of Homer—

> Adde Heliconiadum comites; quorum unus Homerus
> Sceptra potitus [2]—

is as great a fortune as that which has fallen to the lot of any writer. If any one ever succeeded in securing that which

---

[1] ' Who shall say what share the turning over and over in their mind, and masticating, so to speak, in early life as models of their Latin verse, such things as Virgil's
> Disce, puer, virtutem ex me, verumque laborem,
or Horace's
> Fortuna saevo laeta negotio,
has not had in forming the high spirit of the upper class in France and England, the two countries where Latin verse has most ruled the schools, and the two countries which most have had, or have, a high upper class and a high upper class spirit?' High Schools and Universities in Germany, by M. Arnold.

[2] 'Add too the companions of the Muses of Helicon, amongst whom Homer, the peerless, after holding the sceptre—.'

Tacitus says 'should be to a man the one object of an insatiable ambition,' to leave after him 'a happy memory of himself[1],' that may be truly said of Virgil.    Though his name may henceforth be less famous, it cannot be deprived of its lustre in the past.    Nor does it seem possible that this reputation could have been maintained so long, in different ages and nations, without some catholic excellence, depending on original gifts as well as trained accomplishment, which could unite so many diversely-constituted minds of the highest capacity in a common sentiment of veneration.    The secret of his long ascendency is, in the words of Sainte-Beuve, that ' he gave a new direction to taste, to the passions, to sensibility : he divined at a critical period of the world's history what the future would love.'

It is only in the present century that the question has been asked whether this great reputation was deserved.    But the earliest witness who might be called against his claims to this high distinction is Virgil himself.    In the Eclogues and Georgics the delight which he finds in the exercise of his art is qualified by a sense of humility, arising from a feeling of some want of elevation in his subject.    In his last hours he desired that the Aeneid should be burned: and that this was not a mere impulse arising from the depression of illness may be inferred from the request which he made to Varius, before leaving Italy, ' that if anything happened to him he should destroy the Aeneid.'    A letter written to Augustus is quoted by Macrobius, in which Virgil speaks of himself as having undertaken a work of such vast compass ' almost from a perversion of mind[2].'    No poet could well be animated by a loftier ambition than Virgil ;  yet few great poets seem to have been so little satisfied with their own success.    It was not in his nature to feel or express the confident sense of superiority which sustained Ennius and Lucretius in their self-appointed tasks, nor even that satisfaction with the work he had done and that assurance of an abiding place in the memory of men which relieve the ironical self-disparagement of Horace.

[1] Tac. Ann. iv. 38.                    [2] i. 24. 11.

The most obvious explanation of this passionate and pathetic desire that the work to which he had given eleven years of his maturest power should not survive him, is the unfinished state, in respect of style, in which the poem was left. He had set aside three years for the final revision of the work and the removal of those temporary 'make-shifts,' which had been originally inserted with full knowledge of their inadequacy, in order not to check the ardour of composition. After having devoted three years of his youth to the execution of a work so slight in purpose and so small in compass as the Eclogues, he might well feel depressed by the thought that a work of such high purpose and so vast a scope as the Aeneid—and a work of which such expectations as those expressed by Propertius were entertained—should be given to the world before receiving the final touch of the master's hand.

Yet the words in the letter to Augustus,—' that I fancy myself to have been almost under the influence of some fatuity in engaging on so great a work'—if they are to be taken as a true expression of his feeling, imply a deeper ground of dissatisfaction with his undertaking. Horace, in the estimate which he forms of his own work, seems to maintain the due balance between the self-assertion and the modesty of genius. But his modesty arises from his thorough self-knowledge, and from his understanding the limits within which a complete success was attainable by him. That of Virgil seems to be a weakness incidental to his greatest gifts, his sense of perfection, his appreciation of every kind of excellence. His large appreciation of the genius of others, from the oldest Greek to the latest Latin poet, his regard for the authority of the past, his attitude of a scholar in many schools, his willing acceptance of Homer as his guide through all the unfamiliar region of heroic adventure, were scarcely compatible with the buoyant spirit, as of some discoverer of unknown lands, which was needed to support him in an enterprise so arduous and so long-sustained as the composition of a great literary epic. The task which he set himself required of him to combine into one harmonious work of art,

which at the same time should bear the stamp of originality,—
of being a new thing in the world,—the characteristics and
excellences of various minds belonging to various times.  With
such aims it was scarcely possible that the actual execution of
his work should not fall below his ideal of perfection.  Especially must he have recognised his own deficiency in the pure
epic impulse, which apparently sustained Homer without conscious effort.  He could not feel or make others feel the culminating interest in the combat between Turnus and Aeneas,
which Homer feels and makes others feel in the combat between
Hector and Achilles.  In his earlier national poem he had vin-
dicated the glory of the ploughshare in opposition to the glory
of the sword; and, in his later battle-pieces, he must have felt
his immeasurable inferiority to the poet of the Iliad.  And yet
neither the precedents of epic poetry nor his purpose of celebrating the national glory of Rome permitted him to leave this
part of his task unattempted.  To describe a battle or a single
combat in the spirit and with the fellow-feeling of Homer has
been granted to no poet since his time.  Among modern poets
perhaps Scott has approached nearer to him than any other.
Among Roman authors, Ennius, who gained distinction as a
soldier before he became known as a writer, was more fitted to
succeed in such an attempt than the poet whose earliest love
was for ' the fields and woods and running streams among the
valleys.'

As the comparison of his own epic poem with the greatest
of the Greek epics is the probable explanation of Virgil's own
dissatisfaction with the Aeneid, so it is the cause of the adverse
criticism to which the poem has been exposed in recent times.
Of these adverse criticisms, that expressed by Niebuhr, both in
his History of Rome and in his Historical Lectures, was among
the earliest.  In the former he expresses his belief that Virgil,
at the approach of death, wished ' to destroy what in those
solemn moments he could not but view with sadness, as the
groundwork of a false reputation [1].'  In the latter he says, ' The

---

[1] Vol. i. p. 197, Hare and Thirlwall's translation.

whole of the Aeneid, from the beginning to the end, is a mis-
conceived idea.' 'Virgil is one of the remarkable instances of
the way in which a man can miss his true calling. His was
lyric poetry.' 'It is a pity that posterity so much overrated the
very work which was but a failure[1].'

Although the service rendered to the study of antiquity by
the historical insight of Niebuhr is probably as great as that
rendered by the genius of any scholar of this century, yet the
opinions expressed by him on literature are often more arbitrary than authoritative. Still this verdict on the merits of the
Aeneid was in accordance with the most advanced criticism of
the time when it was written, both in Germany and England.
The writer by whom the critical taste of England was most
stimulated and enlarged about the same time was Coleridge;
and in his 'Table Talk' such disparaging dicta as this occur
more than once: 'If you take from Virgil his diction and
metre, what do you leave him?' The whole tone of the criticism which arose out of the admiration of German thought and
poetry was thoroughly opposed to the spirit in which Latin
literature had been admired. Mr. Carlyle also expressed in one
of his earliest works—the Life of Schiller—an estimate of the
value of Virgil, which was not uncommon among younger
scholars at the Universities some thirty years ago. 'Virgil
and Horace,' he writes, 'he (Schiller) learned to construe accu-
rately, but is said to have taken no deep interest in their poetry.
The tenderness and meek beauty of the first, the humour and
sagacity and capricious pathos of the last, the matchless elegance of both would of course escape his inexperienced perception; while the matter of their writings must have appeared
frigid and shallow to a mind so susceptible.' Even the warmest
admirers of Virgil about that time, such as Keble, are content
to claim for him high excellence as the poet of outward nature.
The late Professor Conington, while showing the finest appreciation of 'the marvellous grace and delicacy, the evidences of
a culture most elaborate and most refined,' in the poet to the

---

[1] Lectures on Roman History, vol. iii. p. 131 et seq. (London, 1855.)

interpretation of whose works he devoted the best years of a scholar's life, has questioned 'the appropriateness of the special praise given to Virgil's agricultural poetry, and conceded though with more hesitation to his pastoral compositions.' He speaks also of it as an admitted fact that 'in undertaking the Aeneid at the command of a superior, Virgil was venturing beyond the province of his genius.' And he describes this disparaging estimate as the opinion 'which is now generally entertained on Virgil's claims as an epic poet[1].' Mr. Keightley is also quoted by him as speaking of Virgil as 'perhaps the least original poet of antiquity[2].' It is certainly not in the spirit of an ardent admirer that the author of Virgil's life in the 'Dictionary of Classical Biography and Mythology' approaches the criticism of his poetry. But it is by German critics and scholars that Virgil's claim to a high rank among the poets of the world is at the present day most seriously impugned. Thus to take two or three conspicuous instances of their disparaging criticism : Mommsen in his History of Rome[3] speaks contemptuously of the 'successes of the Aeneid, the Henriade, and the Messiad;' Bernhardy in his *Grundriss der Römischen Litteratur* (1871) brings together a formidable list of German critics and commentators unfavourable to the merits of the Aeneid, in which the illustrious name of Hegel appears; Goss- rau in his edition of the Aeneid quotes from Richter (as a specimen of the unfavourable opinions pronounced by many critics) the expression of a wish that, with the exception of the descriptions and episodes, the rest of the poem had been burned[4]; and W. S. Teuffel, among other criticisms which 'damn with faint praise,' has the following : 'Aber er ist zu weich und zu wenig genial als dass er auf dem seiner Natur zusagendsten Gebiete hätte beharren und darauf Ruhm ernten können.'

[1] Conington's Virgil, Introduction to vol. ii.
[2] Introduction to Éclogue v.
[3] Book iii. chap. xiv.
[4] He adds the comment, 'Equidem dubito num legerit. Nam et philo- logos ita iudicare audivi de Virgilio ut non legisse eos appareret.'

The chief, as well as the most obvious, cause of the revolt against Virgil's poetical pre-eminence, which, though yielding apparently to a revived sentiment of admiration, has not yet spent its force, is the great advance made in Greek scholarship in England and Germany during the present century. Familiarity with Latin literature is probably not less common than it was a century ago, but it is much less common relatively to familiarity with the older literature. The attraction of the latter has been greater from its novelty, its originality, its higher intrinsic excellence, its profounder relation to the heart and mind of man. The art of Homer and that of Theocritus are felt to be an immediate reproduction from human life and outward nature; the art of Virgil seems, at first sight, to be only a reproduction from this older and truer copy. The Roman and Italian character of his workmanship, the new result produced by the recasting of old materials, the individual and inalienable quality of his own genius, were for a time obscured, as the evidences of the large debt which he owed to his Greek masters became more and more apparent.

Again, the greater nearness of the Augustan Age, not in time only but in spirit and manners, to our own age, which in the last century told in Virgil's favour in the comparison with Homer, tells the other way now. The critics of last century were interested in other ages, in so far as they appeared to be like their own. The rude vigour and stirring incident of the Homeric Age or the Middle Ages had no attraction for men living under the *régime* of Louis XIV. and XV. or of Queen Anne and the first Georges. What an illustrious living Frenchman says of the great representative of French ideas in the last century might be said generally of its criticism. 'Voltaire,' says M. Renan, 'understood neither the Bible, nor Homer, nor Greek art, nor the ancient religions, nor Christianity, nor the Middle Ages [1].' And yet he was prepared to pronounce his judgment on them by the light of that admirable. common

---

[1] Questions Contemporaines.   L'Instruction Supérieure en France.

sense which he applied to the questions of his own day.   One of the great gains of the nineteenth century over former centuries consists in its more vital knowledge of the past.   The imaginative interest now felt in times of nascent and immature civilisation all tells in favour of Homer and against Virgil.   The scientific study of human development also tends more and more to awaken interest in a remote antiquity.   Even the ages antecedent to all civilisation have a stronger attraction for the adventurous spirit of modern enquiry than the familiar aspect of those epochs in which human culture and intelligence have reached their highest level.   This new direction given to imaginative and speculative curiosity, while greatly enhancing the interest felt, not in the Iliad and Odyssey only, but in the primitive epics of various races, has proportionately lowered that felt in the literary epics belonging to times of advanced civilisation.   Recognising the radical difference between the two kinds of representation, some recent criticism refuses to the latter altogether the title of epic poetry, and relegates it to some province of imitative and composite art.   There is a similar tendency in the present day to be interested in varieties of popular speech,—in language before it has become artistic. Both tendencies are good in so far as they serve to draw attention to neglected fields of knowledge.   They are false and mischievous in so far as they lead to the disparagement of the great works of cultivated eras, or to any forgetfulness of the superior grace, richness, and power which are imparted to ordinary speech by the labours of intellect and imagination employed in creating a national literature.

Other causes connected with a great expansion of human interests acting on the imagination, and with the revolt against the prevailing poetical style, which arose about the beginning of the present century, have tended to lower the authority of writers who formed the standard of taste to previous ages. The desire of the new era was to escape from the exhausted atmosphere of literary tradition, and to return again to the simplicity of Nature and human feeling.   The genius of

Roman literature is more in harmony with eras of established order, of adherence to custom, of distinct but limited insight into the outward world and into human life, than to eras of expansive energy, of speculative change, of vague striving to attain some new ideal of duty or happiness.   The genius of Greece exercised a powerful influence on several of the great English and German poets who lived in the new era.   But neither Goethe nor Schiller, Byron nor Scott, Shelley nor Keats were at all indebted, in thought, sentiment, or expression, to the poets of the Augustan Age.   Among the great poets of this new era the only one known to have greatly admired Virgil, and who in his poems founded on classical subjects was influenced by him, is the one who most decidedly proclaimed his revolt against the artificial diction and representation of the school of classical imitators,—the poet Wordsworth.

The very perfection of Virgil's art, combined with the calmness and moderation of his spirit, was out of harmony with the genius of such a time.   He seemed to have nothing new to teach the eager generation which regarded the world and speculated on its own destiny with feelings altogether unlike to those of the generations that went before it.   The truth of his sentiment, its adaptation to the spiritual movement of his own age, in which it gained ascendency like a new revelation, had caused it to pass into the modes of thought and feeling habitual to the world.   This too may be said of the ethical feeling and common sense of Cicero's philosophical treatises.   Moral speculation has been so long and so deeply permeated by the thought expressed in these treatises that it now appears trite and common-place.   So too the moderation and unfailing propriety of Virgil's language had no attraction of freshness or novelty to stimulate the imagination.   The direct force of language in Homer or Lucretius never can become trite or common-place. It affects the mind now as powerfully and immediately as in the day of its creation.   There is also a kind of rhetorical style which produces its effect either of pleasure or distaste immediately.   It does not conceal its true character, but tries to

force the reader's admiration by startling imagery, or strained
emphasis, or tricks of allusive periphrasis.    Whether this style
is admired or detested, it does not lose its character with the
advance of years.    Juvenal and Persius probably affect their
readers in much the same way as they did three centuries or
seventeen centuries ago.    But this is not the style of Virgil and
of Horace.    They produce their effect neither through that
direct force which causes a thought to penetrate or an image to
rise up immediately before the mind, nor by strained efforts at
rhetorical effect.    As their language became assimilated with
the thought and feeling of successive generations, it may have
lost something of the colouring of sentiment and association, of
the delicate shades of meaning, of the vital force which it
originally possessed.    It has entered into the culture of the
world chiefly through impressions produced in early youth,
when the mind, though susceptible of graceful variations of
words and harmonious effects of rhythm, is too immature to
realise fulness of meaning half-concealed by the well-tempered
beauty and musical charm of language.    The style of Virgil is
the fruit of long reflection, and it requires long reflection and
familiarity to draw out all its meaning.    The word 'meditari,'
applied by him to his earlier art, expresses the process through
which his mind passed in acquiring its mastery over words.    In
apprehending the charm of his style it is not of the spontaneous
fertility of Nature that we think, but of the harvest yielded to
assiduous labour by a soil at once naturally rich and obedient
to cultivation—'iustissima tellus.'    These characteristics of his
art were not unlikely to be overlooked in an age which
demanded from the literature of imagination a rapid succession
of varied and powerful impressions.

### III.

Though some of the causes which tended to lower the estimation in which Virgil was held were only temporary in their
operation, yet it can hardly be doubted that his claim to pre-

eminence in Latin literature and to a high rank among the greatest poets of all times must, if put forward at all, be maintained on somewhat different grounds from those on which his position formerly rested.   He never again can enter into rivalry with Homer as the inspired poet of heroic action.   He cannot again enjoy the advantage of being widely known, while access to his predecessor is confined to a few scholars not much in sympathy with the poet of an age so far separated from their own.   The art of Virgil in so far as it is a copy of the art of Homer has already produced all the effect on the culture of the world which it is destined to produce.   The life of the heroic age will continue to be known to all future times as it was originally fashioned by the creative mind of Homer, not as it was modified by the after-thought of Virgil.

What charm Virgil had for his countrymen as the reviver of the early poetry of Greece and as the first creator of the early romance of Italy, what permanent value he has as one of the great interpreters of the secret of Nature and of the meaning of human life, will appear in the course of the detailed examination of his various poems.   But there are some considerations, from an historical point of view, which may be stated provisionally as grounds for assigning to him the place of most importance in Latin literature.   He is, more than any other Latin writer, a representative writer,—representative both of the general national idea and of the sentiment and culture of his own age.   One clear note of this representative character is that he absorbs and supersedes so much of what went before him, and that he anticipates and also supersedes much that came after him.   The interest which Rome and Italy have for all times, the interest which the Augustan Age has as the epoch of the maturest civilisation of ancient times and as a great turning-point in the history of mankind, will secure the attention of the world to an author who sets before it, in forms of pure art and with elaborate workmanship, the idealised spectacle of the marvellous career of Rome, and best enables it to feel the charm of natural beauty and ancient memories associated with Italy; and who has interpreted, as no one else has done, the meaning and tendency of his age, and of the change which was then preparing for the human spirit and for the nations of the future.

(1.) The Aeneid brings home to us, in a way in which no other work of Latin literature can do, all those elements in the idea of the destiny, the genius, and character of Rome which most powerfully move the imagination, while it enables us for a time to forget those elements of hardness, unscrupulous injustice, and oppressive domination on which the historian is forced to dwell, and which alienate the sympathies as much as her nobler aspect compels the admiration of mankind. The grandeur and dignity of the Imperial State appear softened and mellowed by Virgil's marvellous art and humane feeling. 'The Aeneid,' says Hallam, 'reflects the glory of Rome as from a mirror[1].' 'It remains,' says Mr. Merivale, 'the most complete picture of the national mind at its highest elevation, the most precious document of national history, if the history of an age is revealed in its ideas, no less than in its events and incidents[2].' 'Virgile,' writes M. Sainte-Beuve, 'a été le poëte du Capitole[3].' 'Dans ce poëme,' writes M. de Coulanges of the Aeneid, 'ils (les Romains) se voyaient, eux, leur fondateur, leur ville, leurs institutions, leurs croyances, leur Empire[4].' M. Patin again describes the same poem as 'expression de Rome, de Rome entière, de la Rome de tous les temps, de celle des Empereurs, des Consuls, des Rois[5].' He might have added that it had anticipated the idea of the Rome of the Popes, in some at least of its aspects. The type of character which Virgil has conceived in Aeneas is more like that of the milder among the spiritual rulers of mediaeval Rome than that either of the Homeric heroes or of the actual Consuls and Imperators who commanded the Roman armies and administered the affairs of

[1] Introduction to the Literature of Europe, Part II. chap. v.
[2] Roman Empire, chap. xli.          [3] Étude sur Virgile.
[4] La Cité antique.
[5] Études sur la Poésie latine.

the Roman State.   It has been said of him by another Frenchman that he was more fitted to be the founder of an order of
monks than of an Empire.   Virgil's object is to make his
readers believe in the mission of Rome, as appointed by Divine
decree, for the ultimate peace and good government of the
world.   The work of Rome in the past, the present, and the
future is conceived by him as a manifestation of the Deity in
his justice, authority, and beneficence.

(2.) The spell which Rome exercises over the imagination is
quite distinct from the charm which the thought of Italy has for
the hearts of men.   The love of Italy was a sentiment as
deeply rooted in Virgil's nature as his pride in Rome.   This
sentiment pervades all his works and inspires some of his
noblest poetry.   In his pastoral poems, under all the borrowed
imagery of the Greek idyl, it reveals itself in his sensibility to
the beauty of the Italian climate ('caeli indulgentia'), to the
charm of the various seasons, to the distinctive graces of the
plants and wild flowers native to the soil, and in the expression
of the deep attachment with which the peasant-proprietor clung
to his little plot of ground as the sphere alike of his cares and
of his happiness.   In the Aeneid this patriotic feeling shows
itself, as a similar feeling shows itself in the poetry of Scott,
in the enthusiasm with which the martial memories of famous
towns and tribes are recalled in association with the picturesque
features of the land.   But by no work of art, ancient or
modern, is the complete impression, moral and physical, of the
old Italian land and people,—

Terra antiqua potens armis atque ubere glaebae[1],—

produced with such vivid truthfulness and such enduring charm
as by the Georgics.   To express the whole meaning of Italy, it
was necessary that the poet should feel a pride in her stubborn
industry[2] as well as in her warlike energy; that he should

---

[1] 'A land of old renown, mighty in arms and the richness of its soil.'
[2] 'Perseverantissimo agrorum colendorum studio veteres illi Sabini
Quirites atavique Romani,' etc.   Columella.

cherish for the whole land, now united as one nation, an impartial love; and that he should be deeply susceptible of that beauty of season and landscape which was a more self-sufficing source of pleasure [1] to the cultivated Italian than even to the ancient Greek. Some sympathy with the 'Itala virtus'—the courage and discipline of the Marsian and other Sabellian races —Ennius had already expressed in his national epic; but he was interested solely in military and political life, in the activity of the camp and battle-field, the forum and senate-house. Virgil was the first and the only Roman poet to realise the full inspiration of that thought, to which he gives utterance in the close of one of his noblest passages,—

> Salve, magna parens frugum, Saturnia tellus,
> Magna virum [2].

(3.) Virgil has also found a truer poetical expression than any other for the political feeling and tendency of his time. He could not indeed teach the whole lesson of the early Empire, or foresee, in the prosperity and glory that followed the battle of Actium, the oppression experienced under the rule of Tiberius, the degradation experienced under Nero. But his imagination was moved by all those influences which, in the Augustan Age, were giving a new impulse and direction to human affairs. His poems, better than any other witnesses, enable us to understand how weary the Roman world was of the wars, disturbances, and anarchy of the preceding century, how ardently it longed for the restoration of order and national unity, how thankfully it accepted the rule of the man who could alone effect this restoration, and how hopefully it looked forward to a new era of peace and prosperity, of glory and empire, under his administration. The poetry of Virgil co-operated with the policy of the Emperor in the work effected in that age. As Augustus professed to give a new organisation

---

[1] Cf. Lucretius, iii. 105-106:
> Quod faciunt nobis annorum tempora, circum
> Cum redeunt fetusque ferunt variosque lepores.
[2] 'Hail mighty mother of harvests, Saturnian land, mighty mother of men.'

to the political life of the Republic, Virgil gave a new direction
to its spiritual life, a new significance to its ancient traditions.
Augustus, in depriving Rome of her liberty, confirmed for centuries her empire over the world : Virgil, in abnegating the
independent position of Lucretius and Catullus, established the
ascendency of Roman culture and ideas for a still longer time.
As Augustus shaped the policy, Virgil moulded the political
feeling of the future.  It is in his poems that loyalty to one
man, which soon became, and, till a comparatively recent
period, continued to be the master-force in European politics,—
apparently a necessary stage in the ultimate evolution of free
national life on a large scale,—finds its earliest expression.
And the loyalty of Virgil is not merely a natural emotion
towards one who is regarded as the embodiment of law as
well as of power, but is a religious acknowledgment of a
government, sanctioned and directed by the Divine will.  Perhaps one reason why he is read with less sympathy in the
present than in previous centuries, is that his political ideal
appears to us a lower ideal than that of a free Commonwealth.
But in Virgil's time faith in the Republic had become impracticable, and, though the sentiment continued to ennoble the life
of individuals, it was powerless to change the current of events.
Loyalty to a person appealed to the imagination with the
charm of novelty, and might be justified to the conscience of
the world, as being, for that time and the times that came after,
the necessary bond of civil order and union.

(4.) As Virgil first expressed the political tendency of his
age, so he is the purest exponent of its ethical and religious
sensibility.  He recalls the simpler virtues of the olden time, he
represents the humanity of his own age, he anticipates something of the piety and purity of the future faith of the world.
As in the development of Roman law, the spirit of equity
fostered by Greek studies gradually gained ascendency over the
native hardness of the Roman temper, so, from the time of
Laelius and the younger Scipio, the expansion through intellectual culture of the humane and sympathetic emotions, ex-

pressed by the word 'humanitas,' continued to prevail, in opposition to the spirit of national exclusiveness habitual to the Roman aristocracy, and in spite of the cruel experience of the Civil Wars.   In no writers is this quality more conspicuous than in Cicero and in Lucretius.   In Lucretius this feeling inspires his passionate revolt against the ancient religions.   The humane feeling of Virgil, on the other hand, is in complete harmony with his religious belief.   His word *pietas*, as is observed by M. Sainte-Beuve, is the equivalent both of our 'piety' and of our 'pity.'   The Power above man is regarded by him not as an unreal phantom created by our fears, but as the source and sanction of justice and mercy, of good will and good faith among men.

This view of the relation between the supernatural world and human life is not indeed the only one which Virgil shows us. He endeavours, by the union of imagination, philosophy, and tradition, to establish religious opinion as well as to kindle religious emotions ; nor is he quite successful in reconciling these various factors of belief.   The 'Fates,' which are the medium through which man's happiness or misery is allotted, are sometimes stern and inflexible, as well as beneficent in their action.   They accomplish their purposes with no regard to individual rights or feelings.   But though Virgil failed, as much as other exponents of religious systems, in reconciling the necessities of his creed with the instincts of human sensibility, it remains true that in regard to much both of his feeling and intuition, in his firm faith in Divine Providence, in his conviction of the spiritual essence in man and of its independence of and superiority to the body, in his belief that the future state of the soul depends on the deeds done in the body, in his sense of sin and purification for sin, in the value which he attaches to purity and sanctity of life, his spirit is much more in unison with the faith and hopes which were destined to prevail over the world, than with the common beliefs or half-beliefs of his own time.   In his religious and ethical, no less than his political sentiment, 'il a deviné à une heure décisive du monde ce

qu'aimerait l'avenir.' If it was as a great national poet, the
rival of Homer, Hesiod, and Theocritus, that he exercised the
most powerful spell over his contemporaries, it was rather as
the 'pius vates,' the prophetic teacher, that, in spite of themselves, he gained ascendency over the cultivated minds of the
early Latin and the mediaeval Churches [1].

(5.) Though other periods of ancient history, and notably the
fifth century B.C. in Greece, were richer in genius and enjoyed
a happier and nobler life than the Augustan Age, yet this latter
age, as the latest of the great literary epochs of antiquity, inherited the science, wisdom, power, and beauty stored up in all
the art and writings of the past. The Augustan Age was pre-
eminently an age of culture, and Virgil was pre-eminently the
most cultivated man belonging to the age. In early youth he
had learned from Greek masters all they could teach him in
poetry and rhetoric, in science and philosophy; and through
all his life he combined the productive labours of an artist with
the patient diligence of a student. He was familiar with the
successive schools of Greek poetry, from Homer and Hesiod
down to the epic and didactic poets of Alexandria. He was
acquainted with all the physical sciences known in his time,
especially, it is said, with astronomy and medicine. His earlier
writings show the influence of the philosophical system of
Epicurus, while his later convictions are more in agreement
with the Platonic philosophy. The oratory of the later books
of the Aeneid breathes the spirit of Stoicism. We are told that
he proposed to devote the years that might remain to him after
the completion of the Aeneid to the further study of philosophy, perhaps with the view of writing a great poem, which
might rival and answer Lucretius. The extant fragments of
Naevius, Ennius, Pacuvius, Attius, and Lucilius, and of later
and obscurer writers such as Hostius and Varro Atacinus, show

---

[1] 'Virgile fut en effet une des âmes les plus chrétiennes du Paganisme.
Quoique attaché de tout son cœur à l'ancienne religion, il a semblé quel-
quefois pressentir la nouvelle, et un Chrétien pieux pourrait croire qu'il ne
lui manqua pour l'embrasser que de la connaître.' Gaston Boissier.

that he had read their works, and could skilfully adapt what he
found in them to his own national epic.   The Georgics, again,
show a careful study and assimilation of the thought and
language of Lucretius.   And to the pursuits of a scholar he
united the research of an antiquary.   He collected from many
sources the myths and traditions connected with the origin of
ancient customs and ceremonies, or attaching to the towns and
tribes of Italy, famous in early times.   He was especially well
versed in the ceremonial lore of the Priestly Colleges.   Thus,
in addition to his higher claims on the admiration of his
countrymen, his poems were prized by them as a great repertory of their secular and sacred learning.   Many fancies
and dim traditions of a remote antiquity, many vestiges of
customs and ceremonies which have disappeared from the
world, many thoughts and expressions of men who have left
scarcely any other memorial of themselves, still survive, because
the mind of Virgil discerned some element of interest in them
which fitted them to contribute to the representative character
of the work to which his life was dedicated.

(6.) Virgil's pre-eminence as a literary artist and master of
poetical expression is so generally acknowledged that it is not
necessary to illustrate it in this preliminary statement of the
position which he holds in Roman literature.   The Augustan
Age was characterised by a careful study and application of the
principles of art, as well as by an elaborate culture.   By the
labours and reflection of three or four generations the Latin
language had been gradually changed from a rude Italian dia-
lect into a great organ of law, government, and literature.
The efforts of the generation preceding the Augustan Age to
attain to perfection in form and style received their fulfilment in
the work accomplished by Virgil and Horace.   Each of them,
in his own way, obtained a complete success ; but the sustained
perfection of a long poem, epic or didactic, is a much greater
result than the perfection shown in the composition of an ode.
Virgil, alone among his countrymen, discerned the true conditions in accordance with which a long continuous poem, epic

or didactic, could as a whole gain, and permanently retain, the ear of the world: and, in accordance with these conditions, he worked the various materials, descriptive, meditative, narrative, and commemorative, of the Georgics and Aeneid into poems of large compass, sustained interest, and finished execution.  His style marks the maturity of development after which the vital force animating the growth of the Latin language begins to decay.  One of the most sensible causes of this decay in the idiomatic structure of the language both of verse and prose is the predominance of Virgil's influence over the later writers. He and Horace introduced into Latin all that it could well bear of the subtlety and flexibility which characterise the Greek tongue.  When first introduced, this infusion of a new force into the Latin language, modifying the use of words and alter- ing the structure of sentences, probably appeared to the literary class at Rome a new source of wealth, colouring words and phrases with the gleam of old poetic association.  But this new infusion, though an immediate source of wealth, tended to cor- rupt the pure current of native speech.  The later poetical style of Rome never regains the lucidity and volume which it has in Lucretius, or the ease and sparkling flow of Catullus. The maturity of accomplishment immediately preceded and partly occasioned the decay in vital force.

In other arts the maturest excellence often foreruns a rapid and inevitable decline.  One cause of this seems to be, that the great masters, having once for all expressed in the happiest manner whatever is best worth expressing within the range and vision of their own era, leave to their successors the choice of tamely imitating them or of striving to gain attention, by a strained way of expressing it, for what is not worth expressing in any way.  Into the first of these pitfalls the imitative poets of the Flavian era sank; the more ambitious *littérateurs* of the Neronian Age fell into the second.  Another cause of the close connexion between the maturity and the decay of art is that the representation of man and Nature produced by a great master is coloured by his own thought and feeling.  The representation thus established gains ascendency over the future. Each new reproduction of this departs further from reality. Art becomes thoroughly conventional. It revives only after a new range of interests, some vital change in belief and ideas, has arisen in the evolution of national life, accompanied by a new birth of original genius, and powerful enough to divert the minds of men from the contemplation of the old to the novel spectacle of the world in which they live. The emotions thus excited force out for themselves a fresh channel: the sound of poetry is again heard in the land, and the hearts of men are refreshed :—

> Illa cadens raucum per levia murmur
> Saxa ciet, scatebrisque arentia temperat arva[1].

The imaginative literature of Greece, of England, and of France has thus renewed itself at various epochs in the history of these nations. Either the life of the ancient world was too much exhausted, or the ascendency of Virgil in the literature of his country was too powerful, to permit the appearance of any new spring of Latin poetry.

## IV.

Whether the gifts of intellect and feeling by which Virgil represented his country and his age entitle him to a place among the greatest poets of the world, will be answered variously according to the degree in which men recognise in him the presence of that diviner faculty of imagination which no analysis can explain. If we look to him for the original force of creative imagination which we find in Homer, Aeschylus, and Sophocles on the one hand, and in the greatest poets of modern times on the other, we shall fail to establish his equality with them. But as there have been various types of philosophical intellect in the world, so there have been various types

---

[1] 'As it falls it awakens a hoarse murmur among the smooth stones, and with its bubbling waters cools the parched fields.'

of imaginative power. And among these types we may distinguish those characteristic of the Hellenic, the Germanic, and
the Italian races. The genius of the ancient Latin race is
further removed from that of the modern Germanic race, than
either is from the genius of ancient Greece. The peculiar
richness of our own poetic literature arises from its combining
some of the great characteristics of each type. While Scott
and Byron, for instance, are among the greatest representatives
of the purely modern imagination, the works of Pope and Gray
are essentially of the Latin type ; and those of Dryden, Milton,
and Spenser blend Roman strength or the culture of Latin
ideas with English boldness and modern exuberance of fancy :
while, again, Shelley, Keats, and all the greatest among our
living poets have received a powerful impulse from Greek art
and Greek ideas. It must be admitted by students of Latin
literature that the intellectual movement and sensibility of the
present time has a closer affinity with the ancient Greek than
with the ancient Latin culture. Students of Homer and
Aeschylus, as well as those who have once felt the spell of

'Goethe's sage mind and Byron's force,'

of Wordsworth's contemplative elevation and the impassioned
ideality of Shelley, find, in turning to Virgil, that their range
of feeling and of contemplation has become narrower. They
no longer enjoy the same illimitable prospect, they no longer
breathe the same keen air, which buoyed them up on the higher
altitudes of poetry. Greek and modern works of imagination
manifest a profounder feeling, a more varied contemplation
of the mystery of life, than is compatible with the more realistic
tendencies of Latin poetry. And though the representation of
the outward world in Virgil is, in its serene beauty, suggestive
of a secret unceasing life which appeals to the human spirit in
its more tranquil moods, yet it does not move the mind to that
profounder sense of an affinity between the soul of man and the
soul of Nature which the great modern poets awaken. The
charm and power of Latin poetry consists, for the most part,

in the vital strength of feeling with which it invests a limited
and definite range of interests. What the Roman poets cared
for, they cared for with all their heart, and strength, and mind.
They seem to have written from more enduring, if less abundant, sources of affection than other poets. Their hearts
thoroughly realised what they idealised in imagination. This
strong realism and constancy of feeling explains the labour
with which they perfected their art, as the strong love of his
small portion of land explains the labour which the ideal husbandman of the Georgics bestows on it. Through that vividness of feeling with which they cherished the thought of what
gave actual joy to their lives, Catullus and Horace were able
to invest the names of Sirmio, of Lucretilis and Digentia, with
an interest which attaches to the favourite residences of no
other poets: though perhaps future generations will find a
similar classic charm attaching to the homes of Wordsworth
and of Scott, and to the hills, dales, and streams which they
have endowed with the wealth of their strong affection. The
human objects of their passionate love excited in several of the
Roman poets this same vital warmth of feeling. The 'spirat
adhuc amor' is still true of all the poetry which the love of
Lesbia and of Cynthia inspired. Even Ovid, whose want of
seriousness and profound feeling is the chief flaw in his poetic
temperament, had the most vivid sense of the pleasure and of
the pain of his own existence. It is this capacity in the imagination of being vitally interested in and possessed by its object,
which enabled Lucretius to breathe the breath of enduring life
into the dry bones of the atomic philosophy. And that this
strong realism of feeling is a characteristic of the race to which
these poets belonged is proved by the pathetic force of the
numerous sepulchral epitaphs of persons altogether undistin-
guished, preserved from the times of the early Empire. It is
owing to the power of producing a strong and abiding impression that Latin has retained the function of being the language
of great epitaphs and of great inscriptions in modern times.

Virgil too possessed this gift of vividly realising the objects

which interested him; and his singularly receptive nature
enabled him to feel a much larger number of interests than
the other poets of his country. What his speculative system
was to Lucretius in its power of concentrating on itself all his
capacity of feeling; what 'Lesbia' and 'Sirmio' and the few
objects associated with the happiness and pain of his life were
to Catullus; what the valley in the Sabine hills was to Horace[1];
what Cynthia in life and death was to Propertius; what the
remembrance of past joy in the midst of sorrow was to Ovid;
that the thought of Rome and the memories associated with it,
the charm of the land and air of Italy, the strength and sanctity
of human affection, the mystery of the unseen world, were to
Virgil. The necessities of his art require him to introduce into
his poem materials which touch his own nature less deeply, and
which come to him through the reflex action of literary association; and these, though he always treats them gracefully, he
does not invest with the same sense of reality. But when his
imagination is moved by the thought of Rome, of Italy, of a
remote antiquity, of human affection, of the unseen world, then
his art becomes truly and vividly creative. The depth of feeling with which these things affect him reveals itself in the
blended majesty and sweetness, the tenderness and pathos of
his tones, occasionally in some more solemn cadence and a
kind of mystic yearning.

If a return to the high admiration once felt for Virgil involved
any detraction from the high admiration with which the great
poets of Greece and of the modern world are regarded,
anything like his claims to his old rank would generally be
set aside. If for no other reason, yet because they have more
in common with the general ideas and movement of the
modern world, these last-named poets have a stronger hold
on students of literature in the present day. But, happily, the
'sacrum litterarum studium'—to use a phrase of Macrobius—

---

[1] It is in the poems connected with this theme that Horace writes most
from the heart; yet even where he writes chiefly from the head he imparts
the same vital realism to the results of his reflection.

the religion of the world of letters, is not a jealous or in-tolerant faith. The object of that religion is to keep alive the sentiment of reverence for every kind of excellence which has appeared in the literature of the world. That Virgil was once the object of the greatest reverence is a reason for not lightly putting his claims aside now. In our study of the great writers of old, it is well to realise the true lesson taught in the sad beauty of the lines,—

Οὐχ ἀμὶν τὰ καλὰ πράτοις καλὰ φαίνεται εἶμεν
οἱ θνατοὶ πελόμεσθα τὸ δ' αὔριον οὐκ ἐσορῶμες[1].

The course of time brings with it losses as well as gains in sensibility. Though the thoughts of the Latin poet may not help us to understand the spirit of our own era, they are a bond of union with the genius and culture of Europe in other times. If poetry ever exercises a healing and reconciling influence on life, the deep and tranquil charm of Virgil may prove some antidote to the excitement, the restlessness, the unsettlement of opinion in the present day. And as it is by the young especially that the imaginative art of Virgil, in comparison with the imaginative art of other great poets, is most questioned, they may be reminded that the words of such a writer are best understood after long study and experience of life have enabled us to feel 'their sad earnestness and vivid exactness[2].' The wise and generous counsel of Burke should induce some diffidence in their own judgment on the part of those to whom the power and charm of this poet have been slow in revealing themselves.

'Different from them are all the great critics. They have taught us one essential rule. I think the excellent and phi-losophic artist, a true judge as well as perfect follower of Nature, Sir Joshua Reynolds, has somewhere applied it or something like it in his own profession. It is this, that if ever

---

[1] 'We are not the first to whom things of beauty appear beautiful,—we who are mortal men, and behold not the morrow.'
[2] *Grammar of Assent*, by J. H. Newman.

we should find ourselves disposed not to admire those writers and artists, Livy and Virgil for instance, Raphael or Michael Angelo, whom all the learned had admired, not to follow our own fancies, but to study them until we know how and what we ought to admire; and if we cannot arrive at this union of admiration with knowledge, rather to believe that we are dull than that the rest of the world has been imposed on[1].'

[1] Appeal from the New to the Old Whigs.

# CHAPTER III.

## LIFE AND PERSONAL CHARACTERISTICS OF VIRGIL.

### I.

THE most trustworthy sources for our personal knowledge of the great writers of antiquity are their own writings, and accidental notices in the works of contemporaries and writers of a succeeding generation. But besides these sources of information some short biographies of eminent Latin writers, written long after their deaths, have reached modern times. In cases where their actual biographies have been lost, fragments or summaries of them have been preserved in Jerome's continuation of the Eusebian Chronicle, and occasionally in commentaries or scholia appended to their own works. Roman literature from a comparatively early period produced a large number of grammarians, commentators, and rhetoricians. In the Ciceronian Age, Varro wrote several books on literary history and the earlier poets; and Cornelius Nepos included in his Biographies the lives of men of letters, among others of his own contemporary, Atticus. Jerome, in the prefatory letter to his own work 'De Viris Illustribus[1],' mentions the names of Varro, Santra, Nepos, Hyginus, and Suetonius as authors of literary biography, and proposes to follow in his own work the precedent set by the last of these authors. Of the work of Suetonius 'De Viris Illustribus,' written in the second century, and containing the lives of eminent poets, orators, historians, philosophers, grammarians, and rhetoricians, considerable portions have been preserved; among others complete biographies of Terence and Horace. This work became the chief authority

---

[1] Quoted by Reifferscheid in his Suetonii Reliquiae.

to later commentators for the facts recorded about the earlier
Roman poets, and was the source from which Jerome himself
drew the materials for the continuation of the Eusebian Chronicle.   The question remains as to how far Suetonius himself,
writing under the rule of Hadrian, is a trustworthy authority
for the lives of poets who lived nearly two centuries before his
own era.   The answer to this question will depend on the
access which he may have had to contemporary sources,
transmitted to his time through an uninterrupted channel, and
on the evidence of credulity or trustworthiness in accepting or
rejecting gossip and scandalous anecdotes which his other
writings afford.   He appears to have been diligent in his
examination of original authorities.   On the other hand, his
'Lives of the Caesars' indicate a vein of credulity in regard
to the details of unverifiable charges at which Tacitus only
hints by general innuendo.   But the main question in regard
to the life of each particular poet is, whether there was in
existence written evidence dating from contemporary sources
on which Suetonius could have based his narrative.   In the
case of some poets, notably of Virgil, it is quite certain that
there was such evidence.   In the case of others, notably of
Lucretius, there is no hint whatever of the existence of any
such evidence.   The poets who immediately succeeded him
and who were diligent students of his poem concur in absolute
silence as to the story of that poet's unhappy fate, told in the
continuation of the Eusebian Chronicle, and now received by
the most competent critics as resting on the authority of
Suetonius.   But even when we substitute Suetonius for Jerome
as the original voucher for the facts stated, the uncertainty as
to any contemporary evidence available to the former, and the
sensational character of the story itself, justify at least a suspense
of judgment in accepting or rejecting this meagre fragment of
personal history; while on the other hand there is no ground
for distrusting the main features, whatever may be said of
some details, of the ancient life of Virgil, equally acknowledged
to rest ultimately on the authority of Suetonius.

In addition to these materials for the biography of Latin writers, in some few cases the imagination is assisted in realising their character and genius by the preservation from ancient times of their statues, busts, images impressed on gems, or other kinds of portraiture.   But in the case of men of letters, it is not often that reliance can be placed on the authenticity of such memorials, except in such instances as that of Cicero, where a great name in literature was combined with prominence in public life.

The data for a knowledge of the life, circumstances, and personal characteristics of Virgil are supplied partly by direct statements contained in his poems or inferences founded on them; partly by the indirect impression of himself stamped on these poems; partly by casual notices in the works of other poets, and especially of Horace; and partly by statements in the Life of the poet originally prefixed to the Commentary of Aelius Donatus,—a grammarian who flourished in the fourth century A.D.,—and founded on, if not an actual reproduction of, the Life originally contained in the work of Suetonius.

The directest record of his tastes and feelings is contained in one or two of the minor poems published among the Catalepton[1], which may without hesitation be treated as genuine.   A fragment of a prose letter to Augustus has been preserved by Macrobius, which confirms the traditional account of the poet's estimate of the Aeneid and of his devotion in later life to philosophical studies[2].   The Eclogues and Georgics add something to our information, but as the representation in the first of these works is for the most part dramatic, and as the purpose of the second is purely didactic, the evidence they supply is much less vivid and direct than that supplied by Horace,

---

[1] For the name *Catalepton* cp. Professor Nettleship's *Vergil* in *Classical Writers*, p. 23.

[2] 'Sed tanta inchoata res est, ut paene vitio mentis tantum opus ingressus mihi videar, cum praesertim alia quoque studia ad id opus multoque potiora impertiar.' Macrob. Sat. i. 24. 11.   The 'potiora studia' seem clearly to mean the philosophical studies, to which his biographer says he meant to devote the remainder of his life after publishing the Aeneid.

Catullus, and the elegiac poets in regard to their lives and pursuits; and even where the allusions to matters personal to himself are unmistakeable, they require to be interpreted by knowledge derived from other sources.

The Georgics and those parts of the Aeneid which are specially ethical and didactic, as that part of Book VI. from line 264 to 751, throw most light on Virgil's spiritual nature and on his convictions on the questions of most vital interest to man. But in these parts of his works Virgil has not revealed himself with such distinctness and consistency as Lucretius has done in his great philosophical poem. The personality of Lucretius was simpler and more forcible : the passion to utter his strong convictions prevailed in him over all considerations of art. The colouring of his own heart and spirit, of his enthusiasm or melancholy, appears in Virgil rather as a pervading and subtly interpenetrating influence, than as the direct indication of his true self. His artistic taste enforced on him reserve in express-ing what was personal to himself; his nature was apparently more open to varied influences of books and men than that of Lucretius; he was endowed with the many-sided susceptibility of a poet, rather than with the simpler, more energetic, but narrower consistency of a philosophical partisan. Equally with Lucretius he throws his whole heart and being into the treat-ment of his subject; but in Lucretius the two streams of what is personal to himself and what is inherent in his subject are still distinguishable. In Virgil the imaginative sentiment of the poet and the strong tender heart of the man seem to be inseparably united. It would be impossible to distinguish them by analysis,—to abstract from the bloom of his poetry the delicate sweetness which may have pervaded his performance of the common duties and his share in the common intercourse of life.

Of the contemporary poets and critics whose works are extant, much the most important witness of the impression produced by Virgil on those with whom he lived is the poet Horace. And he is an admirable witness, from the clearness of his judgment, the calmness of his temperament, and the intimate terms of friendship on which he lived with the older poet.   Unlike Virgil, who from reasons of health, or natural inclination, or devotion to his art had chosen

Secretum iter et fallentis semita vitae [1],

and cherished few, but close, intimacies, Horace lived in the world, enjoyed all that was illustrious, brilliant or genial, in the society of his time, and while still constant to the attachments of his earlier years, continued through all his life to form new friendships with younger men who gave promise of distinction. His Odes and Epistles are addressed to a great variety of men, to those of highest social or political position, such as Agrippa, Pollio, Munatius Plancus, Sallustius Crispus, Lollius, etc.; to old comrades of his youth or brother poets, such as Pompeius Grosphus, Septimius, Aristius Fuscus, Tibullus; to the men of a younger generation, such as Iulus Antonius, Julius Florus, and the younger Lollius: and to all of them he applies language of discriminating, but not of excessive appreciation.   To the men of eminence in the State he uses expressions of courteous and delicate compliment, never of flattery or exaggeration. His old comrades and intimate associates he greets with hearty friendliness or genial irony: to younger men, without assuming the airs of a Mentor, he addresses words of sympathetic encouragement or paternal advice.   But among all those whom he addresses there are only two—unless from one or two words implying strong attachment, we add one more to the number, Aelius Lamia—in connexion with whom he uses the language of warm and admiring affection.   These are Maecenas and Virgil.   Whatever may have been the date or circumstances connected with the composition of the third Ode of Book I., the simple words 'animae dimidium meae' establish the futility

---

[1] 'A way remote from the world and the path of a life that passes by unnoticed.'
   Cp. 'Along the cool sequestered vale of life
         They kept the noiseless tenour of their way.'

of the notion, that the subject of this Ode is not the poet but
only the same merchant or physician whom Horace in the
twelfth Ode of Book IV. invites, in his most Epicurean style, to
sacrifice for a time his pursuit of wealth to the more seasonable
claims of the wine of Cales.

Two short Lives of Virgil written in prose have reached our
time, one originally prefixed to the Commentary by Valerius
Probus, a grammarian of the first century A.D., the other, much
longer and more important, prefixed to that of Donatus.
There is also a Life in hexameter verse, written by a grammarian named Phocas, about one half of which is devoted to
an account of the marvellous portents that were alleged to have
accompanied the birth of the poet.   The Life of Donatus was
in the later MSS. of Virgil so much corrupted by the intermixture of mediaeval fictions, that it is only in recent times that
modern criticism has successfully removed the interpolations,
and restored the original Life based on that of Suetonius [1].
What then were the materials available to Suetonius?   The
earliest source of his information was a work referred to by
Quintilian (x. 3. 8), written by the older contemporary and life-
long friend of Virgil, the poet Varius, entitled 'De ingenio mo-
ribusque Vergilii.'   Aulus Gellius (xvii. 10) speaks of the
'memorials which the friends and intimates of Virgil have left
of his genius and character.'   Among those who contributed to
the knowledge of his habits, etc., the name of C. Melissus, a
freedman of Maecenas, is quoted as an authority for a statement
that 'in ordinary speech he was very slow and almost like an
uneducated man '—a trait which calls to mind what is recorded
of Addison.   Melissus could not fail to be an authority as to
the relations of Virgil to Maecenas, and it is probably on his
evidence that the statement rests of the direction given to the
poet's genius in the choice of the subject of the Georgics.

---

[1] Cf. Reifferscheid, Quaestiones Suetonianae, p. 400.   Hagen, De Dona-
tianae Vergilii vitae Codicibus, prefixed to his edition of the Scholia
Bernensia.   De vita et scriptis P. Vergili Maronis narratio, prefixed to
Ribbeck's text in the Teubner edition of Virgil.

A still more important work was that of the grammarian Asconius Pedianus, born at the commencement of our era, who wrote ' Contra obtrectatores Vergilii.' These ' maligners,' beginning with those whose names have been condemned to everlasting fame, as Bavius and Maevius, had assailed the art of Virgil by flippant parodies, or had traduced his character by imputations, which, though they might have called for no remark if made against any other poet of the time, were believed by those who had the best means of knowing the truth to be incompatible with the finer nature of Virgil. In regard to one of these charges Asconius was able to procure the evidence of an emphatic denial from the only surviving person who could have known anything about the matter [1].

The certainty that the biographical notices of Virgil and the accounts transmitted of his personal characteristics can be traced to contemporary sources and to information derived from contemporaries, gives to the main statements of Donatus a value which does not attach to the meagre notice of Lucretius preserved in the writings of Jerome. On the other hand, while it is believed by his English Editor that the actual features of Lucretius have been transmitted, engraved on a gem, no reliance can be placed on the authenticity either of the busts, such as that shown in the Capitoline Museum, or of the portraits prefixed to various MSS., and all different from one another, which profess to transmit the likeness of Virgil.

## II.

The testimony of inscriptions, of the earliest MSS., and of the Greek rendering of the word, has led to the general adoption in recent times of the name P. Vergilius Maro, as that by which the poet should be known [2]. Yet it is an unnecessary disturbance of old associations to change the abbreviation so

---

[1] Ribbeck, Prolegomena, cap. viii.
[2] Gossrau, in his edition of the Aeneid (1876), argues and quotes authorities in favour of retaining the older form *Virgilius*.

long established in all European literature into the unfamiliar *Vergil*. He was born on the 15th of October in the year 70 B.C., the first consulate of Pompey and Crassus. The Romans attached a peculiar sacredness to their own birth-days and to those of their friends; and the birth-day of Virgil continued long after his death to be regarded with the sanctity of a day of festival[1]. The year of his birth is the first year of that decade in which many of the men most eminent in the Augustan era were born. Virgil was a little younger than Pollio and Varius; a little older than Gallus, Agrippa, Horace, and Augustus, and perhaps Maecenas. All of these men obtained high distinction, and took their place as leaders of their age in action or literature in early youth. The distinction of Virgil was acquired at a somewhat later period of life than that of any of his illustrious contemporaries.

This year is also important as marking the close of the wars and disturbances which arose out of the first great Civil War, and the commencement of a short interval of repose, though hardly of order or security. Lucretius in his childhood and early youth had witnessed the Social War, the bloody strife of Marius and Sulla, and the prolongation of these troubles in the wars of Sertorius and Spartacus: and the memory of the first Civil War seems to have impressed itself indelibly on his imagination and powerfully to have affected his whole view of human life, as the horrors of the first French Revolution imprinted themselves indelibly on the imagination of those whose childhood had been agitated or made desolate by them. Virgil's childhood and early youth were passed in the shelter of a quieter time. He had reached manhood before the second of the great storms which overwhelmed the State passed over the Roman world. The alarm and insecurity felt at Rome during the interval may have caused some agitation of the calmer atmosphere which surrounded his childhood; but the peace of his earliest and most impressible years was marred by no

[1] Cf. Pliny, Ep. iii. 7. Martial, xii. 67 :—
Octobres Maro consecravit Idus.

scenes of horror, such as the massacre at the Colline Gate, the
memory of which perhaps survives in those lines of Lucretius in
which the miseries of a savage life are contrasted with those
of times of refinement :—

> At non multa virum sub signis milia ducta
> Una dies dabat exitio[1].

His birth-place was in the 'pagus,' or 'township,' of Andes
in the neighbourhood of Mantua.   The exact situation of
Andes is unknown, though a tradition, as old as the time of
Dante, identifies it with the village of Pietola, about three miles
lower down the Mincio than Mantua.   But it is only in the
Life by Probus that Andes is described as a 'vicus,' and there
it is said to be distant from Mantua 'xxx milia passuum.'   The
word *pagus*, which is generally used in reference to Andes,
never seems to be used as equivalent to *vicus*, but as a 'country-
district,' which might include several villages.   The tradition
which identifies Andes with any particular village in the neighbourhood of Mantua does not therefore carry with it any guarantee of
its truth.   In the Eclogues the conventional scenery of pastoral
poetry is blended so inseparably with the reproduction from
actual scenes, that it is impossible to determine with certainty
the characteristic features of Virgil's early home.   The immediate neighbourhood of Mantua presents no features to
which the lines of the first Eclogue,

> Maioresque cadunt altis de montibus umbrae[2],

or

> Hinc alta sub rupe canet frondator ad auras[3],

can apply.

The most characteristic objects familiar to Virgil's early
years appear to have been the green banks and slow windings
of the Mincio, which he recalls with affectionate memory in
passages of the Eclogues and Georgics.   From the fact that

---

[1] 'But no single day used then to give to their doom many thousands
of men marshalled under their standards.'   Lucret. v. 999.

[2] 'And larger shadows are falling from the lofty mountains.'

[3] 'From here, under some high rock, the song of the woodsman will rise
into the air.'

the farm on which he lived formed part of the Mantuan land
added to the confiscated territory of Cremona, the inference
seems obvious that it was on the right bank of the Mincio, i. e.
on the side nearest Cremona.   The use of the word ' depellere'
(Ecl. i. 21) might perhaps justify the inference that it was either
on higher ground, or was situated higher up the river than
Mantua, though the other interpretation of ' driving our weaned
lambs' forbids our attaching much force to this problematical
inference.   But the lines which produce more than any other
the impression of describing the actual features of some familiar
place are those of the ninth Eclogue, 7–10 :—

> Certe equidem audieram qua se subducere colles
> Incipiunt mollique iugum demittere clivo,
> Usque ad aquam et veteres, iam fracta cacumina, fagos,
> Omnia carminibus vestrum servasse Menalcan[1].

There seems no motive, certainly none suggested by the Sicilian
idyl, for introducing the hills gradually sinking into the plain,
unless to mark the actual position of the place referred to.
The only hills in the neighbourhood of the Mincio to which
these lines can apply are those which for a time accompany
the flow of the river from the foot of the Lago di Guarda, and
gradually sink into the plain a little beyond 'the picturesque
hill and castle of Vallegio,' about fifteen miles higher up the
river than Mantua.   Eustace, in his Classical Tour, finds many
of the features introduced into the first and ninth Eclogues in
this neighbourhood, though the wish to find them may have
contributed to the success of his search.   A walk of fifteen
miles seems not too long for young and active shepherds, like
Moeris and Lycidas, while such expressions as

> Tamen veniemus in urbem;
> Aut si nox pluviam ne colligat ante veremur[2],—

---

[1] 'I had indeed heard that from the spot where the hills begin to draw
themselves away from the plain, sinking down with a gentle slope, as far as
the river and the old beeches, with their now withered tops, your Menalcas
had saved all his land by his songs.'

[2] 'Yet we shall reach the town: or if we fear that night may first bring
the rain—'

seem inapplicable to the shorter distance between Pietola and Mantua.

The 'sacri fontes' which are spoken of in Eclogue I., the existence of which is further confirmed by the

> Non liquidi gregibus fontes, non gramina deerunt[1]

in the description from the Georgics (ii. 200), of the pastoral land which Mantua lost, are more naturally to be sought in the more picturesque environment of the upper reaches of the river than in the level plain in the midst of which Mantua stands[2]. The accurate description of the lake out of which the Mincio flows—

> Fluctibus et fremitu adsurgens Benace marino[3],—

the truth of which is attested by many modern travellers, Goethe among others—may well be the reproduction of some actual impression made in some of Virgil's early wanderings not far distant from the home of his youth. The passage in the Georgics just referred to, in which, speaking of the land most suitable for rearing herds and flocks, he introduces the lines

> Et qualem infelix amisit Mantua campum,
> Pascentem niveos herboso flumine cycnos[4],

proves the tender affection with which he recalled in later life the memory of his early home.

Some analogy has been suggested between the quiet beauty of the scenery which first sank into his soul, and the tranquil meditative cast of his genius. And though it is easy to push such considerations too far, and to expect a closer correspond-

---

[1] 'The herds will not lack their clear springs, nor their pasture.'

[2] Cf. Eustace, vol. i. chap. v.   Compare also the following characteristic passage quoted from Dickens by Mr. Hare in his Cities of Northern and Central Italy: 'Was the way to Mantua as beautiful when Romeo was banished thither, I wonder?  Did it wind *through pasture land as green, bright with the same glancing streams,* and dotted with fresh clumps of graceful trees?  *Those purple mountains lay on the horizon,* then, for certain.'  Dickens certainly was not looking for Virgilian reminiscences in writing this description.

[3] 'And thou, Benacus, uprising with waves and roar like that of the sea.'

[4] 'And such a plain as ill-fated Mantua lost, a plain which fed its snow-white swans on its weedy river.'

ence than ever exists between the development of genius and the earliest impression of outward nature on the soul, in a poet like Virgil, unusually receptive and retentive of such impressions, whose days from childhood to death were closely bound 'each to each by natural piety,' in whom all elements of feeling were finely and delicately blended with one another, such influences may have been more powerful than in the case of men of a less impressionable and more self-determining type.

The district north of the Po, of which Virgil was a native, had enjoyed the 'ius Latii' since the end of the Social War, but did not obtain the full rights of Roman citizenship till the year 49 B.C., when Virgil was in his twenty-first year. The national poet of the early Empire, like the national poet of the Republic, had thus in all probability no claim by birth to be a member of the State of whose character and destiny his voice has been the truest exponent. It may be doubted whether Virgil belonged by birth to the purely Italian stock. He claims for Mantua a Tuscan origin[1]; but the Etruscan race in the region north of the Po had for a long time previously given way before the settlements of the Gauls; and, although Roman conquest had established several important colonies north of the Po, the main stock between that river and the Alps must have been of Celtic blood, although assimilated in manner of life and culture to the purely Italian inhabitants of the Peninsula. Zeuss, in his Celtic Grammar, recognises the presence of a Celtic root, which appears in other Gallic names, and which he supposes to be the root also of *virgo*, and *virga*, and *Vergiliae*, in the name Vergilius[2]. Some elements in Virgil's nature and genius which seem to anticipate the developments of modern feeling, as, for instance, his vague melancholy, his imaginative sense of the mystery of the unseen world, his sympathy with the sentiment, as distinct from the passion, of love,

---

[1] Aeneid, x. 204.

[2] 'Vergilius—nomen vix dubiae originis Gallicae. Cf. Vergiliae (stellae), Propert. i. 8. 10, Plin. fq. Οὐεργιλία (Oppid. Hispan.), Ptol. 2. 5. Radix vetust. Camb. *guerg.* (efficax) gl. Ox. extat etiam in vetusto nomine apud Caes.' Zeuss, Grammatica Celtica, p. 11, edit. altera: Berol. 1871.

the modes in which his delight in nature manifests itself, the
vein of romance which runs through his treatment of early
times, may perhaps be explained by some subtle intermixture
of Celtic blood with the firmer temperament of the old Italian
race.   Appreciated as his genius has been by all the cultivated
nations of Europe, it is by the nation in whom the impressible
Celtic nature has been refined and strengthened by the discipline of Latin studies that his pre-eminence has been most
generally acknowledged.

It is to be noticed that, while in the Ciceronian Age the
names of the men eminent in literature belong, with one or two
exceptions, either to the pure Roman stock or to the races of
central Italy which had been longest incorporated with Rome,
in the last years of the Republic and in the Augustan Age
Northern Italy contributed among other names those of Catullus, Cornelius Gallus, Quintilius Varus, Aemilius Macer, Virgil,
and the historian Livy to the roll of Latin literature.   Since the
concessions which followed the Social War the whole people
inhabiting the Peninsula had become thoroughly united in spirit
with the Imperial city, and Latin literature as well as the
service of the State thus received a great impulse from the
liberality with which Rome, at different stages in her history,
extended the privileges of her citizenship.   The culture of which
Rome had been for two generations the centre became now
much more widely diffused; and as the privilege of citizenship,
or of that modified citizenship conferred by the 'ius Latii,' was
more prized from its novelty, so the attractions of literary
studies and the impulses of literary ambition were felt more
strongly from coming fresh and unhackneyed to a vigorous
race.   It was a happier position for Virgil and for Horace, it
fitted them not only to be truer poets of the natural beauty of
Italy, but also to feel in imagination all the wonder associated
with the idea of the great city, to have spent their earliest and
most impressible years among scenes of peace and beauty,
remote from contact with the excitement, the vices, the routine
of city life, than if, with the friend of Juvenal, they could have

applied to themselves the words—'our childhood drank in the air of the Aventine.'

There is still one point to be noticed in connexion with the district in which Virgil was born and passed his early youth. It was from Julius Caesar that Gallia Transpadana received the full Roman citizenship.  But before he established this claim on their gratitude, the 'Transpadani,' as we learn from Cicero's letters, were thoroughly devoted to his cause [1], and it was among them that his legions were mainly recruited.  One of the spiteful acts by which the aristocratic party showed its animosity to Caesar was the scourging of one of the inhabitants of the colony of Novum Comum (Como) by order of the Consul Marcellus,—an act condemned by Cicero on the ground that the victim of this outrage was a 'Transpadanus [2].'  Caesar was in the habit of passing the winters of his proconsulate in this part of his province, especially at Verona, where he was the guest of the father of Catullus.  The name of Caesar must thus have become a household word among this people.  They must have soon recognised his greatness as a soldier, and felt the fascination of his gracious presence.  They must have been grateful for his championship of the provinces against the oppressive rule of the Senate, and for the protection afforded by his army from dangers similar to those from which their fathers had been saved, after many disasters, by his great kinsman, Marius.  They did not share the sentiments of distrust excited among the aristocracy at Rome by Caesar's early career, and had no reason to regard the permanent ascendency of one man as a heavier burden than the caprices of their temporary governors.  From the favour which Virgil received from leaders of the Caesarean cause before his fame was established, and from his intimacy with Varius the panegyrist of Julius Caesar, it may be inferred that in adhering to the cause of the Empire he was true to the early impressions of his boyhood.  He was one of the first to feel and make others feel the spell which the

[1] Cic. Epp. ad Att. vii. 7; ad Fam. xvi. 12.
[2] Cic. Epp. ad Att. v. 2.

name of Caesar was destined henceforth to exercise over the world.

Latin literature in the Augustan Age drew its representatives not only from a wider district than the preceding age, but also from a different social class. The men eminent as poets, orators, and historians in the last years of the Republic were for the most part members of the great Roman or Italian families. They were either themselves actively engaged in political life, or living in intimacy with those who were so engaged. Whatever tincture of letters was found in any other class was confined to freedmen or learned Greeks, such as Archias and Theophanes, attached to the houses of the nobility. The fortunes of the two great poets of the Augustan Age prove that no barrier of class-prejudice and no necessary inferiority of early education prevented free-born men of very humble origin from attaining the highest distinction, and living as the trusted friends of the foremost men in the State. Virgil and Horace were the sons of men who by the thrift and industry of a humble occupation had been able to buy small farms in their native district. Virgil's father had not indeed, like the father of Horace, risen from a servile position. He is said to have begun life as a hired assistant to one Magius, who, according to one account, was a potter, according to another a 'viator' (or officer whose duty it was to summon prisoners before magistrates). He married the daughter of his master, being recommended to him, as is said by his biographer, by his industry (ob industriam). The name of Virgil's mother was Magia Polla. His father is said to have increased his substance among other things by keeping bees (silvis coemendis et apibus curandis),—a fact which perhaps explains the importance given to this branch of rural industry in the Georgics. Virgil thus springs from that class whose condition he represents as the happiest allotted to man, and as affording the best field for the exercise of virtue and piety. He and Horace, after living in the most refined society of Rome, are entirely at one in their appreciation of the qualities of the old Italian husbandmen or

small landowners,—a class long before their time reduced in
numbers and influence, but still producing men of modest worth
and strong common sense like the 'abnormis sapiens' of the
Satires, and like those country neighbours whose lively talk and
homely wisdom Horace contrasts with the fashionable folly of
Rome; and true and virtuous women, such as may have
suggested to the one poet the lines—

> Quod si pudica mulier in partem iuvet
> Domum atque dulces liberos,
> Sabina qualis aut perusta solibus
> Pernicis uxor Appuli[1],

and to the other—

> Interea longum cantu solata laborem
> Arguto coniunx percurrit pectine telas[2].

These poets themselves probably owe that stronger grain of
character, their large share of the old Italian seriousness of
spirit (gravitas), which distinguishes them from the other poets
of their time, to the traditions of virtue which the men of this
class had not yet unlearned. It is remarked by M. Sainte-
Beuve how strong the attachment of such men usually is to
their homes and lands, inherited from their fathers or acquired
and enriched by their own industry. He characterises happily
'cette médiocrité de fortune et de condition morale dans la-
quelle était né Virgile, médiocrité, ai-je dit, qui rend tout mieux
senti et plus cher, parcequ'on y touche à chaque instant la
limite, parcequ'on y a toujours présent le moment où l'on a
acquis et celui où l'on peut tout perdre.' The truest human
feeling expressed in the Eclogues is the love which the old
settlers had for their lands, and the sorrow which they felt when
forced to quit them. The Georgics bear witness to the strong
Italian passion for the soil, and the pride in the varied results

---

[1] 'But if a chaste and blooming wife, beside,
    His cheerful home with sweet young blossoms fills,
    Like some stout Sabine, or the sunburnt bride
    Of the lithe peasant of the Apulian hills.'   Martin.
[2] 'Meanwhile, cheering her long task with song, his wife runs over the
web with her sounding shuttle.'

of his skill which made a life of unceasing labour one of contentment and happiness to the husbandman.

As has happened in the case of other poets and men of
poetic genius, tradition recorded some marvellous circumstances
attending his birth, which were believed to have portended his
future distinction.   These stories may have originated early in
his career from the promise of genius afforded by his childhood : or, like the mediaeval belief in his magical powers, they
may be a kind of mythological reflection of the veneration and
affection with which his memory was cherished.   The character
of these reported presages implies the impression produced by
the gentleness and sweetness of his disposition[1], as well as by
the rapid growth and development of his poetic faculty[2].

A more trustworthy indication of his early promise is afforded
by the care with which he was educated.   Like Horace, he was
fortunate in having parents who, themselves of humble origin,
considered him worthy of receiving the best instruction which
the world could give ; and, like Horace, he repaid their tender
solicitude with affectionate gratitude.   By his father's care he
was from boyhood dedicated to the high calling which he faithfully followed through all his life.   At the age of twelve he was
taken to Cremona, an old Latin colony ; and, from the lines in
one of his earliest authentic poems (the address to the villa
of Siron)—

Tu nunc eris illi<br>
Mantua quod fuerat, quodque Cremona prius[3]—

implying a residence at Cremona, it seems probable that his
father may have accompanied him thither, as Horace's father
accompanied him to Rome for the same purpose.   On his

---

[1] Ferunt infantem, cum sit editus, neque vagisse, et adeo miti vultu fuisse,
ut haud dubiam spem prosperioris geniturae jam tunc indicaret.

[2] Siquidem virga populea more regionis in puerperiis eodem statim loco
depacta ita brevi evaluit tempore ut multo ante satas populos adaequasset,
quae arbor Virgilii ex eo dicta atque etiam consecrata est summa gravi-
darum ac fetarum religione.

The resemblance of the name to the word virga is probably at the root
of this story.

[3] ' You will now be to him what Mantua and Cremona were before.'

sixteenth birth-day—the day on which, according to Donatus, Lucretius died—Virgil assumed the 'toga virilis,' and about the same time went to Milan, and continued there, engaged in study, till he removed to Rome in the year 53 B.C., when he was between sixteen and seventeen years of age.   It was in this year of his life that he is said to have written the 'Culex.' There are many difficulties which prevent the belief that Virgil is the author of the poem which has come down to us under that name.   But the consideration of these must be reserved for a later examination of the poem.

At Rome he studied rhetoric under Epidius, who was also the teacher of the young Octavianus.   As the future Emperor made his first public appearance at the age of twelve, by delivering the funeral oration over his grandmother Julia, it may have happened that he and Virgil were pupils of Epidius at the same time, and were not unknown to each other even before the meeting of ten years later which decisively affected Virgil's fortunes and determined his career.   The time of his arrival at Rome was of critical importance in literature.   The recent publication of the poem of Lucretius, the most important event in Latin literature since the appearance of the Annals of Ennius, must have stimulated the enthusiasm of the younger generation, among whom poetry and oratory were at that time conjointly cultivated.   Mr. Munro has shown the influence exercised by this poem on the later style of Catullus, who collected and edited his own poems about the time when Virgil came to Rome, and died shortly afterwards.   One or two of the minor poems among the Catalepton, attributed to Virgil with more probability than the Culex, are parodies or close imitations of the style of Catullus, and are written in a freer and more satiric spirit than anything published by him in later years.   But it is a little remarkable that, while reproducing the language and cadences of both these poets in his first acknow-ledged work, Virgil never mentions the name either of Lucretius or Catullus.   The poets mentioned by him with admiration in the Eclogues are his living contemporaries,

Varius and Cinna, Pollio and Gallus. Is it on account of the
Senatorian and anti-Caesarean sympathies of the older poets
that the poets of the new era thus separate themselves abruptly
from those of the previous epoch ? If it was owing to the
jealousy of the new *régime* that the two great Augustan poets,
while paying a passing tribute to the impracticable virtue of
Cato, never mention the greater name or allude to the fate of
Cicero, there seems to have been nothing in the political action
or expressed opinions of Lucretius to call for a similar reticence. If, on the other hand, the boldness of his attack on the
strongholds of all religious belief had the effect of cutting him
off for a time from personal sympathy, as similar opposition to
received opinions had in modern times in the case of Spinosa
and Shelley, it did not interfere with the immediate influence
exercised by his genius on the thought and art of Virgil.

The most interesting of the minor poems among the Catalepton is one written at the time when the young poet entered
on the study of philosophy under Siron the Epicurean. This
poem expresses the joy felt by him in exchanging the empty
pretension and dull pedantry of rhetorical and grammatical
studies for the real enquiries of philosophy :—

> Ite hinc, inanes rhetorum ampullae,
> Inflata rore non Achaico verba,
> Et vos, Stiloque, Tarquitique, Varroque,
> Scholasticorum natio madens pingui,
> Ite hinc, inanis cymbalon iuventutis.
> \*      \*      \*      \*      \*
> Nos ad beatos vela mittimus portus,
> Magni petentes docta dicta Sironis,
> Vitamque ab omni vindicabimus cura[1].

These lines are the earliest expression of that philosophical
longing which haunted Virgil through all his life as a hope
and aspiration, but never found its realisation in speculative

---

[1] 'Hence, away, empty phrases of the Rhetoricians, words swollen with
water not from a Greek source, and you, ye Stilos, and Tarquiti, and Varros,
tribe of grammarians oozing over with fat, away hence tinkling cymbal of
our empty youth ... I shape my course to the blessed harbours, in search
of the wise words of great Siron, and will redeem my life from every care.'

result.   The motive which he professes for entering on the study,

Vitamque ab omni vindicabimus cura,

is the same as that which acted on Lucretius—the wish to secure an ideal serenity of life.   The same trust in the calming influence of the Epicurean philosophy appears in the

Felix qui potuit rerum cognoscere causas, etc.

of the second Georgic.   But in different ways, by the deep feeling of melancholy in the one, by the revolt and spiritual reaction in the other, Lucretius and Virgil both show that these tenets could not secure to 'the passionate heart of the poet' that calmness and serenity of spirit which they gave to men of the stamp of Atticus, Velleius, or Torquatus.   The final lines of the poem express the lingering regret with which he bids a temporary farewell to the Muses.   These few lines, more than any other poem attributed to Virgil, seem to bring him in his personal feelings nearer to us.   There is a touch of the graciousness of his nature, recalling the cordial feeling of Catullus to all his young comrades, in the passing notice of those who had shared his studies :—

Iam valete, formosi.

At a time when the poetry of the younger generation was universally free and licentious in tone, the purity of Virgil's nature reveals itself in the prayer to the Muses to revisit his writings 'pudenter et raro,' chastely and seldom.   The whole poem is the sincere expression of the scholar and poet, even in youth idealising the austere charm of philosophy, while feeling in his heart the more powerful attraction of poetry.   In the

Nam, fatebimur verum,<br>Dulces fuistis[1],

is the literal expression of that deep joy which afterwards moved him in uttering the lines—

Me vero primum dulces ante omnia Musae, etc.

[1] 'For, I shall own the truth, ye were dear to me.'

and
> Sed me Parnassi deserta per ardua dulcis
> Raptat amor[1];

and which sustained him stedfastly in the noble harmony of all his later life.

Of the next ten years of his career nothing is known with certainty; but the outbreak of the Civil War is likely to have interrupted his residence at Rome, and he is next heard of living in his native district and engaged in the composition of the Eclogues. He took no part in the war, nor ever served as a soldier; and he seems to have appeared only once in the other field of practical distinction open to a young Roman who had received so elaborate an education—that of forensic pleading. He is said to have wanted the readiness. of speech and self-possession necessary for success in such a career; and he was thus fortunate in escaping all temptation to sacrifice his genius to the ambition of practical life, or to divide his allegiance, as Licinius Calvus did, between the claims of poetry and of oratory. His first literary impulse was to write an historical epic on the early Roman or Alban history, and to this impulse he himself alludes in the lines of the sixth Eclogue,—

> Cum canerem reges et proelia, Cynthius aurem
> Vellit et admonuit[2].

He gave up the idea, feeling the unsuitable nature of the material for poetic treatment,—'offensus materia,' as the Life of Donatus expresses it; and he resolutely resisted the projects often urged upon him of giving a poetical account of contemporary events, in celebration of the glory of Pollio, Varus, or Caesar. But it is noticeable as a proof of the persistence with which his mind continued to dwell on ideas once projected, till they finally assumed appropriate shape, that in the Aeneid he really combines these two purposes of vivifying the ancient traditions of Rome and Alba, and of glorifying the great results

---

[1] 'But me a passionate delight hurries along over the lonely heights of Parnassus.'

[2] 'When I would sing of kings and battles, Apollo pulled my ear and warned me.'

of his own era. It is by this capacity of forecasting some great work, and dwelling on the idea till it clears itself of all alien matter and assimilates to itself the impressions and interests of a life-time, that the vastest and most enduring monuments of genius are produced.

In the year of the battle of Philippi, Virgil was living in his native district, engaged in the composition of his pastoral poems. Of his mode of life, taste, and feelings about this time we perceive only that he continued to be a student of the Alexandrine literature, that he had, by natural gift and assiduous culture, brought the technical part of his art—the diction and rhythm of poetry—to the highest perfection hitherto attained, that he enjoyed the favour and patronage of the Governor of the province, Asinius Pollio, and that he was united by strong ties of affection and warm admiration to Cornelius Gallus, who, while still in early youth, had obtained high distinction in poetry and a prominent position in public life. There are in the Eclogues notices of other poets of the district, whose friendship he enjoyed or whose jealousy he excited. The Mopsus of the fifth is said to be the didactic poet, Aemilius Macer. The mention of Bavius and Maevius, the 'iurgia Codri,' and the allusion in a later poem to Anser the panegyrist of Antony, are the nearest approaches to anything like resentment or personal satire that Virgil has shown. It may be that in the lines where Amaryllis and Galatea and other personages of the poems are introduced he refers to some personal experiences; but as compared with all the poets of this era, Virgil either observed a great reticence, or enjoyed an exceptional immunity from the passions of youth. The whole tone of the earlier poems, and numerous expressions in all of them, such as 'tu, Tityre, lentus in umbra,' are suggestive of a somewhat indolent enjoyment of the charm of books, of poetry, and of the softer beauties of Nature.

The following year was the turning-point in his career, and gave a more definite aim to his genius and sympathies. In that year his own fortunes became involved in the affairs which were determining the fate of the world. The Triumvirs, in assigning grants of land to their soldiers, had confiscated the territory of Cremona, which had shown sympathy with the Senatorian cause, and when this proved insufficient, an addition was made from the adjoining Mantuan territory, in which the farm of Virgil's father was situated. The Commissioners appointed to distribute the land were Pollio, Varus, and Gallus, all friendly to Virgil, and by their advice he went to Rome, and obtained the restitution of his land by personal application to Octavianus. On his return to his native district he found that Varus had succeeded Pollio as Governor of the province. He appears to have been unfriendly to the Mantuans, and was either unable or unwilling to protect Virgil, who was forced at the imminent peril of his life to escape, by swimming the river, from the violence of the soldier who had entered on the possession of the land. Two of the Eclogues, the first and the ninth, are written in connexion with these events. Though he still adheres to an indirect and allusive treatment of his subject, these poems possess the interest of being based on real experience. They give expression to the sense of disorder, insecurity, and distress, which we learn from other sources accompanied these forced divisions and alienations of land. The first expresses also the gratitude of the poet to 'the god-like youth' to whom he owed the exceptional indulgence of being, though only for a short time, reinstated in the possession of his land. It is characteristic either of some weakness in Virgil's nature, or of a great depression among the peaceful inhabitants of Italy, that he had no thought of resisting violence by violence, that he does not even express resentment against the intruder, but only a feeling of wonder that any man could be capable of such wickedness. To most readers the vehemence with which the author of the 'Dirae,' under similar circumstances, curses the land and its new owners, appears, if less sweet and musical, more natural than this mild submission to superior force expressed by Virgil. But in these personal experiences that strong sympathy with the national fortunes, which henceforward animates his poetry, originates. Virgil may thus in a sense be numbered among the poets who ' are cradled into poetry by wrong.'

After this second forcible expulsion from his old home, he took refuge, along with his family, in a small country-house which had belonged to his old teacher Siron. The poem numbered X. in the Catalepta,

> Villula quae Sironis eras, et pauper agelle,
> Verum illi domino tu quoque divitiae[1],

was written at this time. It expresses anxiety and distress about the state of his native district, to which, as in Eclogue i., he applies the word *patria*, and affectionate solicitude for those along with him, ' those with⸱ me whom I have ever loved,' and especially for his father. His own experience at this time may have suggested to him the feelings which he afterwards reproduced in describing the flight of Aeneas from the ruins of Troy.

He seems never after this time to have returned to his native district. The liberality of Octavianus [2] compensated him for his loss, nor was the even tenor of his life henceforward broken by any new dangers or hardships. Through the gift of friends and patrons he acquired a fortune, which at his death amounted to 10,000,000 sesterces (about £90,000); he possessed a house on the Esquiline near the gardens of Maecenas, a villa at Naples, and a country-house near Nola in Campania; and he seems to have lived from time to time in Sicily and the South of Italy.

The Eclogues, commenced in his native district in the year 42 B.C., were completed and published at Rome probably in the year 37 B.C. They were at once received with great favour, and recited amid much applause upon the stage. They established the author's fame as the poet of Nature and of rural life,

---

[1] 'Cottage that belonged to Siron, and poor plot of ground, although deemed great riches by your former owner.'
[2] Hor. Ep. ii. 1. 246.

as Varius was accepted as the poet of epic, Pollio of tragic
poetry :—

> Molle atque facetum
> Vergilio annuerunt gaudentes rure Camenae[1].

For a short time afterwards Virgil lived chiefly at Rome, as one
of the circle of which Maecenas was the centre, consisting of
those poets and men eminent in the State whom Horace
(Sat. i. 10) mentions as the critics and friends whose approval
he valued.  Our knowledge of Virgil at this time is derived
from the first Book of the Satires of Horace.  It was by Virgil
and Varius that Horace himself was introduced to Maecenas.
They were all three of the party who made the famous journey
to Brundisium in 37 B.C.   While Horace starts alone from
Rome, Virgil and Varius join him at Sinuessa.   Virgil may
already have begun to withdraw from habitual residence in
Rome to his retirement in Campania, where he principally lived
from this time till his death.   One line in this Satire confirms
the account of the weakness of his health which is given by his
biographer,—the line, namely, in which Horace describes himself and Virgil as going to sleep, while Maecenas went to enjoy
the exercise of the 'pila' :—

> Lusum it Maecenas, dormitum ego Vergiliusque,
> Namque pila lippis inimicum et ludere crudis[2].

There is no notice of Virgil in the second Book of the Satires,
written between the years 35 and 30 B.C., at which time he had
withdrawn altogether from Rome, and was living at Naples,
engaged in the composition of the Georgics.   Two of the
Odes of Book I., however, the third and the twenty-fourth,
throw some light on his circumstances and character, and on
the relations of friendship subsisting between him and Horace.
There is some difficulty in determining the occasion that gave

---

[1] 'Tenderness and grace have been granted to Virgil by the Muses who
delight in the country.'

[2] 'Maecenas goes to play at fives, Virgil and I to sleep, for that game
does not agree with those suffering from dyspepsia and weak eyes.'

rise to the first of these Odes. It is addressed to the ship which was to bear Virgil to Attica. As we only know of one voyage of Virgil to Attica, that immediately preceding his death, and as the first three Books of the Odes were originally published some years before that date, we must suppose either that this Ode refers to an earlier voyage contemplated or actually accomplished by Virgil; or that the Virgil here spoken of is a different person; or that the publication of the edition of the Odes which we possess was of a later date than that generally accepted. The reason for rejecting the second of these alternatives has been already given. Two reasons may be given for rejecting the third,—first, the improbability that one of the latest, if not the latest, in point of time among all the Odes in the three Books should be placed third in order in the first Book, among Odes that all refer to a much earlier period; and secondly, that this Ode, in respect of the somewhat conventional nature of the thought and the character of the mythological allusions, is clearly written in Horace's earlier manner. There is no improbability in accepting the first alternative, that as Virgil travelled to and resided in Sicily, so he may have made, or at least contemplated, an earlier voyage to Greece. One object for such a voyage may have been the desire of seeing the localities which he represents Aeneas as passing or visiting in the course of his adventures between the time of leaving Troy and settling in Latium. The Aeneid indicates in many places the tastes of a cultivated traveller; and parts of the sea-voyage of Aeneas look as if they were founded on personal reminiscences.

It may be noticed in several of the Odes of Horace how he adapts the vein of thought running through them to the character or position of the person to whom they refer. The revival of the old Hesiodic and theological idea of the sin and impiety of that spirit of enterprise which led men first to brave the dangers of the sea, and to baffle the purpose of the Deity in separating nations from one another by the ocean,—an idea to which Virgil himself gives expression in the fourth Eclogue,—

> Pauca tamen suberunt priscae vestigia fraudis,
> Quae temptare Thetim ratibus, etc.[1],—

is not unsuited to the unadventurous disposition of the older poet.

The twenty-fourth Ode is addressed to him on the occasion of the death of their common friend Quintilius Varus, probably the Varus of the tenth poem of Catullus, and thus one of the last survivors of the friendly circle of poets and wits of a former generation.   While a high tribute to the pure character of their lost friend, it is at the same time a tribute to the pious and affectionate character of Virgil.

It is a delicate touch of appreciation that Horace dwells more on the thought of the depth of Virgil's sorrow for their common friend than on his own.   Both of these Odes give evidence of the strong affection which Virgil inspired ; the second affords further evidence of the qualities in virtue of which he inspired that feeling.   Similar proof of affection and appreciation is afforded by the words in which Horace in the fifth Satire of Book I. characterises Virgil ('Vergilius optimus,' as he elsewhere calls him), and his two friends Plotius and Varius,—

> Animae quales neque candidiores
> Terra tulit, neque queis me sit devinctior alter[2].

The word 'candidiores' suggests the same qualities of a beautiful nature,—the unworldly simplicity and sincerity, which are ascribed to Quintilius in the words ' pudor, incorrupta fides, nudaque veritas.'

The seven years from 37 B.C. to 30 B.C. were devoted by Virgil to the composition of the Georgics, a poem scarcely exceeding 2000 lines in length.   His chief residence at this time was Naples :—

> Me dulcis alebat
> Parthenope, studiis florentem ignobilis oti[3].

---

[1] ' Yet there will remain some vestiges of the ancient sin, which will induce men to tempt the sea in ships.'

[2] 'No more sincere souls has the earth ever borne, nor any to whom there is a more devoted friend than I.'

[3] 'I then had my home in sweet Parthenope, happy in the pursuits of an inglorious idleness.'

He possessed also at this time a country-house or estate in the neighbourhood of Nola; and the fourth Book affords evidence of some time spent at or in the neighbourhood of Tarentum, which is confirmed by the lines in Propertius,—

> Tu canis umbrosi subter pineta Galaesi
> Thyrsin et attritis Daphnin harundinibus [1],—

the region prized by Horace as second only to his beloved Tibur. In the year 29 B.C. he read the whole poem to Augustus, on his return from Asia, at the town of Atella. The reading occupied four days. Maecenas was of the party, and relieved the poet in the task of reading.

The remaining years of his life were spent in the composition of the Aeneid. One of the poems of the Catalepta (vi.) gives expression to a vow binding the poet to sacrifice a bull to Venus if he succeeded in accomplishing the task which he had imposed on himself. So early as the year 26 B.C., Augustus while engaged in the Cantabrian war, had desired to see some part of the poem. It was in answer to that request that Virgil wrote the letter of which the fragment, quoted in the previous chapter, has been preserved by Macrobius [2]. At a later time, after the death of the young Marcellus (23 B.C.), he read three Books to Augustus and the other members of his family.

After spending eleven years on the composition of his great epic, he set aside three more for its final correction. In the year 19 B.C. he set out with the view of travelling in Greece and Asia. Meeting Augustus at Athens, he was persuaded to abandon his purpose and return with him to Italy. While visiting Megara under a burning sun he was seized with illness. Continuing his voyage without interruption, he became worse, and on the 21st of September, a few days after landing at Brundisium, he died in the fifty-first year of his age. In his

---

[1] 'You sing, beneath the pine-woods of the shaded Galaesus, Thyrsis and Daphnis on your well-worn reeds.'
[2] Cf. supra, p. 69.

last illness he showed the ruling passion of his life—the craving for perfection—by calling for the cases which held his MSS., with the intention of burning the Aeneid.   It is in keeping with the absence of self-assertion in his writings that his final hours were clouded by this sad sense of failure, rather than brightened by such confident assurances of immortality as other Roman poets have expressed.   In the same spirit of dissatisfaction with all imperfect accomplishment, he left directions in his will that his executors, Varius and Tucca, should publish nothing but what had been already edited by him.   This direction, which would have deprived the world of the Aeneid, was disregarded by them in compliance with the commands of Augustus.

He was buried at Naples, where his tomb was long regarded with religious veneration and visited as a temple; and tradition has associated his name, as that of a magician, with the construction of the great tunnel of Posilippo, in its immediate neighbourhood.

### III.

The interest of the life of Virgil lies in the bearing of his circumstances on the development of his genius, in the view which it affords of his whole nature as a man, and in the relation of that nature to the work accomplished by him as a poet.   The biography of Horace has an independent value as affording insight into social life and character, irrespective of the light which it reflects on the art of the poet.   But no separate line of action, adventure, or enjoyment runs through and intermingles with the even course of Virgil's poetic career. And this may have been a drawback to him as the poet of political action, of heroic adventure, and of human character. His career in this respect is unlike that of other great poets who have been endowed with the epic or dramatic faculty, who either took part in the serious action of their age, or gave proof in their lives of some share of the adventurous spirit or of the rich social nature which they have delineated in their works. In the same way the life of Livy was that merely of a man of letters, and thus different from that of the other great historians of antiquity, who had either passed through a career of adventure, like Herodotus and Xenophon, or had been actively engaged in public affairs, like Thucydides and Polybius, Sallust and Tacitus. The 'inscitia Reipublicae ut alienae' thus betrays itself in Livy more than in any of those historians who have been named. Virgil's life was as much one of pure contemplation or absorption in his art, as that of Lucretius or Wordsworth. The first half of his career, from childhood to maturity, was an education, passive and active, for the position he was destined to fill as the greatest literary artist and greatest national poet of Rome. His later career, from the age of twenty-eight till his too early death, was the fulfilment of the office to which he had dedicated himself. With the exception of one troubled year of his early manhood, which proved the turning-point of his fortunes, he lived, undistracted by business or pleasure, the life of a scholar and poet, combining the concentrated industry of the first with the sense of joyful activity and ever-ripening faculty which sustains and cheers the second. In youth his means of living must have been moderate, yet sufficient to enable him to forsake everything else for his art: in later life, through the munificence of Augustus, he was rich enough to enjoy exemption from the cares of life, and to gratify freely the one taste by which his poetical gifts were fostered—that of living and varying his residence among the fairest scenes of Southern Italy. The one drawback to his happiness, viz. that he suffered during all his life from delicate or variable health[1], was not unfavourable to the concentration of his whole nature on his self-appointed task. It saved him from ever sacrificing the high aim of his existence to the

---

[1] 'Nam plerumque a stomacho et a faucibus ac dolore capitis laborabat, sanguinem etiam saepe rejecit.' Cf. what Sainte-Beuve says of Bayle : ' Il lui était utile même d'avoir cette santé frêle, ennemi de la bonne chère, ne sollicitant jamais aux distractions.'

pleasures in which his contemporaries indulged, and to which
the imaginative temperament of the poets and artists of a
southern land is powerfully attracted. The abstemious regi-
men which from necessity or inclination he observed, the fact
recorded of him that he 'took very little food and wine,' must
have quickened the finer sources of emotion by which his
genius was nourished. Had he received from nature a robuster
fibre and more hardihood of spirit, or had his character been
more tempered by collision with the active forces of life, his
epic poem might have shown a more original energy, and
greater power in delineating varied types of character : but in
combination with a robuster or more energetic temper, much
of the peculiar charm of Virgil would have been lost.

He is said to have been of a tall and awkward figure, of
dark complexion, and to have preserved through all his life
a look of rusticity. He wanted readiness in ordinary conversation, and never overcame the shyness of his rustic origin
or studious habits. It is reported that in his rare visits to
Rome he avoided observation, and took refuge in the nearest
house from the crowds of people who recognised or followed
him. The 'monstrari digito praetereuntium' ·was to him a
source of embarrassment rather than of that gratification which
Horace derived from it.

Both his parents lived till after the loss of his farm, when the
poet was in his twenty-ninth year. Two brothers died before
him, one while still a boy, the other after reaching manhood.
To his half-brother Valerius Proculus he left one half of his
estate. Augustus, Maecenas, and his two friends Varius and
Tucca also received legacies. He was never married, nor is
there any record in connexion with him of any of those temporary liaisons which the other poets of the Augustan Age formed
and celebrated in their verse. Some modern critics arguing
from a single expression in the Life by Donatus, and giving to
a tradition connected with the subject of the second Eclogue
a meaning which, even if the tradition was trustworthy, need
not apply to it, have written of Virgil as if throughout his

whole life he yielded to a laxity of morals from which perhaps
some of his eminent contemporaries were not free, but which
was condemned by the manlier instincts of Romans, as of all
modern nations. The expression of Donatus is probably a
mere survival of the calumnies against which Asconius vindi-
cated Virgil's character. The statement of the same biographer, that on account of his purity of speech and life he was
known in Naples by the name 'Parthenias,' is at least as trustworthy evidence as that on which the imputations on his
character have been revived. The levity and mendacity with
which such calumnies were invented [1], and the attractions which
they have for the baser nature of men in all times, sufficiently
explain both the original existence and the later revival of
these imputations. We are called upon not merely to disregard
them as unproved, or irrelevant to our estimate of the poet's
art, but to reject them as incompatible with the singular purity
and transparent sincerity of nature revealed in all the maturer
works of his genius [2].

The cordial and discriminating language both of the Satires
and the Odes of Horace confirms the impression of delicacy
and simplicity of character suggested by the general tone of
Virgil's writings. The appreciation of Horace for Virgil reminds us of the touching tribute which the great comic poet of
Athens pays to her greatest tragic poet, where he speaks of him
as showing the same disposition among the Shades as he had
shown in the world above—

'Ο δ' εὔκολος μὲν ἐνθάδ', εὔκολος δ' ἐκεῖ [3]—

and of that similar tribute paid by his friend and fellow-dramatist
to our own great poet, in the words 'my gentle Shakespeare.'

[1] Cp. Journal of Philology, Part III. Article on the twenty-ninth poem
of Catullus.
[2] The German historians of Roman literature are more just in their judgment of Virgil's character than of his genius. Thus W. S. Teuffel puts
aside these scandals with the brusque and contemptuous remark—'Der
Klatsch bei Donatus über sein Verhältniss zu seinen Lieblingssklaven
Alexander und Kebes, so wie zu Plotia Hieria, einer amica des L. Varius,
beurtheilte nach sich selbst das was ihm an Vergil unbegreiflich war.'
[3] 'He was gentle here on earth, and is gentle there.' Aristoph. Frogs, 82.

The affection and admiration of the greatest of his contemporaries, surviving in the tradition handed on to future times,
testify to Virgil's exemption from the personal frailties and
asperities to which the impressible and mobile temperament of
genius is peculiarly liable.

His works do not present any single distinct impression of
the poet himself, in his own character and convictions, separable from his artistic representation.   Yet from the study of
these works we are able to form a general conception of the
disposition, affections, and moral sympathies which distinguish
him from the other great writers of his country.   We might
perhaps without undue fancifulness express the dominant
ethical or social characteristic—the ideal virtue or grace—of
some of the great Roman writers by some word peculiarly
expressive of Roman character or culture, and of frequent use
in these writers themselves.   Thus, in regard to Cicero, the
man of quick susceptibility to praise and blame, to sympathy
and coldness, who, except where his personal or political antagonism was roused, had the liveliest sense of the claims of
kind offices and kind feeling which men have on one another,
the word *humanitas* seems to sum up those qualities of heart
and intellect which, in spite of the transparent weaknesses of
his character, gained for him so much affection, and which,
through the sympathy they enabled him to feel and arouse in
others, were the secret of his unparalleled success as an advocate.   To Lucretius we might apply the word *sanctitas*, in
the sense in which he applies the word *sanctus* to the old
philosophers, as expressive of that glow of reverential emotion
which animates him in his search after truth and in his contemplation of Nature.   His own words '*lepor*' and '*lepidus*' express the graceful vivacity, artistic and social rather than ethical,
which we associate with the thought of Catullus.   The quality,
mainly intellectual and social, but still not devoid of ethical
content, of which Horace is the most perfect type, is '*urba-
nitas*.'   The full meaning of the great Roman word '*gravitas*'
—the vital force of ethical feeling as well as the strength of

character connoted by it, and by its sister-qualities 'dignity and authority'—is only completely realised in the pages of Tacitus. And so it is only in Virgil, and especially in that poem in which he deals with types of human character and motives originating in human affection, that we understand all the feelings of love to family and country, and of fidelity to the dead, and that sense of dependence on a higher Power, sanctioning and sanctifying these feelings and the duties demanded by them, which the Romans comprehended in their use of the word '*pietas.*'

With this recognition of man's dependence on a wise and beneficent Power above him, is perhaps connected another moral characteristic strongly indicated in many passages of the Aeneid, and mentioned among the personal attributes of Virgil in some of the editions of Donatus's Life, though it does not appear in that accepted by the latest critics as resting on the best MS. authority[1]. This quality is the stoical power of endurance which he attributes to his hero, but which in him is combined with nothing either of the austerity or pedantry of Stoicism. The passage in the biography, which, if an interpolation in the original Life, is one that is at least 'well invented,' is to the following effect:—'He was in the habit of saying that there was no virtue of more use to a man than patience, and that there was no fortune so harsh, that a brave man cannot triumph over it by wisely enduring it.' Mr. Wickham, in his edition of Horace, refers to this passage as illustrating the maxims of consolation addressed by Horace to Virgil on the death of their friend Quintilius. Many lines in the Aeneid, such as the

> Quidquid erit, superanda omnis fortuna ferendo est—
> Disce, puer, virtutem ex me verumque laborem,
> Fortunam ex aliis [2]—

indicate that the gentleness of Virgil, if combined with a peace-

---

[1] Cf. Reifferscheid, p. 67.

[2] 'Whatsoever it shall be, every fortune must be mastered by bearing it.'
'Learn, my son, from me to bear yourself like a man and to strive earnestly, from others learn to be fortunate.'

loving disposition, was not incompatible with Roman fortitude and resolute endurance.

The reproach from which it is impossible entirely to clear his memory is that of undue subservience to power. It was in the qualities of independence and self-assertion that his character was deficient. It is to the excess of his feeling of deference to power, and not to any insincerity of nature, that we attribute the language occasionally—as in the Invocation to the Georgics —transcending the limits of truth and sobriety, in which the position of Augustus is magnified. It is for ever to be regretted that he was induced to sacrifice not only the tribute of admiration originally offered to the friend of his youth, but even the symmetrical conception of his greatest poem, to the jealousy which Augustus entertained of the memory of Gallus. Virgil, again, has no sympathy with political life, as it realised itself in the ancient republics, or with the energetic types of character which the conflicts of political life develope. His own somewhat submissive disposition, his personal attachments and admirations, his hatred of strife, his yearning after peace and reconcilement, made him a sincere supporter of the idea of the Empire in opposition to that of the Republic. To a character of a more combative energy and power of resistance it would have been scarcely possible to have been unmoved by the spectacle of the final overthrow of ancient freedom, though that freedom had for a long time previously contributed little to human happiness. But the nobleness of Virgil's nature is not the nobleness of those qualities which make men great in resistance to wrong, but the nobleness of a gentle and gracious spirit.

By no poet in any time has he been surpassed in devotion to his art. Into this channel all the currents of his being, all fresh sources of feeling, all the streams of his meditation and research were poured. The delight in poetry and the kindred delight in the beauty of Nature were the main springs of his happiness. With the high ambition of genius and the unceasing aim at perfection he combined a remarkable modesty and a generous appreciation of all poets who had gone before him.  But distrust in himself never led to any flagging of energy.  The stories told of his habits of composition confirm the impression of his assiduous industry.  In writing the Georgics he is said to have dictated many lines early in the morning, under the first impulse of his inspiration, and to have employed the remainder of the day in concentrating their force within the smallest compass.  Of no poem of equal length can it be said that there is so little that is superfluous.  He himself described this mode of composition by the phrase 'parere se versus modo atque ritu ursino'—'that he produced verses by licking them into shape as a bear did with her cubs.'  The Aeneid was first arranged and written out in prose: when the structure of the story was distinct to his mind, he proceeded to work on different parts of it, as his fancy moved him.  Another statement in regard to his manner of reading is worth mentioning, as indicating the powerful inspiration of the true ἀοιδός, which he added to the patient industry of the conscientious artist.  It is recorded on the authority of a contemporary poet, that he read his own poems with such a wonderful sweetness and charm ('suavitate tum lenociniis miris'), that verses which would have sounded commonplace when read by another, produced a marvellous effect when 'chanted to their own music[1]' by the poet himself. Similar testimony is given of the effect produced by the reading or recitation of their own works by some among our own poets, Wordsworth, Scott, and Byron among others.  This large, musical, and impassioned utterance—the 'os magna sonaturum'—is a sure note of that access of emotion which forces the poet to find a rhythmical expression for his thought.

It was through the union of a strong and delicate vein of original genius with a great receptive capacity and an unwearied love of his art that Virgil established and for a long time re-

---

[1] Compare the lines of Coleridge on hearing 'The Prelude' read aloud by Wordsworth :—

'An Orphic song indeed,
A song divine of high and passionate thoughts
To their own music chanted.'

tained his ascendency as one of the two whom the world
honoured as its greatest poets.  Though his supremacy has
been shaken, and is not likely ever again to be fully re-
established, the examination of his various works will show
that it was not through accident or caprice that one of the
highest places in the dynasty of genius was allotted to him,
and that his still remains one of the few great names which
belong, not to any particular age or nation, but to all time and
to every people.

# CHAPTER IV.

## THE ECLOGUES.

### I.

THE name by which the earliest of Virgil's recognised works is known tells us nothing of the subject of which it treats. The word 'Eclogae' simply means selections. As applied to the poems of Virgil, it designates a collection of short unconnected poems. The other name by which these poems were known in antiquity, 'bucolica,' indicates the form of Greek art in which they were cast and the pastoral nature of their subjects. Neither word is used by Virgil himself; but the expressions by which he characterises his art, such as 'Sicelides Musae,' 'versus Syracosius,' 'Musa agrestis' and 'silvestris,' show that he writes in a pastoral strain, and that he considered the pastoral poetry of Greece as his model. He invokes not only the 'Sicilian Muses,' but the 'fountain of Arethusa.' He speaks too of Pan, and Arcadia, and the 'Song of Maenalus.' His shepherd-poets are described as 'Arcadians.' The poets whom he introduces as his prototypes are the 'sage of Ascra,' and the mythical Linus, Orpheus, and Amphion. He alludes also to Theocritus under the name of the 'Syracusan shepherd.' The names of the shepherds who are introduced as contending in song or uttering their feelings in monologue—Corydon, Thyrsis, Menalcas, Meliboeus, Tityrus, etc.—are Greek, and for the most part taken from the pastoral idyls of Theocritus. There is also frequent mention of the shepherd's pipe, and of the musical accompaniment to which some of the songs chanted by the shepherds are set.

The general character of the poems is further indicated by the frequent use of the word 'ludere,' a word applied by

Catullus, Horace, Propertius, Ovid, and others to the poems
of youth, of a light and playful character, and, for the most
part, expressive of various moods of the passion of love. Thus
at the end of the Georgics Virgil speaks of himself thus :—

> Carmina qui lusi pastorum, audaxque iuventa,
> Tityre, te patulae cecini sub tegmine fagi[1].

This reference shows further that the poem which stands first
in order was placed there when the edition of the Eclogues
was given to the world. But other references (at v. 86–87 and
vi. 12) seem to imply that the separate poems were known
either by distinct titles, such as Varus, the title of the sixth, or
from their opening lines, as the 'Formosum Corydon ardebat
Alexim,' and the 'Cuium pecus? an Meliboei?' It has been
also suggested, from lines quoted in the ninth, which profess to
be the opening lines of other pastoral poems, that the ten
finally collected together were actual 'selections' from a larger
number, commenced if not completed ('necdum perfecta
canebat') by Virgil. But these passages seem more like the
lines attributed to the contending poets in the third and seventh
Eclogues, i.e. short unconnected specimens of pastoral song.

Nearly all the poems afford indications of the time of their
composition and of the order in which they followed one
another; and that order is different from the order in which
they now appear. It is said, on the authority of Asconius, that
three years, from 42 B.C. to 39 B.C., were given to the composition of the Eclogues. But an allusion in the tenth (line 47)
to the expedition of Agrippa across the Alps in the early part of
37 B.C. proves that a later date must be assigned to that poem.
The probable explanation is that Virgil had intended to end
the series with the eighth, which celebrated the triumph of
Pollio over the Parthini in 39 B.C.,—

> A te principium, tibi desinet,—

but that his friendship for Gallus induced him to add the tenth,

---

[1] 'I, the idle singer of a pastoral song, who in the boldness of youth
made thee, O Tityrus, beneath the shade of the spreading beech, my
theme.'

two years later, either before the poems were finally collected
for publication, or in preparing a new edition of them.  They
were written at various places and at various stages of the poet's
fortunes.  They appear to have obtained great success when
first published, and some of them were recited with applause
upon the stage.  The earliest in point of time were the second
and third, and these, along with the fifth, may be ascribed to
the year 42 B.C.  The seventh, which has no allusion to contemporary events and is a mere imitative reproduction of the
Greek idyl, may also belong to this earlier period, although
some editors rank it as one of the latest.  The first, which is
founded on the loss of the poet's farm, belongs to the next
year, and the ninth and sixth probably may be assigned to
the same year, or to the early part of the following year.  The
date of the fourth is fixed by the Consulship of Pollio to the
year 40 B.C.; that of the eighth to the year 39 B.C. by the
triumph of Pollio over the Parthini.  The opening words of
the tenth show that it was the last of the series; and the reference to the expedition of Agrippa implies that it could not
have been written earlier than the end of 38 B.C. or the beginning of 37 B.C.  The first, second, third, and fifth [1], were in
all probability written by the poet in his native district, the sixth,
ninth, and perhaps the seventh, at the villa which had formerly

---

[1] The lines of Propertius—
　　　　Tu canis umbrosi subter pineta Galaesi
　　　　　　Thyrsin et attritis Daphnin harundinibus,
might suggest the inference that the seventh was composed at the time
when Virgil was residing in the neighbourhood of Tarentum.  But, at the
time when Propertius wrote, Virgil was engaged in the composition of the
Aeneid, not of the Eclogues.  The present 'canis' seems rather to mean
that Virgil, while engaged with his Aeneid, was still conning over his old
Eclogues.  Yet he must have strayed 'subter pineta Galaesi' some time
before the composition of the last Georgic.  It has been remarked by
Mr. Munro that the 'memini' in the line
　　　　Namque sub Oebaliae memini me turribus arcis
looks like the memory of a somewhat distant past.  Could the villa of Siron
have been in the neighbourhood of Tarentum? (a question originally suggested by Mr. Munro); may it have passed by gift or inheritance into the
possession of Virgil, and was he in later life in the habit of going to it
from time to time? or was the distance too great from Mantua for him to
have transferred his family thither?

belonged to Siron ('villula quae Sironis *eras*'), the rest at
Rome.  The principle on which the poems are arranged seems
to be that of alternating dialogue with monologue.  The eighth,
though not in dialogue, yet resembles the latter part of the fifth,
in presenting two continuous songs, chanted by different shepherds.  The poem first in order may have occupied its place
from its greater interest in connexion with the poet's fortunes,
or from the honour which it assigns to Octavianus, whose pre-
eminence over the other competitors for supreme power had
sufficiently declared itself before the first collected edition of the
poems was published.

In the earliest poems of the series the art of Virgil, like the
lyrical art of Horace in his earlier Odes, is more imitative and
conventional than in those written later.  He seems satisfied
with reproducing the form, rhythm, and diction of Theocritus,
and mingling some vague expression of personal or national
feeling with the sentiment of the Greek idyl.  That the fifth
was written after the second and third appears from the
lines v. 86–87, in which Menalcas, under which name Virgil
introduces himself in the Eclogues, presents his pipe to
Mopsus :—

> Haec nos ' Formosum Corydon ardebat Alexin,'
> Haec eadem docuit ' Cuium pecus? an Meliboei [1]?'

From these lines also it may be inferred as probable that the
second poem, 'Formosum pastor Corydon,' was written before
the third, 'Dic mihi, Damoeta, cuium pecus? an Meliboei?'

A tradition, quoted by Servius and referred to (though
inaccurately) by Martial[2], attributes the composition of the
second Eclogue to the admiration excited in Virgil by the
beauty of a young slave, Alexander, who was presented to
him by Pollio and carefully educated by him.  A similar story
is told of his having received from Maecenas another slave,
named Cebes, who also obtained from him a liberal education

---

[1] ' This taught me " the fair Alexis was loved by Corydon," this too
taught me " whose is the flock? is it the flock of Meliboeus?" '
[2] viii. 56. 12.

and acquired some distinction as a poet.  It is not improbable
that Virgil may have been warmly attached to these youths, and
that there was nothing blameable in his attachment.  Even
Cicero, a man as far removed as possible from any sentimental
weakness, writes to Atticus of the death of a favourite slave,
a young Greek, and evidently, from the position he filled in
Cicero's household, a boy of liberal accomplishments, in these
words: 'And, I assure you, I am a good deal distressed.  For
my reader, Sositheus, a charming boy, is just dead; and it has
affected me more than I should have thought the death of a
slave ought to affect one [1].'  It remains true however that in one
or two of those Eclogues in which he most closely imitates
Theocritus, Virgil uses the language of serious sentiment, and
once of bantering raillery, in a way which justly offends modern
feeling.  And this is all that can be said against him.

There are more imitations of the Greek in this and in the
next poem than in any of the other Eclogues [2].  The scenery
of the piece, in so far as it is at all definite, combines the mountains and the sea-landscape of Sicily with Italian woods and
vineyards.  Corydon seems to combine the features of an
Italian vinedresser with the conventional character of a Sicilian
shepherd.  The line

Aspice aratra iugo referunt suspensa iuvenci [3]

applies rather to an Italian scene than to the pastoral district of
Sicily; and this reference to ploughing seems inconsistent with
the description of the fierce midsummer heat, and with the introduction of the 'fessi messores' in the opening lines of the
poem.  These inconsistencies show how little thought Virgil
had for the objective consistency of his representation.  The
poem however, in many places, gives powerful expression to the
feelings of a despairing lover.  There are here, as in the Gallus,
besides that vein of feeling which the Latin poet shares with

---

[1] Ep. ad Att. i. 12.
[2] Dr. Kennedy refers to no less than seventeen parallel passages from
Theocritus, many of them being almost literal translations from the Greek
poet.
[3] 'Look, the steers are drawing home the uplifted ploughs.'

Theocritus, some traces of that 'wayward modern mood' of longing to escape from the world and to return to some vague ideal of Nature, and to sacrifice all the gains of civilisation in exchange for the homeliest dwelling shared with the object of affection :—

> O tantum libeat mecum tibi sordida rura
> Atque humiles habitare casas, et figere cervos[1];

and again,

> Habitarunt di quoque silvas
> Dardaniusque Paris. Pallas quas condidit arces
> Ipsa colat, nobis placeant ante omnia silvae[2].

The third Eclogue, which is in dialogue, and reproduces two features of the Greek idyl, the natural banter of the shepherds and the more artificial contest in song, is still more imitative and composite in character. It shows several close imitations, especially of the fourth, fifth, and eighth Idyls of Theocritus[3]. In this poem only Virgil, whose muse even in the Eclogues is almost always serious or plaintive, endeavours to reproduce the playfulness and vivacity of his original. Both in the bantering dialogue and in the more formal contest of the shepherds, the subjects introduced are for the most part of a conventional pastoral character, but with these topics are combined occasional references to the tastes and circumstances of the poet himself. Thus in lines 40–42,

> In medio duo signa . . . curvus arator haberet,

allusion is made to the astronomical studies of which Virgil made fuller use in the Georgics. In the line

> Pollio amat nostram quamvis est rustica Musam,

and again,

> Pollio et ipse facit nova carmina[4],

---

[1] 'O that it would but please you to dwell with me among the " homely slighted " fields and lowly cottages, and to shoot the deer.'

[2] 'The Gods too were dwellers in the woods, and Dardanian Paris. Leave Pallas to abide in the towers which she has built; let our chief delight be in the woods.'

[3] Dr. Kennedy refers to twenty-seven parallels from Theocritus.

[4] 'Pollio loves my song, though it is but a shepherd's song.' 'Pollio himself too is a poet.'

he makes acknowledgment of the favour and pays honour to
the poetical tastes of his earliest patron, whom he celebrates
also in the fourth and eighth Eclogues.   The line

Qui Bavium non odit amet tua carmina, Maevi[1]

has condemned to everlasting notoriety the unfortunate pair,
who have served modern satirists as types of spiteful critics and
ineffectual authors.   At lines 10–11 there is, as in Eclogue ii.,
an apparent blending of the occupations of the Italian vinedresser with those of the Sicilian shepherd.   In the contest of
song there is no sustained connexion of thought, as indeed
there is not in similar contests in Theocritus.   These contests
are supposed to reproduce the utterances of improvisatori, of
whom the second speaker is called to say something, either in
continuation of or in contrast to the thought of the first.   The
shepherds in these strains seek to glorify their own prowess,
boast of their successes in love, or call attention to some
picturesque aspect of their rustic life.

The fifth Eclogue is also in dialogue.   It brings before us a
friendly interchange of song between two pastoral poets, Mopsus
and Menalcas.   Servius mentions that Menalcas (here, as in the
ninth Eclogue) stands for Virgil himself, while Mopsus stands
for his friend Aemilius Macer of Verona.   Mopsus laments the
cruel death of Daphnis, the legendary shepherd of Sicilian song,
and Menalcas celebrates his apotheosis.   Various accounts were
given in antiquity of the meaning which was to be attached
to this poem.   One account was that Virgil here expressed
his sorrow for the death of his brother Flaccus[2].   Though
the time of his death may have coincided with that of the
composition of this poem, the language of the lament and of
the song celebrating the ascent of Daphnis to heaven is quite
unlike the expression of a private or personal sorrow.   There
seems no reason to doubt another explanation which has come

---

[1] 'Who hates not Bavius may he be charmed with thy songs, O Maevius!'
[2] 'Menalcas Vergilius hic intelligitur, qui obitum fratris sui Flacci deflet,
vel, ut alii volunt, interfectionem Caesaris.'   Comment. in Verg. Serviani
(H. A. Lion, 1826).

down from ancient times, that under this pastoral allegory Virgil laments the death and proclaims the apotheosis of Julius Caesar. It is probable[1] that the poem was composed for his birthday, the 4th of July, which for the first time was celebrated with religious rites in the year 42 B. C., when the name of the month Quintilis was changed into that which it has retained ever since.   The lines 25–26,

> Nulla neque amnem
> Libavit quadrupes nec graminis attigit herbam[2],

are supposed[3] to refer to a belief which had become traditional in the time of Suetonius, that the horses which had been con- secrated after crossing the Rubicon had refused to feed im- mediately before the death of their master[4].   In the lines expressing the sorrow for his loss, and in those which mark out the divine office which he was destined to fulfil after death,—

> Ut Baccho Cererique, tibi sic vota quotannis
> Agricolae facient, damnabis tu quoque votis[5],—

as in the lines of the ninth, referring to the Julium Sidus,—

> Astrum quo segetes gauderent frugibus, et quo
> Duceret apricis in collibus uva colorem[6],—

allusion is made to the encouragement Caesar gave to the husbandman and vine-planter in his lifetime, and to the honour due to him as their tutelary god in heaven.   And these allusions help us to understand the ' votis iam nunc adsuesce vocari' of the invocation in the first Georgic.

Nothing illustrates more clearly the unreal conceptions of the pastoral allegory than a comparison of the language in the

---

[1] See Conington's Introduction to this Eclogue.

[2] 'No beast either tasted the river or touched a blade of grass.'

[3] Compare M. Benoist's note on the passage.

[4] 'Proximis diebus equorum greges, quos in traiciendo Rubicone flumine consecrarat ac vagos et sine custode dimiserat, comperit pertinacissime pabulo abstinere ubertimque flere.' Sueton. lib. i. c. 81.

[5] 'As to Bacchus and to Ceres so to thee shall the husbandmen annually make their vows; thou too wilt call on them for their fulfilment.'

[6] 'The star beneath which the harvest-fields should be glad in their corn-crops, and the grapes should gather a richer colour on the sunny hill- sides.'

'Lament for Daphnis,' with the strong Roman realism of the lines at the end of the first Georgic, in which the omens portending the death of Caesar are described. Nor can anything show more clearly the want of individuality with which Virgil uses the names of the Theocritean shepherds than the fact that while the Daphnis of the fifth Eclogue represents the departed and deified soldier and statesman, the Daphnis of the ninth is a living husbandman whose fortunes were secured by the protecting star of Caesar,—

> Insere, Daphni, piros, carpent tua poma nepotes [1].

The peace and tranquillity restored to the land under this protecting influence are foreshadowed in the lines 58–61—

> Ergo alacris . . . amat bonus otia Daphnis;

and the earliest reference to the divine honours assigned in life and death to the later representatives of the name of Caesar, is heard in the jubilant shout of wild mountains, rocks, and groves to the poet—

> Deus, deus ille, Menalca.

Although the treatment of the subject may be vague and conventional, yet this poem possesses the interest of being Virgil's earliest effort, directed to a subject of living and national interest; and many of the lines in the poem are unsurpassed for grace and sweetness of musical cadence by anything in Latin poetry.

There is no allusion to contemporary events by which the date of the seventh can be determined; but the absence of such allusion and the 'purely Theocritean [2]' character of the poem suggest the inference that it is a specimen of Virgil's earlier manner. Two shepherds, Corydon and Thyrsis, are introduced as joining Daphnis, who is seated under a whispering ilex; they engage in a friendly contest of song, which is listened to also by the poet himself, who here calls himself Meliboeus.

---

[1] 'Graft your pears, Daphnis: your fruits will be plucked by those who come after you.'

[2] Kennedy.

They assert in alternate strains their claims to poetic honours,
offer prayers and vows to Diana as the goddess of the chase
and to Priapus as the god of gardens, draw rival pictures of
cool retreat from the heat of summer and of cheerfulness by the
winter fire, and connect the story of their loves with the varying
aspect of the seasons, and with the beauty of trees sacred to
different deities or native to different localities.  Though the
shepherds are Arcadian, the scenery is Mantuan :—

> Hic viridis tenera praetexit harundine ripam
> Mincius, eque sacra resonant examina quercu[1].

Meliboeus decides the contest in favour of Corydon :—

> Haec memini, et victum frustra contendere Thyrsin.
> Ex illo Corydon Corydon est tempore nobis[2].

These poems, in which the conventional shepherds of
pastoral poetry sing of their loves, their flocks and herds, of
the beauty of the seasons and of outward nature, in tones
caught from Theocritus, or revive and give a new meaning
to the old Sicilian dirge over 'the woes of Daphnis,' may
be assigned to the eventful year in which the forces of the
Republic finally shattered themselves against the forces of
the new Empire.  There is a strange contrast between these
peaceful and somewhat unreal strains of Virgil and the drama
which was at the same time enacted on the real stage of human
affairs.  No sound of the 'storms that raged outside his happy
ground' disturbs the security with which Virgil cultivates his
art.  But the following year brought the trouble and un-
happiness of the times home to the peaceful dwellers around
Mantua, and to Virgil among the rest.  Of the misery caused
by the confiscations and allotments of land to the soldiers of
Octavianus, the first Eclogue is a lasting record.  Yet even in
this poem, based as it is on genuine feeling and a real experience, Virgil seems to care only for the truth of feeling

---

[1] 'Here the green Mincio fringes its bank with delicate reeds, and
swarms of bees are buzzing from the sacred oak.'

[2] 'This I remember, and that Thyrsis was beaten in the contest : from that
time Corydon is all in all with us.'

with which Tityrus and Meliboeus express themselves, without
regard for consistency in the conception of the situation, the
scenery, or the personages of the poem. Tityrus is at once
the slave who goes to Rome to purchase his freedom, and
the owner of the land and of the flocks and herds belonging
to it[1]. He is advanced in years[2], and at the same time a
poet lying indolently in the shade, and making the woods ring
with the sounds of 'beautiful Amaryllis[3],' like the young
shepherds in Theocritus. The scenery apparently combines
some actual features of the farm in the Mantuan district—

> Quamvis lapis omnia nudus
> Limosoque palus obducat pascua iunco[4],

with the ideal mountain-land of pastoral song—

> Maioresque cadunt altis de montibus umbrae[5].

A further inconsistency has been suggested between the time
of year indicated by the 'shade of the spreading beech' in the
first line, and that indicated by the ripe chestnuts at line 81[6].
The truth of the poem consists in the expression of the feelings
of love which the old possessors entertained for their homes,
and the sense of dismay caused by this barbarous irruption on
their ancient domains:—

> Impius haec tam culta novalia miles habebit?
> Barbarus has segetes? En quo discordia civis
> Produxit miseros[7]!

Virgil's feeling for the movement of his age, which henceforth
becomes one of the main sources of his inspiration, has its origin

---

[1] Cf.    Ergo *tua* rura manebunt—
          Ille *meas* errare boves—
          Multa *meis* exiret victima saeptis.

[2]       Candidior postquam tondenti barba cadebat—
          Fortunate senex.

[3] See Kennedy's note on the passage.

[4] 'Though all your land is choked with barren stones or covered with
marsh and sedge.'—P.

[5] 'And larger shadows are falling from the lofty mountains.'

[6] M. Benoist.

[7] 'Shall some unfeeling soldier become the master of these fields, so
carefully tilled, some rude stranger own these harvest-fields? see to what
misery fellow-countrymen have been brought by civil strife!'

in the effect which these events had on his personal fortunes,
and in the sympathy awakened within him by the sorrows of his
native district.

The ninth Eclogue, written most probably in the same year,
and in form imitated from the seventh Idyl—the famous
Thalysia—of Theocritus, repeats the tale of dejection and
alarm among the old inhabitants of the Mantuan district,—

> Nunc victi, tristes, quoniam fors omnia versat [1],—

and touches allusively on the story of the personal danger
which Virgil encountered from the violence of the centurion
who claimed possession of his land. The speakers in the
dialogue are Moeris, a shepherd of Menalcas,— the pastoral
poet, who sings of the nymphs, of the wild flowers spread
over the ground, and of the brooks shaded with trees,—and
Lycidas, who, like the Lycidas of the Thalysia, is also a
poet:—

> Me quoque dicunt
> Vatem pastores, sed non ego credulus illis.
> Nam neque adhuc Vario videor nec dicere Cinna
> Digna, sed argutos inter strepere anser olores [2].

After the account of the fray, given by Moeris, and the com-
ments of Lycidas, in which he introduces the lines referred to
in the previous chapter, as having all the signs of being a real
description of the situation of Virgil's farms—

> qua se subducere colles incipiunt—

Moeris sings the opening lines of certain other pastoral poems,
some his own, some the songs of Menalcas. Two of these—

---

[1] 'Now in defeat and sadness, since all things are the sport of chance.'

[2] 'Me too the shepherds call a bard, but I give no ear to them; for as
yet my strain seems far inferior to that of Varius and of Cinna, and to be
as the cackling of a goose among tuneful swans.' Compare the lines which
Theocritus applies to Lycidas :—

> Καὶ γὰρ ἐγὼν Μοισᾶν καπυρὸν στόμα, κἠμὲ λέγοντι
> πάντες ἀοιδὸν ἄριστον· ἐγὼ δέ τις οὐ ταχυπειθής,
> οὐ Δᾶν· οὐ γάρ πω κατ' ἐμὸν νόον οὔτε τὸν ἐσθλόν
> Σικελίδαν νίκημι τὸν ἐκ Σάμω, οὐδὲ Φιλητᾶν
> ἀείδων, βάτραχος δὲ ποτ' ἀκρίδας ὥς τις ἐρίσδω.
>
> Theoc. vii. 37-41.

'Tityre dum redeo' and 'Huc ades O Galatea'—are purely
Theocritean.   Two others—

> Vare tuum nomen, superet modo Mantua nobis,

and

> Daphni quid antiquos signorum suspicis ortus [1]—

indicate the new path which Virgil's art was striking out for
itself.   There is certainly more real substance in this poem
than in most of the earlier Eclogues.   Lycidas and Moeris
speak about what interests them personally.   The scene of the
poem is apparently the road between Virgil's farm and Mantua.
There seem to be no conventional and inconsistent features
introduced from the scenery of Sicily or Arcadia, unless it be
the 'aequor' of line 57—

> Et nunc omne tibi stratum silet aequor [2].

But may not that be either the lake, formed by the overflow of
the river, some distance above Mantua, or even the great level
plain, with its long grass and corn-fields and trees, hushed in
the stillness of the late afternoon?

The sixth Eclogue was written probably about the same time
and at the same place, the villa of Siron, in which Virgil had taken
refuge with his family.   It is inscribed with the name of Varus,
who is said to have been a fellow-student of Virgil under the
tuition of Siron.   But, with the exception of the dedicatory lines,
there is no reference to the circumstances of the time.   Though
abounding with rich pastoral illustrations, the poem is rather
a mythological and semi-philosophical idyl than a pure pastoral
poem.   It consists mainly of a song of Silenus, in which an
account is given of the creation of the world in accordance
with the Lucretian philosophy; and, in connexion with this
theme (as is done also by Ovid in his Metamorphoses), some
of the oldest mythological traditions, such as the tale of Pyrrha
and Deucalion, the reign of Saturn on earth, the theft and
punishment of Prometheus, etc., are introduced.   The opening

---

[1] 'Varus, thy name provided only Mantua be spared to us.'
'Daphnis, why gazest thou on the old familiar risings of the constellations?'
[2] 'And now you see the whole level plain [sea?] is calm and still.'

lines—Namque canebat uti—are imitated from the song of
Orpheus in the first book of the Argonautics[1], but they bear
unmistakable traces also of the study of Lucretius. There
seems no trace of the language of Theocritus in the poem.

Three points of interest may be noted in this song: (1)
Virgil here, as in Georgic ii. 475, etc., regards the revelation
of physical knowledge as a fitting theme for poetic treatment.
So in the first Aeneid, the 'Song of Iopas' is said to be about
'the wandering moon and the toils of the sun; the origin of
man and beast, water and fire,' etc. The revelation of the
secrets of Nature seems to float before the imagination of
Virgil as the highest consummation of his poetic faculty.
(2) We note here how, as afterwards in the Georgics, he accepts the philosophical ideas of creation, side by side with the
supernatural tales of mythology. He seems to regard such
tales as those here introduced as part of the religious traditions
of the human race, and as a link which connects man with the
gods. In the Georgics we find also the same effort to reconcile, or at least to combine, the conceptions of science with
mythological fancies. In this effort we recognise the influence
of other Alexandrine poets rather than of Theocritus. (3)
The introduction of Gallus in the midst of the mythological
figures of the poem, and the account of the honour paid to
him by the Muses and of the office assigned to him by Linus,
are characteristic of the art of the Eclogues, which is not so
much allegorical as composite. It brings together in the same
representation facts, personages, and places from actual life
and the figures and scenes of a kind of fairy-land. In the
tenth Eclogue Gallus is thus identified with the Daphnis of
Sicilian song, and is represented as the object of care to the
Naiads and Pan and Apollo. While Pollio is the patron whose
protection and encouragement Virgil most cordially acknowledges in his earlier poems, Gallus is the man among his contemporaries who has most powerfully touched his imagination
and gained his affections.

[1] i. 496.

The Eclogue composed next in order of time is the 'Pollio.'
It was written in the consulship of Pollio, B.C. 40, immediately
after the reconciliation between Antony and Octavianus effected
by the treaty of Brundisium, and gives expression to that
vague hope of a new era of peace and prosperity which recurs
so often in the poetry of this age.   In consequence of the
interpretation given to it in a later age, this poem has acquired
an importance connected with Virgil's religious belief second
only to the importance of the sixth Aeneid.   Early Christian
writers, perceiving a parallel between expressions and ideas in
this poem and those in the Messianic prophecies, believed that
Virgil was here the unconscious vehicle of Divine inspiration,
and that he prophesies of the new era which was to begin with
the birth of Christ.    And though, as Conington and others
have pointed out, the picture of the Golden Age given in the
poem is drawn immediately from Classical and not from
Hebrew sources, yet there is no parallel in Classical poetry
to that which is the leading idea of the poem, the coincidence
of the commencement of this new era with the birth of a child
whom a marvellous career awaited.

The poem begins with an invocation to the Sicilian Muses
and with the declaration that, though the strain is still pastoral,
yet it is to be in a higher mood, and worthy of the Consul to
whom it is addressed.   Then follows the announcement of the
birth of a new era.   The world after passing through a cycle
of ages, each presided over by a special deity, had reached the
last of the cycle, presided over by Apollo, and was about to
return back to the Golden or Saturnian Age of peace and
innocence, into which the human race was originally born.
A new race of men was to spring from heaven.   The first-born
of this new stock was destined hereafter to be a partaker of
the life of the gods and to 'rule over a world in peace with the
virtues of his father.'   Then follow the rural and pastoral
images of the Golden Age, like those given in the first Georgic
in the description of the early world before the reign of Jove.
The full glory of the age should not be reached till this child

should attain the maturity of manhood. In the meantime some
traces of 'man's original sin' ('priscae vestigia fraudis') should
still urge him to brave the dangers of the sea, to surround his
cities with walls, and to plough the earth into furrows. There
should be a second expedition of the Argonauts, and a new
Achilles should be sent against another Troy. The romantic
adventures of the heroic age were to precede the rest, innocence, and spontaneous abundance of the age of Saturn. Next
the child is called upon to prepare himself for the 'magni
honores'—the great offices of state which awaited him; and
the poet prays that his own life and inspiration may be prolonged so far as to enable him to celebrate his career.

There seem to be no traces of imitation of Theocritus in
this poem. The rhythm which in the other Eclogues reproduces the Theocritean cadences is in this more stately and
uniform, recalling those of Catullus in his longest poem. The
substance of the poem is quite unlike anything in the Sicilian
idyl. Though this substance does not stand out in the clear
light of reality, but is partially revealed through a haze of
pastoral images and legendary associations, yet it is not altogether unmeaning. The anticipation of a new era was widely
spread and vividly felt over the world; and this anticipation—
the state of men's minds at and subsequent to the time when
this poem was written—probably contributed to the acceptance
of the great political and spiritual changes which awaited the
world [1].

Two questions which have been much discussed in connexion
with this poem remain to be noticed; (1) who is the child

---

[1] Compare Gaston Boissier, La Religion Romaine d'Auguste aux Antonins : 'Il y a pourtant un côté par lequel la quatrième églogue peut être
rattachée à l'histoire du Christianisme ; elle nous révèle un certain état des
âmes qui n'a pas été inutile à ses rapides progrès. C'était une opinion ac-
créditée alors que le monde épuisé touchait à une grande crise et qu'une
révolution se préparait qui lui rendrait la jeunesse. . . . Il regnait alors
partout une sorte de fermentation, d'attente inquiète et d'espérance sans
limite. " Toutes les créatures soupirent," dit Saint Paul, " et sont dans le
travail de l'enfantement." Le principal intérêt des vers de Virgile est de
nous garder quelque souvenir de cette disposition des âmes.

born in the consulship of Pollio of whom this marvellous career is predicted? (2) is it at all probable that Virgil, directly or indirectly, had any knowledge of the Messianic prophecies or ideas?

In answer to the first we may put aside at once the supposition that the prediction is made of the child who was born in that year to Octavianus and Scribonia. The words 'nascenti puero' are altogether inapplicable to the notorious and unfortunate Julia, who was the child of that marriage. If Virgil was sanguine enough to predict the sex of the child, we can hardly imagine him allowing the words to stand after his prediction had been falsified. We may equally dismiss the supposition that the child spoken of was the offspring of the marriage of Antony and Octavia. Not to mention other considerations adverse to this supposition [1], it would have been impossible for Virgil, the devoted partisan of Caesar, to pay this special compliment to Antony, even after he became so closely connected with his rival. There remains a third supposition, that the child spoken of is the son of Pollio, Asinius Gallus, who plays an important part in the reign of Tiberius. This last interpretation is supported by the authority of Asconius, who professed to have heard it from Asinius Gallus himself. The objection to this interpretation is that Virgil was not likely to assign to the child of one who, as compared with Octavianus and Antony, was only a secondary personage in public affairs, the position of 'future ruler of the world' and the function of being 'the regenerator of his age.' Still less could a poem bearing this meaning have been allowed to retain its place among Virgil's works after the ascendency of Augustus became undisputed. Further, the line

Cara deum suboles, magnum Iovis incrementum

(whatever may be its exact meaning [2]) appears an extreme

---

[1] Any child born of this marriage in the year 40 B.C. must have owed its birth, not to Antony, but to Marcellus, the former husband of Octavia.

[2] The application of the words 'magnum Iovis incrementum' by the author of the Ciris (398) to Castor and Pollux suggests a doubt as to Mr. Munro's interpretation of the words, accepted by Dr. Kennedy; though

exaggeration when specially applied to the actual son of a
mortal father and mother.   These difficulties have led some
interpreters to suppose that the child spoken of is an ideal or
imaginary representative of the future race.   But if we look more
closely at the poem, we find that the child is not really spoken
of as the future regenerator of the age; he is merely the first-
born of the new race, which was to be nearer to the gods both
in origin and in actual communion with them.   Again, the words

Pacatumque reget patriis virtutibus orbem[1]

would not convey the same idea in the year 40 B.C. as they
would ten or twenty years later.   At the time when the poem
was written the consulship was still the highest recognised position in the State.   The Consuls for the year, nominally at least,
wielded the whole power of the Empire.   The words 'reget
orbem' remain as a token that the Republic was not yet
entirely extinct.   The child is called upon to prepare himself
for the great offices of State in the hope that he should in time
hold the high place which was now held by his father.   The
words 'patriis virtutibus' imply that he is no ideal being, but
the actual son of a well-known father.   Virgil takes occasion in
this poem to commemorate the attainment of the highest office
by his patron, to celebrate the birth of the son born in the year
of his consulship, and at the same time to express, by mystical
and obscure allusions, the trust that the peace of Brundisium
was the inauguration of that new era for which the hearts of
men all over the world were longing.

In turning to the second question, discussed in connexion
with this Eclogue, the great amount and recondite character
of Virgil's learning, especially of that derived from Alexandrine
sources, must be kept in view.   Macrobius testifies to this in
several places.   Thus he writes, 'for this poet was learned with
not only a minute conscientiousness, but even with a kind of
reserve and mystery, so that he introduced into his works much

at the same time there is nothing improbable in the supposition that Virgil
gave a meaning to the words which was misunderstood by his imitator.
    [1] 'And will rule the world in peace with his father's virtues.'

knowledge the sources of which are difficult to discover[1].'
In another place he speaks of those things, 'what he had
introduced from the most recondite learning of the Greeks[2].'
And again he says, 'this story Virgil has dug out from the
most recondite Greek literature[3].' It is indeed most improbable that Virgil had a direct knowledge of the Septuagint.
If he had this knowledge it would have shown itself by other
allusions in other parts of his works. But it is quite possible
that, through other channels of Alexandrine learning, the ideas
and the language of Hebrew prophecy may have become
indirectly known to him. One channel by which this may
have reached him would be the new Sibylline prophecies,
manufactured in the East and probably reflecting Jewish as
well as other Oriental ideas, which poured into Rome after the
old Sibylline books had perished in the burning of the Capitol
during the first Civil War.

Still, admitting these possibilities, we are not called upon to
go beyond classical sources for the general substance and idea
of this poem. It has more in common with the myth in the
Politicus of Plato than with the Prophecies of Isaiah. The
state of the world at the time when the poem was written produced the longing for an era of restoration and a return to
a lost ideal of innocence and happiness, and the wish became
father to the thought.

There still remain the eighth and tenth Eclogues to be
examined. The first, like the fourth, is associated with the
name of Pollio, the second with that of Gallus. The date
of the eighth is fixed to 39 B.C. by the victory of Pollio in
Illyria and by his subsequent triumph over the Parthini. The
words

> Accipe iussis
> Carmina coepta tuis[4]

---

[1] Fuit enim hic poeta, ut scrupulose et anxie, ita dissimulanter et clan-
culo doctus, ut multa transtulerit quae, unde translata sint, difficile sit cog-
nitu. Sat. v. 18.

[2] Quae a penitissima Graecorum doctrina transtulisset. Ib. 22.

[3] De Graecorum penitissimis literis hanc historiam eruit Maro. Ib. 19.

[4] 'Receive a song undertaken at your command.'

testify to the personal influence under which Virgil wrote these poems. The title of 'Pharmaceutria,' by which the poem is known, indicates that Virgil professes to reproduce, in an Italian form, that passionate tale of city life which forms the subject of the second idyl of Theocritus. But while the subject and burden of the second of the two songs contained in this Eclogue are suggested by that idyl, the poem is very far from being a mere imitative reproduction of it.

Two shepherds, Damon and Alphesiboeus, meet in the early dawn—

> Cum ros in tenera pecori gratissimus herba[1],

(one of those touches of truthful description which reappear in the account of the pastoral occupations in Georgic iii). They each sing of incidents which may have been taken from actual life, or may have formed the subject of popular songs traditional among the peasantry of the district. In the first of these songs Damon gives vent to his despair in consequence of the marriage of his old love Nysa with his rival Mopsus. Though the shepherds who sing together bear the Greek names of Damon and Alphesiboeus, though they speak of Rhodope and Tmaros and Maenalus, of Orpheus and Arion, though expressions and lines are close translations, and one a mistranslation, from the Greek (πάντα δ᾽ ἔναλλα γένοιτο being rendered 'omnia vel medium fiant mare'), and though the mode by which the lover determines to end his sorrows,

> Praeceps aerii specula de montis in undas
> Deferar[2],

is more appropriate to a shepherd inhabiting the rocks over-hanging the Sicilian seas than to one dwelling in the plain of Mantua, yet both this song and the accompanying one sung by Alphesiboeus approach more nearly to the impersonal and dramatic representation of the Greek idyl than any of those

---

[1] 'When the dew on the tender blade is most grateful to the flock.'
[2] 'I shall hurl myself headlong into the waves from the high mountain's crag.'

already examined. The lines of most exquisite grace and tenderness in the poem,—lines which have been pronounced the finest in Virgil and the finest in Latin literature by Voltaire and Macaulay [1],—

> Saepibus in nostris parvam te roscida mala,
> Dux ego vester eram, vidi cum matre legentem :
> Alter ab undecimo tum me iam acceperat annus,
> Iam fragiles poteram ab terra contingere ramos :
> Ut vidi, ut perii, ut me malus abstulit error [2]—

are indeed close imitations of lines of similar beauty from the song of the Cyclops to Galatea :—

> ἠράσθην μὲν ἔγωγα τεοῦς, κόρα, ἀνίκα πρᾶτον
> ἦνθες ἐμᾷ σὺν ματρὶ θέλοισ᾽ ὑακίνθινα φύλλα
> ἐξ᾽ ὄρεος δρέψασθαι, ἐγὼ δ᾽ ὁδὸν ἀγεμόνευον·
> παύσασθαι δ᾽ ἐσιδών τυ καὶ ὕστερον οὐδ᾽ ἔτι πᾳ νῦν
> ἐκ τήνω δύναμαι· τίν᾽ δ᾽ οὐ μέλει, οὐ μὰ Δί᾽ οὐδέν [3].

But they are so varied as to suggest a picture of ease and abundance among the orchards and rich cultivated land of Italy, instead of the free life and natural beauties of the Sicilian mountains. The descriptive touches suggesting the picture of the innocent romance of boyhood are also all Virgil's own.

The song of Alphesiboeus represents a wife endeavouring to recall her truant, though still faithful, Daphnis from the city to his home. Though some of the illustrations in this song also are Greek, yet it contains several natural references to rustic

---

[1] 'But I think that the finest lines in the Latin language are those five which begin—
    Saepibus in nostris parvam te roscida mala.
I cannot-tell you how they struck me. I was amused to find that Voltaire pronounces that passage to be the finest in Virgil.' Life and Letters of Lord Macaulay, vol. i. pp. 371, 372.

[2] 'It was within our orchard I saw you, a child, with my mother gathering apples, and I was your guide : I had but then entered on my twelfth year, I could just reach from the ground the fragile branches : the moment I saw you how utterly lost I was, how borne astray by fatal passion.'

[3] 'I loved you, maiden, when first you came with my mother wishing to gather hyacinths from the mountain, and I guided you on the way : and since I saw you, from that time, never after, not even yet, can I cease loving you ; but you care not, no, by Zeus, not a whit.'

superstitions which were probably common to Greek and Italian peasants; and the fine simile at line 85 (of which the first hint is to be found in Lucretius [1]) suggests purely Italian associations. The final incident in the poem, 'Hylax in limine latrat' (though the name given to the dog is Greek), is a touch of natural life, such as does not often occur in the Eclogues. On the whole, Virgil seems here to have struck on a vein which it may be regretted that he did not work more thoroughly. If, as has been suggested by Mr. Symonds, in his account and translations of popular Tuscan poems, any of the Eclogues of Virgil are founded on primitive love-songs current among the peasantry of Italy, the songs of Damon and Alphesiboeus are those which we should fix on as being the artistic development of these native germs.

The tenth Eclogue was the last in order of composition, probably an after-thought written immediately before the final publication, or perhaps before the second edition, of the nine other poems. In this poem Virgil abandons the more realistic path on which he had entered in the eighth, and returns again to the vague fancies of the old pastoral lament for Daphnis, as it is sung in the first idyl of Theocritus. Nothing can be more remote from actual fact than the representation of Gallus—the active and ambitious soldier and man of affairs, at that time engaged in the defence of the coasts of Italy—dying among the mountains of Arcadia, in consequence of his desertion by Lycoris (a dancing-girl, and former mistress of Antony, whose real name was Cytheris), and wept for by the rocks and pine-woods of Maenalus and Lycaeus. Yet none of the poems is more rich in beauty, and grace, and happy turns of phrase. As the idealised expression of unfortunate love, this poem is of the same class as the second, and as the song of Damon in the eighth. That vein of modern romantic sentiment, already noticed in the second, the longing to escape from the ways of civilised life to the wild and lonely places of Nature, and to

---

[1] Compare 85–86 with Lucret. ii. 355, etc. :—
　　　At mater viridis saltus orbata peragrans.

follow in imagination 'the homely, slighted shepherd's trade,' meets us also in the lines,

> Atque utinam ex vobis unus vestrique fuissem
> Aut custos gregis aut maturae vinitor uvae [1],—

and again in these,

> Certum est in silvis, inter spelaea ferarum
> Malle pati, tenerisque meos incidere amores
> Arboribus [2].

## II.

### *Relation of the Eclogues to the Greek Pastoral.*

The review of the Eclogues in the order of their composition shows that the early art of Virgil, like the lyrical art of Horace, begins in imitation, and, after attaining command over the form, rhythm, and diction of the type of poetry which it reproduces, gradually assumes greater independence in the choice of subject and the mode of treatment. The susceptibility of Virgil's mind to the grace and musical sweetness of Theocritus gave the first impulse to the composition of the Eclogues; but this susceptibility was itself the result of a natural sympathy with the sentiment and motives of the Greek idyl, especially with the love of Nature and the passion of love. He found this province of art unappropriated. He revealed a new vein of Greek feeling unwrought by any of his countrymen. He gave another life to the beings, natural and supernatural, of ancient pastoral song, and awoke in his native land the sound of a strain hitherto unheard by Italian ears. The form of the Greek idyl, whether in dialogue or monologue, suited his genius, as a vehicle for the lighter fancies of youth, and for half-revealing, half-concealing the pleasures and pains personal to himself, better than the forms of lyrical and elegiac poetry adopted by Catullus and his compeers. In the opening lines of the sixth Eclogue,

---

[1] 'And would that I had been one of you, and had been either shepherd of your flock or the gatherer of the ripe grape.'

[2] 'I am resolved rather to suffer among the woods, among the wild beasts' dens, and to carve my loves on the tender bark of the trees.'

Prima Syracosio dignata est ludere versu
Nostra, neque erubuit silvas habitare Thalia[1],

Virgil acknowledges at once the source of his inspiration and
the lowly position which his genius was willing to assume.
He may have consoled himself for this abnegation of a higher
ambition by the thought suggested in the lines addressed to
the ideal poet and hero of his imagination—

Nec te paeniteat pecoris, divine poeta,
Et formosus ovis ad flumina pavit Adonis[2].

In order to understand the pastoral poetry of Virgil, both
in its relation to a Greek ideal and in its original truth of
feeling, it is necessary to remember the chief characteristics of
its prototype in the age of Ptolemy Philadelphus of Alexandria
and in the early years of the reign of Hiero of Syracuse.
The pastoral poetry of Sicily was the latest creation of Greek
genius, born after the nobler phases of religious and political
life, and the epic, lyric, and dramatic poetry which arose out of
them, had passed away.    In ancient, as in modern times, the
pastoral idyl, as an artistic branch of literature, has arisen, not
in a simple age, living in unconscious harmony with Nature,
but from the midst of a refined and luxurious, generally, too, a
learned or rather bookish society, and has tried to give vent to
the feelings of men weary of an artificial life and vaguely longing to breathe a freer air[3].    But there was in ancient times
a primitive and popular, as well as a late and artistic pastoral.
Of the primitive pastoral, springing out of rustic gatherings
and festivals, or from lonely communion with Nature,

---

[1] 'First my Muse deigned lightly to sing in the Sicilian strain, and
blushed not to dwell among the woods.'
[2] 'Nor need you be ashamed of your flock, O Godlike poet; even fair
Adonis once fed his sheep by the river-banks.'
[3] Compare the following passage from one of the prose idyls of G. Sand:
'Depuis les bergers de Longus jusqu'à ceux de Trianon, la vie pastorale est
un Éden parfumé où les âmes tourmentées et lassées du tumulte du monde
ont essayé de se réfugier.    L'art, ce grand flatteur, ce chercheur com-
plaisant de consolations pour les gens trop heureux, a traversé une suite
ininterrompue de *bergeries*.    Et sous ce titre, *Histoire des bergeries*, j'ai
souvent désiré de faire un livre d'érudition et de critique où j'aurais passé
en revue tous ces différents rêves champêtres dont les hautes classes se
sont nourries avec passion.'    Francois le Champi.

Per loca pastorum deserta atque otia dia[1],

and transmitted, from generation to generation, in the mouth of the people, no fragment has been preserved. Yet traces of the existence of this kind of pastoral song, and of the music accompanying it, at a time antecedent to the composition of the Homeric poems, may be seen in the representation, on the Shield of Achilles, of the boy in the vineyard 'singing the beautiful song Linus,'—a representation which is purely idyllic,—and of the shepherds, in the Ambuscade, who appear τερπόμενοι σύριγξι, as they accompany their flocks. The author of the Iliad absorbed the spirit of this primitive poetry in the greater compass of his epic creation, as Shakspeare has absorbed the Elizabethan pastoral within the all-embracing compass of his representation. Much of the imagery of the Iliad, several incidents casually introduced in connexion with the names of obscure persons perishing in battle, some of the supernatural events glanced at, as of the meeting of Aphrodite with Anchises while tending his herds on the spurs of Ida,—a subject of allusion also in the Sicilian idyl,—are of a pastoral character and origin. In the lines which spring up with a tender grace in the midst of the stern grandeur of the final conflict between Hector and Achilles—

οὐ μέν πως νῦν ἔστιν ἀπὸ δρυὸς οὐδ' ἀπὸ πέτρης
τῷ ὀαριζέμεναι, ἅ τε παρθένος ἠίθεός τε,
παρθένος ἠίθεός τ' ὀαρίζετον ἀλλήλοιιν[2]—

the familiar cadences as well as the sweetest sentiment of pastoral song may be recognised.

This primitive pastoral poetry may have been spread over all Greece and the islands of the Aegean, from the earliest settlements of the Hellenic race, or of that older branch of the family to which the name Pelasgic has been vaguely given,

---

[1] 'Among the lonely haunts of the shepherds and the deep peace of Nature.'

[2] 'One may not now hold converse with him from a tree or from a rock, like a maid and youth, as a maid and youth hold converse with one another.'

and may have lingered on the same in spirit, though with many variations in form and expression, among the peasantry and herdsmen of the mountain districts till a late period. But the earliest writer who is said to have adopted this native plant of the mountains and the woods, and to have trained it to assume some form of art, was Stesichorus of Himera, who flourished about the beginning of the sixth century B.C. But nothing more is heard of it till it revived again at Syracuse in the early part of the third century.

Some of the primitive modes of feeling which gave birth to the earliest pastoral song still survive, though in altered form, in this later Sicilian poetry. The song of the βουκόλοι, or herdsmen, like the song of the masked worshippers of Bacchus (τραγῳδία), may be traced to that stage in the development of the higher races in which Nature was the chief object of worship and religious sympathy. Under the symbols of Linus, Daphnis, or Adonis, the country people of early times lamented the decay of the fresh beauty of spring, under the burning midsummer heat[1]. This primitive germ of serious feeling has perpetuated itself in that melancholy mood which runs through the pastoral poetry of all countries. From that tendency of the Greek imagination to give a human meaning to all that interested it, this dirge over the fading beauty of the early year soon assumed the form of a lament over the death of a young shepherd-poet, dear to gods and men, to the flocks, herds, and wild animals, to the rocks and mountains, among which he had lived. In the Daphnis of Theocritus, the human passion of love produces that blighting influence on the life of the shepherd which in the original myth was produced by the fierce heat of summer on the tender life of the year. A still later development of the myth appears in the lament over the extinction of youthful genius by early death. It is not in any poem of Theocritus, but in the 'Lament of Bion,'—the work of a later writer, apparently an Italian-Greek,—

[1] Compare the account of the origin of pastoral poetry in Müller's Literature of the Greeks.

αὐτὰρ ἐγώ τοι
Αὐσονικᾶς ὀδύνας μέλπω μέλος [1],—

that we find the finest ancient specimen of this later development. It is from this new form of the old dirge of Linus or
Daphnis that the fancies and feelings of the ancient pastoral
have been most happily adapted to modern poetry, as in the
Lycidas, the Adonais, and the Thyrsis of English literature.

Another traditional theme of 'pastoral melancholy,' of which
Theocritus makes use, is the unrequited love of the Cyclops for
Galatea. This too had its origin in the personification of natural
objects [2]. But, unlike the song of Daphnis, the myth of which it
was the expression was purely local, and confined to the shores
of Sicily. It also illustrates the tendency of all pastoral song to
find its chief human motive in the passion of love. While the
original motive of the primitive lament for Daphnis or Linus was
the unconscious sympathy of the human heart with Nature, the
most prominent motive of artistic pastoral or idyllic poetry, from
the 'Song of Songs' to the 'Hermann and Dorothea' and 'The
Long Vacation Pastoral' of these later times, has been the passion of the human heart for the human object of its affection,
blending with either an unconscious absorption in outward
scenes or a refined contemplation of them [3].

But there is another very distinct mode of primitive feeling
traceable in Theocritus, which dictates the good-humoured, often
licentious, banter with which the shepherds encounter one another. As the pastoral monologue continued to betray the
serious character of the Lament out of which it sprung, so this
natural dialogue continued to bear traces of that old licence of
the harvest-home and the vintage-season, which

Versibus alternis opprobria rustica fudit [4].

---

[1] 'But I attune the plaintive Ausonian melody.' Incertorum Idyll. I.
100-101. (Ed. Ahrens.)

[2] Compare Symonds' Studies of Greek Poets, First Series, The Idyllists.

[3] Wordsworth's great pastoral 'Michael' is a marked exception to this
general statement. So, too, love can hardly be called the most prominent
motive in Tennyson's 'Dora.'

[4] 'Poured forth its rustic banter in responsive strains.'

The 'lusit amabiliter' of Horace's lines, which soon became inapplicable to the biting and censorious Italian spirit, expresses happily the tone of the dialogue in the fourth and fifth Idyls of Theocritus, which Virgil attempts to reproduce in his third Eclogue.   This source of rural poetry was known to the 'Ausonian husbandmen' as well as to the country people of Greece and Sicily: and its native force passed not only into the Greek pastoral idyl, but into the Sicilian comedy of Epicharmus and the old comedy of Athens, and, through a totally different channel, into Roman satire.   There is, however, another form in which the pastoral dialogue appears both in Theocritus and Virgil, namely, of extemporaneous contests in song.   Probably these more artistic contests and the award of prizes to the successful competitor had their origin in the bantering dialogue of the shepherds; as the tragic contests at the Dionysian festivals had their origin in the rivalry with which the masked votaries of Dionysus poured forth their extemporaneous verses, in sympathy with the sufferings of their god.

Such were the first rude utterances of the deeper as well as the gayer emotions of men, living in the happy security of the country districts or the 'otia dia' of the mountains in Greece, Sicily, and perhaps Southern Italy, which the art of Theocritus and his successors cast into artistic forms and measures suited to the taste of educated readers.   How far, in the manner in which he accomplished this, Theocritus had been anticipated by 'the grave muse of Stesichorus,' and whether this wild product of the mountains was of a native Siculian or an Hellenic stock, it is not possible to determine.   A citizen of Syracuse, in the palmy days of Hiero, before there was any dream of Roman conquest; deeply susceptible of the beauty of his native island, but, like a Greek, seeing this beauty in relation to human associations; familiar with the songs and old traditions of the land, as well as with the fancies of earlier poets; living his life in friendly association with his literary compeers, such as the Alexandrine Aratus[1] and Nicias, the physician and poet[2],—he

---

[1] Idyl vii. 97, vi. 2.          [2] Idyl xi. 2–6, xiii. 2.

sought to people the familiar scenery of mountain, wood, brook, and sea-shore with an ideal race of shepherds, in whom the natural emotions and grotesque superstitions of actual herdsmen should be found in union with the refinement, the mythological lore, the keen sense of the beauty, not unmixed with the melancholy, of life, characteristic of a circle of poets and scholars enjoying their youth in untroubled and uneventful times. All his materials, old and new, assumed the shape of pictures from human life in combination with the representations of the sounds, sights, and living movement of Nature.  The essential characteristic both of his pastoral Idyls and of those drawn from city-life, such as the second, fourteenth, and fifteenth, is what has been well called the 'disinterested objectivity[1]' of Greek art: and this is the chief note of their difference from Virgil's pastorals.  Even where, as in the seventh, the poet introduces himself on the scene, he appears as one, and not the most important, of the personages on it.  He does not draw attention to his own feelings or fortunes, only to his playful converse and rivalry in song with the young shepherd-poet Lycidas, 'with the bright laughing eye and the smile ever playing on his lip[2].'

It may be urged against these Idyls that, as compared with the best modern Idyls, in prose or verse, they are, for the most part, wanting in incident or adventure; and this charge is equally applicable to Virgil's pastorals.  But there is always dramatic vivacity and consistency in the personages of Theocritus, and this cannot equally be said of those introduced into the Eclogues.  It might be urged also against the representations of Theocritus, and still more against those of Virgil. that the 'vestigia ruris' have been too carefully obliterated.  Yet, though not drawn immediately from life, this picture of Sicilian shepherds and peasants, possessed with the vivid belief in Pan and the Nymphs, singing the old dirge of the herdsman Daphnis

[1] Preface to Poems by M. Arnold, First Series.
[2] vii. 19, 20 :—

καί μ' ἀτρέμας εἶπε σεσαρώς
ὄμματι μειδιόωντι, γέλως δέ οἱ εἴχετο χείλευς.

among the mountain pastures, or the love-song of the Cyclops and Galatea on the rocks overhanging the Sicilian sea, or the song of Lityerses among the ripe corn-fields[1], challenging each other to compete in song or plying each other with careless jest, tending their flocks rather as a picturesque pastime than as a toilsome occupation, and living a life of free social enjoyment in the open air, was a genuine ideal of the Greek imagination, not, perhaps, too far removed from the actual reality.

Before the time of Virgil there had been no attempt to introduce this form of art into Italy. Though the germ of a rude rustic poetry existed in the 'Fescennine verses,' no connexion can be traced between them and the highly artificial pastoral of the Augustan Age. The Eclogues of Virgil are in form and even in substance a closer reproduction of a Greek original than any other branch of Latin literature, with the exception of the comedy of Terence. The 'Lament of Daphnis,' the song of unrequited love, the bantering dialogues of the shepherds and their more formal contests in song, reappear in Latin tones and with some new associations of individual and national life, but in such a manner as to recall the memory of the Sicilian idyl rather than to suggest a new experience from life. And yet Virgil is not satisfied, like the authors of Latin comedy, with presenting to the imagination types of Greek life, Greek sentiment and manners, and Greek scenes. He desires not only to reproduce in new words and music the charm which had fascinated him in Theocritus, but to blend the actual feeling and experience of an Italian living in the Augustan Age with this ideal restored from a by-gone time. The result is something composite, neither purely Greek nor purely Italian; not altogether of the present time nor yet of a mythical foretime; but a blending of various elements of poetic association and actual experience, as in those landscapes of the Renaissance which combine aspects of real scenes with the suggestions of classical poetry, and introduce figures of the day in modern dress

---

[1] x. 41 :—
θᾶσαι δὴ καὶ ταῦτα τὰ τῷ θείῳ Λιτυέρσα.

along with the fantastic shapes of mythological invention.  The
scenes and personages of the Eclogues are thus one stage
further removed from actuality than those of the Greek pastoral.
They do not reproduce, as Keats has done, the Greek ideal of
rural life, and they do not create a purely Italian ideal.   There
was, indeed, latent in the Italian imagination an ideal of a
homely rustic life, finding its happiness in the annual round
of labour and in the blessing of a virtuous home, and that ideal
Virgil loved to draw with 'magic hand;' but that was altogether
unlike the ideal of the Greek imagination.   The life of industry
and happiness which Virgil glorifies in the Georgics, — that
of the 'primitive, stout-hearted, and thrifty husbandmen' of
Horace,—whose pride was in their 'glad harvests,' their 'trim
fields,' their 'vineyards,' and in the use which they derived from
their flocks, herds, and beehives, had nothing in common with
that of the 'well-trimmed sunburnt shepherds' whom Greek
fancy first created, and whom Keats has made live for us again,
enjoying the fulness of actual existence in union with the dreams
of an 'Elysian idleness[1].'   Least of all could the pastoral life of
Arcadia or Sicily have been like the habitual ways of men in the
rich plains of Mantua.   The district of Italy most like the scenes
of the Greek idyl was Calabria, where, among the desolate forest-
glades, the herds and flocks of some rich senator or eques were
now tended by barbarous slaves, with whose daily existence the
ideal glories of pastoral song were not likely to intermingle.

[1]                'Next well-trimm'd
        A crowd of shepherds, with as sunburnt looks
        As may be read of in Arcadian books;
        Such as sat listening round Apollo's pipe,
        When the great deity, for earth too ripe,
        Let his divinity o'erflowing die,
        In music, through the vales of Thessaly.'
And again :—
                        'He seem'd,
        To common lookers on, like one who dream'd
        Of idleness in groves Elysian.'
                        Keats, Endymion.

## III.

It is easy for those who wish to depreciate the art of Virgil to point out very many instances of imitation and artificial treatment in the Eclogues, and to establish their manifest inferiority to the Greek idyl in direct truth and vividness of representation. They are not purely objective, like the Greek idyl, nor purely subjective, as the Latin elegy generally is. They are very much inferior to the Greek originals in dramatic power; and the idyl is really a branch of dramatic poetry. Like the pure drama, it depends on the power of living in the thoughts, situations, and feelings of beings quite distinct from the poet himself. Some of the Eclogues, those in which the passion of love and the Italian passion for the land are the motives, are dramatic in spirit, though the conception of the situation is not consistently maintained. But in most cases, where he is not merely imitative, the dramatic form is to Virgil as a kind of veil under which he may partially reveal what moved him most in connexion with his own personal fortunes, and may express his sympathies with literature, with outward nature, and with certain moods and sentiments of the human heart. It is not in virtue of the originality and consistency of their conception, but of their general truth of feeling and the perfection of the medium through which that feeling is conveyed, that those who admire the Eclogues must vindicate their claim to poetic honour.

The reserve with which all his personal relations are indicated, and the allusive way in which the story of his fortunes is told, are in keeping with the delicacy and modesty of Virgil's nature. He tells us nothing directly of his home-life or occupations, though his attachment to the scenes familiar to him from childhood is felt in the language with which Meliboeus felicitates Tityrus on the restitution of his land, and in that in which Moeris and Lycidas discourse together. We know of no actual Galatea or Amaryllis associated with the joy or the pain of his youth; though his subtle perception of the various moods of the passion of love can hardly be a mere poetic intuition. unen-

lightened by personal experience. The eminent men with
whom he was brought into contact, Octavianus, Pollio, Varus,
and Gallus, are not individualised; though the different feelings
of reverential or loyal respect, of colder deference, or admiring
enthusiasm, which they severally excited in him, can be clearly
distinguished. In the undesigned revelation of himself, which
every author makes in his writings, there are few indications of
the religious and moral feeling and of the national sentiment
which are among the principal elements in Virgil's maturer
poems: but we find abundantly the evidence of a mind open to
all tender and refined influences, free from every taint of envy
or malice, serious and pensive, and finding its chief happiness
in making the charm, which fascinated him in books, in Nature,
and in life, heard in the deep and rich music of the language,
of which he first drew out the full capabilities:—

> Saepe ego longos
> Cantando puerum memini me condere soles[1].

The Eclogues also present Virgil to us as not only a poet, but,
as what he continued to be through all his life, a student of the
writings of the past. Like Milton he was eminently a learned
poet, and, like Milton, he knew the subtle alchemy by which the
duller ore of learned allusion is transmuted into gold. The tales
of the Greek mythology and the names of places famous in
song or story act on his imagination, not so much through their
own intrinsic interest, as through the associations of literature.
It is under this reflex action that he recalls to memory the tales
of Pasiphae, of Scylla and Nisus, of Tereus and Philomela; introduces Orpheus, Amphion, and Linus as the ideal poets of
pastoral song; and alludes to Hesiod, Euphorion, and Theocritus in the phrases 'the sage of Ascra,' 'the verse of Chalcis,'
'the Sicilian Shepherd.' It is in this spirit that he associates
the musical accompaniment of his song with the names of
Maenalus and Eurotas, of Rhodope and Ismarus; and that he

---

[1] 'Often, I remember, when a boy I used to pass in song the long
summer days till sunset.'

speaks of bees and thyme as 'the bees and thyme of Hybla,' of doves as 'the Chaonian doves,' of vultures as 'the birds of Caucasus.' He also characterises objects by local epithets, suggestive rather of the associations of geographical science than of poetry. Thus he speaks of 'Ariusian wine,' of 'Cydonian arrows,' 'Cyrnean yews,' 'Assyrian spikenard,' and the like. The interest in physical enquiries appears in the allusion in Ecl. iii. 40,

> In medio duo signa Conon, etc.,

and in the rapid summary of the Epicurean theory of creation at vi. 31, etc.,

> Namque canebat uti magnum per inane coacta, etc.

In these last passages it is not so much by the scientific or philosophical speculations themselves, as by their literary treatment by former writers, that Virgil appears to be attracted. Perhaps the frequent recurrence of these localising epithets, where there is nothing in the context to call up any thought of the locality indicated, may appear to a modern reader an unfortunate result of his Alexandrine studies; yet the grace with which old poetic associations are evoked and new associations created by such lines as these,

> Tum canit, errantem Permessi ad flumina Gallum
> Aonas in montis ut duxerit una sororum,

or these,

> Omnia quae Phoebo quondam meditante beatus
> Audiit Eurotas, iussitque ediscere laurus,
> Ille canit[1],

attests the cumulative force which ancient names, identified with the poetic life of the world, gather in their transmission through the literatures of different ages and nations.

In the Georgics and Aeneid, as well as in the Eclogues,

---

[1] 'Then he tells in song how Gallus as he strayed by the streams of Permessus was led by one of the sisters to the Aonian mount.'
'All those strains, which when attuned by Phoebus, Eurotas heard, enraptured, and bade his laurels learn by heart, he sings.'

Virgil shows a great susceptibility to the beauty and power of
Nature. But Nature presents different aspects and awakens
a different class of feelings in these poems. In the Eclogues
he shows a great openness and receptivity of mind, through
which all the softer and more delicate influences of the outward
world enter into and become part of his being. The 'molle
atque facetum' of Horace denotes the yielding susceptibility [1]
to outward influences, and the vivacity which gives them back
in graceful forms. In the Georgics, the sense of the relation
of Nature to human energy imparts greater nobleness to the
conception. She appears there, not only in her majesty and
beauty, but as endowed with a soul and will. She stands to
man at first in the relation of an antagonist : but, by compliance
with her conditions, he subdues her to his will, and finds in her
at last a just and beneficent helpmate [2]. In the Eclogues she
takes rather the form of an enchantress, who, by the charm of
her outward mien and her freely-offered gifts, fascinates him
into a life of indolent repose. If the one poem may in a sense
be described as the 'glorification of labour,' the other might be
described as the 'glorification of the *dolce far niente*' of Italian
life. The natural objects described by Virgil are often indeed
the same as those out of which the representation of Theocritus
is composed; but in Theocritus the human figures are, after
all, the prominent objects in the picture: the speakers in his
dialogue, though not unconscious of the charm proceeding
from the scenes in which they are placed, yet are not possessed
by it; they do not lose their own being in the larger life of
Nature environing them. Theocritus shows everywhere the
social temperament of the Greeks. It is an Italian, not perhaps
without something of the Celtic fibre in his composition, who
utters his natural feelings in the lines,

---

[1] Compare for this use of *mollis* in the sense of 'impressible' Cicero's
description of his brother Quintus (Ep. ad Att. i. 17): 'Nam, quanta sit in
Quinto fratre meo comitas, quanta iucunditas, quam mollis animus et ad
accipiendam et ad deponendam iniuriam, nihil attinet me ad te, qui ea
nosti, scribere.'

[2]        'Fundit humo facilem victum *iustissima* tellus.'

> ibi haec incondita solus
> Montibus et silvis studio iactabat inani [1].

In Virgil's representation neither the scenes nor the human figures are so distinctly present to the eye; but there is diffused through it a subtle influence from the outward world, bringing man's nature into conformity with itself. The genius in modern times, which shows most of this yielding susceptibility to the softer aspects and motions of Nature, is that of Rousseau; but in the manner in which he gives way to this sentiment there is a want of restraint, a strain of excited feeling, suggestive of the contrast between this transient intoxication of happiness and the abiding unrest and misery of all his human relations. In reading Virgil there is no sense of any such jarring discord; yet it is rather as a pensive emotion, not unallied to melancholy, than as the joy of a sanguine temperament, that his suscep- tibility to outward impressions is made manifest.

The objects through which Nature exercises this spell are, as was said, much the same as those out of which the landscape of Theocritus is composed.  Virgil, like Theocritus, enables us to feel the charm of 'the sparkling stream of fresh water,' of 'mossy fountains and grass softer than sleep,' of 'the cool shade of trees,' and of caves 'with the gadding vine o'ergrown.' The grace and tender hues of wild flowers—violets, poppies, narcissus, and hyacinth—and of fruits, such as the 'cerea pruna' and the 'tenera lanugine mala,'—the luxuriant vegetation clothing the rocks and the ideal mountain glades,—

> Ille latus niveum molli fultus hyacintho [2],—

the plants and trees,—osiers and hazels, ilex and beech,—the woods, and meadow-pastures, and rich orchards of his native district, have communicated the soul and secret of their being to the mellow tones of his language and the musical cadences of his verse.  He makes us hear again, with a strange delight, the murmur of bees feeding on the willow hedge, the moan of

---

[1] 'There all alone he used to fling wildly to the mountains and the woods these unpremeditated words in unavailing longing.'

[2] 'He, his snow-white side reposing on the tender hyacinth,—'

turtle-doves from the high elm tree, the sound of the whispering
south wind, of waves breaking on the shore, of rivers flowing
down through rocky valleys, the song of the woodman plying
his work, the voice of the divine poet chanting his strain.  By
a few simple words he calls up before our minds the genial
luxuriance of spring, the freshness of early morning, the rest of
all living things in the burning heat of noon, the stillness
of evening, the gentle imperceptible motions of Nature, in the
shooting up of the young alder-tree and in the gradual colouring of the grapes on the sunny hill-sides.  If the labour of man
is mentioned at all, it is in the form of some elegant accomplishment or picturesque task—pruning the vine or grafting the
pear-tree, closing the streams that water the pastures, watching
the flocks and herds feeding at their own will.  The new era on
which the world was about to enter is seen by his imagination,
like the vision of some pastoral valley, half hidden, half glorified
through a golden haze.  The peculiar blessings anticipated in
that era are the rest from labour, the spontaneous bounty of
Nature, the peace that is to reign among the old enemies of the
animal kingdom.

　　The human affections which mingle with these representations of Nature are the love of home, and the romantic sentiment, rather than the passion, of love.  The common human
feeling of the love of home Virgil realises more intensely from
his love of the beauty associated with his own home.  Many of
the sayings of Tityrus and Meliboeus bear witness to the strong
hold which their lands and flocks had on men of their class:—

> nos dulcia linquimus arva—
> ergo tua rura manebunt, Et tibi magna satis—
> Ille meas errare boves ut cernis—
> Spem gregis a, silice in nuda conixa reliquit—
> Ite meae, quondam felix pecus, ite capellae[1].

---

[1] 'We leave the dear fields'—'Therefore you will still keep your fields,
large enough for your desires'—'He allowed my herds to wander at their
will, even as you see'—'Ah! the hope of all my flock, which she had just
borne, she left on the bare flint pavement'—'Go on, my she-goats, once a
happy flock, go on.'

In the passage of the same Eclogue, from 68–79,

> En unquam patrios . . . salices carpetis amaras,

Virgil tells, in language of natural pathos and exquisite grace, of the poor man's sorrow in yielding his thatched hut, his well-trimmed fields, his corn crops, his pear-trees and his vines, the familiar sight of his goats feeding high up among the thickets of the rocks, to some rude soldier, incapable either of enjoying the charm or profiting by the richness of the land.

The three poems—the second, eighth, and tenth—of which love is the theme are all of a serious and plaintive cast. There are few touches in Virgil's art descriptive either of the happier or the lighter and more playful experiences of the passion, which are the common theme of Horace's Odes. Still less does he treat the subject in the style of Propertius and Ovid. The sentiment of Virgil is more like that of Tibullus; only Virgil gives utterance, though always in a dramatic form, to the real despair of unrequited affection (indigni amoris), while the tone of Tibullus is rather that of one yielding to the luxury of melancholy when in possession of all that his heart desires. They each give expression to that modern mood of passion, in which the heart longs to exchange the familiar life of civilisation for the rougher life of the fields, and to share some humble cottage and the daily occupations of peasant life with the beloved object[1]. .In Virgil also there appears some anticipation of that longing for lonely communing with Nature in her wilder and more desolate aspects which we associate with romantic rather than with classical poetry.

Though, unlike all other Latin poets, Virgil avoids all reference to the sensual side of this passion, there is no ancient poet who has analysed and expressed, with equal truth and beauty and with such a chivalrous devotion, the fluctuations

---

[1] This is the tone of the whole of the first Elegy of Tibullus, e.g.
Ipse seram teneras maturo tempore vites
   Rusticus et facili grandia poma manu.
Nec tamen interdum pudeat tenuisse bidentem, etc.

between hope and despair, the sense of personal unworthiness, the sweet memories, the heart-felt longings, the self-forgetful consideration and anxieties of an idealising affection. In such lines as these, expressing at once the sense of unworthiness and the rapid sinking of the heart from hope to despair—

> Rusticus es Corydon, nec munera curat Alexis [1],

and again—

> Tanquam haec sint nostri medicina furoris [2];

in the lines in which Damon traces back his love to its ideal source in early boyhood—

> Saepibus in nostris, etc.;

in the fine simile at viii. 85—

> Talis amor Daphnim, qualis cum fessa iuvencum, etc.;

in the tender thought of the dying Gallus for the mistress who had forsaken him—

> A, tibi ne teneras glacies secet aspera plantas [3],—

there is a delicate and subtle power of touch not unworthy of the master-hand which, with maturer art, delineated the queenly passion and despair of Dido.

The supreme excellence of Virgil's art consists in the perfect harmony between his feeling and the medium through which it is conveyed. The style of his longer poems has many varied excellences, in accordance with the varied character of the thought and sentiment which it is called on to express. But the strong and full volume of diction and rhythm and the complex harmonies of the Georgics would have been an inappropriate vehicle for the luxurious sentiment of the Eclogues. The attitude of the poet's mind in the composition of these earlier poems was that of a genial passiveness rather than that of creative activity. There are few poems of equal excellence

---

[1] 'You are but a clown, Corydon, Alexis cares not for gifts.'
[2] 'As if this could heal my madness.'
[3] 'Ah! may the rough ice not cut thy tender feet.'

in which so little use is made of that force of words which
imparts new life to things.   A few such expressions might be
quoted, like that given by Wordsworth as 'an instance of a
slight exertion of the faculty of imagination in the use of
a single word'—

> Dumosa *pendere* procul de rupe videbo;

and we notice a similar exertion of the faculty in the line—

> Hic viridis tenera *praetexit* harundine ripam
> Mincius [1].

But this actively imaginative use of language seldom occurs in
these poems.   The general effect of the style is produced by
the fulness of feeling, the sweetness or sonorousness of cadence,
with which words, used in their familiar sense, are selected and
combined.   Such epithets as ' mollis,' ' lentus,' ' tener' are of
frequent recurrence, yet the impression left by their use is not
one of weakness, or of a satiating luxury of sentiment.   The
soft outlines and delicate bloom of Virgil's youthful style are as
true emblems of health as the firmer fibre and richer colouring
of his later diction.   What an affluence of feeling, what a deep
sense of the happiness of life, of the beauty of the world,
of the glory of genius, is conveyed by the simple use of the
words *fortunatus, formosus, divinus* in the lines—

> Fortunate senex, ergo tua rura manebunt—
> Nunc frondent silvae, nunc formosissimus annus- -
> Formosi pecoris custos, formosior ipse—
> Tale tuum carmen nobis, divine poeta—
> Ut Linus haec illi divino carmine pastor.

The effect he produces by the sound and associations of proper
names is like that produced by Milton through the same
instrument.   Thus, to take one instance out of many, how
suggestive of some golden age of pastoral song are the following lines, vague and conventional though their actual application
appears to be in the passage where they occur:—

---

[1] ' Shall I see you from afar hang from some bushy rock.'
' Here green Mincio forms a fringe of soft reeds along his bank.'

Non me carminibus vincet nec Thracius Orpheus,
Nec Linus, huic mater quamvis atque huic pater adsit,
Orphei Calliopea, Lino formosus Apollo.
Pan etiam Arcadia mecum si iudice certet,
Pan etiam Arcadia dicat se iudice victum [1].

More even in his rhythm than in his diction does Virgil's superiority appear, not only over all the poets of his country, but perhaps over all other poets of past times, except Homer, Milton, and Shakspeare, in those passages in which his dramatic art admits of a richly musical cadence. Our ignorance of the exact pronunciation of Greek in the Alexandrian Age makes a comparison between the effect that would have been produced by the rhythm of Theocritus and the rhythm of the Eclogues in ancient times difficult or impossible. Yet it may be allowed to say this much, that if the rhythm of the Eclogues does not seem to us to attain to the natural and liquid flow of the Greek idyl, yet its tones are deeper, they seem to come from a stronger and richer source, than any which we can elicit from the Doric reed. Rarely has the soothing and reviving charm of the musical sounds of Nature and of the softer and grander harmonies of poetry been described and reproduced more effectively than in these lines :—

Hinc tibi, quae semper, vicino ab limite saepes
Hyblaeis apibus florem depasta salicti
Saepe levi somnum suadebit inire susurro;
Hinc alta sub rupe canet frondator ad auras;
Nec tamen interea raucae, tua cura, palumbes,
Nec gemere aeria cessabit turtur ab ulmo [2]:

and in these which suggest the thought of that restorative

---

[1] 'I shall not yield in song either to Thracian Orpheus or to Linus, though he be aided by his mother, he by his father, Orpheus by Calliope, Linus by the fair Apollo. Even Pan, should he strive with me with all Arcadia as umpire, even Pan would say that he was vanquished, with Arcadia as umpire.'

[2] 'On this side, with its old familiar murmur, the hedge, your neighbour's boundary, on all the sweets of whose willow blossom the bees of Hybla have fed, will often gently woo you to sleep; on that from the foot of a high rock the song of the woodman will rise to the air; nor meanwhile will your darlings, the hoarse wood-pigeons, cease to coo, nor the turtle-dove to moan from the high elm-tree.'

power of genius which a poet of the present day has happily ascribed to Wordsworth [1] :—

> Tale tuum carmen nobis, divine poeta,
> Quale sopor fessis in gramine, quale per aestum
> Dulcis aquae saliente sitim restinguere rivo [2] :

and in these again, which give both true symbols and a true example of the 'deep-chested music' in which the poet gives utterance to the thought which has taken shape within his mind :—

> Quae tibi, quae tali reddam pro carmine dona?
> Nam neque me tantum venientis sibilus austri,
> Nec percussa iuvant fluctu tam litora, nec quae
> Saxosas inter decurrunt flumina valles [3].

The objections often urged against the poetical value of the Eclogues may be admitted. They are imitative in form. They do not reproduce scenes and characters from actual life, nor are they consistent creations of the imagination. They do not possess the interest arising from a contemplative insight into the hidden workings of Nature, nor from reflection on the problems of life. Their originality, their claim to be a representative work of genius, consists in their truth and unity of sentiment and tone. If it be said that the sentiment which they embody is but a languid and effeminate sentiment, the admiration of two great poets, of the most masculine type of genius that modern times have produced, is a sufficient answer to this reproach. The admiration of Milton is proved by the conception and workmanship of his 'Lycidas,' the most richly and continuously musical even among his creations. Of Wordsworth's admiration there is more than one testimony,—this, from

---

[1] Poems by Matthew Arnold. Memorial Verses :—
'He found us when the age had bound
Our souls in its benumbing round,' etc.

[2] 'Such charm is in thy song for us, O Godlike poet, as is to weary men the charm of deep sleep on the grass, as, in summer heat, it is to quench one's thirst in a sparkling brook of fresh water.'

[3] 'What gifts shall I render to you, what gifts in recompense of such a strain : for neither the whisper of the coming south wind gives me such joy, nor the sound of shores beaten on by the wave, nor of rivers hurrying down through rocky glens.'

the recently published Memoir of the daughter of his early friend and associate in poetry, perhaps the most direct: 'I am much pleased to see (writes S. Coleridge) how highly Mr. Wordsworth speaks of Virgil's style, and of his Bucolics which I have ever thought most graceful and tender. They are quite another thing from Theocritus, however they may be based on Theocritus[1].' The criticism which the same writer applies to 'Lycidas' suggests the true answer also to the objections urged against Virgil's originality. 'The best defence of Lycidas is not to defend the design of it at all, but to allege that the execution of it is perfect, the diction the *ne plus ultra* of grace and loveliness, and that the spirit of the whole is as original as if the poem contained no traces of the author's acquaintance with ancient pastoral poetry from Theocritus downwards.' To the names of these two poets we can now add the name of one of the most illustrious, and certainly one of the least effeminate, among the critics and men of letters whom this century has produced—Macaulay; who, after speaking of the Aeneid in one of his letters, adds this sentence, 'The Georgics pleased me better; the Eclogues best,—the second and tenth above all[2].'

The appreciation of Wordsworth is a certain touchstone of the genuineness of Virgil's feeling for Nature. It is true that the sentiment to which he gives expression in the Eclogues is only one, and not the most elevated, of the many modes in which the spirit of man responds to the forms and movement of the outward world. But the mood of the Eclogues is one most natural to man's spirit in the beautiful lands of Southern Europe. The freshness and softness of Italian scenes are present in the Eclogues, in the rich music of the Italian language, while it still retained the strength, fulness, and majesty of its tones. These poems are truly representative of Italy, not as a land of old civilisation, of historic renown, of great cities, of corn-crops, and vineyards,—'the mighty mother of fruits and men;'—but as a land of a soft and genial air, beautiful with the tender

[1] S. Coleridge's Memoirs, vol. ii. p. 411.
[2] Life and Letters, vol. i. p. 371.

foliage and fresh flowers and blossoms of spring, and with the rich colouring of autumn; a land which has most attuned man's nature to the influences of music and of pictorial art. As a true and exquisite symbol of this vein of sentiment associated with Italy, the Eclogues hold a not unworthy place beside the greater work—the 'temple of solid marble'—which the maturer art of Virgil dedicated to the genius of his country, and beside the more composite but stately and massive monument which perpetuates the national glory of Rome.

# CHAPTER V.

## MOTIVES, FORM, NATIONAL INTEREST, AND SOURCES OF THE GEORGICS.

### I.

THE appearance of the Eclogues marked Virgil out among his contemporaries as the poet of Nature and rural life. That province was assigned to him, as epic poetry was to Varius and tragedy to Pollio. It is to the Eclogues only that the lines in which Horace characterises his art can with propriety be applied. These lines were written before the appearance of the Georgics, and probably before any considerable part of the poem had been composed [1]. The epithets which admirably characterise the receptive attitude of Virgil's mind in the composition of his pastoral poems are quite inapplicable to the solid and severe workmanship and the earnest feeling of his didactic poem. The Eclogues are the poems of youth, and of a youth passed in study and in contact with Nature rather than with the serious interests of life. Though Virgil indicates in them the ambition which was moving him to vaster undertakings, yet he shows at the same time his consciousness of the comparative triviality of his art. The class of poem to which the word *ludere* is

---

[1] From the similarity between the lines in Hor. Sat. i. 1. 114,
    Ut cum carceribus missos,
and those at the end of Georg. i. 512,
    Ut cum carceribus sese effudere quadrigae,
it has been argued that Georgic i, at all events, must have appeared before the first Book of the Satires. Ribbeck supposes that the lines of the Georgics may have been seen or heard by Horace before the appearance of the poem, and imitated by him. But is it likely that Horace would have appropriated an image from an *unpublished* poem? Is it not as probable that Virgil was the imitator here, as in other passages where he uses the language of contemporaries, e.g. of Varius, Ecl. viii. 88?

applied was, even when not of a licentious character, regarded
by the more serious minds of Rome, such as Cicero[1] for instance, with a certain degree of contempt, as being among the
'leviora studia,' partaking more of the 'Graeca levitas' than of
the 'Roman gravitas[2].' The genuine Roman spirit demanded
of its highest literature, as of its native architecture, that it
should either have some direct practical use, or contribute in
some way to enhance the sense of national greatness.

The literary impulse directing Virgil to the composition of
the Georgics was probably the wish to be the Hesiod, as he
had already been the Theocritus, of Rome. The poets of the
Augustan Age selected some Greek prototype whose manner
they professed to reproduce and make the vehicle for the expression of their own thought and experience. Thus Horace chose
Alcaeus, Propertius chose Callimachus as his model. Virgil
assigns to Pollio the praise of alone composing poems 'worthy
of the buskin of Sophocles.' In the Georgics he professes to
find his own prototype in Hesiod :—

> Ascraeumque cano Romana per oppida carmen.

Propertius also recognises him as the disciple of the sage of
Ascra :—

> Tu canis Ascraei veteris praecepta poetae,
> Quo seges in campo, quo viret uva iugo[3].

Though Hesiod can scarcely have taken the highest rank as
a poet, yet a peculiar reverence attached to his name from his
great antiquity, and from the ethical and theological spirit of his
writings. As Virgil chose the mould of Theocritus into which
to cast the lighter feelings and fancies of his youth, he naturally
turned to 'The Works and Days of Hesiod' as a more suitable model for a poem on rural life, undertaken with a more
serious purpose, and demanding a severer treatment.

---

[1] Compare the contrast drawn by him between Ennius and the contemporary 'Cantores Euphorionis,' Tusc. Disp. iii. 19.

[2] Cf. also W. F. Teuffel's History of Roman Literature, chap. i. note 1.

[3] 'You sing the lore of the old poet of Ascra, of the field on which the
corn, the hill on which the grape grows.' iii. 32. 77-78.

The change in Virgil's life between the composition of the
Eclogues and the Georgics had however much more influence
in determining the difference in the character of the two poems,
than the mere artistic desire to enter on a new path of poetry.
During the composition of the earlier poems Virgil was living in
a remote district of Italy, associating with the country-people or
with a few young poets like himself, and coming in contact with
the great world of action and national interests only through the
medium of his intercourse with the temporary governors of the
province.   Rome and its ruler and the powerful stream of events
in which his own fortunes were finally absorbed affect his
imagination as they might do that of one who heard of them
from a distance, but who in his ordinary thoughts and sympathies
was living quite apart from them ;

> Urbem quam dicunt Romam Meliboee putavi
> Stultus ego huic nostrae similem[1].

But before undertaking the task of writing the Georgics he
had become an honoured member of the circle of Maecenas, the
intimate friend of Varius and of Horace (who himself owed his
introduction to that circle to the kindly offices of the two older
poets) and of others distinguished in literature and public affairs.
He had lived for a time near the centre of the world's movement,
in close relations to the minds by which that movement was
directed.   As the most genuine of his Eclogues had been inspired by his personal share in the calamities of his country, it
was natural that he should, now when his own fortunes were
restored through the favour of those at the head of affairs, feel
a stronger and more disinterested sympathy with the public
condition, at a crisis to which no one capable of understanding
its gravity could feel indifferent.   It was natural that his new
relations and the impulse of the new ideas which came to him
through them should move him to undertake some work of art
more suited to his maturer faculty, his graver temperament, and
the firmer fibre of his genius.   Nor is there any difficulty in

---

[1] 'The city which is called Rome, O Meliboeus, I thought, in my folly,
was like this city of ours.'

believing that Maecenas may have had some influence in determining him to the choice of a subject which enabled him to
range over the whole of that field of which he had already appropriated a part, which would afford scope to the literary ambition
urging him to write a poem on a greater scale and of more enduring substance, and which, at the same time, might serve
indirectly to advance the policy of reconciliation and national
and social reorganisation which Caesar and his minister were
anxious to promote.   Among 'the ancient arts by which the
Latin name and the strength of Italy had waxed great,' none
had fallen more into abeyance, through the insecurity of the
times, than the cultivation of the land.   The restoration of the
old 'Coloni' of Italy and the revival of the great forms of
national industry, associated with the older and happier
memories of Rome, had been a leading feature in the policy of
the great popular leaders from the Gracchi down to Julius
Caesar.   Among the completed glories of the Augustan Age,
Horace, some twenty years later, specially notes the restoration
of security and abundance to the land :—

> Tutus bos etenim rura perambulat,
> Nutrit rura Ceres almaque faustitas [1],

and in the same Ode :—

> Condit quisque diem collibus in suis,
> Et vitem viduas ducit ad arbores [2].

And in the brief summing up of the whole glories of the
Augustan reign contained in his latest Ode he begins with the
words,—

> Tua, Caesar, aetas
> Fruges et agris rettulit uberes [3].

All Virgil's early associations and sympathies would lead him
to identify himself with this object and with the interests and

---

[1]        'For safe the herds range field and fen,
            Full-headed stand the shocks of grain.'
[2]        'Now each man basking on his slopes
            Weds to the widowed trees the vine.'
[3]        'Thy era, Caesar, which doth bless
            Our plains anew with fruitfulness.'   Martin.

happiness of such representatives of the old rural life of Italy
as might still be found, or might arise again under a secure
administration.   In proposing to himself some serious aim for
the exercise of his poetic gift, it was natural that he should have
fixed on that of representing this life in such a way as to create
an aspiration for it, and to secure for it the sympathy of the
world.   The language in which he speaks of the poem as a task
imposed on him by Maecenas need not be taken literally: but
it is no detraction from Virgil's originality to suppose that he,
like Horace, was encouraged by the minister to devote his genius
to a purpose which would appeal equally to the sympathies of
the statesman and of the poet.   The testimony of Virgil's
biographer on this subject, which may probably be traced to the
original testimony of Melissus, the freedman of Maecenas, is
neither to be disregarded nor unduly pressed, any more than
the language in which Virgil himself makes acknowledgment of
his indebtedness.   It is impossible to say what chance seed of
casual conversation may have been the original germ of what
ultimately became so large and goodly a creation.   If, in the
composition of the Georgics, Virgil employed his art as an instrument of government, we cannot doubt that he did so not
only because he recognised in the subject of the poem one suited
to his own genius, but because his past life and early associations brought home to him the desolation caused in the rural
districts by the Civil Wars, the moral worth of that old class of
husbandmen who had suffered from them, and the public loss
arising from the diminution in their number and influence.   To
idealise the life of that class by describing, with realistic fidelity
and in the language of purest poetry, the annual round of labour
in which it was passed; to suggest the ever-present charm
arising from the intimate contact with the manifold processes
and aspects of Nature into which man is brought in this life of
labour; to contrast the simplicity and sanctity of such life with
the luxury and lawless passions of the great world; and to
associate this ideal with the varied beauty of Italy and the
historic memories of Rome, were objects worthy of one who

aspired to fulfil the office of a national poet. It is no detraction
from the originality of his idea to suppose that some such
suggestion as that attributed to Maecenas gave the original
impulse to the poem. Not only the art, genius, and learning,
but the religious faith and feeling, the moral and national
sympathies, which give to it its peculiar meaning and value, are
all the poet's own. His strong feeling for his subject was as
little capable of being communicated from without, as the genius
with which he adorns it [1].

With such feelings as those which were moving the imagination of Virgil, a modern poet might have shaped his
subject into the form of a poetic idyl, in which the joys and
sorrows of men and women living during this national crisis
might have been represented in union with the varied aspects
of the scenery and the chief modes of rural industry in Italy.
Such a form of art would have enabled the poet to add the
interest of individual character and action to his abstract delineation of the 'acer rusticus' or the 'duri agrestes' engaged
in a hard struggle with the forces of Nature. And one or two
passages, containing some sketch drawn directly from peasant
life, as for instance i. 291–296,

> Et quidam seros hiberni ad luminis ignes, etc.,

and iv. 125–146,

> Namque sub Oebaliae memini me turribus arcis, etc.,

---

[1] Compare Merivale's History of the Romans under the Empire, chap. xli.
'The tradition that Maecenas himself suggested the composition of the
Georgics may be accepted, not in the literal sense which has generally been
attached to it, as a means of reviving the art of husbandry and the cultivation of the devastated soil of Italy; but rather to recommend the principles
of the ancient Romans, their love of home, of labour, of piety, and order;
to magnify their domestic happiness and greatness, to make men proud of
their country on better grounds than the mere glory of its arms and the
extent of its conquests. It would be absurd to suppose that Virgil's verses
induced any Roman to put his hand to the plough, or to take from his
bailiff the management of his own estates; but they served undoubtedly to
revive some of the simple tastes and sentiments of the olden time, and perpetuated, amidst the vices and corruptions of the Empire, a pure stream of
sober and innocent enjoyments, of which, as we journey onward, we shall
rejoice to catch at least occasional glimpses.'

make us regret that the conditions of his art, as conceived by him, did not encourage him to blend something more of idyllic representation with the didactic and descriptive treatment of his subject. But the idyl which treats the incidents of human life in the form either of a continuous poem or of a tale in prose was unknown to the early art of Greece; and Roman imagination was incapable of inventing a perfectly new mould into which to cast its poetic fancies and feelings. Nor is it probable that a poem so truly representative of Italy in all its aspects could have been produced in the form of an idyl, of which the interest would have been concentrated on some family or group of personages.

There was only one form of literary art known to the Greeks or Romans of the Augustan Age which was at all suitable for the treatment on a large scale of such a subject as that which now filled the mind of Virgil. Next after the epic poem of heroic action, the didactic epos was regarded at Rome as the most serious and elaborate form of poetic art. It was more suited than any other form to the Roman mind. It is the only form in which the genius of Rome has produced master-pieces superior not only to anything of the kind produced by Greece but to all similar attempts in modern times. As Roman invention, stimulated by the practical sense of utility, by the passion for vast and massive undertakings, and by the strong perception of order and unity of design, devised a new kind of architecture for the ordinary wants of life, so in accordance with the national bent to reduce all things to rule, to impose the will of a master on obedient subjects, to use the constructive and artistic faculties for some practical end, if it did not create, it gave ampler compass, more solid and massive workmanship, and the associations of great ideas to that form of poetic art which had been the most meagre and unsubstantial of all those invented by the genius of Greece.

Moreover, a new form, or rather a form of more ample capacity, was required to embody the new poetical feelings and experience which now moved the Roman and Italian

mind.  If less interest was felt at Rome in following the
course of individual destiny, the interest felt in contemplating
the outward aspect and secret movement of Nature was now
stronger than it had been in the great ages of Greek literature.
Though the vivid enjoyment of the outward world had unconsciously shaped the tales of the early Greek mythology, and
though this enjoyment had entered directly, as a subordinate
element, into the epic, lyric, and dramatic poetry of Greece,
and, more prominently, into the later poetry of Alexandria,
and although the phenomena and laws of Nature had aroused
the speculative curiosity of the early Greek philosophers, no
poet before Lucretius had treated of Nature, in the immensity
of her range, in the primal elements and living forces of her
constitution, and, at the same time, in her manifold aspects of
beneficence and beauty, and of destructive energy, as the
subject of a great poem.  The forms adopted by the great
masters of Greek poetry,—the epic, lyric, and dramatic writers,
—whose essential business it was to represent the actions and
passions of men, were inapplicable to the treatment of this
new subject of man's environment.  Lucretius accordingly had
to take the outline of his form from the early physiological
writers, whom the Greeks scarcely ranked among their poets
at all, and who, though animated by the speculative passion to
penetrate to the secret of Nature, were not specially interested
in her aspects of beauty or power, or in her relation to the life
of man.  If he cannot claim the title of an inventor in art, yet
by adding volume and majesty to the rudimentary type of these
early writers, he gave to the ancient world the unique specimen
of a great philosophical poem.

So too Virgil, penetrated with the feeling of Nature in her
relation to human wants and enjoyment, and desirous to give
an adequate expression to this feeling, could derive no guidance
from the nobler genius of Greece.  To find a suitable vehicle,
he had to turn to the earliest and latest periods of her literature.
The didactic, as distinct from the philosophic or contemplative
poem, was the invention of a time prior to the existence of

prose composition.  It seems to have arisen out of the impulse
to convey instruction and advice on the management of life
generally, and especially on the best means of securing a livelihood from the cultivation of the soil.  The use of the language
of poetry for a purpose essentially practical and prosaic was
justified, in that primitive time, not only by the absence of any
other organ of literary expression, but also by the fact that, in
such a time, all literary effort was the result of animated feeling,
and that the most common aspects of Nature, such as the
changes of the seasons or of night and day, and what seem
now the most familiar occupations of life, were apprehended
by the lively mind of the Greek with a fresh sense of wonder,
which use deadens in eras of more advanced civilisation.  But
while this sense of wonder imparts a poetical colouring to the
language of early didactic poetry, and while sufficient harmony
was secured for it by the training of the ear during centuries of
epic song, the form and structure of this kind of art was, as
compared with the other forms of Greek poetry, essentially
rudimentary.  The sole specimen which has reached our times
appears in the form of a personal address, treating of a number
of subjects not closely connected with one another, interspersed
with various episodes, and producing the impression of a connected whole solely through the vivid personality of the writer.
Didactic poetry was absolutely rejected in the maturity of Greek
genius, after the rise of a prose literature had marked off clearly
the separate provinces of prose and poetry, and after Greek
taste had become more exacting in its demand of unity of
impression and symmetry of form in every work of art.  It
was revived again in the Alexandrian epoch, when the creative
impulse was lost, and life and its interests had become tamer,
while at the same time knowledge had greatly increased, and a
kind of literary dilettanteism was one of the chief elements in
refined enjoyment.  By the Alexandrine writers the irregular
and desultory treatment of Hesiod was abandoned.  The
didactic poem was treated by them as one of the recognised
branches of poetical art.  It still retained the general character

of a personal address, which accident may have first suggested
to Hesiod, and which either his example or their own taste had
imposed on the early philosophic poets.   The Alexandrine
type of poem differed from that of Hesiod by professing to
convey systematic instruction on some definite branch of knowledge, instead of offering practical directions on the best method
of carrying on some occupation, combined with a medley of
precepts, moral, religious, and ceremonial.   The change may
be compared to that which the Roman satire underwent, from
the inartistic medley of Ennius and Lucilius to the systematic
treatment of some special subject in the satire of Persius and
Juvenal.   The primary aim of such writers as Aratus and
Nicander was not to communicate ideas capable of affecting
the imagination, but to satisfy intellectual curiosity by communicating interesting information.   So soon as this information
ceased to be interesting, the value of their work was gone.
Thus although accident has handed down several specimens
of the Alexandrine type of didactic poetry, their chief literary
use is to enable us, by contrast, better to appreciate the genius
which, by interfusing with the materials used by them other
elements deeply affecting the heart, the imagination, and the
moral sympathies, has given the world, instead of the temporary
gift of a little useful information, the κτῆμα ἐς ἀεί which it possesses in the Georgics.

   In that poem Virgil combines something of the spirit of the
older or primitive type of didactic poetry with the systematic
treatment of their subject employed by the Alexandrine Metaphrastae.   He retains the old form of a personal address, not
only in the dedication of the poem to Maecenas, but in the
manner in which he inculcates his precepts on the husbandman,
or indicates what he himself would do in particular circumstances[1].   Yet he bears more resemblance to the poets of
Alexandria in his systematic treatment and arrangement of

---

[1] E. g. Aus*im* vel tenui vitem committere sulco ;
and again,
     Neve *tibi* ad solem vergant vineta cadentem, etc.

his materials. He aims, like them, at communicating a large
body of unfamiliar knowledge, as well as conveying practical
precepts founded on experience. By combining these two
aims, but much more by making the aims of conveying
precept and instruction altogether subsidiary to that of moving
the imagination and the affections, Virgil, if he has not created
a new type of didactic poetry, has at least produced almost the
only specimen of it which the world cares to read. He is
apparently conscious of the difficulty of imparting to a poem
of this type a continuous poetical charm; as Lucretius, with
more reason, is conscious of the difficulty of securing a sustained poetical interest for his argumentative processes and his
investigations into the first principles of things. Virgil's difficulty is to maintain his subject on the level of poetical feeling,
while at the same time adhering to the necessities of practical
instruction. And this difficulty attaches to every kind of didactic
poetry. He had to associate with a poetic charm, not only
the fair results of the husbandman's labour, the 'heavy harvests and the Massic juice of the vine,' but the processes
and mechanical appliances through which these fair results
were obtained. Although his idea of his art did not demand
an exhaustive treatment of all the operations of rural industry, such as was demanded of the prose writers on the
subject, yet it did demand that, in making his selection, he
should regard the importance of each topic in connexion with
the work of the farm as well as its adaptation to poetic treatment. It cannot be denied that this necessary infusion of
prosaic matter deprives even the most perfect specimen of
didactic poetry of that purity of imaginative interest which
pervades the masterpieces of epic, lyrical, and dramatic genius:
but it is, on the other hand, a great triumph of art to have
redeemed so much as Virgil has done from the homely realities
of life into the more sacred ground of poetry, and that without
sacrifice either of the truth of fact or of the dignity and sobriety
of expression.

## II.

While the title 'Georgica' reminds us that the form of the poem, like the form of the 'Bucolica' and the 'Aeneis,' was derived from the Greeks, the subject of which it treats was one of peculiarly national interest.   As the Aeneid may be said to be inspired by the idea of Rome and her destiny, and as the practical purpose of that poem was to confirm the faith of the Romans in their Empire and in the ruler in whom that Empire was vested, so the Georgics may be said to be inspired by the idea of Italy; and the true aim of the poem was to revive and extend the love of the land, and to restore the fading ideal of a life of virtue and happiness, passed in the labours of a country life.   But while much of the materials and of the workmanship of the Aeneid is originally due to Greek invention, the general substance of the Georgics and the most essentially poetical passages are of native origin.

The chief modes of rural industry treated in the various books are those which flourished in Italy,—the tillage of the land for various crops, the cultivation of the vine and the olive, the breeding and rearing of cattle, sheep, and horses, and the tending of bees.   It is noticed by Servius that the agricultural precepts of the poem apply only to Italy and not to other lands : 'Sane agriculturae huius praecepta non ad omnes pertinent terras, sed ad solum situm Italiae.'   The frequent references to the products of other lands serve to suggest by contrast the superiority of Italy in those which are the special subject of the poem and which are most essential to human well-being.   Cato also is represented by Cicero[1] as resting the charm of a country life in the contemplation of the same operations of Nature as those indicated in the opening lines of the Georgics:—

> Quid faciat laetas segetes, quo sidere terram
> Vertere, Maecenas, ulmisque adiungere vites
> Conveniat [2],—

[1] De Senectute, xv. xvi.
[2] 'What makes the cornfields glad, beneath what constellation, Maecenas, it is right to turn up the soil, and wed the vine to the elms,'—

The number of Roman writers who treated in prose of this subject, both before and after Virgil, testifies further to the strong national interest attaching to it.   Among these writers, Varro, the immediate predecessor of Virgil, associates the subject directly with the pride which the Romans felt in their country.   He introduces the speakers in his Dialogue as holding their conversation in the Temple of Tellus, and examining a map or painting of Italy on the wall.   One of the speakers addresses the others in these words, ' You who have travelled over many lands, have you ever seen any more richly cultivated than Italy ?   I, indeed, have never seen any so richly cultivated.' He especially characterises the excellence of its corn-crops, its vines, olives, and fruit-trees: ' What spelt shall I compare to the Campanian? what wheat to the Apulian? what wine to the Falernian? what oil to that of Venafrum? is not Italy planted with trees, so that the whole of it seems an orchard[1]?' Other authors, Virgil himself among them[2], and Columella in the Introduction to his treatise[3], testify to the pride which the Italians took in their breed of horses and herds of cattle.   And though the Italian bees and their product were not so famous in poetry as the bees of Hymettus and ' the honey of Hybla,' yet Horace speaks of the country near Tarentum as one ' where the honey yields not to the honey of Hymettus ;' and in another Ode, in which he contrasts his own moderate estate with the resources of richer men, he mentions Calabrian honey along with the wine of Formiae and the fleeces of Gallic pastures among the chief sources of wealth :—

> Quanquam nec Calabrae mella ferunt apes
> Nec Laestrygonia Bacchus in amphora
> Languescit mihi, nec pinguia Gallicis
> Crescunt vellera pascuis[4].

---

[1] De Re Rustica, i. 2.

[2] Georg. ii. 145, etc. ; Aen. iii. 537.

[3] ' Nec dubium quin, ut ait Varro, ceteras pecudes bos honore superare debeat, praesertim autem in Italia, quae ab hoc nuncupationem traxisse creditur, quod olim Graeci tauros Ἰταλοὺς vocabant.'

[4] ' Although neither Calabrian bees produce honey for me, nor does my

This branch of his subject moreover enables Virgil to celebrate the floral beauties of Italy, and to exhibit on a small
scale a picture of a community at once warlike, politic, and
industrious, such as had been realised on the soil of Italy, and
especially in the old Roman Commonwealth, more completely
than among any other people.

The subject was moreover intimately associated with the
national history. Several of the early legends, such as those of
Cincinnatus, and, in more historical times, of Atilius Regulus
and Curius Dentatus, attest the prominence which agriculture
enjoyed among the pursuits of the foremost men in the
Republic. The surnames of many noble families, patrician
and plebeian, such as the Lentuli, Stolones, Bubulci, Pisones,
Dolabellae, and the name of the great Fabian Gens, are connected etymologically with agricultural occupations, products,
or implements, and afford evidence of a time when the men
who filled the great offices of the State lived on their own
lands[1], and were known for the success with which they
improved their farms. The passion to possess and subdue the
land was, in the early history of the Republic, the main motive
power both of the political and military history of Rome.
Even down to the establishment of the Empire there was no
question which more divided the two great parties in the State
than that of the Agrarian laws. And though, after the conquest of Italy, Roman wars were fought for dominion rather
than for new territory, yet the hope of owning land, if not on
Italian yet on some foreign soil, which he should hold by his
sword as well as cultivate by his plough, supported the Roman

wine grow mellow in a Formian jar, nor fleeces grow rich in Gallic pastures.' Compare too

Ego apis Matinae
More modoque, etc.

The importance of honey as a source of wealth is referred to by Mommsen
in his History of Rome, book v. chap. xi. 'A small bee-breeder of this
period sold from his thyme-garden, not larger than an acre, in the neighbourhood of Falerii, honey to an average annual amount of at least 10,000
sesterces (100*l.*).'

[1] 'Illis enim temporibus proceres civitatis in agris morabantur.' Columella.

soldier, even under the Empire, through the long years of his
service.    The Roman 'colonies,' the origin of so many famous
European cities, were settlements of 'Coloni' or cultivators
of the soil.

Thus in the selection of his subject Virgil appealed to old
national associations and living tastes in a way in which no
Greek poet could have done in choosing any mode of practical
industry for poetic treatment.    Even the details of direct instruction would attract a Roman reader by reminding him of
labours which he may often have watched and perhaps have
shared.    Though Virgil found new sources of attraction by
references to Greek mythology and science, and though he
availed himself of the diction of Greek poets much inferior to
himself in their perception of beauty and their power over
language, yet his materials are mainly drawn either from
personal observation, or from Italian writers who had put on
record the results of what they had seen and done.    There is
a thoroughly Roman character in the technical execution of
the poem, in the command over details, in the power of orderly
arrangement with a view to convenience rather than logical
symmetry, and in the combined sobriety and dignity of the
workmanship.    But it is in the longer episodes, in which the
deeper meaning of the poem is most brought out, that the
intimate connexion between the various topics treated in it and
the national character and fortunes becomes most apparent.
There is indeed one marked exception to the maintenance of
this unity of impression.    The long episode in Book iv, from
line 315 to 558, has no national significance.    And this is an
undoubted blot on the artistic perfection of the work.    This
episode not only adds nothing to its representative character,
but it suggests fancies and associations utterly alien from the
Italy of the Augustan Age.    The space given to such a theme
is opposed to the truer taste of the poet, expressed in such
lines as these—

> Non hic te carmine ficto
> Atque per ambages et longa exorsa tenebo,

and
>     Cetera quae vacuas tenuissent carmina mentes,
>     Omnia iam volgata [1].

But it is not the judgment of the poet, but the despotic will
of the Emperor, that is responsible for this imperfection.  The
fourth Book originally ended with an episode which afforded
scope for the expression of personal feeling, for awakening an
interest in that land which was now of vast importance to the
State, and which affected the imagination of cultivated Romans
as it does that of cultivated men in modern times [2], and for
illustrating the national greatness and the recent history of
Rome.  In the first edition the mention of Egypt at line 287
had led Virgil to celebrate the administration of that province
under his early friend Cornelius Gallus.  When Gallus fell into
disgrace and was forced to commit suicide in 26 B.C., Virgil
was required to re-edit the poem with a new concluding
episode [3].  The subject treated in the earlier edition of the
poem would have enabled Virgil to give renewed expression
to his admiration and affection for the Gallus of the Eclogues,
to tell the tale of the downfall of Cleopatra, and to magnify the
greatness of Rome in the conquest and government of her
provinces.  The episode as it now stands is a finished piece of
metrical execution; it illustrates the attraction which the Greek
mythological stories had for educated Romans; it is expressed
in those tones of tender pathos of which Virgil was a master;
but it is at the same time a standing proof of the malign

[1] ‘I shall not here detain you with any tale of fancy, and winding digressions and long preambles.’
‘The other themes that might have charmed the vacant mind, are all
hackneyed now.’
[2] Cf. Tac. Ann. ii. 59–61 : ‘M. Silano, L. Norbano consulibus Germanicus Aegyptum proficiscitur *cognoscendae antiquitatis.*’  The whole account
of the tour of Germanicus illustrates the cultivated taste for foreign travel
among the Romans of the later Republic, the Augustan Age, and early
Empire, and also the mysterious interest which has attached to Egypt from
the earliest times known to history.
[3] This is distinctly stated by Servius in two places, his introductory com-
ments on Eclogue x, and on Georgic iv, and seems sufficiently attested.
Besides, the introduction into the Georgics of such an episode as the ‘Pastor
Aristaeus’ requires some explanation.

influence which the Imperial despotism already exercised on
the spontaneous inspiration. of genius, as well as 'on all sincere
expression of feeling.

## III.

If the idea of the poem and of the national interests associated with it arose in Virgil's mind during his life in Rome, it
was in his retirement in Campania that he prepared himself
for and executed his task. Like the Aeneid it was a work
of slow growth, the result of careful study and meditation.
Besides the great change of the concluding episode, there are
some slight indications that the poem was retouched in later
editions; and perhaps a very few lines added to the original
work may have been either left finally unadjusted to their
proper place, or may have been transposed in the copying of
the manuscript[1]. Although regard for his art was a more
prominent consideration in the mind of Virgil than of Lucretius, yet he did not, any more than his predecessor, wish to

---

[1] Both the nexus of the sense and the rhythm condemn the latitude of
transposition which Ribbeck allows himself. Perhaps the only alteration
which is absolutely demanded is at iv. 203–205. The lines there, as they
stand, clearly interrupt the sense, and are more in place either after 196 or
after 218. The strong line,
        Tantus amor florum et generandi gloria mellis,
is a fitting conclusion for the fine paragraph beginning
        Nunc age, naturas apibus quas Iuppiter ipse, etc.
Either of these places seems more suitable for the lines than that after 183.
It is possible that the conjecture which Ribbeck adopts from Wagner,
'absoluto iam opere in marginem illos versus a poeta coniectos esse,' may
give the true explanation of the misplacement of the lines, though this
does not seem to apply to any other passage in the poem. Such bold
changes as those introduced by Ribbeck at ii. 35–46, and again at iii. 120–
122, are not required by the sense, and are condemned by rhythmical considerations. The line 119,
        Exquirunt calidumque animis et cursibus acrem,
is weak for the concluding line of the paragraph, which ends much more
naturally with that transposed from 122 to 99,
        Neptunique ipsa deducat origine gentem,
as it is Virgil's way to introduce his mythological illustrations after his
real observations are finished. The paragraph of four lines, Quare agite o
proprios . . . . Taburnum, stands bald and bare in the position Ribbeck
assigns it, between 108 and 109. The minor changes for the most part
disturb old associations and throw no new light on the poet's thought.

separate the office of a teacher from that of a poet. How far
the experience of his early years in the farm in the district of
Andes or of his later residence on his land near Nola may
have contributed to his knowledge of his subject, we ·have no
means of knowing ; but probably the delicacy of his health as
well as his devotion to study may have limited his experience
to the observation of the labours of others.    But the power
of vividly realising and enjoying the familiar sights and work
of the farm,—the life which he gives to the notices of seed-
time and harvest, of the growth of trees and ripening of fruits,
of the habits of flocks, herds, and bees, etc.,—the deep love for
his subject in all its details—

> Singula dum capti circumvectamur amore [1]—

were gifts which could not come from any study of books. The
poetry of manhood is, more often perhaps than we know, the
conscious reproduction of the unconscious impressions of early
years, received in a susceptible and retentive mind.   Virgil, in
common with all great poets, retained through life the ' child's
heart within the man's.'    Through this geniality of nature he
was able—

> angustis hunc addere rebus honorem [2]—

to glorify trite and familiar things by the light reflected from
the healthy memories and the idealising fancies of boyhood and
early youth.

But while his feeling is all his own,—the happy survival
probably of the childhood and youth passed in his home in the
district of Andes,—he largely avails himself of the observation,
the thought, and the language of earlier writers, both Greek and
Roman.   His poem is eminently a work of learning as well as
of native feeling.   He combines in its varied and firm texture
the homely wisdom embodied in the precepts and proverbs of
Italian peasants ('veterum praecepta '),—the quaint and oracular
dicta of Hesiod,—the scientific knowledge and mythological

---

[1] ' While charmed with the love of it, we travel round each detail.'
[2] ' To invest these poor interests with a new glory.'

lore of Alexandrine writers,—the philosophic and imaginative conceptions of Lucretius,—with the knowledge of natural history contained in the treatises of Aristotle and Theophrastus, and the systematic practical directions of the old prose writers on rural economy, such as the Carthaginian Mago [1], whose work had been translated into Latin,—Democritus and Xenophon among Greek prose writers,—Cato, the two Sasernae, Licinius Stolo, Tremellius, and Varro among Latin authors. The purely practical precepts of the Georgics were apparently selected and condensed from these writers [2]. But no literary inspiration or ideas were likely to have come from any of these last-named authors, unless the Invocation in the first Book may have been suggested by the example of Varro, who begins his treatise with an invocation to the XII Di consentes. The proverbial sayings or rustic songs embodying the traditional peasant lore, such as the 'Quid vesper serus vehit?' and the 'hiberno pulvere, verno luto, grandia farra, Camille, metes [3],' which add an antique and homely charm to the poem, may have become known to Virgil from the book of the Sasernae, who are quoted by Varro as authorities for many of the old charms used by the primitive husbandmen, such as 'Terra pestem teneto, salus hic maneto,' which is to be repeated 'ter novies.' Servius notes that the words 'sulco attritus splendescere vomer' recall an old saying of Cato, 'Vir bonus est, mi fili, colendi peritus, cuius ferramenta splendent [4].' The notices of ceremonial observances, such as

---

[1] Cf. Col. iii. 15 : 'Ut Mago prodit, quem secutus Vergilius tutari semina et muniri sic praecepit,' etc.

[2] Cf. Col. iv. 9: 'Nam illam veterem opinionem non esse ferro tangendos anniculos malleolos quod aciem reformidant, quod frustra Vergilius et Saserna, Stolonesque, et Catones timuerunt,' etc. Also ix. 14: 'Ceterum hoc eodem tempore progenerari posse apes iuvenco perempto Democritus et Mago nec minus Vergilius prodiderunt.' As a trace of Virgil's imitation of Varro, compare the passage where, after speaking of the injury done by goats to the vine, Varro says, 'Sic factum ut Libero Patri repertori vitis hirci immolarentur,' with Georgic ii. 380, 'Non aliam ob culpam,' etc.

[3] 'From dust in winter, from mud in spring time, you will reap great crops, Camillus.'

[4] 'He, my son, is a worthy man, and a good farmer, whose implements shine brightly.'

the account of the Ambarvalia, and the enumeration of things that might lawfully be done on holy days[1], were probably derived from the pontifical books and the sacred books of the other priestly colleges, of which Virgil made large use also in the Aeneid.   In all the writers on practical farming, from Cato to Varro, he found that strong appreciation of the supreme worth of rural industry and that strong interest in its processes and results which justified him in identifying his subject with the thought of the national life.

Among the sources of literary inspiration from which Virgil drew in the Georgics, the oldest, and not the least abundant, was the 'Works and Days' of Hesiod.   Yet a comparison of the two poems shows immediately that the Georgics do not, either in form or substance, stand in that close relation to their prototype, in which the Eclogues on the one hand, and the Aeneid on the other, stand to the idyls of Theocritus and to the epic poems of Homer.   The immediate influence of Hesiod is most apparent in the first Book of the Georgics, in which the subject is treated in connexion with theological ideas; while in the second Book and in the later Books, in which the philosophical conception of Nature, though in subordination to the conception of a supreme Spiritual power, becomes more prominent, the spirit of Hesiod gives place to the spirit of Lucretius.   There is, however, a real affinity between the primitive piety of the old Boeotian bard and the attitude in which Virgil contemplated the world, though the faith of Virgil has become more rational under the speculative teaching and enquiry which had taken the place of earlier modes of thought among the Greeks.   Virgil is ever seeking to produce a poetical reconcilement between primitive tradition and more enlightened views both of moral and physical truth.   Thus he introduces the old fable of the creation of the present race of men in immediate juxtaposition with the assertion of the 'laws and eternal conditions imposed by Nature on certain places.'   He accepts the belief in a Golden Age and in the blight which fell on the

---

[1] i. 269.

world under the dispensation of Jove; but he regards this
blight as sent, not in anger, but as a discipline and incentive to
exertion. He describes the natural progress of the various arts
of life under this stimulus, but still leaves room for divine inter-
vention in the more important discoveries :—

> Prima Ceres ferro mortalis vertere terram
> Instituit[1].

Again, the teleological view of Nature, which appears in the
Georgics in antagonism to the teaching of Lucretius, in such
passages as i. 231—

> Idcirco certis dimensum partibus orbem, etc.,

and i. 351—

> Atque haec ut certis possemus discere signis—

is in the spirit of Hesiod, though in advance of his conception
of Zeus, who appears in him not as a beneficent Providence,
but rather as a jealous task-master. So too the constant inculcation of prayer and ceremonial observances—

> Umida solstitia atque hiemes orate serenas,
> Agricolae—
>
> Votisque vocaveris imbrem—
>
> In primis venerare deos, atque annua magnae
> Sacra refer Cereri[2]—

the specification of lucky and unlucky days, the reference to
the old Greek fables of Coeus, Iapetus, and Typhoeus, are,
though not directly imitated from Hesiod, yet conceived in his
spirit.

But, besides appealing to primitive religious and mythological associations, the poet of Andes aims at reproducing
some flavour of the sentiment of a remote antiquity and of
the quaint *naïveté* characteristic of the sage of Ascra. The
very use of such an expression as ' *quo sidere* terram Vertere,'

---

[1] ' Ceres first taught mortals to turn up the earth with iron.'

[2] ' Pray, farmers, for wet summers and dry winters '—' And may have
called forth the rain by vows '—' Especially worship the Gods, and offer the
yearly sacrifices to mighty Ceres.' Cf. Ἔργ. καὶ Ἡμ. 463 :—
Εὔχεσθαι δὲ Διὶ χθονίῳ Δημήτερί θ' ἁγνῇ.

—the thought of the husbandman's labours as being regulated not by the Roman Calendar[1], with its prosaic divisions of the month by kalends, nones, and ides, but by the rise and setting of the constellations,—the picturesque signs of the change of the seasons, as in the line

> Candida venit avis longis invisa colubris[2],—

the use of such quaint expressions as 'nudus ara, sere nudus,' —seem all intended to remind the reader that the subject is one 'antiquae laudis et artis,'—the most ancient and unchanging of the great arts of life,—that too in which man's dependence on Nature and the Spiritual power above Nature is most vividly realised[3].     This infusion into the practical realities and prosaic details of his subject of something of the wonder and 'freshness of the early world' Virgil derives from the relation which he establishes between himself and his Boeotian prototype.

Though in spirit and poetical inspiration Virgil's debt to Hesiod is greater, yet the Georgics present more direct traces of imitation of the Alexandrine poets.     It is in accordance with the learning and science of Alexandria that the subject is illustrated by local epithets, such as 'Strymoniae grues,' by reference to the products of distant lands—

> nonne vides croceos ut Tmolus odores, etc.,—

by recondite mythological and astronomical allusions and by the substitution of the names of various deities, such as Liber and Ceres, for the natural products which were supposed to be

---

[1] The great confusion into which it had fallen before its reformation by Julius Caesar may have made this return to the primitive 'Shepherd's Calendar' familiar to Virgil's youth.

[2] 'When the white bird, abhorred by the long snakes, has come.'   Cf. Ἔργ. καὶ Ἡμ. 448 :—

Φράζεσθαι δ' εὖτ' ἂν γεράνου φωνὴν ἐπακούσῃς.

[3] The same suggestion of the ancient and unchanging nature of this art is vividly conveyed in the Chorus of the Antigone :—

Θεῶν τε τὰν ὑπερτάταν Γᾶν
ἄφθιτον ἀκαμάταν ἀποτρύεται,
ἰλλομένων ἀρότρων ἔτος εἰς ἔτος, ἱππείῳ γένει πολεύων.

their gifts.  But to several special authors his debt is more
direct.  Thus the passage, i. 233—

> Quinque tenent caelum zonae, etc.,—

is copied from Eratosthenes.  The account of the signs of
the weather, from i. 355 to 465, is taken from the Διοσημεία
of Aratus, a work so popular at Rome, that it was not only
imitated and almost incorporated in his poem by Virgil, but
had been translated by Cicero in his youth, and was subsequently translated by Germanicus.  Again, the description
at iii. 425, of the dangerous serpent that haunts the Calabrian pastures, is closely imitated from the extant Θηριακά of
Nicander; nor can we doubt that there were in the fourth
Book imitations of the lost Μελισσουργικά of the same author,
who probably anticipated Virgil in the use which he made of
Aristotle's observations on the habits of bees.

A comparison of the passages in the Georgics with those
of which they are imitations produces the impression not only
of Virgil's immense superiority as a poet over the Alexandrine
Metaphrastae, but of the immense superiority of the Latin
hexameter, as an organ for expressing the beauty and power
of Nature, over the exotic jargon and unmusical jingle which
those writers compounded out of their epic studies and their
scientific nomenclature.  To take one or two instances of
Virgil's imitations from these writers:—in the passage Georg.
i. 233–246, Virgil reproduces very closely scientific statements
of Eratosthenes and Aratus.  But of the five lines which
follow—

> Illic, ut perhibent, aut intempesta silet nox
> Semper et obtenta densentur nocte tenebrae,
> Aut redit a nobis Aurora diemque reducit;
> Nosque ubi primus equis Oriens adflavit anhelis,
> Illic sera rubens accendit lumina Vesper [1],—

---

[1] 'There, as they say, there is either the silence of midnight, and a
thicker darkness beneath the canopy of night, or else the dawn returns to
them from us and brings back the day; and when the morning sun breathes
on us with the first breath of his panting steeds, there the glowing star of
evening is lighting up her late fires.'

where through the evanescent mists of early science we discern
the enduring substance of poetic creation, there is no trace in
either of the Greek writers. Again, in the passage at i. 410,
imitated from Aratus—

> Tum liquidas corvi presso ter gutture voces, etc.,—

the mere natural phenomenon is given in greater detail in the
original passage; but the lines which communicate to it the
touch of tender sympathy—

> iuvat imbribus actis
> Progeniem parvam dulcesque revisere nidos [1],—

and the following lines—

> Haud equidem credo quia sit divinitus illis, etc.,—

which elevate the whole description into the higher air of
imaginative contemplation, are entirely Virgil's own. So too
in nearly all the indications of stormy or bright weather,
whether taken from natural phenomena or the habits of
animals, we find in the Latin poet some suggestion of poetical
analogy giving new life to the thing described, or some touch
of tender feeling, of which his original supplied him with no
hint whatever.

For the true poetry of the Georgics—the colour of human
and sympathetic feeling, the atmosphere of contemplative
ideas, the ethical and national associations with which the
subject is surrounded—Virgil owes very little to Greek inspiration. Much of this poetry is the mode in which his own
spirit interprets Nature and human life. But much also is
due to the genius of his great predecessor in Latin poetry,
who, though 'unnamed,' is 'not unowned,' but felt to be a
pervading presence in the thought and feeling, the creative
diction and the grander cadences, of the Georgics. Yet this
influence is perhaps as potent in the antagonism as in the
sympathy which it evokes. Virgil is no mere disciple of
Lucretius, either as regards his philosophy or his art. Though

---

[1] 'They are glad, now that the rains are over, to revisit their young
brood and their dear nests.'

his imagination pays homage to that of the older poet; though he acknowledges his contemplative elevation; though he has a strong affinity with the deep humanity of his nature; yet in his profoundest convictions and aspirations he proclaims his revolt from him. The key to the secret of much in the composition of the Georgics,—of the condition of mind out of which this work of genius assumed the shape it has as a great literary possession,—is to be sought in the collision between the force of thought, imagination, and feeling which the active spirit of Lucretius stored up and left behind him as his legacy to the world, and the nature, strongly susceptible indeed, but, at the same time, firm in its own convictions, which first felt the shock of that force, in its attractive, stimulating, and repellent power.

# CHAPTER VI.

## STRUCTURE AND COMPOSITION OF THE POEM, IN RELATION TO THE POEM OF LUCRETIUS.

### I.

THE influence, direct and indirect, exercised by Lucretius on the thought, composition, and even the diction of the Georgics was perhaps stronger than that ever exercised, before or since, by one great poet on the work of another. This influence is of the kind which is oftener seen in the history of philosophy than of literature. It was partly one of sympathy, partly of antagonism. Virgil's conception of Nature has its immediate origin in the thought of Lucretius; his religious convictions and national sentiment derive new strength by reaction from the attitude of his predecessor. This powerful attraction and repulsion were alike due to the fact that Lucretius was the first not only to reveal a new power, beauty, and source of wonder in the world, but also to communicate to poetry a speculative impulse, opening up, with a more impassioned appeal than philosophy can do, the great questions underlying human life,—such as the truth of all religious tradition, the position of man in the Universe, and the attitude of mind and course of conduct demanded by that position.

Nor was it a poetical and speculative impulse only that Virgil received from his predecessor. A new didactic poem, dealing largely with the same subject-matter as that treated by Lucretius, —such as the earth, the heavens, the great elemental forces, the growth of plants, the habits of animals, and the like—contemplating, among other objects, that of determining the relation of man to the sphere in which he is placed, and seeking to invest the ordinary processes of Nature with an ideal charm,—could not help assuming a somewhat similar mould to that which had been originally cast for the philosophic thought and realistic observation of the older poet.

Again, in regard to the technical execution of his work, rhythm and expression, Virgil inherited the new wealth introduced into Latin literature by Lucretius. Lucretius had given to the Latin Hexameter a stronger and more unimpeded flow, a more sonorous and musical intonation than it had before his time. He stamped the force of his mind on new modes of vivid expression and of rhythmical cadence, which, though they might be modified, could not be set aside in any future representation of the 'species ratioque,' the outward spectacle and the moving principle of Nature.

Many circumstances conduced to bring Virgil, more powerfully than any other Latin poet, under the spell of Lucretius. As is remarked by Mr. Munro[1], when the poem of his predecessor first appeared Virgil was at, or near, the age which is most immediately impressed and moulded by a contemporary work of genius. The enthusiasm for philosophy, expressed in the short poem written immediately before he began to study under Siron, implies that he had been already attracted by the subject of which Lucretius was the only worthy[2] Latin exponent; and his studies under that teacher must have prepared his mind to receive the higher instruction of the 'De Rerum Natura.' The song of Silenus in the sixth Eclogue and many expressions and cadences in other poems of the series attest the poetical, if not the speculative, impression thus produced. But the clearest testimony of Virgil's recognition of the influence of his predecessor is found in that passage of the Georgics in which he speaks of himself most from his heart,—

Me vero primum dulces ante omnia Musae, etc.,—(II. 475.)

---

[1] Introduction to Notes, ii. p. 315.

[2] Compare the contemptuous expressions used by Cicero, Tusc. Disp. ii. 3, of those who had written on the Epicurean philosophy in Latin. It seems strange, if he had any hand in editing his poems, that he makes no exception there in favour of Lucretius.

and in which he declares his first wish to be that the Muses
should reveal to him the secrets of Nature ; but, if this were
denied him, he next prays that 'the love of the woods and running streams in the valleys' might be his portion.   He may not
have meant the lines

> Felix qui potuit rerum cognoscere causas, etc.,—(II. 490.)

to be taken as a description of the individual Lucretius, or those
containing the other picture, placed by its side,

> Fortunatus et ille, deos qui novit agrestis,
> Panaque Silvanumque senem Nymphasque sorores, etc.,—(II. 493.)

as a description of himself.   Such direct personal references are
not in keeping with the allusive style in which he writes of himself and others.   He seems rather in these passages to set forth
two ideal states of mind, that of philosophic contemplation, on
the one hand, that of the pure love of Nature and conformity
with the simple beliefs of country-people, on the other, as
equally capable of raising men above the vulgar passions and
pleasures of the world.   But it is evident that he thought of
Lucretius as the poet who had held up the one ideal to the imagination and the severer mood of his countrymen, and of himself as holding up the other to their poetical feeling and their
human affections.

He would thus seem to have looked on Lucretius with something of that veneration with which Lucretius regards Epicurus,
Empedocles, and Ennius, and with which Dante long after
regarded Virgil himself.   The two greatest among the Roman
poets had many feelings in common,—the love of Nature, the
love of study, especially the study of ancient poetry and of
science, a natural shrinking from the pomp and luxury of city-
life and from the schemes of worldly ambition, an abhorrence
of the crimes and violence of civil war.   They felt the charm of
the same kind of outward scenes,—of rivers flowing through
green pastures, of meadow and woodland, of rich corn-fields
and vineyards.   They had the same strong sympathy with the
life of animals associated with man's labour, the same fellow-

feeling with the pain and the happiness of which human affection
is the source.   The numerous passages in which phrases or
cadences, thought or imagery in the Georgics recall phrases or
representation in the earlier poem[1], leave no doubt that Virgil
found in Lucretius a heart and spirit with which his own largely
receptive nature could in many ways sympathise, as well as that
he recognised in him a guide whom he could follow in imagination 'among the lonely heights of Parnassus[2].'

Yet, on the other hand, it is quite true that both the character
and genius of Virgil are essentially of a different type from those
of Lucretius.—They are both thoroughly original representatives
of different elements in the Roman and Italian character.—So
far as he represents the mind and temper of Rome, Lucretius
represents the old order which had passed away.   Though
scarcely anything is known of the circumstances of his life, yet
his *gentile* name (as is shown by Mr. Munro), his relation of
equality to Memmius, the stamp of his powerful personality
impressed on his poem, point to the conclusion that he was one
of the old Roman aristocracy, born into a time when many of
its members had begun to retire in disgust from active interest
in the Republic, which they were no longer able to govern.   It
was, as has been already remarked[3], to this class among the
Romans, almost exclusively, that the taste for literature was confined in the last age of the Republic; and it was among men of
this class, such as the Luculli and Hortensius, and the Velleius
and Torquatus of Cicero's Dialogues, that the Epicurean philosophy found its chief adherents.   The poem of Lucretius shows
all the courage and energy, the power of command, the sense of
superiority and the direct simplicity of manner emanating from
it, which are the inheritance of a great governing class.   He is
the one man of true genius for poetry whom that class gave to
Rome.   His lofty pathos and tenderness of feeling are the
graces of his own nature, refined and purified by the most

---

[1] Compare Munro's notes *passim*, and specially the note on Lucret. iii. 449.
[2] Compare Georg. iii. 291 with Lucret. i. 926.
[3] Chap. iii. p. 109.

humanising studies.  His profound melancholy is a mood natural to one who looks on the passing away of a great order of things, political, social, and religious, in the midst of scenes of turbulence and violence, and takes refuge from an alien world in the contemplation of another order of things, infinitely more majestic than either the old social state which was shaken and tottering to its fall, or the new which was yet 'powerless to be born.'

There could scarcely be any greater contrast, in social relations and the dispositions arising out of them, between any two men, than between the representative of the old governing families of the Republic, and the humbly-born native of the Cisalpine province,—delicate in health, modest and self-distrustful, yet endowed with a deep consciousness of genius and a resolution to follow that guidance only,—entering on manhood and beginning his career as poet contemporaneously with the events which determined the ascendency of the new order of things, and identified with it through his personal relations to the leading men of the new Empire,—a poet who derived from his birth and early nurture 'the spirit of the ages of Faith[1],'—one too who had been happy in his early home-affections and in the friendships of his manhood, and who was able to dedicate his mature years to his art under conditions of the greatest personal and national security.  In considering the influence of the ideas of Lucretius on the mind of Virgil, we must accordingly make large allowance for the medium of alien sympathies, personal, social, and political, through which they were refracted.  We must take into consideration also the wide difference between the philosophic poet and the pure poetic artist. The feeling of Virgil towards philosophy was apparently one of aspiration rather than of possession.  He shows no interest in the processes of enquiry,—in tracing the operation of great laws in manifold phenomena,—in investigating one obscure subject after another, with the confident assurance that every discovery

---

[1] Merivale's Roman Empire.

is a step towards the light and the ultimate revelation of the whole mystery. Virgil recognises the source of his own strength in the words

Flumina *amem* silvasque.

It is the power of love which quickens his intuition and enables him to perceive the tenderness and beauty revealed in the living movement of Nature. He receives and applies the complete ideas of Lucretius, but he does not follow them with the eagerness of their author through the various phases of their development. Certain results of a philosophic system affect his imagination, but he does not seem to feel how these results necessarily exclude other conclusions which he will not abandon. Hence arises his prevailing eclecticism,—the existence of popular beliefs side by side in his mind with the tenets of Epicureans, Stoics, and Platonists,—of some conclusions of the Lucretian science along with the opposing doctrines expressed in the poetry of Alexandria. Even in the arrangement of his materials and the grouping of his landscapes, some chance association or rhythmical cadence seems to guide his hand, more often than the perception of the orderly connexion of phenomena with one another.

II.

The idea which Lucretius revealed to the world in fuller majesty and life than any previous poet or philosopher, was the idea of Nature, apprehended, not as an abstract conception, but as a power omnipresent, creative, and regulative throughout the great spheres of earth, sky, and sea, and the innumerable varieties of individual existence. The meaning conveyed by the Greek word φύσις, as employed by Democritus, Heraclitus, Empedocles, etc., is powerless to move the imagination or enlarge the sense of beauty, when compared with the illimitable content of 'Natura daedala rerum' as conceived by the Latin poet. Nature is to him the one power absolutely supreme and independent in the Universe, too vast and too manifold to be subject to any will but her own,—

.Libera continuo dominis privata superbis.

Her independent existence is incompatible with that of the multitude of beings, of limited power and intelligence, which the old mythologies established as lords over the world and man. The gods, abiding in a state of blessed ease and indifference, are themselves dependent on a power infinitely transcending their own. But in what relation does man stand to this power? He too is within her sphere, altogether subject to her, but no special object of her regard. He exists only through compliance with and resignation to her conditions. And these conditions are on the whole unfavourable to him. He can gain only a scanty subsistence by a continual struggle with reluctant and rebellious forces in the earth; and even after all his toil and care, causes over which he has no control, such as the inclemency of the skies and incalculable vicissitudes of heat and cold, frustrate his endeavours.

> Quod superest arvi *tamen id natura sua vi*
> *Sentibus obducat*, ni *vis humana resistat*
> Vitai causa valido consueta bidenti
> *Ingemere et terram pressis proscindere aratris.*
> Si non fecundas *vertentes* vomere glebas
> *Terraique solum subigentes* cimus ad ortus,
> *Sponte sua nequeant liquidas* existere in auras.
> Et tamen interdum *magno quaesita labore*
> Cum iam per terras frondent atque omnia florent,
> Aut nimiis torret fervoribus aetherius sol
> Aut subiti perimunt imbris gelidaeque pruinae,
> Flabraque ventorum violento turbine vexant[1].

[1] ' What remains of tilled land, even that Nature by its own force would overgrow with briars did not the force of man resist it, inured, for the sake of living, to ply, with pain and labour, the stout mattock, and to split up the new earth with the deep-sunk ploughs: did not we, by turning up the fruitful clods with the plough-share, and subduing the soil of the earth, call forth the seeds to the birth, they could not of their own impulse come forth into the clear air. And after all, sometimes the products of much toil, when they are already in blade and in beauty over the earth, either the Sun in heaven scorches with excessive heat, or sudden rains and chill frosts ruin them, and the blasts of the winds in wild hurricane make them their sport.' Lucret. v. 206–217 (See Munro's note on the passage). Cf.

How deeply the thought expressed in these lines—the thought of the hard struggle which man is forced to carry on with an unsympathetic Power—sank into the mind of Virgil, is evident from the various passages in the Georgics in which the phraseology as well as the idea expressed by Lucretius is reproduced. These lines in which the struggle between the 'vis humana,' impersonated in the husbandman, and the resistance offered by Nature to his energetic labours, is vividly described, suggest whatever there is of speculative thought in the Georgics. And though it would be misleading to speak of that poem as, in any sense, a philosophical poem, yet, as in all other great works of genius, some theory of life—of man's relation to his circumstances and of his place, either in a spiritual or natural dispensation—pervades and gives its highest meaning to the didactic exposition.

Lucretius further regards this state of things, so far from being remediable by man, as necessarily becoming worse. Each new generation of husbandmen and vinedressers finds its burden heavier :—

> Iamque caput quassans grandis suspirat arator
> Crebrius, incassum manuum cecidisse labores[1], etc.

The earth which, under the genial influence of sun and rain, produced fair crops without the labour of the ploughman and vinedresser[2], can now scarcely produce its fruits in sufficient quantity, though the strength of men and oxen is worn out by labouring on it[3]. The cause of this decay in productiveness he attributes to the waste or dissipation of the elemental matter of our world, which has become much greater and more rapid than the supply of new materials. 'In the long warfare waged from infinite time'—

> Ex infinito contractum tempore bellum—

Georg. ii. 411; i. 198; i. 208; ii. 237; ii. 47; i. 197. Compare also Virgil's use of *subigere* and *vertere* as applied to the soil.

[1] 'And now the aged peasant, shaking his head, often sighs forth the complaint, that the labour of his hands has come to naught.' Lucret. ii. 1164, etc.

[2] v. 932, etc.     [3] ii. 1160, etc.

the destructive forces are gaining the superiority over the
restorative forces of Nature; and this process is hastening on
the advent of that 'single day' which will overwhelm in ruin
the whole framework of earth, sea, and sky [1].

What then under these irremediable conditions is it best
for man to do? Lucretius has no other answer to give him
than to study the laws of Nature, so as to understand his
position, and thus to limit his wants and reconcile himself to
what he cannot alter. Yet in other passages of the poem,
which Virgil also remembered [2], he did recognise the fact that
human skill and the knowledge acquired by observation had
done much to enrich and beautify the earth :—

> Inde aliam atque aliam culturam dulcis agelli
> Temptabant, fructusque feros mansuescere terram
> Cernebant indulgendo blandeque colendo [3].

But he seems to have no idea of further progress. Though
he contemplates with imaginative sympathy the trials of the
'grandis arator' and the 'vetulae vitis sator,' he has no
guidance to offer them. The lessons taught by Lucretius are
not those of active energy, applicable to every condition of life,
but the lessons of a resigned quietism and a contemplative
energy, adapted only to men of leisure, enjoying ample resources for the gratification of their intellectual tastes.

That this opinion of the decay in the natural productiveness
of the earth made a strong impression on the Roman mind
may be inferred from the fact that Columella opens his treatise
by arguing against it. And that the idea of the struggle with
Nature was one familiar to the prose writers on such subjects
appears from an expression in the first book of the same
writer : 'that the land ought to be weaker than the husbandman,
since he has to struggle with it.' Cicero too puts into Cato's

---

[1] ii. 1146; v. 95.

[2] Compare Lucret. v. 1367-1369 with Georg. ii. 36. Compare also Virgil's use of *indulgere* and *indulgentia*.

[3] 'After that they essayed now one, now another, mode of tilling the
dear plot of ground, and they saw that the earth made wild fruits into
fruits of the garden, by a kindly and caressing culture.'

mouth[1] the sentiment that the earth, if rightly dealt with, never refuses the 'imperium' of man.   And this too is Virgil's doctrine: and it was to give that guidance which Lucretius, though he discerned the evil, did not supply, that the didactic directions of the Georgics were given.

The Lucretian idea of Nature, both in its philosophical and poetical significance, runs through the Georgics; but it is modified by other considerations, and it is rather latent than prominent in the poetry and in the practical teaching of the poem.   The mind of Virgil is not possessed, as the mind of Lucretius was possessed, by the thought of the immensity of her sphere and the universality of her presence.   He sees her presence in the familiar scenes and objects around him.   The idea adds variety, grace, and liveliness to his description of every detail of rural industry.   A sense of the ministering agency of Nature is a more pervading element in his poetry than that of her power and majesty.   Objects are still regarded by him as separate and individual.   The conceptions of Nature which created mythology contend in his mind with the half-apprehended conceptions of universal law and of the inter-dependence of phenomena on one another.   Thus the poetical element in his descriptions of the life of plants and trees, or of the forces of flood and storm, does not spring from such deep sources in the imagination as the same element in the descriptions of the older poet.   But neither is it limited to the perception of the 'outward shows' of things which gratify the eye, or the sounds which delight the ear.   Even in the Eclogues the intuition into Nature is deeper than that.   The study of Lucretius has enriched the Georgics with the most pervading charm of the poem—the sense of a secret, unceasing, tranquil power (like that ascribed by Wordsworth to May—

> Thy help is with the weed that creeps
> Along the barest ground, etc.),

communicating to outward things the grace and tenderness

---

[1] De Senectute, xv.

of human sentiment, the variety and vivacity of human energy.

But the Lucretian conception of Nature in its relation to human wants has been greatly modified by the religious tendency of Virgil's thought, his respect for traditional opinion, his sense of man's dependence on a higher Spiritual Power. Nature he regards as no more independent in her sphere than man is in his.   The laws and conditions imposed on her have been appointed with reference to the relation in which she stands to man.   Where these conditions are unfavourable, they have been appointed to quicken man's faculties and force him into the ways of industry.   Lucretius dwells on the fact that two-thirds of our globe are unsuited for human habitation, as disproving the opinion of a Divine creation of the world for the benefit of man [1] : Virgil dwells on the fact that two temperate regions have been assigned to weak mortals as a proof of Divine beneficence [2].   Virgil also accepts the idea that the earth once was more productive than it is [3], but he accepts it in the spirit of Hesiod rather than of Lucretius.   In the Golden Age, under Saturn, the earth bore all things spontaneously. It was Jove—or Providence—who imposed on man, and continues to impose on him, the necessity of labouring for his subsistence ; and this he did, not, as Hesiod believed, in anger at the deceit of Prometheus, but as a discipline and incentive to exertion.   The poetical references to the Saturnian Age and the subsequent reign of Jove need not imply a literal belief in the fables of mythology, any more than the allusion at Georg. i. 62 to the fable of Pyrrha and Deucalion implies the literal acceptance of the explanation there given of the existence of the present race of men.   But as that allusion seems meant to convey the belief in a Divine creative act, so the former allusion seems to convey a belief in a Divine moral dispensation.   The idea of Providential guidance, of a Supreme Father, wielding the forces of Nature, shaping the destinies of man, acting for the most part by regular processes in order

---

[1] v. 204, etc.        [2] Georg. i. 237–8.        [3] Ib. 128.

that man may learn to understand his ways[1], but making his personal agency more manifest from time to time, as after the death of Caesar, by signs and wonders interrupting the order of Nature, supersedes or largely modifies the conception of natural law. The other powers of the Greek Olympus and of the Roman Pantheon are no longer, as the former are in the Iliad, at war with one another, but all work in harmony with the Supreme Will. Like the fables just referred to, the names of these deities seem to be introduced symbolically, to signify the different modes of activity of the one Supreme Spiritual Power, and the different forms under which he is to be reverenced.

The speculative idea of the Georgics is thus rather a theological than a philosophical idea. The ultimate fact which Virgil endeavours to set forth and justify is the relation of man to Nature, under a Divine dispensation. He too, as well as Lucretius, recognises the tendency of all things to degenerate; but this tendency he attributes, not to natural loss of force, but to the fiat of Omnipotence—

> sic omnia fatis
> In peius ruere.

He too recognises the liability to failure and loss from causes over which man has no direct control,—the violence of storms, the inclemency of seasons, etc.,—as well as from others which he is able to provide against by constant vigilance. What resource has he against these untoward conditions? First he is bound to watch the signs of impending change which Providence has appointed, so as to leave as little as possible at the mercy of the elements. Next he has the resource of prayer, and the power of propitiating Heaven by customary rites and sacrifices, and by a life of piety and innocence. The ethical precepts of the poem, as is said by a distinguished French

---

[1] Cf. Georg. i. 351–353:—
   Atque haec ut certis possemus discere signis,
   Aestusque pluviasque et agentis frigora ventos,
   Ipse Pater statuit, quid menstrua Luna moneret.

writer, may be summed up in the medieval maxim, 'Laborare
est orare [1].'

To inculcate the necessity of a constant struggle with the
reluctant forces of Nature, and to show how this struggle may
be successfully conducted by incessant labour, vigilance, pro-
pitiation of the Supreme Will by prayer and piety, thus appears
to be the main ethical teaching of the Georgics.   And this
statement of Virgil's aim is not inconsistent with the interpretation of his meaning, first suggested by Mr. Merivale, and
accepted and admirably illustrated by Conington.   But the
phrase 'glorification of labour' suggests modern rather than
ancient associations.   Labour is not glorified as an end in
itself; it is inculcated as a duty, as the condition appointed by
Providence for attaining the peace, abundance, happiness, and
worth of the life of the fields.   As of old

Τῆς ἀρετῆς ἱδρῶτα θεοὶ προπάροιθεν ἔθηκαν,

so now they make the sweat of man's brow the means through
which the ' divini gloria ruris ' can be realised.   By the labour
spent in drawing into actual existence the glory and beauty of
the land man best fulfils his duty and secures his happiness.
There is no truer source for him of material and moral good,
of simple pleasures, of contemplative delight.   Yet if we wish
rightly to appreciate the purely didactic parts of the poem, it is
impossible, as has been fully shown by Conington in his
General Introduction to the Georgics, to overrate the stress
which Virgil puts on the ceaseless industry, foresight, vigilance,
and actual force [2] which must be put forth by the husbandman,
as the condition of success in the struggle in which he is

---

[1] ' Travailler et prier, voilà la conclusion des Georgiques.'   From an
article in the Revue des Deux Mondes (vol. 104), called Un Poëte Théologien, by Gaston Boissier.

[2] Compare, among many other similar instances, such expressions as
these :—
                           Labor actus in orbem
        Agricolis redit.
        Omnia quae multo ante memor provisa repones.
        Quae vigilanda viris.
        Continuo in silvis magna vi flexa domatur, etc.

engaged. The very style of the Georgics bears the impress of this predominant idea. It is this idea which seems to give Roman strength to the workmanship of the poem ; as it is the sense of the rich and tender life of Nature which gives to it the softness of Italian sentiment, so marvellously blended with that Roman strength. The imperial tone of conquest and command and civilising influence makes itself heard in such lines as these :—

> Exercetque frequens tellurem atque imperat arvis.
>                     Tum denique dura
> Exerce imperia et ramos compesce fluentes.
> In quascumque voces artes haud tarda sequentur [1].

This idea of the need of a struggle with Nature, latent under all the special precepts of the Georgics, is thus seen to arise out of the philosophical thought of Lucretius. But the lesson inculcated by Virgil is directly opposite to that state of quietism and pure contemplation in which Lucretius finds the ideal of human life. Virgil's teaching is that best adapted to the strenuous temperament of his countrymen and to the general condition of men in all times. And it will be found that this idea of a hard struggle, ordained by Supreme Power, against adverse circumstances, in which man receives Divine guidance by prayer and patient interpretation of the will of Heaven, and through which he attains to a state of final rest, runs through the Aeneid as well as the Georgics. Virgil reaches a practical result opposed to that which Lucretius reaches, by subordinating the Lucretian conception of man's relation to Nature to the Platonic belief in the supremacy of a Spiritual Will and in the moral dispensation under which man is placed. It is this belief which appears to underlie Virgil's acceptance of the religious traditions of antiquity, which might have been expected to have received, for all educated minds, their death-blow at the hands of Lucretius.

---

[1] 'And is incessantly drilling the land, and exercising command over the fields '—' Then at length exercise a stern command, and restrain the wild luxuriance of the branches '—' They will, with no reluctant obedience, adopt any ways you bid them.'

The science of Lucretius, as distinct from his philosophy of
Nature and human life, is also partly accepted by Virgil, and
partly rejected in favour of the tenets of an opposite school.
In such passages as i. 89–90,

> Seu pluris calor ille vias et caeca relaxat
> Spiramenta, novas veniat qua sucus in herbas[1], etc.,

i. 415–423,

> Haud equidem credo, etc.,

iii. 242,

> Omne adeo genus in terris hominumque ferarumque, etc.,

we recognise the Lucretian explanation of the constitution of
the earth, of the material elements of the mind, of the physical
influence of love.   Other passages again, such as i. 247, etc.,

> Illic ut perhibent aut intempesta silet nox,

and iv. 219–227,

> His quidam signis, etc.,

are in harmony with the Stoical doctrines and in direct opposition to the Epicurean science.   Some of these apparent
inconsistencies of opinion may be explained on the supposition
that Virgil changed his allegiance from one school to another
during the composition of the Georgics.   But probably the
truer explanation is that he was

> Nullius addictus iurare in verba magistri[2],

and that he accepted certain results of science which impressed
his imagination, without caring for their consistency with others
which he equally accepts.   There is a constant tendency in him
to allow his belief in the miraculous to interfere with his belief
in natural law; as for instance in the account he gives of the
birth of bees (iv. 200), and again of their spontaneous generation
from the blood of slain bullocks (iv. 285).   He has not the firm
faith in natural agency which Lucretius had.   Phenomena are

---

[1] 'Whether it is that the heat opens up various ways of access and re-
laxes the secret pores, where the sap may enter into the young plants.'
[2] 'That he owed allegiance to no master.'

still regarded by him as isolated, not interdependent. The ordinary course of Nature he supposes to be interrupted by marvels and portents. The signs of coming things are represented, not as Lucretius would have represented them, as natural antecedents or concomitants of the things portended, but as arbitrary indications appointed for the guidance of man.

## III.

For the technical execution of his poem Virgil could gain little help from his Greek models. The mass of materials which he had to reduce to order was much larger and more miscellaneous than the special topics selected for their art by the Alexandrians. The subject treated in the Georgics would have afforded scope for several poems treated on the principle on which Aratus and Nicander treated their subjects; and not only was the mass of materials larger and more varied, but the whole purpose of the Georgics was more complex. Virgil's artistic aim was not only to combine into one work the topics which he treats successively in the four books of the Georgics, but to interweave with them the poetry of personal and national feeling, of speculative ideas, of ethical and religious teaching, of science, of the living world of Nature. In Lucretius, on the other hand, he found an example of the systematic treatment of a vaster range of topics,—a range so vast, indeed, that the principal topics of Virgil's art enter as subsidiary elements into one part of his representation. Lucretius too had shown how to combine with the systematic exposition of his abstract theme a strong personal interest and a strong ethical purpose. He had shown how, out of the treatment of this abstract theme, opportunities naturally arose for uttering the poetry and pathos of human life, and for delineating in all its beauty and majesty the outward face and revealing the inner secret of Nature. He thus supplied the general plan which Virgil might follow, with modifications suited to his narrower range of subject and his more purely didactic office. We see how Virgil adopts this

plan, modified to suit his own ideas, in the personal dedication;
in the Invocation and short introduction to his various books;
in his manner of arranging, connecting, and illustrating the successive stages of his exposition; and, lastly, in the use which he
makes of episodes, chiefly at the end of various books, with the
view of enabling his readers to feel the intimate connexion of
his subject with the most valued interests of life,—with religion
and morality, with family affection, with peace, prosperity, and
national greatness.

The first parallel to be noticed, in the comparison between
the two poems, is in the personal address.    Maecenas stands
in the same relation to the Georgics as Memmius does to the
'De Rerum Natura.'   But as Memmius in the body of the poem
is often merged in the ideal philosophical student, so Virgil, after
the lines of compliment at the opening of his various books, for
the most part directs his instructions to some imaginary husbandman.    In the tones in which Memmius and Maecenas are respectively addressed there may be an equal sincerity of feeling.
But a difference in the relation in which the poets stand to those
whom they address makes itself felt in the contrast between such
lines as these,

> Sed tua me virtus tamen et sperata voluptas
> Suavis amicitiae,

and

> O decus, O famae merito pars maxima nostrae[1].

In the one case we recognise the man, born into the equal
relations of an aristocratic Republic, who knows of no social
superior in the world, and is attracted to him whom he honours
by his dedication solely by the charm of friendship.    In the
other case, though the affection may not be less sincere, there is
the unmistakeable note of deference to a social superior.

The difference between the position which the two poets

---

[1] 'But your excellence and the hope of the delightful enjoyment of your
friendship.'  'O my pride, O thou, to whom I justly ascribe the greatest
share of my renown.'

occupied and of the times in which they lived is still more manifest in the selection of the person whom they each fix on as the object of their reverential homage.  Though the poem of Lucretius is inscribed to Memmius, it is really dedicated to the glory of Epicurus.  His image presides over the massive temple raised to the Power of Nature.  He is the great benefactor of the world, exalted by his service to mankind, not only above all living men, but above those whom the popular religion had in early times elevated to the rank of gods—

> deus ille fuit, deus, inclyte Memmi.

In every book of the poem his praises are repeated in language of enthusiastic devotion.  In the poem of Virgil the living Caesar occupies the place of a tutelary deity—

> In medio mihi Caesar erit, templumque tenebit.

He is ranked above all living men, and above the great men of the past by whom Rome had been saved from her enemies : he is addressed as the immediate object of care to the native gods of Italy, and as destined after death to rank among the ruling powers of Heaven.  Something is said in his honour in every book of the poem.  The lines near the end,

> Caesar dum magnus ad altum
> Fulminat Euphraten bello, victorque volentis
> Per populos dat iura, viamque adfectat Olympo [1],

seem intended to leave the thought of his actual greatness as the abiding impression on the mind of the reader; as the con-cluding lines of the Invocation seem intended to make his presence felt as that of its inspiring deity.  While we cannot doubt that the admiration expressed by Lucretius is the sincere and generous tribute of genius acknowledging a great debt and unconsciously exaggerating the nobleness of its benefactor, it is impossible to determine how far Virgil's language is the

---

[1] ' While mighty Caesar is hurling the thunder-bolts of war by the deep Euphrates, and, a conqueror, issues his laws among willing subjects, and is already on the way which leads to Heaven.'

expression of sincere conviction, and how far it is dictated by
the necessities of his position.

But it is in their invocations of a Superior Power to aid
them in their task that we recognise the strongest contrast
between the philosophic poet, who, while denying all supernatural agency, is yet carried away by his imagination to attribute consciousness, will, and passion to the great creative
Power of Nature,—the source of all life, joy, beauty, and art,—
and the 'pius vates,' influenced by the religious sense of man's
dependence on a Spiritual Power, deeply feeling the poetical
charm of the old mythology, and striving to effect some
reconcilement between the fading traditions of Polytheism
and the more philosophical conceptions prevalent in his time.
Lucretius for the moment adopts the symbolism of ancient
mythology, and probably the actual figures of pictorial art
(which elsewhere he speaks of as a great source of human
delusion), to impart visible presence, colour, and passion to his
thought; but he leaves no doubt on the reader's mind that his
representation is merely symbolical. Virgil, on the other hand,
appears in the opening lines of the Georgics to attribute a
distinct personality to the beings of that composite Polytheism
which had gradually grown up out of the union of Greek art
and Roman religion, but which it is difficult to comprehend as
having any real hold over the minds of men who had received
any tincture of Greek philosophy. In the divine office which he
assigns to Caesar he adopts the latest addition to this eclectic
Pantheon; and this new divinity he introduces in the midst of
the old gods, just as he fancifully introduces Gallus in the
Eclogues amid the choir of Apollo and the Muses.

But in the Eclogues there is no feeling of doubt in our
minds that the representation is purely fanciful. The strain
in the Georgics is altogether too serious; the juxtaposition
of Caesar with the gods of Olympus and the protecting deities
of the husbandman is too carefully meditated to admit of our
supposing the lines from 'Tuque adeo' to 'adsuesce vocari' to
be intended to be taken as a mere play of fancy. We cannot

think of Lucretius, perhaps not even of Cicero, reading Virgil's Invocation, and especially the concluding lines of it, without a certain feeling of scorn. We cannot help asking how far could the pupil of Siron, the student of Epicurus and Lucretius, the enlightened associate of Maecenas, Augustus, Pollio, Horace, etc., attach any serious meaning to the words of this Invocation. How far was he simply complying with an established convention of literature? how far using these mythological representations as symbolism? how far was he identifying himself in imagination with the beliefs of his ideal husbandman?

To answer these questions we must endeavour to realise the very composite character which the Pagan religion, the accumulation of many beliefs from the earliest and rudest fancies of primitive times to the studied representations of Greek art and the later symbolical explanations of philosophical schools, presented to men living in the Augustan Age. In this Invocation and in the body of the poem we can trace three or four distinct veins of belief, existing together, without producing any sense of inconsistency, and combining into a certain unity for the purpose of artistic representation.

Religion in the Augustan Age presented a different aspect to the dwellers in the town and in the country; to the refined classes whose tastes were formed by Greek art and poetry, and to men of the old school,—senators like Cotta or antiquarians like Varro,—who sought to conform to the ancient Roman traditions; to students of philosophy, who either, like the Epicureans, denied all Divine agency, or like the Stoics, resolved the many divinities of the popular belief into one Divine agency under many forms. The peculiarity of Virgil's mind is that his belief, at least as expressed in his poetry, was a kind of syncretism composed out of all these modes of thought and belief. Like Horace and Tibullus, he sympathises in imagination with that rustic piety which expressed the natural thankfulness of the human heart for protection afforded to the flocks and the fruits of the field, by festivals and ceremonial observances like the Palilia and Ambarvalia, by sacrifice of a

kid to Faunus, or offerings of flowers and fruit to the Penates.
The feelings connected with this vein of belief as they are
represented in the poetry of the Augustan Age,—

> Faune nympharum fugientum amator, etc.,—

and again in Tibullus,

> Di patrii, purgamus agros, purgamus agrestes, etc.,—

are of a happy and generally of a genial and festive character,
and not altogether devoid of such elements of simple piety as
find expression in the

> Caelo supinas si tuleris manus, etc.,

of Horace.   Poetical sympathy with the beliefs and picturesque
ceremonies of the peasants among whom they lived enhanced
the real enjoyment derived from their country life by men of
refined feeling like Horace and Tibullus.   But Virgil's feeling
in regard to the religious trust and observances of the country
people appears to be stronger than mere poetical sympathy.
He sees in them a class of men more immediately dependent
than others on the protection of some unseen Power, and thus
forced, as it were, into more immediate relation with that
Power.   The modes in which they endeavoured to gain the
favour of that Power or to express their thankfulness for its
protection were probably among the influences which had
moulded his own early belief and character in his Mantuan
farm.   In the prayer

> Dique deaeque omnes studium quibus arva tueri[1],

as in the later exclamation,

> Fortunatus et ille deos qui novit agrestes[2],

he is identifying himself in imagination with a living mode of
popular belief, and one to which he may have been attracted by
his early associations as well as by poetical sympathy.

But the Invocation recognises the creations of Greek art

---

[1] 'Gods or Goddesses whose task it is to watch over the fields.'
[2] 'Blessed too was he who knew the Gods of the country.'

along with the ruder and simpler objects of Italian worship.
The 'Fauni Dryadesque puellae' assume to Virgil's fancy the
forms of Greek art and poetry. The legend of Neptune producing the horse by the stroke of his trident suggests the attributes of Ποσειδῶν ἵππιος, not of the Italian Neptunus. It is not
the Roman Minerva, but ἁ γλαυκῶπις Ἀθάνα, who is associated in
poetry and legend with the olive,—

> Φύτευμ' ἀχείρωτον αὐτόποιον
> γλαυκᾶς παιδοτρόφου φύλλον ἐλαίας.

He calls upon Pan to leave his native groves and the woodland
pastures of Lycaeus, just as Horace describes him as passing
nimbly from his Arcadian haunt to the Sabine Lucretilis. These
gods, nymphs, and satyrs of an alien belief were now to Romans
as to Greeks the recognised materials which art and song had
to shape into new forms. In the vigorous prime of Greek
poetry, so late even as the age of Sophocles and Herodotus,
there was a real belief in the personal existence and active
agency of these supernatural beings. This real belief first gave
birth to, and was afterwards merged in, the representations of
art. Art, which owed its birth to religious sentiment, superseded it. But after a time and under new conditions the strong
admiration for the beauty or significance of the objects represented in art produces a strong wish to revive the belief in their
reality; and in minds peculiarly susceptible of such influences
the wish tends to fulfil itself.

Probably Virgil himself would not have cared to probe too
deeply the state of half-belief in which his heart and mind
realised the bright existence and kindly influence of beings consecrated to him by the most cherished associations of living art
and the poetry of the past. Even Lucretius, while sternly
rejecting all belief in their existence as absolutely incompatible
with truth, feels from time to time attracted by their poetical
charm. Horace, we can see, from the absence of anything in
his Satires, or Epistles, implying a real belief in the gods of
mythology, keeps his literary belief apart from his true convic-

tions. In the case of Virgil, it is not possible, at all events for
a modern reader, distinctly to separate them. The power of the
old mythology over the fancy and the weakness of scientific
thought in ancient times to overthrow that power is nowhere
more visible than in his poetry.

But there was another mode of Greek influence acting on the
educated minds of Rome, stronger than that of the ancient mythology. That influence was the religious speculations of the
various philosophical schools [1]. There was, on the one hand,
the Epicurean acceptance of an infinite number of gods dwelling in the 'Intermundia,' enjoying a state of supreme calm,
apart from all concern with this world or the labours and pursuits of men. They might be objects of pure contemplation,
and pious reverence to the human spirit; but they were capable
neither of being propitiated nor made angry by anything that
men could do. The Stoic doctrine, on the other hand, recognised the incessant agency and forethought of a Supreme
Spiritual Power over human life. It accepted the stories and
beings of the traditional religion, but explained them away.
The various deities worshipped by the people are the various
manifestations and functions of this one Supreme Spiritual
Power, whether called by the name of Zeus, or by the abstract
name of Providence (πρόνοια). This is the Power addressed in
the famous hymn of Cleanthes, and that appealed to in the
familiar τοῦ γὰρ καὶ γένος ἐσμέν of Aratus. It is part of Virgil's
eclecticism to combine the science of Epicurus with the theology
of the more spiritual schools. The Supreme Spiritual Power in
the Georgics is generally spoken of under the title of 'Pater.'
It is noticeable that the word Iuppiter is used either with a purely
physical signification, as in

> Iuppiter umidus austris—
> Et iam maturis metuendus Iuppiter uvis—

or as in the phrases 'sub Iove,' 'ante Iovem,' in reference to
the stories of the ancient mythology. Even in this Invocation,

---

[1] Compare the first book of Cicero's De Natura Deorum.

the object of which seems to be to assign function and personality to the gods of Olympus and of Italy, the influence of
the Stoic theology was recognised in ancient times in the identification of the sun and moon—'clarissima mundi lumina'—
with Liber anớ Ceres [1].  The rhythm of the lines 5–7 can leave
no doubt whatever as to this identification, notwithstanding the
appeal to Varro's example, who distinguishes the various deities
whom he invokes.  It is characteristic of Virgil's art to introduce
such a variation in any passage which he imitates, and also to
suggest a thought which he does not distinctly develope.  In
the lines 95–96,

> neque illum
> Flava Ceres alto nequiquam spectat Olympo [2],

he reproduces a thought which Callimachus had expressed in
his hymn to Artemis [3]—

> Οὓς δέ κεν εὐμειδής τε καὶ ἵλαος αὐγάσσηαι
> κείνοις εὖ μὲν ἄρουρα φέρει στάχυν [4].

The 'flava Ceres' of Virgil's description seems to call up
before our mind a picture of the harvest-moon looking down
on the corn-fields of the prosperous husbandman.

The national religion of Rome was something distinct both
from the rustic Paganism of Italy, and from that aesthetic
amalgamation of Greek and Roman beliefs and that semi-
philosophical rationalism which art and literature made familiar
to the Romans of the Augustan Age.  The great symbol of
that national religion was the Temple of Jove on the Capitol [5].

---

[1] Servius has the following note on the passage:—'Stoici dicunt non esse
nisi unum deum, et unam eandemque (esse) potestatem, quae pro ratione
officiorum nostrorum variis nominibus appellatur.  Unde eundem Solem,
eundem Liberum, eundem Apollinem vocant.  Item Lunam, eandem Dia-
nam, eandem Cererem, eandem Iunonem, eandem Proserpinam dicunt;
secundum quos, pro Sole et Luna, Liberum et Cererem invocavit.'

[2] 'Nor is it without good result that golden-haired Ceres beholds him
from Heaven on high.'

[3] Quoted by M. Benoist.

[4] 'But on whom she gazes with bright and favourable aspect, for them
the field bears the ear of corn abundantly.'

[5] Cf. 'Incolumi Iove et urbe Roma.'  Hor. iii. 5. 12.  Cf. also iii. 3. 42;
iii. 30. 8.

Cf. also 'Sedem Iovis Optimi Maximi auspicato a maioribus pignus im-

That religion was based on the idea that the wide empire and eternal duration of Rome had been appointed by Divine decree. As distinguished from the national religion of Greece, which expressed itself in new and varied forms of art, Roman religion was one which adhered to ancient rites and expressed itself in the pomp of outward ceremonial and other impressive symbols. It acted on the imagination through the sense of vastness, pomp, stateliness, and solemnity; that of Greece through the sense of life, joy, beauty, and harmony animating its ceremonial and embodying itself in its symbols. The objects of Roman worship were almost innumerable. In addition to the greater divinities which it shared with the Greek worship, and besides the various native divinities common to it with the religion of other Italian races, Roman religion had erected temples to various abstract qualities, such as Peace, Faith, Concord, and the like. This tendency to multiply their deities, to deify mere abstractions, and to recognise a distinct deity as presiding over every common act and process of life, weakened or destroyed the sense of the personality of the gods, and thus indirectly promoted that advance to Monotheism which philosophy had made in a different direction. While the Greeks conceived of each local god or hero as a distinct person, endowed with his own human qualities and his own visible shape, and thus naturally adapted for the representations of dramatic poetry or plastic art, the Romans worshipped rather one Divine impersonal power .with many attributes and functions. The need which the popular imagination feels of some personal embodiment of the idea of Godhead probably explains the readiness with which, in the dissolution of older faiths, the worship of the Emperor became the chief symbol of the national faith.

perii conditam,' etc.  Tac. Hist. iii. 72 ; and ' Sed nihil aeque quam incendium Capitolii, ut finem imperio adesse crederent, impulerat,' iv. 54.
   The Capitol is the symbol of the eternal duration of the Empire to Virgil also :—

> Dum domus Aeneae Capitoli immobile saxum
> Accolet, imperiumque pater Romanus habebit.
> > Aen. ix. 448-9.

So far as the conceptions of the national religion of Rome, which have a powerful influence on the action of the Aeneid, enter into this Invocation, it is in the recognition of the divinity of Caesar. But here he is associated with the rural gods, who listen to the prayers of the husbandman, rather than, as elsewhere both in Horace and Virgil, with the majesty of the Roman State. The passage probably, as is suggested by Ribbeck, owes its origin to the decree of the Senate in 36 B.C., —after the naval victory gained by Agrippa over Sextus Pompeius,—by which the worship of Caesar, 'inter municipales deos,' was established. There is probably no passage in Virgil, scarcely any in Latin poetry, which must strike the modern reader as so unreal as this, or so untrue to the actual convictions of educated men. There is none in which the language of adulation appears so palpably, or in which the love of mythological allusion, as one of the conventional ornaments of poetry, appears to exercise so unfortunate an influence on the truthful feeling of the poet. It seems strange that a man of the commanding understanding of Augustus should have derived any pleasure from the supposition that he might become the son-in-law of Tethys, from the statement that the glowing Scorpion was already beginning to make room for him in the sky, or from the appeal made to him to resist the ambition of supplanting Pluto as the future ruler of Tartarus. In contrast with this state of feeling we learn to respect the masculine sense and dignity with which Tiberius disclaims the attribution of divine honours: 'I, Conscript Fathers, call you to witness and desire posterity to remember, that I am but a mortal, and am performing human duties, and consider it enough if I fill the foremost place[1]. But though it is not possible that the lines from 'Tuque adeo' to 'adsuesce vocari' should ever appear natural to us, or that we should ever read them without some feeling that they are unworthy of the manliness of a great poet, we may yet recognise some symbolical meaning in them

---

[1] Tac. Ann. iv. 38.

beyond the mere expression of overstrained eulogy. In such expressions as

>     Auctorem frugum tempestatumque potentem [1],

Virgil associates the idea of the power of Caesar with the main subject of his poem; and probably, as is pointed out by Ribbeck, he suggests the thought of the dependence of Rome and Italy for subsistence on the vigilance of their ruler [2]. In the mention of Tethys there is a reference to recent naval successes; and in the 'tibi serviat ultima Thule' there may be an allusion to the contemplated expedition to Britain, and certainly, as in so many other passages of the poetry of the age, there is a recognition of the wide empire of Rome. In the lines

>     Anne novum tardis, etc.,

we recognise the idea which connected the apotheosis of Julius Caesar with the appearance of the 'Iulium Sidus' (see Ecl. ix); while the lines

>     Nam te nec sperant Tartara regem, etc.,

read in connexion with those at the end of Book I,

>     Hunc saltem everso iuvenem succurrere saeclo
>     Ne prohibete, etc.,

are evidently prompted by the conviction that the well-being and security of the world are dependent on a single life.

In this apparent acceptance of new and old modes of belief, —in this neopaganism of art,—it is difficult to say how far we are to recognise the representations of fiction, conscious that it is fiction, as in the mythological art of the Renaissance, or how far we are in the presence of a temporary revival of a faith which satisfied a simpler time, in inconsistent conjunction with incompatible modes of modern thought. Probably not even the poets themselves, and least of all Virgil, could have given an

---

[1] 'Giver of fruits, and lord over the seasons.'
[2] Cf. Tac. Ann. iii. 54. 'At Hercule nemo refert quod Italia externae opis indiget, quod vita populi Romani per incerta maris et tempestatum cotidie volvitur. . . . Hanc, Patres Conscripti, curam sustinet princeps, haec omissa funditus rem publicam trahet.'

explanation of their real state of mind.  The dreams of an
older faith were still haunting them, though its substance was
gone.  The traditions of the Greek mythology survived, endowed with what, in the absence of any new creed, might seem
immortal life, in the pages of poets, and in the paintings and
other works of art which afforded a refined pleasure to educated
men.  The national faith of Italy and Rome still kept the outward show of life in many visible symbols, and still retained a
hold over the mass of the people.  The herds and flocks were
still believed to flourish under the kindly protection of Pales
and Faunus.  The festive pleasures of country life at the
harvest-home or the vintage season were enjoyed on old religious holidays, and formed part of ceremonies handed down
from immemorial antiquity.  The pomp and ceremonial of what
was peculiarly the Roman worship still met the eye on all great
occasions within the walls of the city :—

> Hinc albi, Clitumne, greges et maxima taurus
> Victima, saepe tuo perfusi flumine sacro,
> Romanos ad templa deum duxere triumphos[1].

The magnificent temples of deities blending the attributes of
native Italian gods with those of the gods of Olympus seemed
to preside over the tumult and active business of the Forum;
and the majesty of the Capitoline Jove was still recognised as
the manifestation of the stability and power of the State.  But
the Roman imagination was at the same time beginning to be
impressed by a new symbol of Divine agency, which was felt in
all national concerns.  The ideal majesty of Jove was merging,
as an object of veneration, in the actual majesty of Caesar, regarded as the vicegerent of the Supreme Power.  All these
phases of religious belief, Greek and Italian, old and new, some
appealing to the popular, some to the educated mind, meet in
the poetry of the Augustan Age, and nowhere in more close
conjunction than in this Invocation.  They appear in still

---

[1] 'From this land thy white herds, Clitumnus, and the bull, most stately
victim, after bathing often in thy sacred stream, have led the procession
of the Roman triumphs to the temples of the Gods.'

stranger connexion with the later results of science and philosophic thought.   It is impossible to find any principle of reconcilement in accordance with which their proper place in the reasonable intelligence of the age may be assigned to each. They came together in Virgil as a composite result of the union of his literary and philosophic tastes with his religious feeling and national sympathies.   So far as we can attach any truth of meaning to this Invocation, we must look upon it as a symbolical expression of Divine agency and superintendence in all the various fields of natural production.

Virgil is much more sparing than Lucretius in the proems to his other books.   In the second book there is a brief invocation to Liber, who is introduced, with rich pictorial colouring, as the special god of the vintage; and at lines 39–46 there is an appeal to Maecenas, which disclaims, perhaps not without some reference to the contrary practice of Lucretius, all intention to detain his hearer 'through digressions from the main theme and long preambles.'   In the fourth there is again a brief appeal to Maecenas, a statement of the subject, an admission of its homely character,—'In tenui labor,'—an expression of the hope that, even out of these materials, great glory may ensue if Apollo hears the poet's prayer and no unpropitious powers impede the course of his song.   The introduction to the third book is more extended, and more interesting from the light which it throws on the motives which determined Virgil to the choice of the subject of his epic poem.   Here, too, as in the first and second books, there is an appeal to the tutelary deities of the herds and flocks, the Italian Pales, and the 'Pastor ab Amphryso,'—the Apollo νόμιος of Greek legend and rural worship.   The associations of Greek poetry are also evoked in the reference to the woods and streams of Lycaeus, to the lowing herds of Cithaeron, to the dogs that range over Taygetus, and to the famous horses of the Argive plain.   The choice of the subject is justified by the contrast suggested between its novelty—'silvas saltusque sequamur Intactos'—and the hackneyed poems founded on mythological subjects which his immediate predecessors in poetry had written in imitation of their Alexandrine prototypes. But he indicates here, with a new application of the words of Ennius, the aspiration to compose a great national epic in celebration of the exploits of Caesar :—

> temptanda via est, qua me quoque possim
> Tollere humo victorque virum volitare per ora[1].

Under the allegory of the games which he proposed to celebrate, and the marble temple which he proposed to raise on the banks of the Mincio, he associates the thought of his early home with his ambition to rival the great works of Greek genius (for this seems to be the meaning of the lines

> Cuncta mihi, Alpheum linquens lucosque Molorchi,
> Cursibus et crudo decernet Graecia cestu)[2],—

and to spread the fame of Caesar through distant ages. This invocation must have been written later than the crowning victory of Actium, but before the plan of the Aeneid had definitely assumed shape in the poet's mind. From the allegorical representations of the designs in gold, ivory, and marble for the ornaments of the temple, and still more clearly from the direct statement

> Mox tamen ardentis accingar dicere pugnas
> Caesaris[3],

it may be inferred that his first idea was to make the contemporaneous events the main subject of his epic, and to introduce the glories of the Trojan line as accessories. Under what influence he changed this purpose, making contemporary events subsidiary and the ancient legend the main argument of his poem, will be considered in the chapters devoted to the examination of the Aeneid.

---

[1] 'I too must try to find some way by which I may rise aloft, and be borne triumphant through the mouths of men.'

[2] 'I shall have all Greece to quit Alpheus and the groves of Molorchus, and to contend before me in the race and with the cestus of raw hide.'

[3] 'Soon I shall gird myself up to celebrate the fiery battles of Caesar.'

## IV.

As affecting the arrangement and illustration of their materials, there is this essential difference between the poems of
Lucretius and Virgil, that the one is a great continuous argument, the development of speculative truths depending on one
another; and its professed aim is purely contemplative,—the
production of a certain state of mind and feeling.   The other is
the orderly exposition of a number of precepts, depending on
experience and special knowledge ; its professed aim is the
mastery over a great practical occupation.   Lucretius uses
poetry as the vehicle of science, Virgil as the instrument of a
useful art.   In the first we expect, and we find, in so far as
the poem was left completed, rigorous concentration of thought,
and an exhaustive treatment of the subject.   In the second we
expect, and we find, an orderly and convenient arrangement,
and such a selection of topics as, while producing the impression of a thorough mastery of the subject, leaves also much to
be filled up by the imagination or experience of the reader.
Still, that Virgil regarded Lucretius as his technical model may
be inferred from the use which he makes of several of his for-
mulae, such as ' Principio,' ' Quod superest,' ' His animadversis,'
' Nunc age,' ' Praeterea,' by which the framework of his argument is held together.   Virgil uses these more sparingly, and
with a more careful selection, so as, while producing the impression of continuity of thought, not to impede the pure flow of his
poetry with the mechanism of logical connexion.   He follows
Lucretius also, who here observed the practice of the Greek
didactic poets, in maintaining the liveliness of a personal address
by the frequent use of such appeals as these, ' Nonne vides,'
' Contemplator,' ' Forsitan et . . . quaeras,' ' Vidi,' ' Ausim,' etc.

In illustrating and giving novelty to his various topics Virgil
has the example of Lucretius to justify him in catching up
and dwelling on every aspect of beauty or imaginative interest
which they are capable of presenting.   And it is here that the

more careful art of Virgil, and the fact that he attached more value to the perfection of his art than to the knowledge he imparts, give him that technical superiority over the older writer which, notwithstanding the tamer interest of his subject, and perhaps the tamer character of his own genius, has made the Georgics a poem much more familiar to the world than the 'De Rerum Natura.' Virgil, for one thing, enjoys greater freedom of omitting any set of topics,—any of those details on which Cato or Varro would have felt themselves bound to be specially explicit,—which would detract unduly from the beauty and general amenity of his exposition; or by a simple touch (such as the 'Ne saturare fimo pingui,' etc.) he can suggest the necessity of attending to such topics, while leaving their full realisation to the reader. He thus, by greater selection and elimination of his materials, avoids the monotony and the long prosaic interspaces between the grander bursts of poetry which his vast argument imposes on Lucretius. But, further, he avails himself of many more resources to give variety of interest and literary charm to the topics which he successively deals with. Each and all of these topics,—the processes of ploughing and sowing, the signs of the weather, the grafting of trees and the pruning of the vine, the qualities of horses and cattle, the tending of sheep and goats, the observation of the habits of bees,— bring him into immediate contact with the genial influences of the outward world. The vastness as well as the abstract character of his subject forces Lucretius to pass through many regions which seem equally removed from this genial presence and from all human associations. It is only the enthusiasm of discovery —the delight in purely intellectual processes—that bears him buoyantly through these dreary spaces; and it is only the knowledge that from time to time glimpses of illimitable power and wonder are opened up to him, and admiration for the energy and clear vision of his guide, that compel the flagging reader to accompany him. But Virgil leads his readers through scenes, tamer indeed and more familiar, yet always bright and smiling with some homely charm, or rich and glowing with the 'pomp of cultivated nature,' or fresh and picturesque with the charm of meadow, river-bank, or woodland pasture.

The secret of the power of Lucretius as an interpreter of Nature lies in his recognition of the sublimity of natural law in ordinary phenomena. The secret of Virgil's power lies in the insight and long-practised meditation through which he abstracts the single element of beauty from common sights and the ordinary operations of industry. Thus, to take one or two instances of the way in which the charm of Nature is communicated to the drudgery of rural labour :—what a sense of refreshment to eye and ear is conveyed by the lines which describe the practical remedies by which the farmer mitigates the burning drought of summer :—

> Et cum exustus ager morientibus aestuat herbis,
> Ecce supercilio clivosi tramitis undam
> Elicit ; illa cadens raucum per levia murmur
> Saxa ciet, scatebrisque arentia temperat arva[1].

Again, what a picture of rich woodland beauty is created out of the occurrence, in the midst of practical directions, of some homely traditional maxims, in accordance with which farmers judged of the probable abundance of their crop :—

> Contemplator item, cum se nux plurima silvis
> Induet in florem et ramos curvabit olentis :
> Si superant fetus, pariter frumenta sequentur,
> Magnaque cum magno veniet tritura calore[2].

So too, in a technical account of the different varieties of soil, he brings before the mind, by a single descriptive touch, a picture of abundant harvest-fields,—

---

[1] 'And when the parched field is all hot and its blades of corn are withering, look! from the brow of its sloping channel he tempts forth the rushing stream : it as it falls awakens a hoarse murmur among the smooth stones, and with its bubbling waters cools the tilled land.' i. 107–110.

[2] 'Mark too, when in the woods, the walnut, in great numbers, clothes itself in blossom and weighs down the fragrant branches, if there is abundance of fruit, the corn crops will likewise be in abundance, and there will come a great threshing with a great heat.' i. 187–190.

> non ullo ex aequore cernes
> Plura domum tardis decedere plaustra iuvencis[1];

and enables us to feel the charm of a rich pastoral country,—
with its lonely woodland glades, its brimming river flowing past
mossy and grassy banks, and the shelter and shade of its caves
and rocks, in the midst of homely directions for the care of
mares before they foal :—

> Saltibus in vacuis pascunt et plena secundum
> Flumina, muscus ubi et viridissima gramine ripa,
> Speluncaeque tegant, et saxea procubet umbra[2].

In the inculcation of his practical precepts his aim is even
more to exalt the dignity and to exhibit the delight of rural
labour, than to explain its methods or inculcate its utility.

He imparts a peculiar vivacity, grace, and tenderness to his
treatment of many topics by the analogy which he suggests
between the life of Nature and of man. The perception of
analogy originates in the philosophical and imaginative thought
of Lucretius; and it is in the second Book, in the composition
of which, as Mr. Munro has shown, Virgil's mind was saturated
with the ideas, feelings, and language of his predecessor, that
this element of poetical interest is most conspicuous. The following examples, occurring in the technical exposition of the
growth and tending of trees, are all taken from the second
Book; and two of them, those marked *g* and *h*, are immediately suggested by Lucretius :—

[3] *a.* Parva sub ingenti matris se subicit umbra.
 *b.* tenero abscindens de corpore matrum.
 *c.* Exuerint silvestrem animum.

---

[1] 'There is no other kind of plain from which you will see more wains
wending their way home with the lagging steers.' ii. 205–206.

[2] 'They let them feed in lonely pastures, and by the bank of brimming
rivers, where moss abounds and the grass is greenest, and where caves give
shelter, and the shadow of some rock is cast far in front.' iii. 143–145.

[3] *a.* 'The young plant shoots up under the mighty shadow of its
mother.'

 *b.* 'Rending them from the loving body of their mother.'

 *c.* 'Will cast off their woodland spirit.'

[1] *d.*  Miraturque novas frondes et non sua poma.
  *e.*  Mutatam ignorent subito ne semina matrem.
  *f.*  atque animos tollent sata.
  *g.*  Viribus eniti quarum et contemnere ventos
     Adsuescant.
  *h.*  Ac dum prima novis adolescit frondibus aetas,
     Parcendum teneris.
  *i.*  Ante reformidant ferrum.
  *k.*  Praecipue dum frons tenera imprudensque laborum.

Many more examples might be added from the other Books.
The force of many of the epithets applied to material objects,
such as 'ignava,' 'laeta et fortia,' 'maligni,' 'infelix,' etc., consists in the suggestion of a kind of personal life underlying and
animating the silent processes of Nature.

Virgil, too, like Lucretius, shows the close observation of
a naturalist, and a genuine sympathy with the pains and pleasures of all living things, especially of the animals associated
with the toil or amusement of men.   The interest of the third
Book arises, to a great degree, from the truth and vivacity of
feeling with which he observes and identifies himself with the
ways and dispositions of these fellow-labourers of man,—with
the pride and emulation of the horse, the fidelity and companionship of the dog, the combative courage of the bull and
his sense of pain and dishonour in defeat, the patience of the
steer and his brotherly feeling for his yoke-fellow in toil, and
with the attachment of sheep and goats to their offspring and
to their familiar haunts [2].   The interest of the fourth Book,
again, turns on the analogy implied between the pursuits,

---

[1] *d.*  'And marvels at its strange leaves and fruits not its own.'
  *e.*  'Lest the plants through the sudden change should fail to recognise
     their mother.'
  *f.*  'And the plants will lift up their hearts.'
  *g.*  'By their strength they may become accustomed to mount aloft and
     despise the winds.'
  *h.*  'And while they are still in the first stage of growth or their
     leaves are new, you must spare their infancy.'
  *i.*  'Before that they shrink from the steel.'
  *k.*  'Especially while the leaf is still tender, and all unwitting of its
     trials.'
[2] As an instance of the last, cf. iii. 316, 317 :—
     Atque ipsae memores redeunt in tecta, suosque
     Ducunt.

fortunes, wars, and state-policy of bee-communities and of
men.   It is the sense of this analogy that imparts a meaning
deeper than that demanded by the obvious force of the words—
a more pathetic feeling of the vanity of all earthly strife—to
that final touch in the description of the combat in mid-air
between two hosts, led by rival chiefs :—

> Hi motus animorum atque haec certamina tanta
> Pulveris exigui iactu compressa quiescunt [1].

In thus relieving the dryness of technical detail, by availing
himself of every aspect of beauty associated with it, and by
imparting the vivacity of human relations and sensibility to
natural objects, Virgil makes use of the same resources as
elicit springs of poetic feeling from many of the dry and stony
wastes through which the argument of Lucretius leads him.
There are others however employed by Virgil, which Lucretius
uses more sparingly or not at all.   There are, in the first place,
all those which arise out of the conception of the 'human force,'
impersonated in the 'sturdy ditcher,' the 'farmer roused to
anger,' the 'active peasant,' contrasting with and conflicting
with that other conception of the life of Nature.   And as in
Lucretius the speculative ideas, penetrating through every
region of the wide domain traversed by him, elicit some poetic
life out of its barrenest places, so the two speculative ideas,
of Nature as a living force, and of man's labour, vigilance,
forethought in their relation to that force, impart a feeling of
imaginative delight to Virgil's account of the most common
details of the husbandman's toil.   The strength and vivacity
thus imparted to the style has been well illustrated by Professor Conington in his Introduction to the Georgics.   It may
be noted however that, even in this imaginative recognition
of the strength and force of man in conflict with the force of

---

[1] 'These passions of their hearts and these desperate battles are all
stilled to rest, by the check of a little handful of dust.'   Compare Horace's
line, Od. i. 28. 3 :—
> *Pulveris exigui* prope litus parva Matinum
> **Munera.**

Nature, Virgil is still following in the tracks of Lucretius.
Such expressions as

> Ingemere et terram pressis proscindere aratris—
> ferro molirier arva—
> magnos manibus divellere montes—

in the older poet first opened up this vein which was wrought
with such effectual results by his successor.  But Conington
has, in his notes, drawn attention to another vein of feeling,
which is all Virgil's own, and which enables him to give further
variety and charm to these homely details.  The husbandman
has not only his hard and incessant struggle—'labor improbus'
—but he has the delight of success, the joy of contemplating
the new beauty and richness, created by the strength of his
arm.  This feeling breaks out in the 'Ecce' of the line already
quoted,—

> Ecce supercilio clivosi tramitis undam;

in the 'iuvat' of

> iuvat Ismara Baccho
> Conserere, atque olea magnum vestire Taburnum[1];—

and in the 'canit' of the line

> Iam canit effectos extremus vinitor antes[2].

Another set of associations, interwoven with the rich and
firm texture of the poem, are those derived from earlier science
and poetry.  Of the resources of learned allusion Lucretius
makes a singularly sparing use.  The localising epithets and
mythological names in which Virgil's poem abounds possessed
no attraction for his austerer genius, nourished by the severe
models of an older time, and rejecting the ornaments and
distractions from the main interest familiar to Alexandrine
literature.  Virgil had already shown in the Eclogues this
tendency to overlay his native thought with the spoils of Greek
learning.  Such phrases as 'Strymoniae grues,' 'Pelusiacae
lentis,' 'Amyclaeum canem,' 'Idumaeas palmas,'—the refe-

---

[1] 'What joy to plant Ismarus with the vine, or to clothe the mighty
sides of Taburnus with the olive.'
[2] 'And now the last vintager sings with joy at completing all his rows.'

rences to the 'harvests of Mysia and Gargarus,' to the 'vines of Ismarus,' 'Cytorus, waving with boxwood,' etc. etc., must have been charged, for Virgil's contemporaries, in a way which they cannot be for a modern reader, with the memories of foreign travel or of residence in remote provinces, or with the interest attaching to lands recently made known. To us their chief interest is that by their strangeness they enhance the effect with which the more familiar names of Italian places are used. Thus the contrasted pictures of the illimitable pastures of Libya and of the wintry wastes of Scythia enable us to realise more exquisitely the charm of that fresh[1] Italian pastoral scene immediately preceding, the description of which combines the tender feeling of the Eclogues with the deeper realism of the Georgics. Thus too the great episode on the beauty and riches of Italy (ii. 136–176) is introduced in immediate contrast to the account of the prodigal luxuriance of Nature in the forests and jungles of the East. But even to a modern reader such expressions as these—

> Vos silvae amnesque Lycaei—
>   vocat alta voce Cithaeron—
>     O, ubi campi
> Spercheusque, et virginibus bacchata Lacaenis
> Taygeta, etc.,

seem to bear with them faint echoes from a far-off time, of some ideal life of poetry and adventure in the free range and 'otia dia' of pastoral scenes,—of some more intimate union of the human soul with the soul of mountains and woodland than is granted to the common generations of men. On Virgil himself, to whom the whole of Greek poetry and legend was an open page, the spell which they exercised was of the same kind as that exercised by the magic of classical allusion on the poets and painters of the Renaissance.

The contrast between Lucretius and Virgil, as regards their relation to the ancient mythology, has already appeared in the examination of the Invocations to their respective poems. This

---

[1] iii. 321–338.

contrast is still more brought out by the large use which Virgil makes of mythological allusions in the body of his poem, as compared with the rare, and generally polemical, references to the subject in Lucretius.  Virgil recalls the tales and poetical representations of mythology sometimes by some suggestive epithet, or other qualifying expression, as in speaking of 'poppies steeped in the sleep of Lethe,' 'Halcyons dear to Thetis,' 'the Cyllenian star,' 'the slow-rolling wains of the Eleusinian mother,' and the like.  More frequently however he does this by direct mention of some of the more familiar, and occasionally of some of the more recondite, tales which had supplied materials to earlier poets and painters.  Thus, in connexion with the topic of lucky and unlucky days, he hints at the tale of the war of the Giants with the Olympian gods, at that of Scylla and Nisus in connexion with the signs of the weather, at that of the Centaurs and Lapithae—the 'brawl fought to the death over the wine cup'—in the account of the vine, at that of the daughter of Inachus tormented in her wanderings by the vengeance of Juno in connexion with the plague of flies with which cattle were afflicted, etc. etc.  Less familiar stories, of picturesque adventure or of a kind of weird mystery, are revived in the passages—

> Talis et ipse iubam cervice effudit equina
> Coniugis adventu pernix Saturnus, et altum
> Pelion hinnitu fugiens implevit acuto[1],

and

> Munere sic niveo lanae, si credere dignum est,
> Pan deus Arcadiae captam te, Luna, fefellit,
> In nemora alta vocans; nec tu aspernata vocantem[2].

Such allusions came much more home to an ancient than to a modern reader.  They were familiar to him from the pages of

---

[1] 'So too looked even Saturn, when with nimble movement, at the approach of his wife, he let the mane toss on his neck, and, as he sped away, made high Pelion ring with his shrill neighing.'

[2] 'So with the snowy gift of wool, if one may believe the tale, did Pan, the God of Arcadia, charm and beguile thee, O Luna, calling thee into the deep groves; nor didst thou scorn his call.'

poets, or from pictures adorning the walls of his own town and country-houses, or seen in the temples and other sacred places of famous Greek and Asiatic cities, and forming great part of the attraction of those cities to travellers then, as the pictures seen in the galleries, palaces, and churches of Rome, Florence, and Venice do to travellers now.  But though the colours of these poetic fancies have faded for us, they are felt to be a legitimate source of variety in the poem, and to be an element of interest connecting the humbler cares of the country-people with the refined tastes of the educated class.  They are not introduced as a substitute for truthful representation of fact, but rather as adding a new grace to this representation. Neither do they, as in Propertius, overlay the main subject of the poem by their redundant use.  They probably produced the same kind of impression on an ancient reader, as allusions from the works of Latin or Italian poets in Spenser or Milton produce on a modern reader.  Occasionally they may seem weak and faulty from their incongruity with the thought with which they are associated.  Thus in the passage at i. 60, etc.,—

> Continuo has leges aeternaque foedera certis
> Imposuit natura locis, quo tempore primum
> Deucalion vacuum lapides iactavit in orbem,
> Unde homines nati, durum genus[1],

the mind is offended by the juxtaposition of the great thought, which Lucretius had striven so earnestly to impress on the world, with one of the most unmeaning fables that ever violated all possibilities of natural law.  So too the contrast between the artistic and recondite elegance of the lines (iii. 549–550),

> Quaesitaeque nocent artes; cessere magistri
> Phillyrides Chiron, Amythaoniusque Melampus[2],

---

[1] 'These laws and everlasting covenants were at once established by Nature for particular places, from the time when Deucalion first cast stones into the empty world, whence men, a hard race, were born.'
[2] 'The resources of art prove baneful: its masters retired baffled, Chiron, son of Philyra, and Melampus, son of Amythaon.'

and the grand, solemn realism of the parallel passage in the account of the Plague of Athens,—

> Mussabat tacito medicina timore [1],—

makes us feel how unapproachable by all the resources of art and learning is that direct force of insight united to fulness of feeling with which Lucretius was endowed above nearly every poet, ancient or modern.

Equally remote from the practice of Lucretius is the use made by Virgil of that amalgamation of mythological fancy with the rudiments of science which assigned names, personality, and a poetical history to the various constellations :—

> Pleiadas, Hyadas, claramque Lycaonis Arcton.

But Virgil's practice is in accordance with that of all the Greek poets from Homer and Hesiod down to the latest Alexandrine writers. He thus enriches the treatment of his subject with the interest of early science, and with the associations of the open-air life of hunters, herdsmen, and mariners in primitive times. Lucretius is impressed by the splendour, wonder, and severe majesty of the stars as they actually appear to us,— 'aeterni sidera mundi,' 'caeli labentia signa,' 'noctis signa severa,'—without any superadded association of mythology or antiquity. Neither does he use that other resource, by which Virgil adds an antique lustre to his subject—the introduction of quaint phrases and turns of speech, derived from Hesiod, such as 'nudus ara, sere nudus,' 'laudato ingentia rura, Exiguum colito,' or those derived from the traditional peasant-lore of Italy,—'hiberno laetissima pulvere farra,'—which Virgil intermingles with the classic elegance of his style. Still less could Lucretius appeal to the associations of the popular religion. Such expressions as 'fas et iura sinunt,' 'hiemes orate serenas,' 'nulla religio vetuit,' and the mention of old religious ceremonies and practices prevalent in the country districts, such as that at i. 345,

---

[1] ' The healing art muttered in speechless fear.'

> Terque novas circum felix eat hostia fruges[1],

and at ii. 387,

> Et te, Bacche, vocant per carmina laeta, tibique
> Oscilla ex alta suspendunt mollia pinu[2],

not only afford a legitimate relief to the inculcation of practical precepts in the Georgics, but impress on the mind the dignity imparted to the most ordinary drudgery by the sense of its association with the religious life of man.

On the other hand, it is to be noticed how sparingly Virgil uses one of the grandest resources in the repertory of Lucretius,— that of imaginative analogies, through which familiar or unseen phenomena are made great or palpable by association with other phenomena which immediately affect the imagination with a sense of wonder and sublimity. The apprehension of these analogies between great things in different spheres proceeds from the inventive and intellectual faculty in the imagination,— that by which intuitions of vast discoveries are obtained before observation and reason can verify them; and in this faculty of imaginative reason Lucretius is as superior to Virgil, as Virgil is to him in artistic accomplishment. One of the few 'similes' in the Georgics is that often-quoted one, in which the difficulty which man has in holding his own against the natural deterioration of things is compared to the difficulty which a rower has in holding his own against a strong adverse current (i. 201–203):—

> Non aliter, quam qui adverso vix flumine lembum
> Remigiis subigit, si bracchia forte remisit
> Atque illum in praeceps prono rapit alveus amni[3].

There is suggestiveness and verisimilitude in this image. But it does not make us feel the enlargement of mind and the poetic thrill of the thought which are produced by many of the great

---

[1] 'Thrice let the auspicious victim pass around the young crops.'

[2] 'And invoke thee, Bacchus, in their joyous chants, and in honour of thee hang soft faces waving in the wind from the high pine tree.'

[3] 'Just as happens to the rower who scarcely keeps his boat against the stream, if he slackens his stroke, and has it swept headlong down the channel of the river.'

illustrative images in Lucretius.   Virgil too is much inferior to
the older poet, and much less original, in the general reflections
on life which he occasionally introduces,—such as that at iii.
**66,—**

> Optima quaeque dies miseris mortalibus aevi
> Prima fugit ; subeunt morbi tristisque senectus[1].

In so far as the thought here expressed is true, the truth cannot
be said to be either new or profound.

The inferiority of Virgil to Lucretius, in that faculty of imagination, which perceives an inner identity between great forces in
the material and in the spiritual world, is apparent also from a
comparison of their respective diction.   There is often a creativeness, a boldness of invention and insight into the deepest
nature of things, in the language of Lucretius, such as did not
reappear again in Italian poetry till more than thirteen centuries
had passed, and which makes us feel how much nearer he was
in many ways than any other Latin poet to our modern modes
of thought and feeling.   There is, on the other hand, scarcely
any great poem from which so few striking and original images
can be quoted as from the Georgics.   The figurative language
arising out of the perception of the analogy between the vital
processes of Nature and various modes of human sensibility is
rather like that unconscious identification of Nature with humanity out of which mythology arose, than the conscious recognition of some common force or law operating in totally distinct
spheres.   And even this identity or analogy between the life
of Nature and of man is not conceived with such power and
passion in Virgil as in Lucretius.   But if Virgil's language is
inferior to that of his predecessor not only in vivid creative
power, but in clearness and idiomatic purity, it is much superior
in the uniform level of poetical excellence which it maintains.
In this respect Virgil compares favourably with some of the
greatest masters of style among English poets, for example with
Wordsworth, Shelley, and Byron.   There is nothing redundant

---

[1] ' The best days of life are those which fly first from unhappy mortals :
then disease steals on, and sad old age.'

or monotonous in the style of the Georgics, nothing trivial or mean; while always rich and pregnant with suggestion, it is never overstrained or overloaded; while always elevated to the pitch of poetry, it never seems to soar too far above the familiar aspects of the world. Nothing shows the perfect sanity of Virgil's genius more clearly than his entire exemption from the besetting sin of our own didactic poetasters of last century—a sin from which even Wordsworth himself is not altogether free —that of calling common things by pompous names, and of dignifying trifles by applying heroic phrases to them. If he seems sometimes to deviate from this habitual temperance of manner in the account of his bee communities, he does so purposely, to convey through this gentle vein of irony something of that pensive meditativeness of spirit which is produced in him by reflection on the transitory passions, joys, and vicissitudes of our mortal life.

The general superiority of Virgil's art to that of Lucretius is equally apparent in his rhythm. The powerful movement of spirit which Lucretius feels in the presence of the sublimer spectacle of Nature and of the more solemn things of human life does indeed produce isolated effects of majestic speech and sonorously rhythmical cadence, swelling above the deep, strong, monotonous flow of his ordinary verse, which neither Virgil nor any other poet has surpassed. But in variety, equable smoothness and grandeur, in that tempered harmony of sound which never disappoints and never burdens the ear, it may be doubted whether the musical art of any poet has maintained such a uniform level of excellence as that maintained in the Georgics. Virgil produces more varied effects than Lucretius can do even in his more finished passages, while at the same time binding himself by stricter laws in the composition of his verse. This he does by the greater variety and greater frequency of his pauses, by uniformly placing the words of strength and emphasis in the strong positions of the line, and by a skilful regulation of the succession of long and short, of accentuated and unaccentuated syllables, and of lines of a more rapid or slower move-

ment.  The result is that the feeling of his rhythm becomes a
main element in the realisation of his meaning.

The principal resources by which Virgil, in the didactic exposition of his subject, avoids that monotony of effect which was
likely to arise from the strong Roman concentration of purpose
with which his work was executed, and, without deviating from
the true perception of facts, is able to invest a somewhat narrow
range of interests with charm and dignity,—

angustis hunc addere rebus honorem,—

are thus seen to be, first his feeling of Nature, of man's relation
to it, of his joy in the results of his toil, and, secondly, the associations of strange lands, of mythology, of antiquity, and of
religious custom.  The instruments by which these resources
are made available are the careful choice and combinations of
words and the well-practised melody of his verse.  These resources and instruments have been considered in relation to and
contrast with those employed by Lucretius.  There is, moreover, this difference between the method of the two poets, that
Virgil is much more of a conscious artist, that he seems to go
more in search of illustrations and the means of artistic embel-
lishment, that he endeavours to make for himself a wreath,
'undique decerptam;' while the occasional accessions of a
more powerful poetic interest to the ordinary exposition of
Lucretius arise naturally in the process of his argument, from
the habit of his mind to observe the outward world, the ways of
all living things, and the condition of man in their intimate
connexion with the great speculative ideas of his philosophy.
His modes of varying the interest of his subject and adorning
it are thus more simple and homogeneous; they work more in
harmony with the purpose of his poem, so as to produce a
pervading unity of sentiment and impression.  The variety of
resources used by Virgil gives, at first sight, a composite character to his art.  But there is, deeper than this apparent composite character, an inner unity of tone and sentiment pervading
the whole work.  The source of this unity is the deep love and

pride which he feels in every detail of his subject, from the great human interests with which these details are associated in his mind. What these human interests are is brought out prominently in the episodes of the poem, which still remain to be considered.

## V.

The finest poetry in the didactic poems of Lucretius and of Virgil and the thoughts which give the highest interest to their respective poems are contained in passages of considerable length, rising out of the general level or undulations of the poem into elevations which at first sight seem isolated and unconnected with one another. It may be doubted whether even the power of thought and style in Lucretius could have secured immortality to a mere systematic exposition of the Atomic philosophy; nor could the mere didactic exposition of the precepts of agriculture, though varied by all the art and resources of Virgil, have gained for the Georgics the unique place that poem holds in literature. It is in their episodes that each poet brings out the moral grandeur, and thereby justifies the choice of his subject. In Lucretius, these passages are introduced sometimes in the ordinary march of his argument, more often at the beginning or completion of some important division of it, and are intended both to add poetical charm to the subject and to show man's true relation to the Universe, and the attitude of mind which that relation demands of him. The object of Virgil in some of his minor and in one or two of his larger episodes may be merely to relieve the dryness of exposition by some descriptive or reflective charm. But even these passages will in general be found to draw attention to the religious, ethical, or national bearing of his subject.

Some of these passages have been suggested by parallel passages either in Hesiod or Lucretius. The largest of all the episodes, that with which the poem concludes, has, for reasons already considered, only a slight and external relation to the

great ideas and interests with which the poem deals. But the
three most important passages, those of most original invention
and profound feeling, viz. those at Book I. 466 to the end of
the Book, Book II. 136 to 177, and also from line 458 to the
end, serve like those great cardinal passages in the Aeneid, in
which the action is projected from a remote legendary past
into the actual present, to bring into light the true central
interest of the poem,—the bearing of the whole subject on the
greatness and well-being of the Italian race.

Any of the passages which are not needed for the special
practical purpose of the poem may be regarded as episodical,
such, for instance, as that thoroughly Lucretian passage in
Book I. in which the feelings of rooks are explained on purely
physical principles, or that passage of Book IV. inspired by the
teaching of an opposite school, in which the theory of a divine
principle pervading the world—the same theory as that accepted
as his own by Virgil in Aeneid VI.—is enunciated as a probable explanation of the higher instinct of the bees. And it
is characteristic of the eclecticism of Virgil's mode of thought,
and also of the lingering regret with which he regards the
evanescent fancies of the old mythology, that he not only combines these tenets of the most materialistic and most spiritualistic
philosophies in the same poem, but that the philosophic or
theosophic solution of Book IV. 219, etc. comes shortly after a
passage in which the same phenomenon is accounted for on
the ground of the service rendered by bees in feeding the
infant Jove in the cavern of Mount Dicte. Another passage
of a scientific rather than a philosophic character is that at
Book I. 233, etc., in which the five zones girding the heaven
and the earth are described in language closely translated from
Eratosthenes. Besides the scientific interest which this passage
must have had to the poet's contemporaries, it serves to draw
forth Virgil's antagonism to the religious unbelief of Lucretius,
in the expression

Munere concessae divom,

and also to imply his dissent from the emphatic denial which

Lucretius gives, at Book I. 1065, to the Stoical belief in the existence of the Antipodes :—

> Illi cum videant solem, nos sidera noctis
> Cernere, et alternis nobiscum tempora caeli
> Dividere, et noctes parilis agitare diebus[1].

Another passage of a semi-philosophical character is that at Book III. 242–283, in which the Lucretian idea of the all-pervading influence of the physical emotion of love over all living things in sea, earth, and air,—an idea in which Lucretius was anticipated by Euripides[2] and by other earlier Greek poets, —appears in combination with the purely mythological conception of the direct personal agency of Venus, and with the legend of 'the mares of Glaucus of Potniae.'

More important than these, as illustrative of the main ideas and feelings of the poem, but still subsidiary to the greater episodes, are the following: Book I. 121–159, Book II. 323–345; and in the same class may be included III. 339–383, and IV. 125–148. The first of these, 'Pater ipse colendi,' etc., is immediately suggested by Hesiod's account of the Golden Age; but the greater part of it, the account of the progress of the various arts of life, is simply a summary of the long account of human progress at the end of the fifth Book of Lucretius. The idea of the purpose with which Providence has imposed labour on man is Virgil's own; and this thought contributes much of its ethical meaning to the poem. The passage 'Ver adeo frondi nemorum,' etc., in which all the glory of Nature as she unfolds herself in the exuberant life of an Italian spring is described in lines of surpassing beauty and tenderness, is thoroughly Lucretian in feeling, idea, and expression. The charm of climate, of vegetation, and of life is in complete harmony with the specially Italian character of

---

[1] 'When they behold the Sun, that we see the stars of night, and that they share alternately with us the divisions of the sky, and pass their nights parallel to our days.'

[2] The passage in the Georgics may be compared with those passages which Mr. Munro quotes in his note to Lucret. i. 1.

the second Book. The digression at Book III. 339, 'Quid tibi pastores Libyae,' containing the elaborate picture of a Scythian winter, suggested by the winter scene in Hesiod, also serves through the effect of contrast to heighten the charm of the fresh pastoral life of Italy described in the lines immediately preceding.

The actual description of winter has been criticised unfavourably, and not altogether without justice, by one of the most independent and at the same time most scholarly of English critics[1], who compares it with a corresponding passage in Thomson. It is inferior in simplicity and direct force of representation to the corresponding picture in Hesiod. Virgil's imagination seems to require that even where the objects or scenes he describes are taken from books, they should be such that he could verify them in his own experience. It is this apparent verification, where the subject is not originally suggested by his own observation, that imparts the marvellous truthfulness to his art. Such lines as those—

> Aeraque dissiliunt volgo—

to

> Stiriaque impexis induruit horrida barbis—[2]

convey a less real impression of winter than the single line— an idealised generalisation from many actual winters—which ends the description of the various occupations and field-sports which an Italian winter offers to the husbandman :—

> Cum nix alta iacet, glaciem cum flumina trudunt[3].

Perhaps none of the minor episodes recurs to the mind so often with so keen a feeling of delight as the passage at IV. 125 to 148, beginning 'Namque sub Oebaliae,' etc. Virgil here introduces himself in his own person, and draws a picture

---

[1] W. Savage Landor.
[2] 'And their brazen vessels constantly split asunder, and the rough icicle froze on their unkempt beards.'
[3] 'When the snow lies deep, when the rivers force the masses of ice slowly down.'

of one whom he had known, and who had interested him as
actually realising that life of labour and of happiness in the
results of his labour, which in the body of the poem is held
up as an abstract ideal.   The scene of this vivid reminiscence,
—the district

> Qua niger umectat flaventia culta Galaesus [1],—

seems to have had peculiar attraction both for Virgil and
Horace.   It is there—

> umbrosi subter pineta Galaesi—

that Propertius pictures to himself Virgil meditating his Aeneid
and still conning over his earlier Eclogues—

> Thyrsin et attritis Daphnin harundinibus.

It is to 'that nook of earth' that Horace looks, if the unkind
Fates forbid his residence at his favourite Tibur, for a resting-
place for his ' age to wear away in.'   But it is not only to the
local charm that attention is drawn, and to the beauty of plant,
flower, and fruit, created by the labour of love which the old
Cilician gardener—some survivor probably from the Eastern
wars of Pompey—bestowed on his neglected spot of ground.
Here also the true moral of the poem is pointed, that in the
life of rural industry there is a deep source of happiness altogether independent of wealth, and which wealth cannot buy :—

> Regum aequabat opes animis, seraque revertens
> Nocte domum dapibus mensas onerabat inemptis [2].

A more prominent place is assumed by the two episodes
with which the third and fourth Books close.   In the first of
these, which extends from line 478 to 566, and which describes
a great outbreak of cattle-plague among the Noric Alps and
the district round the Timavus,—a locality which seems to
have had a special attraction to Virgil's imagination [3],—he
aims at painting a rival picture to that of the plague at Athens

---

[1] 'Where dark Galaesus waters the yellowing cornfields.'
[2] 'In his heart he enjoyed wealth equal to the wealth of kings; and
as he returned late at night he loaded his board with a feast unbought.'
[3] Cf. Ecl. viii. 6; Aen. i. 244.

with which the poem of Lucretius ends.   It would be unfair to
compare the unfinished piece of the older poet, overcrowded
as it is with detail and technical phraseology, with an elaborate
specimen of Virgil's descriptive power, exercised on a kind of
subject in which the speculative genius of the one poet gave
him no advantage over the careful and truthful art of the other.
Yet, as has been already pointed out[1], there are here and there
strokes of imaginative power in the larger sketch, and marks
of insight into human nobleness, roughly indeed expressed, as
at 1243–6—

> Qui fuerant autem praesto, contagibus ibant
> Atque labore, pudor quem tum cogebat obire
> Blandaque lassorum vox mixta voce querellae.
> Optimus hoc leti genus ergo quisque subibat[2]—

in which the sincerity of the older master still asserts itself.
There is great beauty however of pastoral scene, of pathos and
human sympathy, of ethical contrast between the simple wants
of the lower animals and the artificial luxury of human life,
in Virgil's description.   In the lines 520–522 one of those
scenes in which he most delighted is brought before the imagination :—

> Non umbrae altorum nemorum, non mollia possunt
> Prata movere animum, non qui per saxa volutus
> Purior electro campum petit amnis[3].

The last element in the picture suggests at once the ' Saxosas
inter decurrunt flumina valles' of the Eclogues, and the lines
earlier in the book—

> Saltibus in vacuis pascunt et plena secundum
> Flumina.

And the whole feeling of the passage is in harmony with that
in Lucretius, ii. 361 :—

---

[1] Cf. supra, p. 239.

[2] 'Those who ministered to them, came into close contact and bore the
labour, which a feeling of honour compelled them to undergo, and the appealing voice of the weary sufferers, mingling with the voice of their com-
plaining.   It was in this way accordingly that the best men died.'

[3] 'Neither the shade of the high groves, nor the soft meadows can rouse
any feeling, nor the river which rolling over stones in a stream purer than
amber hurries to the plain.'

> Nec tenerae salices atque herbae rore vigentes
> Fluminaque illa queunt summis labentia ripis
> Oblectare animum, sumptamque avertere curam [1].

And in thorough harmony both with the pathos and the ethical feeling in Lucretius are the following :—

> it tristis arator,
> Maerentem abiungens fraterna morte iuvencum [2]:

and

> Quid labor aut benefacta iuvant? quid vomere terras
> Invertisse gravis? atqui non Massica Bacchi
> Munera, non illis epulae nocuere repostae:
> Frondibus et victu pascuntur simplicis herbae,
> Pocula sunt fontes liquidi atque exercita cursu
> Flumina, nec somnos abrumpit cura salubris [3].

[1] 'Nor can the tender willows and the grass fresh with dew, and the rivers gliding level with their banks, delight her heart, and banish her sorrow.'

[2] 'The ploughman goes sadly on his way, separating the sorrowing steer from his dead brother.' The truth of this picture is confirmed by a modern writer, who, in her idyllic stories from the rural life of France, seems from time to time, better than any modern poet, to reproduce the Virgilian feeling of Nature. 'Dans le haut du champ un vieillard, dont le dos large et la figure sévère rappelaient celui d'Holbein, mais dont les vêtements n'annonçaient pas la misère, poussait gravement son *areau* de forme antique, traîné par deux bœufs tranquilles, à la robe d'un jaune pâle, véritables patriarches de la prairie, hauts de taille, un peu maigres, les cornes longues et rabattues, de ces vieux travailleurs qu'une longue habitude a rendus *frères*, comme on les appelle dans nos campagnes, et qui, privés l'un de l'autre, se refusent au travail avec un nouveau compagnon et se laissent mourir de chagrin. Les gens qui ne connaissent pas la campagne taxent de fable l'amitié du bœuf pour son camarade d'attelage. Qu'ils viennent voir au fond de l'étable un pauvre animal maigre, exténué, battant de sa queue inquiète ses flancs décharnés, soufflant avec effroi et dédain sur la nourriture qu'on lui présente, les yeux toujours tournés vers la porte, en grattant du pied la place vide à ses côtés, flairant les jougs et les chaînes que son compagnon a portés, et l'appelant sans cesse avec de déplorables mugissements. Le bouvier dira: "C'est une paire de bœufs perdue: son frère est mort, et celui-là ne travaillera plus. Il faudrait pouvoir l'engraisser pour l'abattre; mais il ne veut pas manger, et bientôt il sera mort de faim."' La Mare au Diable. G. Sand.
The famous picture in Lucret. ii. 355–366,
            At mater viridis . . . . notumque requirit,
shows a similar observation of the strength of bovine affection.

[3] 'What avail all their toil or their services to man? what that they have upturned the heavy earth with the plough-share? and yet they have received no harm from Massic vintages or luxurious banquets; their food is leaves and simple grass, their drink is the water of fresh springs, and rivers kept bright by their speed; and no care breaks their wholesome sleep.'

If the space assigned to the different episodes is to be regarded as the measure of their importance, the long episode at the end of the fourth Book, from line 315 to 558, would have to be regarded as of nearly equal value to all the others put together. And yet, notwithstanding the metrical beauty of the passage, it must be difficult for any one who is penetrated by the pervading sentiment of the Georgics to reach this point in the poem without a strong feeling of regret that the jealousy of Augustus had interfered with its original conclusion. As a Greek fable, composed after some Alexandrine model, mainly concerned with the fortunes of Orpheus and Eurydice,—for the shepherd Aristaeus, the

> cultor nemorum cui pinguia Ceae
> Ter centum nivei tondent dumeta iuvenci [1],

really plays altogether a secondary part in the episode,—it has little to do with rural life, and nothing at all to do with Italy. Its professed object is to give a fabulous explanation of an impossible phenomenon, though one apparently accepted both by Mago and Democritus. To enrich this episode with a beauty not its own, Virgil has robbed his Aeneid—on the composition of which he must have been well advanced when he was called on, after the death of Gallus in 26 B.C., to provide a substitute for the passage written in his honour—of some beautiful lines which are more in keeping with the larger representation and profounder feeling of the epic poem, than with the transient interest attaching to this recast of a well-known story. Even regarded simply as an epyllion or epic idyl, it may be questioned whether the Pastor Aristaeus is of an interest equal to that of the epic idyl of Catullus, 'Peliaco quondam prognatae vertice pinus,' etc. There is this coincidence between the poems, that they each contain one story or idyllic representation within another, and in each case it is to the secondary representation that the most pathetic and passionate interest belongs.

---

[1] 'The guardian power of the groves, for whom three hundred snow-white steers browse in the rich thickets of Cea.'

Opinions may differ as to whether the passion of Ariadne or the sorrow of Orpheus is represented with most skill. There seems this difference between the two, that in the one we feel we are reading a fable, that the situation is altogether remote from experience, that it is one suited for a picture or a poem of fancy. The beautiful picture of Ariadne, on the other hand, appears like one drawn from the life, and her passionate complaint is like that of a living woman. But still more undoubted is the superiority of Catullus in pictorial or statuesque reproduction seen in that part of his poem in which the original subject, the marriage of Peleus and Thetis, is described. Catullus, above all other Latin poets, except perhaps Ovid, can bring a picture from human life or from outward nature before the inward eye; and this power is, much more than Virgil's power of suggesting deep and delicate shades of feeling, appropriate to the more limited compass of the idyl. It is no disparagement to Virgil to say that in this kind of art he is inferior to Catullus. Catullus, though a true Italian in temperament, largely endowed with and freely using the biting raillery —'Italum acetum'—which ancient writers ascribe to the race, had in his genius, more than any Roman writer, the disinterested delight in art, irrespective of any personal associations, characteristic of the Greek imagination. Virgil's art, on the other hand, produces its deepest impressions only when his heart is moved. Even in the Eclogues this is for the most part true. Something must touch his personal sympathies, his moral or religious nature, or his national feeling, before he is roused to his highest creative effort.

In the three cardinal passages which remain to be considered, in the composition of which the deeper elements of Virgil's nature were powerfully moved, the impression which the changing state of the national fortunes produced upon him is vividly stamped. The first of these (i. 464 to the end) was written in the years of uncertainty and alarm preceding the outbreak of the last of the great Civil Wars. The unsettlement all over the Empire, from its eastern boundary to its

furthest limits in Europe,—the agitation and impetuous sweep of
the river before plunging into the abyss,—is described and
symbolised in the concluding lines of the Book :—

> Hinc movet Euphrates, illinc Germania bellum;
> Vicinae ruptis inter se legibus urbes
> Arma ferunt; saevit toto Mars impius orbe:
> Ut cum carceribus sese effudere quadrigae,
> Addunt in spatia, et frustra retinacula tendens
> Fertur equis auriga, neque audit currus habenas [1].

This state of alarm is shown to be connected with the great
national crime which Rome was still atoning,—the murder of
Julius Caesar. The episode arises immediately out of the
enumeration of the signs of the weather, which, from their importance to the husbandman, are treated of at considerable
length in the body of the poem. As the sun is the surest index
of change in the physical, so is he said to be in the political
atmosphere. The eclipse which occurred soon after the murder
of Caesar is regarded as a sign of compassion for his fate and of
abhorrence of the crime. Then follows an enumeration of other
omens which accompanied or preceded that event,—some of
them violations of natural law, such as those which occur in the
narrative of Livy, when any great disaster was impending over
the Roman arms,—

> pecudesque locutae,
> Infandum—
> Et maestum inlacrimat templis ebur, aeraque sudant [2] :—

others arising out of a great sympathetic movement among the
spirits of the dead,—

> Vox quoque per lucos volgo exaudita silentis
> Ingens, et simulacra modis pallentia miris
> Visa sub obscurum noctis [3];

----

[1] 'On the one side Euphrates, on the other Germany sets war afoot:
neighbouring cities, breaking their compacts, are in arms against each
other; Mars, in unhallowed rage, is abroad over all the world; even as
when the chariots have burst forth from the barriers, they bound into the
course, and the charioteer, vainly pulling the reins, is borne along by his
steeds, and the chariot no longer obeys his guidance.'

[2] 'And cattle spoke, horror unutterable'—'And the images of ivory
within the temples weep in sorrow, and the images of bronze sweat.'

[3] 'A voice too was heard by many through the silent groves, speaking
with a mighty sound, and ghosts, wondrous pale, were seen in the dusk.'

others showing themselves in ominous appearances of the
sacrifices, or in strange disturbance of the familiar ways of bird
and beast,—

> Obscenaeque canes importunaeque volucres
> Signa dabant—
>
>                           Et altae
> Per noctem resonare lupis ululantibus urbes [1];

others manifesting themselves through great commotion in
the kingdom of Nature,—earthquakes, volcanic eruptions, great
floods,—

> 'The noise of battle hurtling in the air,'

lightnings in a clear sky, and the blaze of comets portending
doom.    These all succeed one another in Virgil's verse according to no principle of logical connexion, but as they might be
successively announced to the awe-struck citizens of Rome.
The whole passage is pervaded by that strong sense of awe
before an invisible Power—the 'religio dira'—by which the
Roman imagination was possessed in times of great national
calamity.    The issue of all these portents appeared in the second
great battle in which Roman blood fattened the Macedonian
plains.    Then by a fine touch of imagination, and looking
far forward into the future, the poet reminds us of the contrast,
indicated in other passages of the poem, between the peaceful
and beneficent industry of the husbandman and the cruel
devastation of war :—

> Scilicet et tempus veniet, cum finibus illis
> Agricola, incurvo terram molitus aratro,
> Exesa inveniet scabra robigine pila,
> Aut gravibus rastris galeas pulsabit inanis,
> Grandiaque effossis mirabitur ossa sepulchris [2].

Next follows the prayer to the national gods of Italy to preserve

---

[1] 'And dogs of ill omen and dire birds gave signs'—'and mountain-built
cities echoed through the night with the howl of wolves.'

[2] 'Doubtless too the time will come when in those lands the husbandman, as he upheaves the earth with his crooked plough, will find javelins
eaten away by rough rust, or with his heavy mattock will strike on
empty helmets, and marvel at the huge bones in their tombs, now dug
open.'

the life of him who could alone raise the world out of the sin
and ruin into which it had fallen, and alone restore their ancient
glory to the fields, which now lay waste from the want of men
to till them :—

> Non ullus aratro
> Dignus honos, squalent abductis arva colonis,
> Et curvae rigidum falces conflantur in ensem[1].

In the second of the great episodes this sorrow for the pas
and foreboding for the future has entirely cleared away.  The
feeling now expressed is one of pride and exultation in Italy, as
a land of rich crops and fruits, of vines and olives, a land famous
for its herds and flocks and breed of horses, for its genial
climate, for the beauty of the seas washing its coasts, for it:
great lakes and rivers, its ancient cities and other mighty works
of men; famous too for its hardy, energetic, and warlike
races,—

> Haec genus acre virum Marsos pubemque Sabellam,
> Adsuetumque malo Ligurem Volscosque verutos
> Extulit[2],—

for its great men and families who had fought for it in old times,
and for one greater still, who was then in the furthest East
defending Rome against her enemies,—

> Haec Decios magnosque Camillos,
> Scipiadas duros bello, et te, maxime Caesar,
> Qui nunc extremis Asiae iam victor in oris
> Imbellem avertis Romanis arcibus Indum[3].

This passage, introduced as a counter-picture to the description
of the rank luxuriance of Nature in the vast forests and jungles
of the East, concentrates in itself the deepest meaning and

---

[1] 'There is no due honour now to the plough, the fields are desolate,
and those who tilled them are gone, and the crooked pruning-hooks are
forged into the stiff sword.'

[2] 'This land has reared a valiant race of men, the Marsi and Sabellian
youth, the Ligurian trained to hardship, and the Volscian spearmen.'

[3] 'This too bore the Decii and the great Camilli, the Scipios, men of
iron in war, and thee, great Caesar, who now, ere this victorious in the
furthest coasts of Asia, art turning away the unwarlike Indian from the
hills of Rome.'

inspiration of the poem.   The glory of Italy is declared to be
the motive for the revival of this ancient theme—

> *Tibi* res antiquae laudis et artis
> Ingredior [1].

As Varro represents his speakers as looking on the great picture
of Italy in the Temple of Tellus while they discuss the various
ways of tilling and improving the soil, so Virgil in the midst of
his didactic precepts holds up this ideal picture of the land to
the love and admiration of his countrymen.   By a few powerful
strokes he combines the characteristic features and the great
memories of Italian towns in lines which recur to every
traveller as he passes through Italy,—

> Adde tot egregias urbes operumque laborem,
> Tot congesta manu praeruptis oppida saxis,
> Fluminaque antiquos subterlabentia muros [2].

No expression of patriotic sentiment in any language is more
pure and noble than this.   It is a tribute of just pride and
affection to the land which, from its beauty, its history, its great
services to man, is felt to be worthy of the deep devotion with
which Virgil commends it to the heart and imagination of the
world.

In the last of the great episodes which remains to be considered, all the higher thoughts and feelings by which beauty,
dignity, and moral grandeur are given to the subject are found
concurring ; and the presence of Lucretius is again felt as a
pervading influence, though modified by Virgil's own deepest
convictions and sympathies.   The charm of peaceful contemplation, of Nature in her serenest aspect and harmony with the
human soul, of an ethical idea based on religious belief and
national traditions, of a life of pure and tranquil happiness,
remote from the clash of arms and the pride and passions of the

---

[1] 'It is in thy honour that I enter on the task of treating an art of ancient
renown.'

[2] 'Besides many famous cities, with their massive workmanship, many
towns piled by the hand of man on steep crags, and rivers gliding beneath
walls that have been from of old.'

world, is made present to us in a strain of continuous and modulated music, which neither Virgil himself nor any other poet has surpassed. Virgil creates a new ideal of happiness for the contemplation of his countrymen by combining the old realistic delight in the husbandman's life with the imaginative longing for the peace and innocence of a Saturnian Age, and with that new delight in the living beauty of the world and in the charm of ancient memories which it was his especial office to communicate. This ideal is contrasted, as is the older poet's ideal of 'plain living and high thinking,' with the pomp and magnificence of city life,—

> Si non ingentem foribus domus alta superbis
> Mane salutantum totis vomit aedibus undam—
>
> Si non aurea sunt iuvenum simulacra per aedes
> Lampadas igniferas manibus retinentia dextris [1],—

and, as in the older poet also, with the distractions, the restless passions, and the crimes of ambition. Virgil, as in other passages, compresses into a few lines the thought which Lucretius with simpler art follows through all its detail of concrete reality. Thus the

> Gaudent perfusi sanguine fratrum [2]

of Virgil is intended to recall and be explained by the more fully developed representation of the old cruelties of the times of Marius and Sulla, contained in the lines—

> Sanguine civili rem conflant divitiasque
> Conduplicant avidi, caedem caede accumulantes;
> Crudeles gaudent in tristi funere fratris;
> Et consanguineum mensas odere timentque [3].

In their protest against the world both poets are entirely at

---

[1] 'Though no lofty mansion with proud portals pours forth from all its chambers its wave of those who pay their court in the morning.'— 'Though there are no golden statues of youths through their chambers, holding blazing torches in their right hands.'

[2] 'They revel in the bloodshed of their brethren.'

[3] 'By the bloodshed of their fellow-citizens they amass an estate, and covetously double their riches, heaping murder upon murder: they take a cruel joy in the sad death of a brother; and hate and fear the board of their kinsmen.' Lucret. iii. 70–73.

one.  But the ideal of Virgil's imagination, on its positive side, is more on the ordinary human level than that of lonely contemplation in accordance with which Lucretius lived and wrote. The Virgilian ideal, like that of Lucretius, recognised a heart at peace and independent of Fortune as a greater source of happiness than any external good.  But this peace the one poet sought for in a superiority to the common beliefs of men; the other rather in a more trusting acceptance of them.  Some other elements in Virgil's ideal Lucretius too would have ranked among the supreme sources of human happiness.   The lines

> Interea dulces pendent circum oscula nati,
> Casta pudicitiam servat domus [1],

beautiful as the thought and picture is, are not more true to human feeling, scarcely touch the heart and imagination so vividly, as the lines which suggested them—

> Iam iam non domus accipiet te laeta, neque uxor
> Optima, nec dulces occurrent oscula nati
> Praeripere [2].

Other elements in Virgil's ideal Lucretius would have sympathised with, as he did with all natural human pleasure ; but the elements of social kindliness expressed in the lines—

> Ipse dies agitat festos, etc.

could mix only as an occasional source of refreshment with his

---

[1] 'Meantime his dear children hang with kisses round his lips; a pure household keeps well all the laws of chastity.'

[2] 'Soon no longer shall thy home receive thee with glad greeting, nor thy most excellent wife, nor thy dear children run to meet thee to snatch the first kiss.'

The most classical of our own poets seems to combine both representations with the thought and representation of an earlier passage of the Georgics

(Et quidam seros hiberni ad luminis ignes, etc.)
in the familiar stanza—

> For them no more the blazing hearth shall burn,
>   Or busy housewife ply her evening care;
> No children run to meet their sire's return,
>   And climb his knees the envied kiss to share.

lonely contemplation. The great difference between the two
men is that Virgil's ordinary feelings and beliefs are in unison
with the common ways of life; he has a more active sympathy
with the toils and pleasures of simple men ; and, above all, he
regards it as the highest good for man, not to secure peace of
mind for himself, but to be useful in supporting others, in contributing to the well-being of his country, of his family, even of
the animals associated with his toil :—

> hinc patriam parvosque Penates
> Sustinet, hinc armenta boum meritosque iuvencos[1].

This ideal Virgil seems to regard as one that might be attained
by man, if he only could be taught how to appreciate it[2];
nay, that has been attained by him in happier times when the
land was cultivated by free men, each holding his own plot of
ground. This was the life of the old Italian yeomen, the life
by which Etruria waxed strong and brave, the life to which
Rome herself owed the beginning of her greatness[3]. It is the
life which the national imagination, in its peaceful mood, and
yearning to return into the ways of innocence and piety, discerned in that distant Golden Age, when all men lived in
contentment and abundance under the rule of the old god,

---

[1] 'Hence he supports his country and his humble home, hence his herds
of cattle, and his well-deserving steers.'

[2] Cp. 'Le mot triste et doux de Virgile : "O heureux l'homme des
champs, s'il connaissait son bonheur" est un regret, mais, comme tous les
regrets, c'est aussi une prédiction. Un jour viendra où le laboureur pourra
être aussi un artiste, si non pour exprimer (ce qui importera assez peu
alors) du moins pour sentir le beau.' G. Sand.

[3] Virgil rightly connects this greatness with the site of Rome in the line,
> Septemque una sibi muro circumdedit arces.
It was from the necessities imposed by that site that Rome at an early
period became the largest urban community in Italy, and was forced, in
consequence of the contiguous settlements of other races, to begin that
incorporating and assimilating policy which ultimately enabled her to
establish universal empire. Cp. 'Rome herself, like other cities of Italy,
Gaul, and elsewhere, grew out of the primitive hill-fortresses ; the distinction between Rome and other cities, the distinction which made Rome all
that she became, was that Rome did not grow out of a single fortress of
the kind, but out of several.' Historical and Architectural Sketches, by
E. A. Freeman, D.C.L., etc.—Walls of Rome, p. 160.

from whom the land received the well-loved name 'Saturnia tellus [1].'

> Hanc olim veteres vitam coluere Sabini,
> Hanc Remus et frater, sic fortis Etruria crevit
> Scilicet, et rerum facta est pulcherrima Roma,
> Septemque una sibi muro circumdedit arces.
> Ante etiam sceptrum Dictaei regis et ante
> Impia quam caesis gens est epulata iuvencis,
> Aureus hanc vitam in terris Saturnus agebat;
> Necdum etiam audierant inflari classica, necdum
> Impositos duris crepitare incudibus enses [2].

[1] Cf. 'Itaque in hoc Latio et Saturnia terra, ubi Dii cultus agrorum progeniem suam docuerunt.' Columella.

[2] 'Such was the life that the old Sabines lived long ago, such the life of Remus and his brother; thus in truth brave Etruria grew strong and Rome became the glory of the world, and though a single city enclosed seven hills within her wall. Nay, even before the Sovereign-lord, born on Dicte, wielded the sceptre, and an unholy generation feasted on slaughtered steers, this was the life of Saturn on earth in the golden age. Not yet had men heard the blare of the war-trumpet, not yet had they heard the clang of the sword on the hard anvil.'

# CHAPTER VII.

## The Georgics as the representative poem of Italy.

The consideration of the motives which influenced Virgil to undertake the composition of the Georgics, of the form of art adopted by him, of the national interest attaching to his subject, of the materials used by him and the sources from which he derived them, of the author who most influenced him in speculative idea and in the general manner of treating his subject, leads to the conclusion that, in its essential characteristics, the poem is a genuine work of Italian art and inspiration. If the original motive influencing him was the ambition to treat of rural life in the serious spirit of Hesiod, as he had done in the lighter vein of Theocritus, that motive was soon lost in the strong impulse to invest with charm and dignity the kind of life in which the Italian mind placed its ideal of worth and happiness. By thus identifying himself with a great national object Virgil raised himself to a higher level of art than that attained by poets whose interests are purely personal and literary.

Next to satire, there was no form of poetry which had more of a Roman character than didactic poetry. By becoming a province of Roman art, this form acquired all its dignity and capacity of greatness. And though the Georgics, being a work of Italian culture as well as of Italian inspiration, could not escape some relation, not in form only but in materials and mode of expression, to Greek originals, there is no great work of Latin genius, except the Satires and Epistles of Horace, in which the debt thus incurred is so small. And not only is the debt small in quantity, but it is incurred to authors much inferior to Virgil in creative power and poetical feeling.   In using borrowed materials he makes the mind of Greece tributary to his own national design.   But his most valuable materials are derived either from personal observation, or from Latin authors who had put on record the results of their observation: and his largest debt, in imaginative feeling and conception, is incurred not to any Greek author, but to the most powerful and original of Roman poets and thinkers.   The speculative idea, which gives something of philosophical consistency to the poem, was, if not one of pure Italian conception, yet made more truly real and vital through the experience of the force and endurance exercised by the strong men of Italy in subduing the earth to their will, and in constructing their great material works ('operum laborem'), such as their roads, baths, aqueducts, harbours, encampments, and great draining works, by which they provided the comforts of life ('commoda vitae') and defended themselves against their enemies or the maligner influence of the elements.

The language of Virgil himself and the testimony of ancient commentators confirm the impression, that the object of which he was most distinctly conscious in the composition of the poem was the 'glorification of Italy,'—of the land itself in its fertility and beauty, and of the life most congenial to Italian sentiment. Even to a greater extent than he may have intended, Virgil, through the national mould in which his thought was cast and the national colour of his sympathies, fulfils this representative office.   Where the poem seems to a modern reader to fail in human interest, the interest which it had for the poet's countrymen is revived by dwelling in thought on this representative character.   When the associations appealed to are of Greek rather than of Italian origin, we have to remember that the poem was addressed to a highly educated class of readers, at the time when the Roman mind had been most enlarged and enriched, but had not yet been satiated by Greek studies.   Yet this kind of appeal is quite subsidiary to that made to the native sensibilities of the Romans. It is to commend to their love and admiration a purely Italian ideal that Virgil employs the resources of Greek learning, as well as all the strength and delicacy of his own genius.

A rapid review of the tastes, sympathies, and affections on the part of his readers to which Virgil appeals, both in the body of his poem and in its finer episodes, will show that they all contribute to produce this representative character. Where some of the details of the poem seem to fail in poetic interest, they still have the interest of being characteristic of the Italian mind.

1. The poem professes to impart practical instruction on the best method of cultivating the land, of propagating trees, of breeding cattle, horses, etc., of profiting by the industry of bees :—

> Quare agite, O, proprios generatim discite cultus,
> Agricolae[1].

This is the obvious and ostensible purpose of the poem; and the truth and accuracy of the instruction were important elements in the estimate which the countrymen of the poet formed of its value. Columella and Pliny, while controverting him on a few minor points[2], attest his practical knowledge as an agriculturist and a naturalist. Similar testimony is given by some modern writers competent to speak with authority on these subjects[3]. Neither ancient nor modern critics regard him as

---

[1] 'Come then, ye tillers of the soil, learn the special modes of husbandry, each according to its kind.'

[2] E. g. Col. iv. 9 : 'Nam illam veterem opinionem damnavit usus non esse ferro tangendos anniculos malleolos, quod aciem reformidant, quod frustra Vergilius, et Saserna, Stolonesque et Catones timuerunt.' Virgil is there quoted along with the recognised authorities on agriculture. This is often done in matters on which Columella agrees with him, e. g. i. chap. 4 : 'Si verissimo vati velut oraculo crediderimus dicenti.'

[3] Cp. Gisborne's 'Essays on Ancient Agriculture,' and 'Forest Trees and Woodland Scenery,' by W. Menzies, Deputy Surveyor of Windsor Forest and Parks. The following extracts from the last-named work—a work which combines thorough practical knowledge with true poetical feeling— support the statement in the text: 'All the methods, both natural and artificial, of propagating trees are described in graphic language. Virgil also fully describes the self-sowing of trees, artificial sowing, propagating by transplanting of suckers, propagating by pegging down the branches till

free from liability to mistake, and the tendency of his mind to believe in marvellous deviations from natural law exposed him to errors into which less imaginative writers were not likely to fall; but the substantial accuracy of his observations and acquired knowledge seems to be attested both by positive and negative evidence.   It is not a question as to whether the operations described in Virgil satisfy the requirements of skilled or even of unskilled farming in the present day, or whether he does not fall into mistakes in natural history which a modern reader, with no scientific knowledge of the subject, may easily detect; but whether he has adequately represented the methods of ancient Italian agriculture, and whether he is a trustworthy exponent of the scientific beliefs of his age, and an accurate observer of those phenomena which were as accessible to an ancient as to a modern enquirer.   On these points he satisfied the best critics among his countrymen.   The general truth of his observation is further attested by the survival in Southern Europe, into comparatively recent times, of some of the processes described by him, which seem most remote from our ordinary experience [1].   It is attested also by the accuracy of his description of the unchanging phenomena of Nature, and of the habits of animals.

A modern reader may think the value of his poetry little, if at all enhanced, by the rank which he may claim among the 'scriptores rei rusticae.'   It may seem matter for regret that so much of the faculty, which should have given permanent delight

---

they strike root at the point of contact with the earth, and propagating by simply cutting off a small branch from the top and placing it in the moist warm earth.   All these are correct.   Indeed, the art is little advanced since the time of Virgil,' p. 46.   Mr. Menzies suggests an ingenious explanation of Virgil's mistake as to what trees could be grafted on one another.   In speaking of the Aeneid he bears further testimony to the accuracy of Virgil's observation : ' The poet was equally great and observant of the details of woodcraft, and must have watched keenly the details of the foresters around him,' p. 50.   This remark reminds us of the fact that one of his father's means of livelihood was ' silvis coemendis.'   At p. 53 Mr. Menzies draws special attention to the description of the mistletoe in Book vi, and of the aged elm under which the Shades are described as resting.

[1] Cp. Holdsworth's Remarks and Dissertations on the Georgics.

to the world, should have been employed in conveying temporary instruction.   His very fidelity to the office of a teacher
detracts somewhat from his poetic office.   Though it satisfies
our curiosity to know how the ancient Italians tilled their lands
and cultivated the vine, yet this satisfaction is quite distinct from
the joy which the poetical treatment of a poetical subject gives
to the imagination.   It is not as repertories of useful information that the great writers of Greece and Rome are to be
studied.   Their importance in this way has long since been
superseded.   Each generation adds to the stock of knowledge
in the world, modifies the results arrived at by the preceding
generation, and dispenses with the works in which these results
have been embodied.   But a work of power, stimulating moral
and intellectual feeling,—whether in the form of poem, history,
speech, or philosophic dialogue,—may acquire from long antiquity even a stronger hold over the imagination than it originally possessed[1].   In the didactic poems of Lucretius and
Virgil the information conveyed by them possesses permanent
value, in so far as it is coloured by human feeling,—in so far as
we recognise the passion or affection by which the poet was
stirred in acquiring his knowledge and in conveying it to sympathetic readers.   And as the scientific enthusiasm of Lucretius
animates the driest details of his argument, so the love entertained for his subject by Virgil,—as an Italian, the son of a
small Italian land-holder,—

Veneto rusticis parentibus nato inter silvas et frutices educto[2],—

writing for Italians, for whom every detail of farm labour had
a fascination unintelligible to us,—brightens with the gleam of
human and poetical feeling the technical teaching of the traditional precepts of Italian husbandry.   The position of a
teacher assumed by him,—a position which no great Greek or

---

[1] Compare the distinction drawn out by De Quincey, and originally suggested by Wordsworth, between the literature of knowledge and the literature of power.
[2] 'A Venetian born of peasant parents, reared in a rough woodland
country.'   Macrobius, v. 2.

English poet could gracefully maintain,—impresses us with the
thorough adaptation of the form of the poem to the sober practical understanding of the Italian race.    Horace mentions this
love of teaching and learning as one of the notes distinguishing
the Roman from the Greek genius :—

> Maiores audire, minori dicere per quae
> Crescere res posset, minui damnosa libido [1].

It adds to our sense of Virgil's thoroughness as an artist to
know that he faithfully performed the office which he undertook;
and the fact of his undertaking this office helps to bring home
to us the practical, unspeculative genius of those to whom his
poem was in the first place addressed.

2.  Not only the instruction directly conveyed in the poem,
but the frequent illustrations from geography, mythology, and
astronomy, have much less meaning to us than they had to the
contemporaries of the poet.    Yet they help to make us realise
the relation in which the Rome and Italy of the Augustan Age
stood to the rest of the world and to the culture of the past.
By the references to the varied products of other lands we are
reminded of the active commercial intercourse between Rome
and the East,—a feature of the age of which we are also often
reminded in the Odes, Satires, and Epistles of Horace.    We
see how the success of the Roman arms had made the products
of the whole world—the 'saffron dye of Tmolus,' the 'ivory of
India,' the 'spices of Arabia,' the 'iron of the Chalybians,' the
'medicinal drugs of Pontus,' the 'brood-mares of Epirus [2]'—
part of the possessions of Rome.    We are reminded too of the
fact that many Romans and Italians were settled as colonists
in the provinces of the Empire, and that Virgil had them also
in view in the instruction which he imparts [3].    The frequent
allusions to Greek mythology and to the constellations, on the

---

[1] 'To listen to their elders, to point out to younger men the ways by
which their substance might be increased, the passions that lead to ruin be
weakened.'  Ep. ii. 1. 106–107.                    [2] Georg. i. 56–59.
[3] E. g. iii. 408 :—
> Aut impacatos a tergo horrebis Hiberos.

other hand, help to remind us that the art and science of the past, as well as the material products of the world, had now been diverted to the enjoyment and use of the new inheritors of intellectual culture.

3. It was seen how assiduously Virgil, in the body of his poem, inculcates the necessity and duty of labour. And though the 'glorification of labour' was found to be rather a derivative and tributary stream than the main current of interest in the poem, yet it is impossible to doubt that to the mind of Virgil this assiduous toil of the husbandman, on a work so congenial and surrounded with such accessories of peaceful happiness, had a special attraction, even independent of its results. This recognition of the dignity of labour owes nothing to a Greek original. A life of intellectual leisure was the ideal of the Greeks. Hesiod indeed does dwell on the necessity of labour, as the ground both of worldly well-being and divine approval,—and this is another point of affinity between him and Virgil,—but the line in which he claims consideration for work,

Ἔργον δ' οὐδὲν ὄνειδος, ἀεργίη δέ τ' ὄνειδος [1],

is apologetic in tone; and, moreover, Hesiod can hardly be regarded as a typical Greek. There seems to be no word in the Greek language equivalent to the grave Roman word 'industria.' Perhaps it is owing to the disesteem in which labour was held by Greek writers that industry is scarcely ranked among virtues, nor idleness among vices, even by modern moralists. When long after the time of Homer a new poet arose in Greece, appealing to a great popular sentiment, it was in their passion for the great public games that he found the point of contact with the hearts of his countrymen. The Romans, on the other hand, show a great capacity for labour in every field of exertion,—in war and the government of men, in law and literature, in business transactions, in the construction of vast works of utility, and in cultivating the land. And of these, next to war and government, the last was most congenial

---

[1] Ἔργ. κ. Ἡμ. 310.

to the national mind.   The land was to the Romans the chief
field of their industry and the original source of their wealth, as
the sea was the scene of occupation and adventure to the
Greeks, and, through the outlet which it gave to the results of
their artistic ingenuity, the great source of their prosperity.
The Odyssey is a poem inspired, in a great degree, by the
impulse which first sent the Greek nation forth on its career of
maritime and colonising enterprise.   The Georgics are inspired
by that impulse which first started the Latin race on its career
of conquest, and which continued to animate the struggle with
the reluctant forces of Nature, as it had animated the struggle
with the other races of Italy for the possession of the soil.

4. Again, we find that the poem is pervaded by the poetical
feeling of Nature.   And Virgil, more than any other poet,
presents that aspect of Nature in which the outward world
appeared to the educated Italian mind.   The personality and
individual life attributed to natural objects, such as trees, rivers,
winds, etc., belongs to a stage of conception between the Greek
anthropomorphism and the recognition by the imagination of
universal law and interdependence of phenomena.   Modern poets
consciously personify natural objects with more boldness and
varied sympathy than Virgil.   His conception of the life and
personal attributes of natural objects appears to be less a conscious creative effort of the imagination, than an unconscious
impression from outward things; an impression produced in a
state of passive contemplation, rather than of active adventure;
and an impression produced by qualities of a serene and tender
beauty, rather than by those of a bolder or sublimer aspect.   In
all these respects Virgil represents a stage in the culture of the
imagination between that of the early Greek poets and artists,
and that of the most imaginative poets and painters of modern
times.   The familiar beauty of the outward world, as it was felt
by a Roman or Italian, was expressed in the Latin word
'amoenum.'   Thus Horace describes his retreat among the
Sabine hills, as not only dear to him personally, but as beautiful
in itself:—

Hae latebrae dulces, etiam, si credis, amoenae[1].

And it is to the attributes summed up in that word that Virgil imparts the ideal life of the imagination.

But not only is the feeling of Nature in the Georgics characteristic of the highest culture of the Italian mind, but the spectacle of Nature,—

'The outward shows of sky and earth'

brought before us,—is that which still delights the eye and moves the imagination in the various districts of Italy. The description of Spring at Georg. ii. 323–345,

Ver adeo frondi nemorum, . . . .
. . . exciperet caeli indulgentia terras,

is one of which (though we can always feel its beauty) we cannot often verify the accuracy in our more northern latitudes. It is to an Italian spring, more than to any season in any other European country, that the words of the third Eclogue ' nunc formosissimus annus,' are applicable. The varied pastoral beauty of the long summer day described at Georg. iii. 323–338,—from the early dawn when the fields are fresh beneath the morning-star ; through the gathering warmth of the later hours, when the groves are loud with the chirping of the grasshoppers and the herds collect around the deep water-pools ; through the burning heat of midday, from which the shade of some huge oak or some grove of dark ilexes affords a shelter ; till the coolness of evening tempers the air, and the moon renews with dew the dry forest-glades,— is a beauty quite distinct from the charm of freedom and solitude,—yet not too remote from human neighbourhood,—of the changing aspects of the sky, and of the picturesque environment of hill, river, and moorland, which abides in the pastoral regions of our own and other northern lands. The ' sweet interchange of hill and valley [2],' mountain range and rich

---

[1] 'This retreat—charming to me, nay, if you believe me, even beautiful in itself.'

[2]                          'Sweet interchange
Of hill and valley, rivers, woods, and plains.'
                     Paradise Lost, Book ix. ll. 115–116.

cultivated land, which northern and central Italy exhibits, must have made such scenes as that described at ii. 186-188,

> Qualem saepe cava montis convalle solemus
> Despicere[1], etc.,

and again the opening scene of the poem, at i. 43,

> Vere novo gelidus canis cum montibus umor
> Liquitur, et Zephyro putris se glaeba resolvit[2],

familiar to Roman readers.  And while the ' caeli indulgentia' characteristic of the Italian climate is felt as a pervading genial presence through the various books of the poem, the sudden and violent vicissitudes to which that climate is especially liable form part of the varied and impressive spectacle presented to us.   The passage i. 316–321,

> Saepe ego cum flavis . . . . stipulasque volantis,

records a calamity to which the labours of the Italian husband-man were peculiarly exposed.   In the description of the storm of rain, immediately following, the words ' collectae ex alto nubes' remind us, like the description of a similar storm in Lucretius (vi. 256–261), that Virgil, as Lucretius may have done, must often have watched such a tempest gathering over the sea that washes the Campanian shores.   The inundation of the Po is described among the omens accompanying the death of Caesar, in lines which may have been suggested by some scene actually witnessed by the poet, and which with vivid exactness represent for all times the destructive forces put forth by the great river that drains the vast mountain-ranges of Northern Italy :—

> Proluit insano contorquens vertice silvas
> Fluviorum rex Eridanus, camposque per omnes
> Cum stabulis armenta tulit[3].

---

[1] ' Such as we often look down on in some mountain dale.'

[2] ' In early spring when chill waters are streaming down from the hoary sides of the hills, and the clod breaks up and crumbles beneath the west wind.'

[3] ' Whirling whole forests in its mad eddies, Eridanus, monarch of rivers, swept them before it, and bore over all the plains herds of cattle with their stalls.'

And while the general representation of Nature, in the freshness or serene glory of her beauty and in her destructive energy, is true to that aspect which she presents in Italian scenery, the characteristic features and products of particular localities in the various regions of Italy are recalled to memory with truthful effect.    The love of Nature in Lucretius appears apart from local associations.    In Horace this feeling seems to link itself to places dear to him from the memories of childhood, or from the personal experience of later years.    In Virgil the feeling is both general as in Lucretius, and combined with attachment to or interest in particular places as in Horace.    But Virgil is able to feel enthusiasm not only for places dear to him through personal association, but for all which appeal to his sentiment of national pride.    As was seen in the last chapter, the episode, which perhaps more than any other brings out the inspiring thought of the poem, is devoted to a celebration of the varied beauties of the land ; and the names of Clitumnus, of Larius, and Benacus are still dearer to the world because they are for ever intermingled with ' the rich Virgilian rustic measure [1].'    In the body of the poem also we find many local references to the northern, central, and southern regions of Italy.    The light bark, hollowed out of the alder, is launched on the rapid flood of the

---

[1] The lines,

'And now we passed
From Como, when the light was gray,
And in my head for half the day,
    The rich Virgilian rustic measure
Of Lari Maxume, all the way,
    Like ballad-burthen music, kept,' etc.,

are so familiarly known that they hardly need to be quoted in support of this statement.    But among other testimonies to the power of Virgilian associations, one may be quoted from another great poet, whose mind was less attuned to Latin than to Greek and English poetry.    Goethe, in his ' Letters from Italy,' mentions, on coming to the Lago di Garda, that he was reminded of the line,
    Fluctibus et fremitu adsurgens, Benace, marino.
He adds this remark : ' This is the first Latin verse, the subject of which ever stood visibly before me, and now, in the present moment, when the wind is blowing stronger and stronger, and the lake casts loftier billows against the little harbour, it is just as true as it was hundreds of years ago. Much, indeed, has changed, but the wind still roars about the lake, *the aspect of which gains even greater glory from a line of Virgil.*'

Po ; the starwort, out of which wreaths are made to adorn the altars of the gods, is gathered by shepherds by the winding banks of the Mella (a river in Northern Italy mentioned also by Catullus) ; the meadow-land which unfortunate Mantua lost is adduced as a type of the best kind of pasture, and the land in the neighbourhood of Capua and the region skirting Mount Vesuvius as that most suitable for corn-crops.  We read also of the rose-beds of Paestum,—of the olives clothing the sides of the Samnian Taburnus,—of the woodland pastures of Sila,—of those by the banks of the Silarus, on Alburnus green with ilexes, and by the dry torrent-bed of the Tanager,—and of the yellow corn-fields through which the dark Galaesus flows.  The Aeneid affords further testimony of the interest which Virgil awakens in the region which forms the distant environment of Rome.  But the sentiment of the Georgics is a sentiment of peace inspired by the land, quite different from that inspired by the Imperial City, and from the memories of war and conquest with which the neighbourhood of Rome is associated.  And though the aspect which Nature generally presents in the poem is that of her nobler mood, yet that air of indolent repose which characterises her presence in the Eclogues is not altogether absent from the severer poem.  The sense of rest after toil—'molles sub arbore somni,'—the quiet contemplation of wide and peaceful land-scapes,—'latis otia fundis,'—relieve the strain of strenuous labour which is enforced as the indispensable condition of realising the glory of the land.

5. The religious and ethical thought of the poem is also in accordance with what was happiest and best in the old Italian faith and life.  The poetical belief in many protecting agencies—

Dique deaeque omnes studium quibus arva tueri [1]—

watching over the labours of the husbandman, and present at his simple festival and ceremonies, is in accordance with the genial character of the rustic Paganism of Italy and with the

---

[1] ' All gods and goddesses whose task it is to watch over the fields.'

attributes of the great gods of the land, Faunus and Saturnus. Human life appeared to Hesiod as well as to Virgil to be in immediate dependence on the gods. But the graver aspect of Virgil's faith is purer and happier than that of Hesiod; as the trust in a just and beneficent father is purer and happier than the fear of a jealous task-master. But on the other hand, the faith of Virgil is less noble than that of Aeschylus and of Sophocles. It is more of a passive yielding to the longing of the human heart and to the impulses of an aesthetic emotion, than that union of natural piety with insight into the mystery of life which no great poets, Pagan or Christian (unless it may be Dante), exhibit in equal measure with the two great Athenian dramatists. In the religious spirit of Virgil, which accepts and does not question, which finds its resource in prayer rather than in reverent contemplation and searching out of the ways of God, we may recognise a true note of his nationality,—a submissive attitude in presence of the Invisible Power, derived from the race whose custom it was to veil the head in sacrifice and in approaching the images of their gods [1].

6. Equally true to the national character is the ethical ideal upheld in the Georgics. The negative elements in that ideal were seen to be exemption from the violent passions and pleasures of the world. And in these negative elements the ideal of the Georgics coincides with that of Lucretius. But, on the positive side, Virgil's ideal implies the active performance of duties to the family and to the State. One has only to re-member the low esteem in which women were held and the indifference to family ties in the palmiest days of Athenian civili-

---

[1] Cp. Mommsen, book i. chap. 2: 'As the Greek when he sacrificed raised his eyes to Heaven, so the Roman veiled his head; for the prayer of the former was vision, that of the latter reflection.' Cf. also Lucret. v. 1198:—

> Nec pietas ullast velatum saepe videri
> Vertier ad lapidem atque omnis accedere ad aras;

and Virg. Aen. iii. 405-409 :—

> Purpureo velare comas adopertus amictu.
>
> .      .      .      .      .
>
> Hunc socii morem sacrorum, hunc ipse teneto;
> Hac casti maneant in religione nepotes.

sation, or to recall the ideal State of Plato's imagination, to perceive how true to Italian, and how remote from Greek sentiment, are the pictures presented in such passages as these—

> Interea dulces pendent circum oscula nati ;
> Casta pudicitiam servat domus—

and this—

> Interea longum cantu solata laborem
> Arguto coniunx percurrit pectine telas [1].

Friendship among men, and even the social friendliness which makes life more pleasant and manners more humane, were ranked among the virtues by Greek philosophy; and the first is treated by Aristotle, not only as a single virtue, but as the condition under which all virtue can best be realised: but natural affection is regarded as a mere instinct, and the duties of family life do not fall under any of those conditions with which ethical philosophy concerns itself.  On the other hand, the legendary history of the early Republic, and many great examples, in the midst of the corruption of the later Republic and of the Empire, prove that the ideal of domestic virtue and affection among the Romans was no mere passing fancy or dream of an age of primitive innocence, but was in harmony with the national conscience throughout the whole course of their history.

In devotion to the good of the State no superiority can be claimed for the Romans over the Athenians of the times of Cleisthenes, Themistocles, and Pericles.  And while each people, in its best days, was equally ready to serve the Republic in war and by the performance of public duties, and while the Roman perhaps more than the Athenian regarded the labour of his hands as a service due from him [2], the Athenian freely gave the higher energy of his genius to make the life of his fellow-citizens brighter and nobler.  And it is the peculiar glory of the Athenians of the fifth century B.C.,—the glory claimed for them

---

[1] 'Meanwhile cheering her long task with song his wife runs over her web with shrill-sounding shuttle.'

[2] Compare the double meaning of 'moenia' and 'munia,' as illustrated by Mommsen.

in one of the speeches attributed to their great Statesman by their great Historian,—that they combined this devotion to the common good with a high development of all personal excellence.　But in Athens this union of national and individual energy and virtue was of very brief duration.　On the other hand, the lasting greatness of the Roman Commonwealth was purchased by the sacrifice of the energies and accomplishments which add to the grace and enjoyment of individual existence. The greatness and permanence of the race, not the varied development of the individual, was the object aimed at and attained in the vigorous prime of the Roman Republic[1].

If this aspect of national life is not directly brought before us by Virgil in the Georgics, it is brought into strong light in the representation of his mimic commonwealth—the

> Mores et studia et populos et proelia[2]

of the community of bees.　It scarcely needs the reminder of

> ipsae regem parvosque *Quirites*
> Sufficiunt[3]

to convince us that, in this representation of an industrious and warlike community, earnest in labour from the love of the objects on which it was bestowed and from pride in its results—

> Tantus amor florum et generandi gloria mellis[4],—

resolute and unconquerable in battle, sacrificing life rather than abandoning the post of duty, inspired with more than Oriental devotion to their head, Virgil was teaching a lesson applicable to the Roman Commonwealth under its new government.　While labour is shown to be a condition of individual happiness, or at least contentment, it is not in individual happiness, but in the permanent greatness of the community that its ultimate recom-

---

[1] Cp. Mommsen, book i. chap. 2.

[2] 'The characters and tasks and hosts and battles.'

[3] 'They themselves supply the sovereign and tiny citizens of the community.'

[4] 'So great is their passion for flowers, so great is their pride in producing honey.'

pense is to be sought.   Though the individual life may be short and meagre in its attractions, and generation after generation may spend itself in an unceasing round of toil,

> At genus immortale manet, multosque per annos
> Stat fortuna domus et avi numerantur avorum [1].

The training and discipline for the attainment of these virtues are to be sought in plain and frugal living, in hardy pastime as well as hardy industry [2], in obedience to parents and reverent worship of the gods—

> Illic saltus et lustra ferarum,
> Et patiens operum exiguoque adsueta iuventus,
> Sacra deum sanctique patres [3],—

and in abstinence from the luxurious indulgence, the anxious business, and the enervating pleasures of a corrupt civilisation [4]. While the grace and beauty of the poem arise out of the feeling of the life of Nature, the dignity and sanctity with which the subject is invested are due to the sense of the intimate connexion between the cultivation of the land and the moral and religious life of the Italian race.

7. The poem may be called a representative work of genius in respect also of its artistic execution.   It is the finest work of Italian art, made perfect by the long education of Greek studies. More than any work in Latin literature the Georgics approach to the symmetry of form, the harmony of proportion, the unity of design and tone, characteristic of the purest art of Greece. But it is not in any sense a copy formed after any Greek pattern.   It was seen that out of the more rudimentary attempts of Greek literature in this particular form of poetry Virgil

---

[1] 'But the stock remains eternal, and through long years the fortune of the house stands steadfast, and the grandsires of grandsires are counted up.'

[2] Compare with this the character of the Italian race given in the speech of Remulus, Aen. ix. 603, etc. :—
> Venatu invigilant pueri, etc.

[3] 'There are forests and the lairs of wild beasts, a youth inured to hardship and accustomed to scanty fare, worship of the gods and reverence yielded to parents.'

[4] This abstinence is indirectly inculcated and illustrated in such passages as iii. 209, 524, iv. 197, etc.

created a new and nobler type, which never has been, and probably never will be, improved on. The execution of the poem is characterised by the genial susceptibility and enthusiasm of the Italian temperament, by the firm structure of all Roman work and the practical moderation and dignity of the Roman mind, and by a kind of meditative and pensive grace peculiar to the poet himself. The thought of the poem is not separable from the sentiment pervading it. And in this respect there is a marked difference between the genius of Virgil and of Lucretius. However much the speculative activity of Lucretius is charged with feeling, yet the thought stands out, clearly defined, through the atmosphere surrounding it. The melancholy of Lucretius, though it was the result partly of disposition,—the reaction perhaps of a strongly passionate temperament,—and partly of his relation to his age, was yet a state of mind for which he could assign definite grounds. That of Virgil was probably also in a great measure the result of temperament; but it seems to be a mood habitual to one who meditated much inwardly on the misery of the world, who was moved by compassion for all sights of sorrow or suffering[1], and was yet unable to shape this sense of 'the burthen of the mystery' into articulate thought. The atmosphere of the poem has become one with its substance. The fusion of meditation and feeling derived from the individual genius of the poet imparts a distinctively original charm to the style of the Georgics.

The style is thus, in a great degree, Virgil's own, and owes little to the borrowed beauties of Greek expression. Though the language of the Alexandrine poets is sometimes reproduced, yet the beauty of those transferred passages arises from the grace given to them, not from that borrowed from them. The same

---

[1] It is among the blessings of the countryman's lot enumerated in the passage 'O fortunatos,' etc., that he is removed from the painful sight of the contrasts between poverty and riches which the life of a great city presents—

neque ille

Aut doluit miserans inopem aut invidit habenti.

may be said of the use sometimes made of the quaint diction of Hesiod.   In one or two striking passages, such as that

Ecce supercilio clivosi tramitis, etc.,

Virgil has adopted the language of the Iliad[1]; and though it is impossible to improve on that, yet there is no slavish imitation of it; only a new picture is painted, recalling, by some vivid touches, a former piece by the great master.   If detraction is to be made from the originality of expression in the Georgics, the debt due by Virgil was incurred to his own countryman.   In adopting modes of expression from Lucretius, Virgil brings down the bold creativeness of his original to a tone more suited to the habitual sobriety of the Italian imagination.   He often fixes into the form of some general thought what appears in Lucretius as a living movement or individualised action.   And this tendency to abstract rather than concrete representation is in accordance with the Roman mould of mind.   We notice also how much more sparingly he uses such compound words as 'navigerum,' 'silvifragis,' etc., by which the earlier poets endeavoured to force the harder metal of the Latin language into the flexibility of Greek speech.   Virgil felt that these innovations were unsuited to the genius of the Latin tongue, and endeavoured to enlarge its capacities by novel constructions and by using old words with a new application rather than by novel formations of words.   But this gain was perhaps more than compensated by the loss which the language suffered in idiomatic purity and clearness.

In rhythmical movement the poem exhibits the highest perfection of which Latin verse is capable.   Of Homer's verse it has been happily said that it has 'a tranquil deep strength, reminding us of his own line,

Ἐξ ἀκαλαρρείταο βαθυρρόου ὠκεανοῖο[2].

---

[1] Il. xxi. 257–262.

[2] 'Out of the tranquil deep current of ocean.'   Professor Lushington's Inaugural Lecture delivered to the Students of the Greek Classes in the University of Glasgow, November, 1838.

The movement of Virgil's verse reminds us rather of his own
river—

> qui per saxa volutus
> Purior electro campum petit[1].

Occasionally we catch the sound of some more rapid rush and
impetuous fall, as in the hurry and agitation and culminating
grandeur of these lines—

> Continuo, ventis surgentibus, aut freta ponti
> Incipiunt agitata tumescere, et aridus altis
> Montibus audiri fragor, aut resonantia longe
> Litora misceri et nemorum increbrescere murmur[2];—

but generally the stream flows on, neither in rapid torrent nor
with abrupt transitions, but 'with a tranquil deep strength,' fed
by pure and abounding sources of affection, of contemplation,
of moral and religious feeling, of delight from eye and ear,
from memory and old poetic association.

---

[1] 'Which rolling over rocks in stream purer than amber makes for the
plain.'

[2] 'Forthwith as the winds are rising, either the channels of the sea begin to
boil and swell, and a dry crashing sound to be heard on the lofty mountains, or the shores to echo far with a confused noise, and the uproar of
the woods to wax louder.'   G. i. 356–9.

# CHAPTER VIII.

## THE ROMAN EPIC BEFORE THE TIME OF VIRGIL.

THE distinction between what is called the primitive and the literary epic has become one of the commonplaces of criticism. The two kinds of narrative poem belong to totally different epochs in civilisation; they are also the products of very different national temperaments and faculties. It is somewhat remarkable that those literatures which are richest in literary epics—the ancient Latin, the modern Italian, and the English— are those which possess few or no native poems either of the type realised in the Nibelungen-Lied, the Song of Roland, and poems of that class, or of the type realised in the Iliad and Odyssey; nor is there, in connexion with the earlier traditions of the Italian or the English race, that cycle of heroic adventure and personages in which such poems have their origin. The composition of the Aeneid and of the Paradise Lost implies powers of combination, of arranging great masses of materials, of concentration of the mind on a single object, more analogous to those which produced the vast historical work of Livy and 'The Decline and Fall' of Gibbon, than to the spontaneity, the *naïveté,* the rapidity of conception and utterance, and that immediate sympathy between poet and people, to which we owe the continuous poems developed out of some germ of popular ballad or national legend. It was the peculiar glory of Greece, that in the earlier stage of her literary development she manifested not only a perfection of expression and of art, but a maturity of intelligence, a true insight into the meaning of life, a nobility of imagination in union with a clearness and sanity of judgment, which the most advanced eras of other literatures scarcely equal. Thus the two great Greek epics are unique in character, and, while they have, in the highest degree, the excellences of each class, they can properly be ranked under neither. While exhibiting, better than any other writings, man and the outward world in 'the first intention,'—man in the energy and buoyancy of the national youth, and Nature in the vividness of impression which she makes on the mind and sense in their most healthy activity,—they are at the same time masterpieces of art and great monuments of the national mind. The Greek imagination with no appearance of effort produced works of such compass and harmonious proportion as only long years of labour and reflection in collecting and combining materials in accordance with a predetermined purpose produced in other literatures.

We are not called upon to consider here the conditions out of which the earlier type of epic poetry is developed, or to enquire why the Latin race failed to create at least some inartistic legendary poem of sufficient length to be ranked in that form of literature. Perhaps no answer could be given to the question excepting that the Latin race had not sufficient creative force to produce such a work,—which is simply another way of stating the fact that it did not produce epic poems. The Romans were from a very early period interested in their past history and traditions. They seem to have shaped, either out of real incidents in their national and family history, or out of their chief national characteristics, stories of strong human interest[1], which only want the 'vates sacer' to be converted into poems. Every great family seems to have had its own traditions, glorifying the exploits and preserving the memory of illustrious ancestors; and whatever may have been the case in regard to the legendary stories connected with the fortunes of the State, some of these traditions were undoubtedly expressed in rude Saturnian verse, and chanted at family gatherings and at funeral banquets. The memory of these ancestral lays—if we may apply that word to them—survived till the time of

[1] E. g. those of Lucretia, Virginia, Coriolanus, Brutus, T. Manlius, etc.

Cicero, Horace, and apparently even of Tacitus[1], though no actual trace of them appears to have existed even in the age of the elder Cato. But the influence of these rude germs of poetry—if they exercised any influence on Latin literature at all —was confined to the structure of Roman history. An enquiry into the origin and growth of Roman epic poetry need not concern itself with them.

Neither is it necessary here to go back into the vexed and probably insoluble question of the genesis of the Homeric poems. That these stand in most intimate relation with the Virgilian epic is a patent fact; and the nature of this intimate relation will be examined in some of the subsequent chapters. But they first began to act on the Roman imagination and art many centuries after they assumed their present form. The Romans accepted them as they did the lyrical and dramatic poetry of Greece, and were absolutely unconcerned with the questions as to their origin which interest modern curiosity. For the adequate understanding of the form and substance of the Roman epic as it was shaped by its greatest master, a competent knowledge of the Iliad and Odyssey must be presupposed; but it is unnecessary in a work on Latin literature to discuss the origin and character of the epic poetry of the Greeks on the same scale on which their idyllic and didactic poetry has been discussed in previous chapters.

But just as historical composition, regarded as a branch of art, though originating in the imitation of Greek models, has assumed in the works of Livy and Tacitus a distinctively Roman type, in conformity with certain characteristics of the race and with the weight of new matter which it has to embody, so, too, the type of epic poetry realised by Virgil has acquired a distinctive character as a vehicle of Roman sentiment and material. To appreciate the native, as distinct from the foreign element in the mould in which Virgil's representation is cast, it is necessary to attend to certain instincts and tendencies which

---

[1] Cf. Annals, iii. 5, 'Veterum instituta ... meditata ad virtutis memoriam carmina,'—quoted by Teuffel.

were calculated strongly to affect any form of narrative poetry amongst the Romans, and also to take a rapid survey of the history of their narrative poetry from the beginning of their literature to the Augustan Age.

In the first place, the strong national sentiment of Rome was a feeling which could not fail to be appealed to in any works which aimed at securing both general and permanent interest. The heroic story of Greece was indeed able for a time to attract general attention at Rome from the novelty of the dramatic representations in which it was introduced. But even Roman tragedy, to judge from the testimony of Cicero and others, seems to have owed more of its popularity to the grave spirit by which it was animated and the Roman strength of will exhibited in its personages, than to the legitimate sources of interest in a drama, viz. the play of human motives and the vicissitudes of human fortunes. But to sustain the interest of a long narrative, as distinct from a dramatic poem, it was necessary to act on some deep and general feeling. Not only did the hearers require to be thus moved to attention, but the poet himself could only thus be inspired and sustained in the unfamiliar task of literary composition. Now, looking to other manifestations of Roman energy, we see that whatever force was not employed on present necessities, was given, not as among the Greeks to ideal creation, but to the commemoration of events of public importance, and to the transmission of the lessons as well as of the history of the passing time. The connexion between the past and the future was maintained by monuments of different kinds, by public inscriptions, written annals, fasts, or festivals recording some momentous experience in the history of the State. All that we know and can still see of Roman work suggests the thought of a people who had an instinctive consciousness of a long destiny; who built, acted, and wrote with a view to a distant future. A national history was the legitimate expression of this impulse; but before the language was developed into a form suited for a continuous work in prose, it was natural that the tendency to realise the past and hand down the memory of the present should find an outlet for itself in various forms of narrative poetry.

Again, the Romans had a strong personal feeling of admiration for their great men. They were animated by that generous passion to which, in modern times, the term hero-worship has been applied. And corresponding with this feeling on the part of his countrymen, there was in the object of it a strong love of glory, a strong passion to perpetuate his name. Through the whole course of Roman history we recognise this motive acting powerfully on the men most eminent in war, politics, and literature, and on no one more powerfully than on the Emperor Augustus. The memory of the great men of Rome and of their actions was kept alive by monuments, statues, coins, waxen images preserved in the atrium of the family house, by the poems sung and speeches delivered among funeral ceremonies, by inscriptions on tombs (such as that still read on the tomb of Scipio Barbatus), by family names (such as that of Africanus) derived from great exploits, and, under the Empire, by the great triumphal arches and columns which still excite the admiration of travellers. The Roman passion for glory received its highest gratification in the triumph which celebrated great military exploits. The culmination of the tendency to glorify actual living men, or men recently dead, is witnessed in the deification of the Emperors. With the development of literature we find, as we should expect, this tendency of the imagination allying itself with poetry, from the time when Ennius devoted one work to the celebration of Scipio down to the panegyrists of Augustus, Messala, or Agrippa [1] under the early Empire. A new direction and a new motive were thus given to narrative poetry—a direction and motive which had no inconsiderable influence in determining Virgil to the choice of the subject of the Aeneid.

Another characteristic of the race was likely to impress itself on the form and execution of their narrative poetry, viz.

---

[1] Cf. Horace's Ode, 'Scriberis Vario,' etc., which shows at least that Agrippa desired to have a poem written in honour of his exploits.

their love of works of large compass and massive structure. Vastness of design and solid workmanship are as distinctive properties of Roman art, as harmony of proportion and beauty of form are of the works of Greek imagination.  To compose a literary work which should be representative of the genius of Rome, it was necessary that the author should be not only imbued with Roman sentiment and ideas, but also endowed with the Roman capacity for patient and persevering industry.  Concentration of purpose on works conceived and executed on a great scale, with a view both to immediate and permanent results, was an essentially Roman quality.  The Romans built their aqueducts and baths for the commonest needs of life, and constructed their roads and encampments, in such a way as to astonish the world after the lapse of nearly two thousand years. With similar energy and persistence of purpose they built up their greatest literary works.  This characteristic favoured the growth among them of a type of epic poetry as distinct from that of Greece as the Coliseum was from the Parthenon.

If Roman epic poetry was not to be a mere imitation of the Greek epic, we should accordingly expect that it should exhibit some or all of these characteristics,—that it should seek that source of interest which secures permanent attention to a long narrative poem in national sentiment; that it should strive to restore the memory of the past history and traditions of the State and at the same time to give expression to the ideas of the present time; that it should magnify the greatness of eminent living men or of those who had served their country before them; and that it should be conceived on a large scale, and be executed perhaps with rude, but certainly with strong and massive workmanship.  The first original narrative poem in Latin literature—the Punic War of Naevius—treated of a subject of living interest, and at the same time glorified the mythical past of Rome; and, while rude in design and execution, it was conceived and executed on a scale of large dimensions.  The example was thus given of a Roman epic based on a legendary foundation, but mainly built out of the materials of contemporary history. We can imagine that, at the time when this poem was composed, a more vivid interest would be felt in the fictitious connexion between Rome and Troy from the fact that it was in the First Punic War that this connexion appears first to have been generally recognised. The legend had not as in Virgil's time the prestige of two centuries, but it had the force of novelty to recommend it for poetic purposes. At the same time the great struggle between Rome and Carthage, on which the attention of the world was fixed at the time when Naevius wrote, must have given a peculiar meaning to the early relations between the two imperial States, as they were first represented in his poem.

The poem of Naevius gave the germinative idea and some of the materials to the first and fourth Books of the Aeneid; it established also the principle of combining in one work a remote mythical past with a subject of strong contemporary interest. At the same time it gave the example, followed by the Roman national epic, before the time of Virgil, of taking the main subject of the poem from the sphere of actual history. This confusion between the provinces of poetry and prose had been avoided by the instinct of Greek taste. Among the large number of Greek epic writers from the age of Homer to that of Nonnus, we hear of only one or two who treated of actual historical events. The general neglect of those poems which in ancient and modern times have treated of historical events and characters in the forms of epic poetry shows that the Greek instinct in this, as in all other questions of art, was unerringly right. The choice and treatment of such a subject are equally fatal to the truth and completeness of historical representation and to the ideality and unity of a work of art. Though the objection does not equally apply to dramatic art, yet the modern instinct, which selects for that mode of representation subjects remote from our own times, confirms the judgment in accordance with which the Athenians fined their tragic poet for reminding them of a too recent sorrow.

The Roman writers recognised the analogy between epic and

historic narrative,—and the way in which they apprehended the alliance between them was as injurious to the truthfulness of their history as to the symmetry of their early poetry,—but they did not before the time of Virgil recognise the artistic distinction between them.  The Roman epic and Roman history originated in the same feeling and impulse—the sentiment of national glory, the desire to perpetuate the great actions and the career of conquest, which were the constituent elements of that glory.  The impulse both of poets and historians was to build up a commemorative monument ; not, as among the Greeks, to present the spectacle of human life in its most animated, varied, and noble movements.  To a Roman historian and to a Roman poet the character and the fate of individuals derived their chief interest from their bearing on the glory and fortune of the State.  In the Greek epic, on the other hand, the interest in Achilles and Hector is much more vivid than that felt in the success of the Greek or Trojan cause.  In Herodotus the interest felt in the most important historical crisis through which the world has ever passed is inseparably blended with that felt in a great number of individual men, among the enemies of Greece, no less than among Greeks themselves.  In the History of Livy we do not expect to find truthful delineation or sagacious analysis of the characters of the leading men of Rome; still less do we expect to find impartial and sympathetic delineation of the enemies of Rome ; but we seek in his pages the image of the nation's life in its onward career of conquest and internal change, as pride and affection shaped it on the tables of the national memory.  The idea of Rome, as the one object of supreme interest to gods and men, in the past, present, and future, imparts the unity of sentiment, tone, and purpose which is characteristic of the type of Roman epic poetry and of Roman history.

Naevius in selecting for his epic poem the subject of the First Punic War, and in connecting that war with the events which were supposed to connect the Roman State immediately with a divine origin and destiny, was the first Roman who was moved

to write by this powerful impulse.   But the man who first gave
full expression to the national idea and feeling, who first made
Rome conscious of herself, and who was the true founder of
her literature, was Ennius.   The title which he gave to his epic
—Annales—perhaps the most prosaic title ever given to a work
of genius, indicates the character of his work and his mode of
treatment.   The inspiration under which it was written is more
truly indicated by the other name—Romais—by which, according to the testimony of an ancient grammarian [1], it was sometimes known.   He took for his subject the whole career of
Rome, from its mythical beginning in the events which followed
the Trojan war onward to the latest events in his own day.
The work was recognised as a great epic poem, and at the same
time fulfilled the part of a contemporary chronicle.   It was a
true instinct of genius to feel that the only material suitable for
a Roman epic was to be sought in the idea of the whole national life.   That alone could supply the essential source of epic
inspiration, the sympathy between the poet and those to whom
his poem is addressed, by which the epic poet receives from,
as well as gives back to, his audience.   But on the other hand,
while he has the true poetic impulse,—the ' vivida vis ' and the
strong conceptions of a poet,—he came too soon to acquire the
tact and delicacy of conception and execution equally essential
to the creation of works destined for immortality.   The subject
was too vast to be treated within the compass of a poem, which
demands to be read as a whole, and to be contemplated as one
continuous mental creation.   The treatment of a long series of
actions in chronological order is incompatible with artistic
effect; the treatment of contemporary history is incompatible
with the ideality of imaginative representation.   The workmanship of the poem, as exhibited in many fragments, is powerful,
but at the same time rude and unequal.   Yet Ennius was a
true representative writer.   He appealed powerfully to the
national sentiment; he revived the mythical and historic fame
of the past; he perpetuated the memory and interpreted the

[1] Diomedes, quoted by Teuffel.

meaning of his own time; he enhanced the glory of the great men and the great families of Rome; and he produced a work of colossal proportions and massive execution. Till his place was taken by a successor who united the fervour of a national poet to the perfect workmanship of an artist, he was justly regarded as the truest representative in literature of Roman character, sentiment, and ideas.

Other narrative and historical poems were known by the name of 'Annales;' one in three Books, written by Accius, the tragic poet; another written by A. Furius of Antium, which extended to a greater length, as Macrobius (ii. 1. 34 [1]) quotes from the tenth and the eleventh Books lines appropriated by Virgil,—one of many proofs of the manner in which the genius of Virgil, acting upon great reading, absorbed the thoughts and diction of his predecessors. The most important of the historical poems which continued the mistake of treating recent history in the form of a metrical chronicle appears to have been the Istrian War of Hostius, the grandfather of the Cynthia of Propertius, and alluded to by him in the line,

> Splendidaque a docto fama refulget avo.

This poem was written early in the first century B. C., in three Books, and took up the treatment of Roman history where the Annals of Ennius ended.

In the earlier part of the Ciceronian Age, the decay of public spirit, and the strong tendency which had set in of advancing individual claims above the interest of the State, and of looking to individual leaders rather than to established institutions, gave a new direction to narrative verse. The passion for personal

---

[1]     Rumoresque serit varios ac talia fatur.  Aen. xii. 228.
Furius in decimo:
Rumoresque serunt varios et multa requirunt.
Nomine quemque vocans reficitque in proelia pulsos.  Aen. xi. 731.
Furius in undecimo:
Nomine quemque ciet; dictorum tempus adesse
Commemorat.
Deinde infra:
Confirmat dictis simul atque exuscitat acres
Ad bellandum animos reficitque ad proelia mentes.

glory became the principal motive of those poems which treated of recent or contemporary history. Eminent families and individuals secured for themselves the services of poets, native or Greek. Even before this time, Accius, as we learn from Cicero[1], was closely associated with D. Brutus, and it seems not unlikely that the choice of the subject of one of his tragedies,—Brutus, —was made as a compliment to his friend and patron. The Luculli and Metelli retained the services of Archias, as their panegyrist,—a fact referred to by Cicero in one of his letters to Atticus, not without a slight touch of jealousy[2]. Pompey was served in the same way by Theophanes of Mitylene. The patronage of the great to men of letters was thus by no means so disinterested as our first impressions might lead us to suppose. Cicero himself with his extraordinary literary activity wrote in his youth a poem on his townsman Marius, and failing to find any other Greek or Roman to undertake the task, composed a poem in three Books on his own Consulship[3], with a result not fortunate to his reputation either for modesty or good taste. In a letter to his brother Quintus, we find him encouraging him to the composition of a poem on the Invasion of Britain by Julius Caesar. The passage is worth attending to as indicating the materials out of which those poems which aimed at celebrating contemporary events were framed :—'What strange scenes, what opportunities for describing things and places, what customs, tribes, battles. What a theme too you have in your general himself[4]!' This passage may be compared with two passages in Horace, showing that the same kind of thing was expected from a poetical panegyrist under Augustus. The first of these is from Sat. ii. 1, lines 11 etc., where Trebatius advises Horace,

> Caesaris invicti res dicere—

[1] Pro Arch. 11.
[2] Ep. ad Att. i. 16: 'Epigrammatis tuis, quae in Amaltheo posuisti, contenti erimus, praesertim quum et Chilius nos reliquerit, et Archias nihil de me scripserit; ac vereor, ne, Lucullis quoniam Graecum poema condidit, nunc ad Caecilianam fabulam spectet.'
[3] Also one on his exile.
[4] Epist. ad Q. Fratrem, lib. ii. 16.

to which advice the poet answers,

> Cupidum, pater optime, vires
> Deficiunt: neque enim quivis horrentia pilis
> Agmina, nec fracta pereuntes cuspide Gallos,
> Aut labentis equo describat vulnera Parthi [1].

The other passage from Horace (Epistles, ii. 1. 250) has a closer resemblance to the passage in Cicero:—

> Nec sermones ego mallem
> Repentes per humum quam res componere gestas,
> Terrarumque situs et flumina dicere, et arces
> Montibus impositas, et barbara regna, tuisque
> Auspiciis totum confecta duella per orbem [2], etc.

Horace expresses his contempt for this style of poem in other passages of his Satires, as (ii. 5. 41),

> seu pingui tentus omaso
> Furius hibernas cana nive conspuet Alpes [3];

and also (Sat. i. 10. 36–37),

> Turgidus Alpinus jugulat dum Memnona, dumque
> Defingit Rheni luteum caput [4].

The most prolific writer of epics in the latter half of the Ciceronian Age was Varro Atacinus, the first Transalpine Gaul who appears in Roman literature; the same who is mentioned by Horace as having made an unsuccessful attempt to revive the satire of Lucilius:—

> Hoc erat, experto frustra Varrone Atacino [5], etc.

---

[1] 'Though anxious to do so, worthy father, I have not strength enough; for it is not every one who can describe the lines bristling with pikes, nor the Gauls dying in the fight with broken spear point, or the wounded Parthian falling from his horse.'

[2] 'Nor should I choose rather to write prosaic discourses than to treat of historic deeds, and to describe the scenes of other lands and rivers and castles perched on mountains, and barbarous realms, and the wars brought to an end over the whole world under thy auspices.'

[3] 'Or whether gorged with rich tripe (*al.* with huge paunch distended) Furius will spit his white snows over the Alps in winter-time.' The 'Furius' mentioned here is supposed to be M. Furius Bibaculus, the reputed author of a poem on the Gallic War, as well as of the Epigrams, 'referta contumeliis Caesarum,' of which Tacitus speaks (An. iv. 34).

[4] 'While blustering Alpinus strangles Memnon, and disfigures and bemires the source of the Rhine by his description.'     [5] Sat. i. 10. 46.

He had served under Julius Caesar in Gaul, and wrote a poem
on the war against the Sequani in the traditional form.   He
also opened up to his countrymen that vein of epic poetry
which had been wrought by the Alexandrians.   The most
famous poem of this kind in the literature of the Republic was
the Jason of Varro, imitated probably from the Argonautics of
Apollonius.   Propertius speaks of this poem in a passage where
he classes Varro also among the writers of amatory poetry
before his own time, such as Catullus, Cinna, Gallus, and Virgil
in his Eclogues :—

> Haec quoque perfecto ludebat Iasone Varro,
> Varro Leucadiae maxima flamma suae[1].

He is thus as a writer of epic poems, on the one side, of the
native school of Ennius and the Annalists; on the other, he is
the originator of that other type of Roman epic which appears
under the Empire in the Thebaid and Achilleid of Statius and
the Argonautics of Valerius Flaccus.

The two great poets of the later Ciceronian era introduced a
great change into Roman poetry,—the practice of careful composition.   They are the first artistic poets of Rome.   The
rapidity of composition which characterised all the earlier writers
was, in the rude state of the language at that time, incompatible
with high accomplishment.   We read of Cicero writing five
hundred hexameters in a night, and of his brother Quintus
writing four tragedies in sixteen days.   The true sense of
artistic finish first appeared in Lucretius, and to a greater degree
in Catullus, and the younger men of the Ciceronian Age, Licinius Calvus, Helvius Cinna, etc.   The contempt with which
the younger school regarded the old fashion of composition
appears in Catullus' references—neither delicate nor complimentary—to the 'Annales Volusi,' the ponderous annalistic
epic of his countryman (conterraneus) Tanusius Geminus[2].
But in this younger school, poetry separated itself entirely from

---

[1] 'Such love songs Varro too composed after finishing his Jason, Varro,
the great passion of his own Leucadia.'

[2] Schwabe, Quaestiones Catullianae, p. 279.

the national life, or dealt with it only in the form of personal
epigrams on the popular leaders and their partisans.   The
dignity of the hexameter was reserved by them for didactic
or philosophic poetry and short epic idyls treating of the
heroic legends of Greece.   Didactic poetry, directing the attention to contemplation instead of action, established itself as
a successful rival to the old historical epic, in the province of
serious literature.

The latter, however, still found representatives in the following generation.   Thus Anser, the panegyrist of Antony, is
familiarly known, owing to one of the few satiric allusions which
have been attributed to Virgil :—

> Nam neque adhuc Vario videor nec dicere Cinna
> Digna, sed argutos inter strepere anser olores[1].

Varius, with whom he is by implication contrasted in those
lines, is characterised by Horace as 'Maeonii carminis ales,'
at a time when Virgil was only famous as the poet of rural
life.   He was the author of a poem on the death of Julius
Caesar.   We hear also of other specimens of the contemporary epic produced in the Augustan Age, one by Cornelius
Severus treating of the Sicilian Wars, one by Rabirius treating of the Battle of Actium, and one by Pedo Albinovanus
treating of the voyage of Germanicus 'per oceanum septen-
trionalem[2].'

We find Horace repeatedly excusing himself with self-
disparaging irony, while exhorting younger poets to the task
of directly celebrating the wars of Augustus,—e. g. Epist. i.
3. 7 :—

> Quis sibi res gestas Augusti scribere sumit?
> Bella quis et paces longum diffundit in aevum[3]?

Horace does indeed celebrate some of the military as well as

---

[1] 'For my strain seems not yet to be worthy of Varius or Cinna, but to
be as the cackling of geese amidst the melody of swans.'

[2] Mentioned by W. S. Teuffel.   Perhaps the best known poem in our own
literature of this type is 'The Campaign' of Addison.

[3] 'Who takes on himself to write the story of Augustus' deeds, who
perpetuates to distant ages the memory of wars waged and the peace
concluded?'

the peaceful successes of the Augustan Age, in the only form in which contemporary or recent events admit of being poetically treated, viz. lyrical poetry. But considering how eager Augustus was to have his wars celebrated in verse and how strong in him was the national passion for glory, and considering that Virgil and Horace were pre-eminently the favourite poets of the time and the special friends both of the Emperor himself and his minister, it is remarkable how they both avoid or defer the task which he wished to impose on them. This reluctance arose from no inadequate appreciation of his services to the world, but from their high appreciation of what was due to their art. Virgil had been similarly importuned in earlier times by Pollio and Varus, and had gracefully waived the claim made on him by pleading the fitness of his own muse only for the lighter themes of pastoral poetry. He seems to have hesitated long as to the form which the celebration of the glories of the Augustan Age should take. How he solved the problem, how he sought to combine in a work of Greek art the inspiration of the national epic with the personal celebration of Augustus, will be treated of in the following chapter.

# CHAPTER IX.

## FORM AND SUBJECT OF THE AENEID.

### I.

THE motives and purpose influencing Virgil to undertake the composition of the Aeneid are to be sought partly in his own literary position, partly in the state of public feeling at the time when he commenced his task, and partly in the direction given to his genius by the personal influence of Augustus. As the author of the Georgics he had established his position as the foremost poetic artist of his time. He had achieved a great success in a great and serious undertaking. He had entered into competition with Greek poets of acknowledged reputation, and had surpassed them in their own province. He had accomplished all that could be accomplished by him as the poet of the peaceful charm of country life. But while in his two earlier works he limits himself to that field assigned to him by Horace,—that over which the 'gaudentes rure Camenae' presided,—the stirring of a larger ambition is observable in both poems :—

> Si canimus silvas, silvae sint consule dignae :

and again :—

> Temptanda via est qua me quoque possim
> Tollere humo victorque virum volitare per ora [1].

He had yet to find a fuller expression for his sympathy with his age, which had deepened with the deepening significance of the

---

[1] 'If our song be of the woods, let the woods be worthy of a consul.'
'I must essay a way by which I too may be able to rise above the ground, and to speed triumphant through the mouths of men.'

times, and for that interest in the contemplation of human life which becomes the dominant influence in all great poets whose faculty ripens with advancing years. He might still aspire to be the Homer, as he had proved himself to be the Theocritus and the Hesiod of his country. The rudeness of the work of Ennius, the limited and temporary scope of the works of Varius, —his only competitor in epic song,—left that place still unappropriated. Virgil's whole previous career prepared him to be the author of a poem of sustained elevation and elaborate workmanship. The composition of the Georgics had trained his faculty of continuous exposition and of massing together a great variety of details towards a common end. It had given him a perfect mastery over the only vehicle suitable to the dignity of epic poetry. He had indeed still to put forth untried capacities, —the faculties of dealing with the passions and movement of human life as he had dealt with the sentiment and movement of Nature, of expressing thought and feeling dramatically and oratorically, and of imparting living interest to the actions and fortunes of imaginary personages. But he was now in the maturity of his powers. He had long lived with the single purpose of perfecting himself in art and knowledge. He had no other ambition but to produce some great work, which should perpetuate his own fame, and be a monument of his country's greatness.

The completion of the Georgics and the first conception of the Aeneid coincided in point of time with the event which not only established a sense of security in the room of the long strain of alarm and anxiety and a sense of national unity in the room of internecine strife in the Roman world, but which, to those looking back upon it after nineteen centuries, appears to be one of the most critical turning-points in all history. The enthusiasm of the moment found expression by the voice of Horace :—

> Nunc est bibendum, nunc pede libero
> Pulsanda tellus.

But Virgil represents more truly the deeper tendencies of his

age than the poet who has most faithfully painted its social
aspects.   He looks beyond the temporary triumph and sense of
relief, and sees in the victory of Actium the culminating point
of all the past history of Rome and the starting point of a
greater future.   There had been no time since the final defeat
of Hannibal so calculated to re-awaken the sense of national
life, of the mission to subdue and govern the world assigned to
Rome, and of the divine guardianship of which she was the
object.   As the joy of a great success had found a representative
voice in Ennius in the age when the State, relieved from all overwhelming danger, started on its career of foreign conquest, so
it found as deep and true a voice in Virgil at the time when the
relief, if not from as imminent a danger, yet certainly from a
much longer strain of anxiety, left Rome free to consolidate her
many conquests into a vast and orderly Empire.

In both the Eclogues and Georgics it was seen that Virgil
allows his genius to be in some measure directed by others in
the choice of his subjects, while he follows his own judgment in
his mode of treating them.   In the earlier poems he acknowledges the direction given to him both by Varus and by Pollio,—

Non iniussa cano—
                                 Accipe iussis
Carmina coepta tuis,—

while at the same time he excuses himself from directly celebrating their actions.   In the Georgics he describes his task
as being commanded by Maecenas—' tua, Maecenas, haud mollia
iussa.'   The desire of Augustus, whether openly expressed or
not, to commemorate his success and to add lustre to his rule
by associating them with the noblest art of his age, must have
acted with more imperious urgency on the will of Virgil than
the wishes of any of his earlier patrons.   His patriotic and
personal feeling to the saviour of the State and his own benefactor must have made the task imposed on him a service of
love as well as of obligation.   But in undertaking this task he
desired to make it subservient to the purpose of producing a
work which should emulate the greatest poetical works of the

Greeks, and which should, at the same time, be a true symbol of Rome at the zenith of her fortunes.

Virgil had now found in his own age a motive for the composition of that epic poem which it had been his boyish ambition to attempt,—

Cum canerem reges et proelia.

He could appeal as Ennius, or even as Homer had done, to hearers animated by the same feeling which moved himself. The two great conditions of a work of art which should gain the ear of the world immediately, and which should interest it permanently, were prepared for him in the enthusiasm of the moment, and in the enduring interest attaching to the career of Rome. His highly-trained faculty, already proved and exercised in other works, was a guarantee for the artistic execution of any design which he should undertake. But two questions remained for him to solve,—what form should his epic poem assume? should he follow absolutely the precedent of Homer, or of Ennius, or endeavour to surpass the contemporary panegyrists like Varius by a direct celebration of the events of his age? And if he adopted the Homeric type, what subject should he adopt so as to impart the interest of personal fortunes and human character to a poem the inspiring motive of which was the national idea?

The problem which Virgil set before himself was really one altogether new in literature. The Alexandrian Age had endeavoured to revive an interest in the heroic adventure of early or mythical times. It had recognised the principle that this distant background was essential to a poem of heroic action, and that events of contemporary or recent history were not capable of epic treatment. But it had not discerned the necessary supplement to that principle, that if such a poem, on a large scale, is to gain a permanent place in literature, it must bear some immediate relation to the age in which it is written, and be associated with some ethical and religious truths or some political cause of vital importance to the world. The epic poet of a cultivated age can maintain his place as a great artist only by being something more than an artist. He must feel more strongly than others, and give expression to the deepest tendencies of his own time. His subject must be charged with the force of the present, and not be mere material for the exercise of his imitative faculty. Virgil might, merely as an artist, have easily surpassed the Jason of Varro, or the Thebaid of Statius; but no technical skill in form, diction, and rhythm could have given to his treatment of such subjects the immediate attraction or the enduring spell which belongs to the Aeneid.

Both Ennius and Naevius had set the example of connecting a continuous narrative of the events of their own time with the mythical glories and the traditional history of Rome. And the Introduction to the third Georgic indicates that some idea of this kind at one time hovered before the imagination of Virgil. But while moved by the same patriotic impulses as these older poets, Virgil must have felt as strongly as Horace did that they were examples to be avoided in the choice of form and mode of treatment. He and Horace acknowledged the Greeks alone as their masters in art. He aspires not only to surpass Ennius and Naevius in the office they fulfilled, but to enter into rivalry with Homer,—to perform for the Romans of the Augustan Age a work analogous to that which Homer performed for the Greeks of his age. To do this, it was necessary to select some single heroic action from the cycle of mythical events, and to connect that with the whole story of Rome and Italy and with the events of the Augustan Age. The action had in some way to illustrate or symbolise the thoughts, memories, and hopes with which public feeling was identified at the time when the poem was written. Thus the original motive of the Virgilian epic was essentially different from that of the Homeric poems. The Iliad and the Odyssey have their origin in the pure epic impulse. The germ of the poems is the story; their purpose is to satisfy the curiosity felt in human action and character. The ' wrath of Achilles,' the ' return of Odysseus,' are, as they profess to be, the primary sources of interest in the poems founded on them; the representative character of the poems, like the representative character of Shakspeare's historical dramas, is accidental and undesigned. The germ of the Aeneid, on the other hand, is to be sought in the national idea and sentiment, in the imperial position of Rome, in her marvellous destiny, and in its culmination in the Augustan Age. The actions and sufferings of the characters that play their part in the poem were to be only secondary objects of interest; the primary object was to be found in the race to whose future career these actions and sufferings were the appointed means. The real key-note to the poem is not the 'Arma virumque' with which it opens, but the 'Tantae molis erat Romanam condere gentem [1]' with which the exordium closes. The choice and conduct of the action were the mechanical difficulties to be overcome by the poet, not the inspiring motives of his genius. This is the main cause of the comparative tameness of the Aeneid in point of human interest. Actors and action did not spring out of the spontaneous movement of the imagination, but were chosen by a refined calculation to fulfil the end which Virgil had in view. What Aeneas and his followers want in personal interest, is supposed to accrue to them as instruments in the hands of destiny. A new type of epic poetry is thus realised. The Iliad and the Odyssey are essentially poems of personal, the Aeneid is the epic of national fortunes.

## II.

Had Virgil's sole object been to write a national epic, which should satisfy popular sentiment, we can imagine several reasons why the tale of Romulus should have been chosen as its subject in preference to that of Aeneas. Though the traditional account of the founder of the city owes some of its features to Greek invention, yet it has a much more *naïve* and indigenous character than that of the Trojan settlement in Latium. It was more firmly rooted in the popular mind. It was still celebrated,

---

[1] 'So vast a toil it was to build up the Roman people.'

as we learn from Dionysius, in national hymns. It had been commemorated in a famous work of art, the bronze she-wolf still extant, at a time antecedent to the origin of Roman literature. It formed the chief subject of the first book of the Annals of Ennius, which, as dealing with the mythical portion of his theme, seems to have had more of an epic character than the later books. It was also a subject which by its relation to famous localities and memorials of the past,—such as the oldest city-wall, the Ruminal fig-tree, the temple of Jupiter Stator, the Palatine and Aventine hills,—and with the religious and social organisation of the State, admitted easily of being connected with the present time. It might have been so treated as to magnify the glory of the Emperor, who desired to be regarded as the second founder of the city, and is said to have debated whether he should not assume the title of Romulus, before deciding on taking that of Augustus. A poet of bolder and more original invention, and one more capable of sympathising with the purely martial characteristics of his hero, might have been attracted by this story of indigenous growth rather than by the exotic legend on which Virgil has bestowed such enduring life.

That legend seems, at first sight, to fail in the elements both of national and human interest. It was mainly of Greek invention. It seems to have been received by the Romans at a later stage in their development than that in which religious or legendary beliefs strike deep root in the popular imagination. It existed in vague and indistinct shape, and was associated with no marked individuality of personages or incidents. It was of composite growth, made up of many incongruous elements, the product rather of antiquarian learning and reflexion than of creative imagination.

The Greek germ out of which the legend arose, and the acceptance of this explanation of their origin by the Romans from the beginning of their literary history, are clearly ascertained. But there is great uncertainty as to the connecting link between these two stages in the development of the legend. The continuance of the line of Aeneas after the destruction of

Troy is announced by the mouth of Poseidon in the twentieth
Book of the Iliad (307–308) :—

> Νῦν δὲ δὴ Αἰνείαο βίη Τρώεσσιν ἀνάξει
> καὶ παίδων παῖδες, τοί κεν μετόπισθε γένωνται[1].

If an historical character may be assigned to any passages in
the Iliad, it may be presumed that the author of these verses
knew of a line of princes ruling over some remnant of the
Trojans, and claiming Aeneas as their ancestor. But these
verses do not imply any removal to a distant settlement. The
Cyclic poet, Arctinus, next spoke of Aeneas as retiring to Mount
Ida and founding a city there. The earliest traditions accordingly point to the Troad as the scene of the rule of his descendants : other traditions however, which must have been known to
Virgil, brought him to Thrace, to various places on the Aegean,
and to Buthrotum in Epirus. The origin of these traditions is
believed to be the connexion of Aeneas with the worship of
Aphrodite, which was widely spread over the Mediterranean, probably as a survival of early Phoenician settlements. This connexion
in worship is supposed to have arisen from a confusion between
the Trojan hero and the title Αἴνεας, denoting one of the attributes of the goddess. But the writer who first gave the idea of
a Trojan settlement in Italy is said to have been Stesichorus,
the lyrical poet of Himera in Sicily, who flourished about the
beginning of the sixth century B. C. One of the representations
in the Ilian table in the Capitoline Museum exhibits the figures
of Aeneas, of his son Ascanius, of the trumpeter Misenus, and
of Anchises carrying the sacred images, just as they are on the
point of embarking on board their ship. The following inscription is written under these figures,—

> Αἰνήας σὺν τοῖς ἰδίοις ἀπαίρων εἰς τὴν Ἑσπερίαν[2],—

and the Ἰλίου πέρσις of Stesichorus is quoted as the authority
for the representation[3]. The motive actuating Stesichorus was

---

[1] 'And now the mighty Aeneas shall rule over the Trojans, and his
children's children who may be born hereafter.'

[2] 'Aeneas with those belonging to him starting for Hesperia.'

[3] Schwegler, Römische Geschichte, vol. i. p. 298.

probably the desire to connect the newly-discovered localities in Italy and Sicily with the cycle of Homeric narrative. But Stesichorus apparently knew nothing of a Trojan settlement in Latium; Siris in Oenotria seems to have been fixed on by him as the place of refuge for the Palladium and the Penates of Troy. It was after the destruction of Siris that the fancy of the Greeks fixed on Lavinium, where there was a worship similar to that established at Siris, as the ultimate resting-place of Aeneas. The first definite statement connecting Rome with Troy was made by Cephalon of Gergis in the Troad (about 350 B. C.), who ascribed the foundation of the city to Romus a son of Aeneas. In the course of the next half century this appears to have become the prevailing belief among the Greeks, whose attention was now attracted by the growing ascendency of Rome in Italy. About the beginning of the third century Timaeus, the Sicilian historian, is said to have shaped the legend into the form adopted by Naevius [1].

It is obvious that there is a great gap in our knowledge of the stages in the development of the legend between Stesichorus, a poet of the sixth century, and Cephalon, an historian of the fourth. And the question suggests itself whether, in the interval between them, the Romans themselves had accepted any similar explanation of their origin. The early connexion between Rome and Cumae renders it not impossible that the Romans had formed some idea of their Trojan descent, before the wars of Pyrrhus brought them into more intimate connexion with the Greeks. It was by the Greek colonists of Cumae that the Isles of the Sirens, the Kingdom of the Laestrygones, and the abode of Circe were localised near Sorrento, the ancient town of Formiae, and the promontory of Circeii. It seems probable that to them also may be ascribed the mythical connexion established between the promontories of Caieta, Misenum, and Palinurum, in their own immediate neighbourhood, with the names of the household or followers of Aeneas. The

---

[1] The account here given of the development of the legend is taken from Schwegler, Römische Geschichte.

mythical traditions which assign a Greek origin to various important Latin towns, such as Tibur, Tusculum, Praeneste, and to the earliest settlement on the Palatine Hill, probably owe their invention to the same source. Alba Longa, as the chief city of the old Latin confederacy, must have been an object of greater interest to the Cumaeans than Tibur or Tusculum, and if we could be sure of the existence of the belief in the Trojan settlement in Latium before the destruction of Alba, we might infer with probability the great antiquity of the legend which ascribed the foundation of that town to the son of Aeneas. This belief might easily have passed to Rome; and Cephalon may have received it, in a somewhat distorted form, from native sources. But it is impossible to take any step in these conjectures without feeling the extreme uncertainty of our ground. We really know nothing of the acceptance of this account of their origin by the Romans before the time of the First Punic War; it is not easily reconcileable with the indigenous belief which certainly struck much deeper roots in the national history: the story as told by Cephalon appears to exclude the connexion between Rome and Alba as an intermediate link in that between Rome and Troy. It seems, on the whole, most probable that the story on which the Aeneid is founded is not only a Greek invention, but is an invention of a late and prosaic time, and was not known to the Romans before the date of their wars with Pyrrhus [1].

But besides the foreign and prosaic origin of the story, there is great vagueness and indistinctness in the incidents and personages connected with it. Homer indeed has supplied a definite, though not a marked, outline to the character of Aeneas; and Stesichorus, in shaping the family group of Anchises, Aeneas, and Ascanius flying from Troy with their household-gods, may have suggested to Virgil the leading characteristic of his hero. But these were nearly all the elements in the legend derived from primitive poetical sources.

[1] The growth of this legend is discussed with learning and ability by Professor Nettleship in his 'Vergil,' pp. 46-61.

There was no individuality of character attaching to any of the followers of Aeneas, nor any incident due to early imaginative invention associated with the dim tradition of his wanderings. The story, as finally cast into shape by Virgil, is one of composite growth, made up of many heterogeneous elements,—some supplied by poetical invention and the impressions of a primitive time, some the products of prosaic rationalism and the antiquarian fancies of a literary age, some suggested by Greek mythology and others by the ritual observances of Rome, some directly borrowed from the Homeric poems, others derived from the traditions of ancient Italy. It need hardly surprise us if out of such indistinct and heterogeneous materials Virgil failed to shape a thoroughly consistent and lifelike representation of human action and character.

But, on other grounds, the judgment of Virgil may be justified in the choice of this legend, vague, composite, and unpoetical as it was, as most adapted to his own genius and to the purpose of his epic poem. It was the only subject, of national significance, connected with the Homeric cycle of events. Not only the epic and dramatic poets of Greece, but the Roman tragic poets had recognised the heroic legends of Greece as the legitimate material for those forms of poetry which aimed at representing human action and character with seriousness and dignity. The personages and events connected with the Trojan War had especially been made familiar to the Romans by the works of their early dramatic poets. The Romans themselves had no mythical back-ground, rich in poetic associations, to their own history. It was impossible for a poet of a literary age to create this back-ground. But it was possible for him to give substance and reality to the shadowy connexion, existing in legend and in the works of older national writers, between the beginnings of Roman history and this distant region of poetry and romance. Virgil's imagination, as was seen in the examination of the Georgics, was peculiarly susceptible of the impressions produced by a remote antiquity and by old poetic associations. If he was deficient in spon-

taneous invention, he possessed a remarkable power of giving
new life to the creations of earlier times.   Next to the invention
of a new world of wonder and adventure,—a work most difficult
of accomplishment in a late stage of human development,—the
most attractive aim which an epic poet could set before himself
was that of reviving, under new conditions and with an immediate reference to the feelings of his contemporaries, an image
of the old Homeric life.   The subject of the wanderings and
subsequent adventures of Aeneas enabled Virgil to tell again,
and from a new point of view, the old story of the fall of Troy,
to present a modern version of the sea-adventures of the Odyssey, and to awaken the interest of a nation of soldiers in the
martial passions of an earlier and ruder age.

Although there is no evidence that the connexion of Rome
with Troy had sunk deeply into the popular mind before the
time of Virgil, yet it had been recognised in official acts of the
State for more than two centuries.   So early as the First Punic
War the Acarnanians had applied to the Romans for assistance
against the Aetolians, on the ground that their ancestors alone
among the Greeks had taken no part in the Trojan War.   The
Senate had offered alliance and friendship to King Seleucus on
condition of his exempting the people of Ilium, as kinsmen of
the Romans, from tribute[1].   T. Flamininus, in declaring all the
Greeks free after the conclusion of the Second Macedonian
War, described himself as one of the Aeneadae[2].   In the
Second Punic War, the prophet Marcius uses the word Troi-
ugena as an epithet of the Romans:—

---

[1] Suetonius says of the Emperor Claudius, ' Iliensibus, quasi Romanae
gentis auctoribus, tributa in perpetuum remisit, recitata vetere epistula
Graeca Senatus populique Romani Seleuco regi amicitiam et societatem
ita demum pollicentis, si consanguineos suos Ilienses ab omni onere im-
munes praestitisset.'   For these and other official recognitions of the
connexion between Rome and Ilium, see Schwegler, Römische Geschichte,
vol. i. p. 305 et seq.

[2] Mommsen (book iii. ch. 14) quotes these two lines from an Epigram
composed in the name of Flamininus:—

Αἰνεάδας Τίτος ὕμμιν ὑπέρτατον ὥπασε δῶρον
Ἑλλήνων τεύξας παισὶν ἐλευθερίαν.

> Amnem Troiugena Cannam Romane fuge [1].

So early as the time of Timaeus, i. e. before the First Punic War, the connexion of Aeneas with the worship of the Penates at Lavinium had been recognised. His own worship also established itself in the religion of the State by his identification with Jupiter Indiges, who seems to have had a temple on the banks of the river Numicius. Many families among the Roman aristocracy, as for instance the Cluentii, Sergii, Memmii [2], claimed to be descended from the followers of Aeneas. From the time of Naevius this account of the origin of the Romans had been the accépted belief in all Latin literature. Ennius begins his annals from the date

> Quum vetȇr occubuit Priamus sub Marte Pelasgo [3].

The poet Accius had written a tragedy called Aeneadae. The Roman annalists started with the tradition as an accepted fact. Thus Livy in reference to this belief uses the expression 'it is sufficiently established.' The great antiquarian Varro wrote a treatise on the Trojan origin of Roman families. Cicero in his Verrine orations (act. ii. 4. 33) speaks of the relationship of the people of Segesta in Sicily, which claimed to be a colony founded by Aeneas, with the Roman people. Even Lucretius, who stands apart from the general traditional beliefs of his countrymen, begins his poem with the words 'Aeneadum genetrix.' Virgil's poem appealed not to the popular taste, but to the national, religious, aristocratic, and literary sympathies of the cultivated classes. The legend of Aeneas, if less ancient and less popular, assigned a more august origin to the Roman race than the tale of the birth of Romulus :—

> Ab Iove principium generis, Iove Dardana pubes
> Gaúdet avo ; rex ipse Iovis de gente suprema
> Troius Aeneas, etc [4].

---

[1] Livy, xxv. 12.                                    [2] Aen. v. 117–123.
[3] 'When old Priam fell beneath the Pelasgian host.'
[4] 'From Jove is the origin of. our race : in Jove, as their fore-father, the Dardan youth exults ; our king himself the Trojan Aeneas is of the high lineage of Jove.' Aen. vii. 219–221.

These considerations may have recommended this subject to Virgil, as the most suitable symbol of the idea of Rome, from both a national and religious point of view.  But the circumstance which must have absolutely determined his choice was the claim which the Julian gens made to be directly descended from Iulus, Aeneas, and the goddess Venus.  This claim Virgil had already acknowledged in the line (Ecl. ix. 47),

> Ecce Dionaei processit Caesaris astrum,

and again (Georg. i. 28),

> cingens materna tempora myrto [1].

Even Julius Caesar had shown the importance which he attached to it by taking the words 'Venus Victrix' for his watchword at the battle of Pharsalia.  A greater tribute was paid to the qualities of Augustus, a more august consecration was conferred on his rule, by representing that rule as a prominent object in the counsels of Heaven a thousand years before its actual establishment, than could have been bestowed on him by the most detailed and ornate account of his actual successes.  The personal, as distinct from the national motive of the poem, is revealed in the prophetic lines attributed to Jupiter,

> Nascetur pulchra Troianus origine Caesar,
> Imperium Oceano, famam qui terminet astris,
> Iulius, a magno demissum nomen Iulo [2].

While the vagueness of the tradition and the absence of definite incident and individual character associated with it were conditions unfavourable to novelty and vividness of representation, yet they allowed to Virgil great latitude in carrying out his purpose of giving body and substance to all that unknown and shadowy past, which survived only in names, customs, and cere-

---

[1] 'Lo the star of Caesar sprung from Dione hath advanced'—'wreathing his brows with the myrtle sacred to his mother.'  Cf. Sic fatus velat materna tempora myrto.  Aen. v. 72.

[2] 'There shall be born of an illustrious line a Trojan Caesar, destined to make ocean the boundary of his empire, the stars the boundary of his fame, Julius, a name handed down from mighty Iulus.'  Aen. i. 286–288.

monies.  He was not limited to any particular district or period.
His plan enabled him to embrace in the compass of his epic the
dim traditions connected with the 'origins' of the famous towns
and tribes of Central Italy and of several of the great Roman
families; it enabled him to imagine the primitive state of places
which had a world-wide celebrity in his own time; to invoke,
as an element of poetic interest, the veneration paid to the
ancient rites of religion; and to cast an idealising light on
events, personages, families, or customs familiar to his own age,
by associating them with the sentiment of an immemorial past.
One great excellence of the Aeneid, as a representative poem,
is the large prospect of Roman and Italian life which it opens
up before us.  The vague outlines of the story which he followed
enabled Virgil to enlarge his conception with an ampler content
of local and national material, than if he had been called upon
to recast a more definite and more vital tradition.  The want
of individuality in the personages of his story justified him in
exhibiting their character in accordance with his own ideal; in
conceiving of Aeneas as the type of antique piety combined
with modern humanity, and of Turnus as the type of the
haughty and martial spirit animating the old Italian race.

Even the composite character of the legend and the heterogeneous elements out of which it was composed, if unfavourable
to unity of impression and simplicity of execution, conduced to
the poet's purpose of concentrating in one representation, of a
Roman vastness of compass, whatever might enhance and
illustrate the greatness of Rome and of its ruler.  The Rome of
the Augustan Age no longer exhibited the political and religious
unity of an old Italian republic; it was expanding its limits so
as to embrace in a much wider unity the various nations that
had played their part in the past history of the world.  As the
glory and wealth of Asia, Greece, Carthage, etc. had all gone to
swell the glory and wealth of Rome, so all the traditions,
historic memories, and literary art of the past were to be made
tributary to her national representative poem.  The first great
epic poem of the ancient world is buoyant with the promise of

the mighty life which was to be; the last great epic is weighty
with the accumulated experience of all that had been.   The
stream of epic poetry shows no longer the jubilant force and
purity of waters—'exercita cursu flumina'—which rise in the
high mountain-land separating barbarism from civilisation; it
moves more slowly and less clearly through more level and cultivated districts; its volume is swollen and its weight increased
by tributaries which have never known the 'bright speed[1]' of its
nobler sources.

### III.

*Composite character of the Aeneid illustrated by an examination
of the poem.*

These considerations lead to the conclusion that the legend
of Aeneas was better suited than any other which he could have
selected for the two objects which Virgil had before his mind in
the composition of the Aeneid; first, that of writing a poem
representative and commemorative of Rome and of his own
epoch, in the spirit in which some of the great architectural
works of the Empire, such as the Column of Trajan, the Arches
of Titus and of Constantine, were erected; and, secondly, that
of writing an imitative epic of action, manners, and character
which should afford to his countrymen an interest analogous to
that which the Greeks derived from the Homeric poems.   The
knowledge necessary to enable him to fulfil the first purpose
was contained in such works as the ceremonial books of the
various Priestly Colleges, the 'Origines' of Cato, the antiquarian
treatise of Varro, and perhaps the 'Annales' and 'Fasti[2]'
which preserved the record of national and family traditions.
In giving life to these dry materials his mind was animated by

[1]        'Oxus forgetting the bright speed he had
         In his high mountain cradle in Pamere.'
                                        Sohrab and Rustum.
[2] Cf. Hor. Od. iii. 17. 2–4 :—
         Quando et priores hinc Lamias ferunt
         Denominatos, et nepotum
         Per memores genus omne fastos, etc.

the spectacle of Rome, and the thought of her wide empire, her genius, character, and history; by the visible survivals of ancient ceremonies and memorials of the past; by the sight of the great natural features of the land, of old Italian towns of historic renown, or, where they had disappeared, of the localities still marked by their name :—

locus Ardea quondam
Dictus avis; et nunc magnum tenet Ardea nomen[1].

As poetic sources of inspiration for this part of his task Virgil had the national epic poems of Naevius and Ennius; and of both of these he made use: of the first, in his account of the storm which drives Aeneas to Carthage and of his entertainment there by the Carthaginian Queen; of the second, by his use of many half-lines and expressions which give an antique and stately character to the description of incidents or the expression of sentiment.  For Virgil's other purpose, his chief materials were derived from his intimate familiarity with the two great Homeric poems: but he availed himself also of incidents contained in the Homeric Hymns, in the Cyclic poems, in the Greek Tragedies, as for instance the lost Laocoon of Sophocles, and in the Argonautics of Apollonius Rhodius.   His own experience of life, and still more the insight which his own nature afforded him into various moods of passion, affection, and chivalrous emotion, enabled him to impart novelty and individuality to the materials which he derived from these foreign and ancient sources.

A minute examination of the various books of the poem would bring out clearly that these two objects, that of raising a monument to the glory of Rome and of Augustus, and that of writing an imitative epic reproducing some image of the manners and life of the heroic age, were present to the mind of Virgil through his whole undertaking.   It will be sufficient in order to show this two-fold purpose to look at the first book, and at some of the more prominent incidents in the later books.

[1] 'The place was called Ardea long ago by our fathers: and now Ardea, a name of might, haunts the spot.'

In the opening lines of the poem—

Arma virumque . . . multa quoque et bello passus—

we find, as in the Odyssey—

ἄνδρα μοι ἔννεπε . . . πάθεν ἄλγεα ὃν κατὰ θυμόν—

an announcement of a poem of heroic adventure, of vicissitudes and suffering by sea and land, determined by the personal agency of some of the old Olympian gods ('vi superum'). The scope of the Aeneid as explained in these lines is however wider than that of the Odyssey, as embracing the warlike action of the Iliad as well as a tale of sea-adventure. But in the statement of the motive of the poems a more essential difference between the two epics is apparent. The wanderings of Odysseus have no other aim than a safe return for himself and his companions. He acts from the simplest and most elemental of human instincts and affections, the love of life and of home,—

ἀρνύμενος ἥν τε ψυχὴν καὶ νόστον ἑταίρων. ]

Aeneas, like Odysseus, starts on his adventures after the capture of Troy,—

Troiae qui primus ab oris—

ἐπεὶ Τροίης ἱερὸν πτολίεθρον ἔπερσεν—

but he starts, 'fato profugus,' on no accidental adventure, but on an enterprise with far-reaching consequences, determined by a Divine purpose. While actively engaged in the personal object of finding a safe settlement for himself and his followers in Italy, he is at the same time a passive instrument in the hands of Providence, laying the foundation, both secular and religious, of the future government of the world:—

Multa quoque et bello passus, dum conderet urbem<br>
Inferretque deos Latio, genus unde Latinum<br>
Albanique patres atque altae moenia Romae[1].

The difference in character of the two epics is perceptible in the very sound of their opening lines. While the Latin moves with

---

[1] 'And after suffering much in war too, before he could found a city, and find a home for his gods in Latium—from whom is the Latin race, and the lords of Alba, and the walls of lofty Rome.'

stateliness and dignity and is weighty with the burden of the
whole world's history, the Greek is fluent and buoyant with the
spirit and life of the ' novitas florida mundi.'   The greatness of
Aeneas is a kind of ' imputed' greatness; he is important to the
world as bearing the weight of the glory and destiny of the
future Romans—

> Attollens humero famamque et fata nepotum.

Odysseus is great in the personal qualities of courage, steadfastness of purpose and affection, loyalty to his comrades, versa-
tility, ready resource ; but he bears with him only his own
fortunes and those of the companions of his adventure; he
ends his career as he begins it, the chief of a small island, which
derives all its importance solely from its early association with
his fortunes.

The double purpose of the Aeneid, and its contrast in this
respect with the Homeric poems, is further seen in the statement
of the motives influencing the Divine beings by whose agency
the action is advanced or impeded.   As in the opening paragraph Virgil had the opening lines of the Odyssey in view, in
the second, which announces the supernatural motive of the
poem—

> Musa, mihi causas memora, quo numine laeso—

he had in view the passage in the Iliad beginning with the
line—

> τίς τ' ἄρ σφωε θεῶν ἔριδι ξυνέηκε μάχεσθαι;

In the Iliad the supernatural cause of the action is the wrath of
Apollo, acting from the personal desire to avenge the wrong
done to his priest Chryses : in the Odyssey, it is the wrath of
Poseidon acting from the personal desire to avenge the suffering
of his son whom Odysseus blinded :—

> ἀλλὰ Ποσειδάων γαιήοχος ἀσκελὲς αἰεί
> Κύκλωπος κεχόλωται, ὃν ὀφθαλμοῦ ἀλάωσεν [1].

---

[1] 'Nay, but it is Poseidon, the girdler of the earth, that hath been wroth
continually with quenchless anger for the Cyclops' sake whom he blinded of
his eye.'   Butcher and Lang.

The gods in both cases act from personal passion without moral purpose or political object.   So too the powers which befriend Odysseus act from personal regard to him and acknowledgment of his wisdom and piety :—

ὃς περὶ μὲν νόον ἐστὶ βροτῶν, περὶ δ' ἱρὰ θεοῖσιν
ἀθανάτοισιν ἔδωκε, τοὶ οὐρανὸν εὐρὺν ἔχουσιν [1].

In the Aeneid, Juno, by whose agency in hindering the settlement of Aeneas in Italy the events of the poem are brought about, acts from two sets of motives; the first bringing the action into connexion with one of the great crises in the history of Rome, the second bringing it into connexion with the Trojan traditions.   Prominence is given to the first motive, in the announcement of which the deadly struggle between Rome and Carthage, 'when all men were in doubt under whose empire they should fall by land and sea [2],' is anticipated :—

Urbs antiqua fuit, Tyrii tenuere coloni,
Karthago . . .
           hoc regnum dea gentibus esse,
Si *qua fata sinant,* iam tum tenditque fovetque.
Progeniem sed enim Troiano a sanguine duci
Audierat, Tyrias olim quae verteret arces ;
*Hinc populum late regem belloque superbum*
Venturum excidio Libyae ; sic volvere Parcas [3].

In two other passages of the Aeneid this great internecine contest for the empire of the world, which left so deep an impression on the Roman memory, is seen foreshadowing itself, viz. in the dying denunciation and prayer of Dido,—

Exoriare aliquis nostris ex ossibus ultor,—

---

[1] 'Who in understanding is beyond mortals and beyond all men hath done sacrifice to the deathless gods who keep the wide heaven.'   Butcher and Lang.
[2] Lucret. iii. 836.
[3] 'There was a city of old, dwelt in by settlers from Tyre, Carthage,— that this should hold the empire of the world, if by any means the fates should allow, is even then the fond desire and purpose of the goddess.   Yet she had heard that a new race was issuing from Trojan blood, destined hereafter to overthrow the Tyrian towers,—and from them should spring a people, wielding wide sway, and of proud prowess in war, who should come to lay waste Libya—so did the Parcae roll on the circling events.'

and in the speech of Jupiter in the great council of the gods in
the tenth book—a passage imitated from Ennius :—

> Adveniet iustum pugnae, ne arcessite, tempus,
> Cum fera Karthago Romanis arcibus olim
> Exitium magnum atque Alpes inmittet apertas[1].

But to this motive are added other motives, both political and
personal,—the memory of her former enmity to Troy arising
out of her love to Argos, of the slight offered to her beauty by
the judgment of Paris, and of the occasion given to her jealousy
by the honour awarded to Ganymede :—

> manet alta mente repostum
> Iudicium Paridis spretaeque iniuria formae,
> Et genus invisum et rapti Ganymedis honores[2].

These two sets of motives bring out distinctly the two-fold
character of the action of the poem, its inner relation to the
future fulfilment of the Roman destiny, its more immediate
dependence on the past events forming the subject of the
Homeric poems.  The prominence in Virgil's mind of the
Roman over the Greek influences, in which his epic had its
origin, is indicated by the position and weight of the line of
cardinal significance—

> Tantae molis erat Romanam condere gentem ;

just as the dominant influence under which Lucretius wrote his
poem is indicated by the position and weight of the line—

> Tantum religio potuit suadere malorum.

In entering on the detailed narrative, which forms the main
body of the poem, Virgil at once attaches himself to Homer.
The action, like the action of the Odyssey, is taken up at that
stage immediately preceding the events of most critical interest,

---

[1] 'There shall come a fitting time for fight, seek not to hasten it on,
when fierce Carthage shall hurl against the Roman towers a mighty ruin,
through the open gateways of the Alps.'

[2] 'There remains deeply rankling in her heart the memory of the decision
of Paris, and of the wrong of her slighted beauty, of the hated family, and
the honours of the ravished Ganymede.'

after which it advances steadily to the final catastrophe.   The slower movement of the story in the years between the fall of Troy and the departure from Sicily is presupposed, and, like the adventures of Odysseus before his departure from the Isle of Calypso, the adventures of Aeneas are subsequently narrated by the principal actor in them.   The storm which drives the Trojan fleet to the Carthaginian coast ·was an incident in the epic of Naevius ; but the original suggestion and the actual description of it are due to the account of the storm raised by Poseidon in the fifth book of the Odyssey.   Juno, in availing herself of the instrumentality of Aeolus, bribes him by a promise similar to that made to Sleep in the fourteenth book of the Iliad.   The description of the harbour in which the Trojan ships find refuge is imitated from that of the harbour to which the Phaeacian ship brings Odysseus; and the success of Aeneas in the chase is suggested by two passages in the Odyssey, ix. 154 *et seq.* and x. 104 *et seq.*

The speech of Aeneas (198–207) again reminds us of the ultimate object of all the vicissitudes and dangers which he encounters :—

> Per varios casus, per tot discrimina rerum
> Tendimus in Latium, sedes ubi fata quietas
> Ostendunt[1].

Immediately afterwards we come upon one of the three great passages of the poem in which the action is prophetically advanced into the Augustan Age.   These three passages (i. 223–296, vi. 756–860, viii. 626–731), like the greater episodes of the Georgics, draw attention directly to what is the most vital and most permanent source of interest in the Aeneid.   They serve, along with the opening lines of the poem, better than any other passages to bring out the relation both of dependence on the Homeric epic and of contrast with it which characterise the Virgilian epic.

The passage before us, the interview between Jupiter and

---

[1] 'Through varied accidents, through so many perils, we hold our course to Latium, where the Fates reveal to us a peaceful settlement.'

Venus, owes its original suggestion to the scene in the first book of the Iliad in which Thetis intercedes with Zeus, to avenge the wrong done to her son. The object of this intercession is a purely personal one; the result of it is the whole series of events which culminates in the death of Hector. The object which Venus claims of Jupiter is the fulfilment of his promise that a people should arise from the blood of Teucer—

> Qui mare, qui terras omni dicione tenerent[1];

the result of her prayer is that Jupiter reveals to her not only the immediate future of Aeneas and the founding of Lavinium and of Alba, but the birth of Romulus, the building of Rome, the ultimate triumph of the house of Assaracus over Pthia, Mycenae, and Argos, the peaceful reign on earth and the final acceptance into heaven of the greatest among the descendants of Aeneas, who is there called, not by his later title of Augustus, but by the earlier name which he inherited from his adoptive father—

> Iulius a magno demissum nomen Iulo[2].

In this passage we note (1) Virgil's relation to the earlier poem of Naevius, who had sketched the outline of the scene which is here filled up; and also the reproduction of the diction of Ennius in the passage—

> Despiciens mare velivolum terrasque iacentis
> Litoraque et latos populos[3];

and in this—

> Olli subridens hominum sator atque deorum
> Voltu, quo caelum tempestatesque serenat[4];

and (2) we note a reference to the closing of the gate of Janus in the line—

> Claudentur Belli portae;

---

[1] 'Who should hold sea and land in universal sway.'
[2] 'Iulius a name handed down from mighty Iulus.'
[3] 'Looking down on the sail-winged sea, and low-lying lands, and the coasts and wide nations.'
[4] 'Smiling on her with that look with which he clears the sky and the storms, the father of men and gods,'—

and apparently to some symbolical representation in the art of
the Augustan Age in the words which follow—

Furor impius intus,
Saeva sedens super arma et centum vinctus aenis
Post tergum nodis, fremet horridus ore cruento[1].

After this digression the action proceeds according to Homeric
precedents. Mercury is sent to Dido, as Hermes is sent to
Calypso in the fifth book of the Odyssey. Then follows the
meeting of Venus with Aeneas and Anchises, the picturesque
and poetical features of which scene are suggested by a passage
in the Homeric Hymn to Aphrodite, describing the meeting of
the goddess with Anchises. The Trojan heroes pass on to
Carthage concealed in a mist as Odysseus makes his way to the
city of the Phaeacians. The pictorial representation of the
events of the Trojan war on the walls of the temple of Juno
is suggested partly by the pictorial art of the Augustan Age,
and partly by the song of the bard in the eighth book of the
Odyssey, celebrating the

νεῖκος Ὀδυσσῆος καὶ Πηλείδεω Ἀχιλῆος.

So too the later banquet in the palace of Dido is suggested
partly by the feast in the hall of Alcinous, partly by the magnificence of Roman entertainments in the Augustan Age, such
as those referred to in the lines of Lucretius—

Si non aurea sunt iuvenum simulacra per aedes, etc.

Finally, the device by which Venus substitutes Cupid for
Ascanius is borrowed from the Argonautics of Apollonius;
the introduction of the various suitors of Dido is suggested by
the part which the suitors of Penelope play in the Odyssey;
and the request of Dido to Aeneas to recount his past adventures owes its origin to the similar request made by Alcinous to
Odysseus.

---

[1] 'Within unhallowed Rage, seated on a heap of cruel arms, and bound
with a hundred knots of brass behind his back, will chafe wildly with
blood-stained lips.' Cf. the note on the passage in Servius: 'In foro
Augusti introeuntibus ad sinistram fuit bellum pictum et furor sedens super
arma aenis vinctus, eo habitu quo poeta dixit.'

It is in the first book that Virgil adheres most closely to his Greek guides; yet even in it we observe many traces of modern invention, which give a new character to the representation. The thought of Italy in the immediate future—

> Est locus, Hesperiam Graii cognomine dicunt,
> Terra antiqua, potens armis atque ubere glaebae;
> Oenotri coluere viri; nunc fama, minores
> Italiam dixisse ducis de nomine gentem [1]—

and the remoter vision of the ' altae moenia Romae ' remind us that we are contemplating no mere recast of a Greek legend, but a great national monument of the race which during the longest period of history has played the greatest part in human affairs.    The old gods of Olympus appear on earth once more, and now with all the attributes of Roman state, as ' principalities and powers ' contending for the empire of the world, and as instruments in the hands of destiny for the furthering of the great work which was only fully accomplished by Augustus.

In the recital of the fall of Troy, which occupies the second book, Virgil is said by Macrobius to have adhered almost verbally [2] to the work of a Greek poet, Pisander, the author of a poetical history of the world from the marriage of Jupiter and Juno down to the events contemporary with the poet himself. There seem to have been three Greek poets of that name, and the only one of them who was likely to have treated at any length of the events of that single night recorded in the second Aeneid is said to have lived after the time of Virgil.    It seems impossible that any earlier poet could have assigned so much space as that demanded by the statement of Macrobius to the personal adventures of Aeneas.    We are on surer ground in recognising the debt which Virgil owed to the account of the wooden horse in the Odyssey, to some of the lost plays of Sophocles, which told the tale of the treachery of Sinon and of

---

[1] ' There is a place named by the Greeks Hesperia, a land of old renown, mighty in arms and the richness of its soil—the Oenotrians dwelt in it.  Now the story is that their descendants have called the nation Italia from the name of their leader.'

[2] Sat. v. 2. 4.

the tragic fate of Laocoon, and to some of the lost Cyclic poems
and the 'Ιλίου πέρσις of Stesichorus.  The vision of Hector to
Aeneas reminds us of that of Patroclus to Achilles ; but in this
resemblance we recognise also the difference between the poem
founded on personal and that founded on  national fortunes.
The care which summons the shade of Patroclus to the couch
of his friend is the care for his own burial; the care which
brings Hector back to earth is the care for the salvation of the
sacred relics of Troy in view of the great destiny which awaited
them.   There is more of human pathos in the vision of Patroclus; more of a stately majesty in that of Hector.   And as in
other passages where Virgil wishes to produce this effect, we
note that he avails himself here of the language of Ennius,—

> Hei mihi, qualis erat. ·

So too, near the end of the book, where the shade of Creusa
gives to Aeneas the first intimation of his settlement in a
western land,—

> Et terram Hesperiam venies, ubi Lydius arva
> Inter opima virum leni fluit agmine Thybris [1],—

the same antique associations are appealed to [2].   So also in
describing the destruction of the palace of Priam, Virgil is said
to have imitated the description by Ennius of the destruction of
Alba [3].   And that feeling of ancient state and majesty with
which the memory of Troy is invested in such lines as

> Urbs antiqua ruit multos dominata per annos [4],

had been first expressed in the 'Andromache' of the older
poet.

Among the sources which Virgil used in the third book were

---

[1] 'And you will come to the land Hesperia, where Lydian Tiber flows
between rich fields of men with tranquil stream.'
[2] The line
> Quod per amoenam urbem leni fluit agmine flumen
occurs among the fragments of Ennius, and has been imitated also by
Lucretius (v. 271).
[3] Serv. Comment. on line 486.
[4] 'An ancient city, that held empire through long years, is falling in
ruins.'

probably the prose accounts of the late Greek historians, who rationalised the traditions of the various settlements of Aeneas which grew out of his association with the worship of Aphrodite. But the whole suggestion of sea-adventure, and still more of the incidents arising out of the visit to the land of the Cyclops, is due to the Odyssey, while the events connected with the landing in Thrace and in Epirus owe their origin to the Hecuba and Andromache of Euripides. But, on the other hand, the exact geographical knowledge displayed in it imparts a thoroughly modern character to the book; and one passage at least (as has been shown by a writer in the Journal of Philology)—the description of the voyage round the eastern and southern shores of Sicily—is so minutely accurate in detail as to give clear indication of being drawn from the personal experience of the author. Again, the frequent mention of Italy in the book, the speech of Helenus which announces the old traditional omen of the white sow, the direction as to the mode of performing religious ceremonies which the Romans should observe in all future times,—

> Hac casti maneant in religione nepotes,—[1]

and the trophy raised by Aeneas on the shores of Actium, help to remind us of the modern meaning which Virgil desired to impart to his representation of antique manners.

The fourth book, in which Virgil deserts the guidance of Homer for that of the Alexandrine epic, is intended to give the most passionate human, as distinct from the pervading national, interest to the poem. But the tragic nature of the situation arises from the clashing between natural feeling and the great considerations of State by which the divine actors in the drama were influenced. The death of Dido gives moreover a poetical justification for the deadly enmity which animated the struggle between Rome and her most dangerous antagonist. The fifth book follows the old tradition—as old at least as the time of Thucydides—which represented Trojan settlements as estab-

---

[1] 'Let their descendants piously observe this ceremony.'

lished in Sicily. The account of the foundation of Segesta by
the followers of Aeneas, and the story of the burning of the
ships by the Trojan women, may have been told by Timaeus;
and it was natural to ascribe to her son the building of the
famous temple of Venus Erycina. But the greater part of the
book is occupied with an account of the funeral games in
honour of Anchises, which, with modifications to suit the
changed locality, reproduce the games which Achilles celebrated
in honour of Patroclus. But the account of these games serves
the purpose of giving some individuality to three of the most
shadowy personages in the poem by establishing their connexion with three illustrious Roman families, and to flatter
Augustus by assigning an ancient origin to the Ludus Troiae,
—a kind of bloodless tournament of noble youths exhibited in
the early years of his reign,—and also, by the invention of a
fabulous ancestor, to add distinction to the provincial family of
the Atii, which was more truly ennobled by the great personal
qualities of the Emperor's mother, Atia.

With the landing in Italy the narrative assumes greater independence. The various localities introduced and the traditions
connected with them, the usages or ceremonies peculiar to
Italy which admit of being referred to an immemorial past, the
mere Italian names of Latinus and Turnus, Mezentius and
Camilla, are able to evoke national and sometimes modern associations. Thus the introduction of the Cumaean Sibyl into
the narrative affords the opportunity of reminding the Romans
of the importance assigned to the Sibylline prophecies in their
national counsels; and the impressive ceremony of the opening
of the gates of war enables the poet to appeal to the patriotic
impulses of his own age, in the lines—

> Sive Getis inferre manu lacrimabile bellum
> Hyrcansive Arabisve parant, seu tendere ad Indos
> Auroramque sequi Parthosque reposcere signa [1].

---

[1] 'Whether they are preparing to bring all the woes of war on the Getae,
or the Hyrcanians, or the Arabs, or to hold their way to the Indians, and
to go on and on towards the dawn, and to claim back the standards from
the Parthians.'

But many of the warlike incidents in the later books—as for instance the night foray of Nisus and Euryalus, the treacherous wounding of Aeneas, the withdrawal by supernatural agency of Turnus from the battle, the death of Pallas and the effect which that event has on Aeneas, and the final conflict between Turnus and Aeneas—show that Virgil was still following in the footsteps of his original guide. The passages, however, which bring out most clearly both this relation of Virgil to Homer and his point of departure from him are those which give an account of the descent into hell and describe the shield of Aeneas. The sixth book of the Aeneid owes its existence to the eleventh book of the Odyssey: but the shadowy conceptions of the Homeric 'Inferno,' suggested by the impulses of natural curiosity and the yearnings of human affection, are enlarged and made more definite, on the one hand, by thoughts derived from Plato, and, on the other, by the proudest memories of Roman history, from the legends of the Alban kings to the warlike and peaceful triumphs of the Augustan Age. The shield of Achilles presents to the imagination the varied spectacle of human life—sowing and reaping, a city besieged, a marriage festival, etc.; the shield of Aeneas presents the spectacle of the most momentous crises in the annals of Rome, culminating in the great triumph of Augustus. We note too in the latter passage the enhancement of patriotic sentiment by the use of the language and representation of Ennius, as at lines 630–634, and the lesson taught of the dependence of national welfare on the observance of religious traditions and of the duties of life sanctioned by religion, in the lines which describe the processions of the Salii and Luperci, and which indicate the punishment awarded to the sin of rebellion and disloyalty in the person of Catiline, and the recognition of civic virtue, even when exercised in defence of a losing cause, in the position assigned to Cato in the nether world—

Secretosque pios, his dantem iura Catonem [1].

---

[1] 'And the good apart, and Cato giving to them laws.'

The Iliad and the Odyssey are thus seen to be essentially epics of human life; the Aeneid is essentially the epic of national glory. The Iliad indeed is the noblest monument of the greatness, as it is of the genius, of the Greeks. And the Aeneid is much more than a monument of national glory. It is full of pathetic situations and stirring incidents which move our human compassion or kindle our sympathies with heroic action. But if we ask what are the most powerful sources of interest in the Greek and in the Roman epic respectively, the answer will be that in the first these spring immediately out of human life; in the second they spring out of the national fortunes. And this distinction is generally recognisable in the art, literature, and history of the two nations. This predominance of national interest and the presence of a large element of living modern interest in the treatment of an ancient legend separate the Aeneid still further from the Alexandrine epic and its later Roman imitations. The compliance with the conditions of epic poetry, as established by Homer and confirmed by the great law-giver of Greek criticism, equally separates it from the rude attempts of Ennius and Naevius, and from the poems which treat of historical subjects of a limited and temporary significance, such as the Pharsalia of Lucan and the Henriade of Voltaire. Though Virgil may be the most imitative, he is at the same time one of the most original poets of antiquity. We saw that he had produced a new type of didactic poetry. By the meaning and unity which he has imparted to his Greek, Roman, and Italian materials through the vivifying and harmonising agency of permanent national sentiment and of the immediate feeling of the hour, he may be said to have created a new type of epic poetry—to have produced a work of genius representative of his country as well as a masterpiece of art.

# CHAPTER X.

## The Aeneid as the Epic of the Roman Empire.

### I.

The Aeneid, like the Annals of Ennius, is a poem inspired by national sentiment, and expressive of the idea of Rome. But the 'Res Romana [1],' the growth of which Ennius witnessed and celebrated, had become greatly extended and had assumed a new form since the epic of the Republic was written. Yet the sentiment of national glory was essentially the same in the age of the elder Scipio and in the age of Augustus, though in the first it may be described as still militant, in the second as triumphant. In each time the Romans had a firm conviction of their superiority over all other nations, and a firm trust in the great destiny which had attended them since their origin, and still, as they believed, awaited them in the future. The ground on which their national self-esteem rested was their capacity for conquest and government; the result of that capacity was only fully visible after the empire over the world was established.

The pride of empire is thus the most prominent mode in which the national sentiment asserts itself in the poetry of the Augustan Age. In that series of Odes in which the art of Horace becomes the organ of the new government this sentiment finds expression by the mouth of the old enemy of the Roman race, the goddess Juno:—

---

[1] Audire est operae pretium procedere recte
Qui rem Romanam Latiumque augescere· vultis.

> Horrenda late nomen in ultimas
> Extendat oras, qua medius liquor
>   Secernit Europen ab Afro,
>     Qua tumidus rigat arva Nilus.
>   *        *        *        *
> Quicunque mundi terminus obstitit,
> Hunc tanget armis, visere gostiens
>   Qua parte debacchentur ignes,
>     Qua nebulae pluviique rores[1].

And while it animates even the effeminate tones of the elegiac poets to a more manly sound, this pride of empire is the dominant mode of patriotic enthusiasm in the Aeneid.   Thus, in the very beginning of the poem, Virgil describes the people destined to spring from the remnant of the Trojans as

> populum late regem belloque superbum.

To them Jupiter himself promises empire without limit either in time or place :—

> His ego nec metas rerum nec tempora pono,
> Imperium sine fine dedi[2].

In the same passage he sums up their greatness in the arts of war and peace in the line

> Romanos rerum dominos gentemque togatam[3].

The earliest oracle given to Aeneas in the course of his wanderings contains the promise of universal dominion :—

----

[1] 'Yes, let her spread her name of fear,
      To farthest shores ; where central waves
  Part Africa from Europe, where
  Nile's swelling current half the year
      The plains with plenty laves.
        *        *        *
      Let earth's remotest regions still
      Her conquering arms to glory call
  Where scorching suns the long day fill,
  Where mists and snows and tempests chill,
      Hold reckless bacchanal.'   Martin.

[2] 'To them I assign no goal to their achievements, no end,—I have given empire illimitable.'   i. 278–9.

[3] 'The Romans, lords of the world, and the people clad in the gown.' i. 282.

> Hic domus Aeneae cunctis dominabitur oris,
> Et nati natorum et qui nascentur ab illis [1].

The sacred images of the gods who are partners of his enterprise make a similar announcement to him :—

> Nos tumidum sub te permensi classibus aequor,
> Idem venturos tollemus in astra nepotes,
> Imperiumque urbi dabimus [2].

In the fourth book Jupiter, who appears rather as contemplating the future course of affairs than as actively influencing it, speaks of Aeneas in these words :—

> Sed fore, qui gravidam imperiis belloque frementem
> Italiam regeret, genus alto a sanguine Troiae
> Proderet, ac totum sub leges mitteret orbem [3].

In the famous passage in the sixth book the mission of Rome is summed up, in contrast to the artistic glories of Greece, in the lines—

> Tu regere imperio populos, Romane, memento
> (Hae tibi erunt artes), pacisque inponere morem,
> Parcere subiectis et debellare superbos [4].

The oracle of Faunus thus announces to Latinus the great future which awaited the race destined to arise from the union of the Trojans and Italians :—

> Externi venient generi, qui sanguine nostrum
> Nomen in astra ferant, quorumque ab stirpe nepotes
> Omnia sub pedibus, qua Sol utrumque recurrens
> Aspicit Oceanum, vertique regique videbunt [5].

---

[1] 'Here the house of Aeneas shall rule in all coasts, and their sons' sons, and they who shall be born from them.' iii. 97-8.

[2] 'We, who under thy protection have traversed the heaving sea in thy fleet, we shall raise to the stars thy descendants in days to come, and shall give empire to thy city.' iii. 157-9.

[3] 'But that he should be one to rule over Italy the mother of empire, echoing with the roar of war, who should transmit a race from the high line of Troy, and bring the whole world beneath his laws.' iv. 229-31.

[4] 'Thine be the task, O Roman, to sway the nations with thy imperial rule—these shall be thy arts—to impose on men the law of peace, to spare those who yield, and to quell the proud.' vi. 852-4.

[5] 'Strangers shall come as thy sons-in-law, destined by mingling their blood with ours to raise our name to the stars—whose descendants shall see all things, where the Sun beholds either Ocean in his course, overthrown beneath their feet and governed.' vii. 98-101.

In the ninth book Virgil for once breaks through the impersonal reserve of the epic singer to claim for Nisus and Euryalus an eternity of fame,—

> Dum domus Aeneae Capitoli immobile saxum
> Accolet imperiumque pater Romanus habebit [1].

In several of these passages it is not merely the pride of conquest and dominion which is expressed, but the higher and humaner belief that the ultimate mission of Rome is to give law and peace to the world. Thus the initiation of Iulus into war is accompanied by the declaration put into the mouth of Apollo—

> iure omnia bella
> Gente sub Assaraci fato ventura resident [2].

In this way Virgil softens and humanises the idea of the Imperial State, representing her as not only the conqueror but the civiliser of the ancient world, and the transmitter of that civilisation to the world of the future. And while he invests the thought of ancient and powerful sovereignty with imaginative associations, and describes acts of heroism with the glow of martial enthusiasm, yet the crowning glory which he ascribes to the Romans is the piety inherited from their Trojan ancestors. The final appeasement of the rancour of Juno is secured by the declaration of Jupiter—

> Hinc genus Ausonio mixtum quod sanguine surget,
> Supra homines, supra ire deos pietate videbis,
> Nec gens ulla tuos aeque celebrabit honores [3].

The national idea of Rome was associated also with the thought of the divine origin, the great antiquity, the unbroken tradition, and the eternal duration of the State. Universal

---

[1] 'While the house of Aeneas shall dwell by the Capitol's immoveable rock, and a Roman lord hold empire.' ix. 448-9.

[2] 'Rightly shall all the wars destined to come hereafter subside in peace beneath the line of Assaracus.' ix. 642-3.

[3] 'The race that mixed with Ausonian blood shall arise from them, thou shalt see transcend men, nay even gods in piety; nor shall any people equally pay homage to thee.' xii. 838-40.

empire, uninterrupted continuity of existence, were the claims of the ancient Imperial as of the modern Ecclesiastical Rome. And this idea, by the strong hold which it had on the minds first of the Romans themselves and afterwards of other nations, went far to realise itself.    The confidence of the Romans in themselves was intimately connected with their belief in their origin.    Ennius had impressed on their minds the belief in the miraculous birth of their founder and in his miraculous elevation after death, and in the protection afforded by the 'augustum augurium' by which the building of their city had been consecrated.    Among no people did ancient customs and ceremonies, of which in many cases the origin was altogether forgotten, survive with such vitality.    In no other people did the memory of their past history, whether of triumph or disaster, exercise so potent an influence on the present time. In no Republic have the pride of birth and the reverence felt to ancestors been so powerful and prevailing sentiments : no State has ever been more loyal to the memory of the men who at successive crises in its history had served it or saved it from its enemies: and no great secular power ever felt so strong an assurance of an unbroken ascendency in the future, and of the dependence of the fate of the world on that ascendency.

The Aeneid appealed to all these sentiments even with more power than the epic of the Republic and than the various national histories in which Roman literature was peculiarly rich. Virgil, while still leaving to his countrymen the pride of their descent from Mars, made them feel the charm of their relation to a more gracious divinity, and even the hereditary claim which they had to regard themselves as special objects of care to the Supreme Ruler of Heaven[1].    The association of their destiny with the fortunes of Aeneas enabled them to look back to a remoter and more famous epoch of antiquity than the legends of their origin which had satisfied the fancy of the older Romans.    Various passages in the poem enable Virgil to invest impressive ceremonies, existing in his own time, with the asso-

[1] vii. 219, etc.

ciations of an immemorial past.  The three great prophetic passages in the first, sixth, and eighth books enable him to revive, as Ennius had done, the thought of the great men and families of Rome, and of the great events both of earlier and more recent history.  The march of Roman conquest during one hundred and fifty momentous years enabled the younger poet to evoke greater, though in some respects less happy, memories than those evoked by his predecessor.  And the security of the Empire established in his day justified him in looking forward to the future with even a more assured confidence, though perhaps in a less sanguine spirit.

The national sentiment manifesting itself in the pride of empire and deeply rooted in the past, was combined with strong local attachments and the attribution of a kind of sanctity to the great natural features of the land or to spots associated with historic memories which had impressed themselves on the hearts of successive generations.  Virgil was, as we saw in examining the Georgics, peculiarly susceptible of such impressions.  There is no passage in any ancient writer which makes us feel so vividly the 'religio loci' which has for more than two thousand years invested the very site of Rome as that in the eighth book of the Aeneid, in which Evander conducts Aeneas over the ground destined to be occupied by the temples and dwellings of Rome.  The feeling which the sight of the Capitoline hill and of the Tarpeian rock calls forth is one rather of religious awe than of any more familiar sentiment.  The feeling, on the other hand, with which the Tiber is introduced—

Caeruleus Thybris, caelo gratissimus amnis—

is one rather of proud affection than of religious veneration. The aspect of the great city itself awed the imagination rather than called forth the affections of her citizens.  But these affections were given to the rivers and streams, the lakes, and mountain-homes of Italy.  Patriotism in the Augustan Age was as much an Italian as a Roman sentiment.  The military greatness of Rome was even more identified with the discipline and cou-

rage of the Marsian and Apulian[1] soldier than with that of the
Latin race[2]. Her moral greatness is more often identified by
the poets with the virtues of the old Sabellian stock than with
those of the 'populus Romanus Quiritium.' While the Georgics
celebrate the peaceful glory and beauty of Italy, the Aeneid
evokes the memory of its old warlike renown—

> quibus Itala iam tum
> Floruerit terra alma viris, quibus arserit armis[3].

The first omen[4] which meets the Trojans on approaching Italy
marks it out as a land 'mighty in arms' as well as 'in the
richness of its soil.' The speech of Remulus in the ninth book
identifies the ancient rural life of Italy with the hardihood and
warlike aptitude of the people, as the Georgics identify it with
their virtue and happiness :—

> Durum ab stirpe genus natos ad flumina primum
> Deferimus saevoque gelu duramus et undis;
> Venatu invigilant pueri, silvasque fatigant ;
> Flectere ludus equos et spicula tendere cornu.
> At patiens operum parvoque adsueta iuventus
> Aut rastris terram domat, aut quatit oppida bello.
> Omne aevum ferro teritur, versaque iuvencum
> Terga fatigamus hasta ; nec tarda senectus
> Debilitat vires animi mutatque vigorem :
> Canitiem galea premimus, semperque recentis
> Comportare iuvat praedas et vivere rapto[5].

---

[1] Hor. Od. iii. 5. 9.

[2] The Latin name seems rather associated with the thought of the other
great distinguishing characteristic of the Romans, their capacity for law.
Cf. Hor. Od. iv. 14. 7, 'Quem legis expertes Latinae,' etc. Virgil may
intend to indicate this peaceful attribute of the Latins, in contradistinction
to the warlike energy of the other Italian races, in the line (Aen. vii. 204),—
Sponte sua veterisque dei se more tenentem.

[3] 'The men in whom even then the Italian land rejoiced as her sons, and
their fiery spirit in war.' vii. 643–4.

[4] iii. 539 :—Bellum, O terra hospita, portas.

[5] 'A hardy stock, we bear our new-born sons to the rivers, and harden
them with the chill cold ; as boys they ply the chase and give the woods
no rest : it is their pastime to rein the steed and aim their arrows from the
bow.   But our warrior youth, patient in toil and inured to scanty fare,
either subdues the soil with the harrow or makes towns shake by their
assault.   Each period of life wears away in arms, and with the butt end of
the spear we goad the steer ; nor does the lethargy of age impair our spirit

In the account of the gathering of the Italian clans in the seventh book, and of the Etruscans and the Northern races in the tenth, the warlike sentiment of the land is appealed to in association with the names of ancient towns, mountain districts, lakes, and rivers :—

> Quique altum Praeneste viri, quique arva Gabinae
> Iunonis gelidumque Anienem et roscida rivis
> Hernica saxa colunt, quos dives Anagnia pascit,
> Quos, Amasene pater [1];

and again :—

> Qui Tetricae horrentis rupes montemque Severum
> Casperiamque colunt Forulosque et flumen Himellae;
> Qui Tiberim Fabarimque bibunt, quos frigida misit
> Nursia, et Hortinae classes populique Latini;
> Quosque secans infaustum interluit Allia nomen [2];

and also :—

> Qui saltus, Tiberine, tuos, sacrumque Numici
> Litus arant, Rutulosque exercent vomere collis,
> Circaeumque iugum, quis Iuppiter Anxurus arvis
> Praesidet et viridi gaudens Feronia luco;
> Qua Saturae iacet atra palus, gelidusque per imas
> Quaerit iter vallis atque in mare conditur Ufens [3].

This union of patriotic sentiment with the love of Nature and with the romantic associations of the past, Virgil has in common with the most distinctively national of the poets of the present

---

or change our vigour: our hoary hairs we press with the helmet, and it is our joy ever to gather fresh booty and to live by foray.'  ix. 603–613.

[1] 'The men who dwell in high Praeneste and the tilled land where Gabii worships Juno, and the Hernican rocks, sparkling with streams, they whom rich Anagnia and thou, father Amasenus, feedest.'  vii. 682–5.

[2] 'They who dwell among the crags of grim Tetrica, and the mount Severus, and Casperia and Foruli and the river of Himella; they who drink of the Tiber and Fabaris, whom cold Nursia sent, and the hosts of Horta and the Latin tribes; and those whom Allia, name of ill omen, divides with its stream flowing between them.'  vii. 713–7.

[3] 'They who plough thy glades, Tiberinus, and the hallowed shore of Numicius, and work the Rutulian hills with the ploughshare, and the ridge of Circeii, the fields of which Jove of Anxur is guardian, and Feronia glorying in her green grove—where the black marsh of Satura lies, and where with cold stream through the bottom of the vales Ufens gropes his way and hides himself in the sea.'  vii. 797–802.

century, from whom in the other characteristics of his art and
genius he is widely removed.

The national sentiment to which Virgil and the other contemporary poets give expression is thus seen to be the sentiment of the Italian race[1].  For two centuries the principal
members of that race had looked to Rome as their chief glory,
rather than as their old rival and antagonist.  The thought of
Rome as their head had become to the other Italian tribes their
basis of union with one another and the main ground of their
self-esteem in relation to other nations.  To that self-esteem
and sense of superiority Virgil was fully alive.  He is not altogether free from the narrowness of national prejudice.  He has
not the largeness of soul which enables Homer, while never
losing his sense of the superiority of the Greeks over the
Trojans, yet to awaken feelings of admiration and of generous
pity for Hector and Sarpedon, for Priam and Andromache.
Yet if Virgil has not this largeness of soul he has the tenderness
of human compassion :—

> Sunt lacrimae rerum et mentem mortalia tangunt[2].

He might have maintained a stronger sympathy for his hero,
and have gratified a sentiment still fresh in the minds of his
countrymen, by attributing to Dido the shameless licence as
well as the dangerous fascination of Cleopatra ; or he might
have painted the Carthaginians in traditional colours of cruelty
and treachery, in which Roman writers represented the most
formidable among the enemies of Rome.  But Virgil's artistic
sense or his humaner feeling saved him from this ungenerous

---

[1] This view of Virgil's pride in the qualities of the Italians is not incompatible with the fact to which Mr. Nettleship has drawn attention (Suggestions Introductory to a Study of the Aeneid, pp. 13 et seq.), that Virgil
represents their earlier condition as one of turbulent barbarism.  Virgil
seems to have regarded ' the savage virtue of his race,' although requiring
to be tamed by contact with a higher civilisation, as the ' incrementum '
out of which the martial virtue and discipline of the later Italians was
formed :—

> Sit Romana potens Itala virtute propago.

[2] ' Tears to human sufferings are due, and hearts are touched by the
common lot.'

gratification of national prejudice.　Yet while more just or
tolerant than other Roman writers to the Carthaginians, and
especially to the memory of their greatest man, he indicates
something like antipathy to the Greeks.　The triumph of Rome
over her Greek enemies is made prominent in the announcement of her future glories :—

> Veniet lustris labentibus aetas,
> Cum domus Assaraci Phthiam clarasque Mycenas
> Servitio premet ac victis dominabitur Argis[1];

and again :—

> Eruet ille Argos Agamemnoniasque Mycenas,
> Ipsumque Aeaciden, genus armipotentis Achilli[2].

The bitterness of national animosity is especially apparent in
his exhibition of the characters of Ulysses and Helen.　The
superiority of the Greeks in the arts and sciences is admitted
not without some touch of scorn ('credo equidem') in contrast
with the superiority of Rome in the imperial arts of conquering
and governing nations.　It may appear strange that the only
race to which Virgil is unjust or ungenerous is the one to which
he himself, in common with all educated Romans, was most
deeply indebted.　But it is to be remembered that there was
a dramatic propriety in the expression of this hostility in the
mouth of Aeneas and of Anchises.　The championship of the
cause of Troy demanded an attitude of antagonism to her
destroyer.　The Greek tragedians had themselves set the example of a degraded representation of two of the most admirable of Homer's creations; and Virgil's mode of conceiving
and delineating character is much nearer to that of Euripides
than to that of Homer.　The original error of Helen and the
craft in dealing with his enemies, which is one of many qualities
in the versatile humanity of Odysseus, gave to these later artists

---

[1] 'There will come a time as the years glide on, when the house of
Assaracus will reduce to bondage Phthia and famous Mycenae, and lord it
over vanquished Argos.'　Aen. i. 283–5.

[2] 'He shall overthrow Argos and the Mycenae of Agamemnon, and the
king himself of the line of Aeacus, descendant of the puissant Achilli.'
vi. 839–40.

the germ, in accordance with which the whole character was
conceived.   They did not adequately apprehend that the most
interesting types of nobleness and beauty of character as imagined by the greatest artists are also the most complex, and the
least capable of being squared with abstract conceptions of vices
or virtues.   The full truth of Homer's delineations of character
was apparently not recognised by the most cultivated of his
Roman readers.   It is enough for Virgil that Ulysses is 'fandi
fictor,' as it is for Horace that Achilles is 'iracundus, inexora-
bilis, acer:' although the worldly wisdom of the last-named
poet makes him comprehend better Homer's ideal of intelligent
than his ideal of emotional heroism :—

> Rursus quid virtus et quid sapientia possit,
> Utile proposuit nobis exemplar Ulixem[1], etc.

Juvenal exhibits the virulence of national animosity towards the
Greeks of his time, as well as a well-founded scorn of the moral
baseness of character exhibited by many of them.   The contempt of Tacitus is shown for their intellectual frivolity, combined with their assumption of intellectual superiority ('qui sua
tantum mirantur[2]') based on the renown of their ancestors.
The deference which Virgil and Horace might pay to the genius
of early Greece was not due to the shadow of that genius as it
existed in their own time.   But the contemporary Greek *littérateurs* were not likely to resign their claim of precedence in
favour of their new rivals.   Neither Greek art[3] nor Greek criticism seems ever to have made any cordial recognition of the
literary genius of Italy.   The light in which Virgil represents
the Greek character may thus perhaps owe something to the
wish to repay scorn with scorn.

---

[1] 'Again he has set before us in Ulysses a profitable example of the power
of courage and wisdom.'   Ep. i. 2, 17, etc.

[2] Annals, ii. 88.

[3] It is remarked by Helbig, in his 'Campanische Wandmalerei,' that
among the many paintings found at Pompeii dealing with mythological and
similar subjects, only one is founded on the incidents of the Aeneid.

## II.

The confidence which the Romans felt in the continued existence of their Empire and in their superiority over all other nations was closely connected with their religious feeling and belief[1]. Horace has expressed the national faith in this connexion with Roman force and conciseness in the single line,

Dis te minorem quod geris imperas[2].

And it was Virgil's aim in the Aeneid to show that this edifice of Roman Empire, of which the enterprise of Aeneas was the foundation, on which the old Kings of Alba and of Rome and the successive generations of great men under the Republic had successively laboured, and on which Augustus placed the coping-stone, was no mere work of human hands, but had been designed and built up by divine purpose and guidance. The Aeneid expresses the religious as it does the national sentiment of Rome. The two modes of sentiment were inseparable. The belief of the Romans in themselves was another form of their absolute faith in the invisible Power which protected them. This invisible Power was sometimes recognised by them under the name of 'Fortuna Urbis,'—the spiritual counterpart of the city visible to their eyes. The recognition of this divinity was not only compatible with, but involved the recognition of, many other divinities associated with it in this protecting office. But to these numerous divinities no very distinct personality was attached. It was the awe of an ever-present invisible Power, manifesting itself by arbitrary signs, exacting jealously certain definite observances, capable of being alienated for a time by any deviation from these observances, and of being again appeased by a right reading of and humble compliance with its will, and working out its own purposes through the agency of the Roman arms and the wisdom of Roman counsels, that was the moving power of Roman religion. The Jove of the

---

[1] Cp. Mr. Nettleship's Suggestions, etc., p. 10, and the passages from Cicero there quoted.

[2] 'Thou rulest the world by bearing thyself humbly towards the Gods.'

Capitol in early times, the living Emperor under the Empire, were the visible representatives of this mysterious Power. But its influence was acknowledged throughout all Roman history in the importance attached to the great priestly offices, and especially to that of Pontifex Maximus, which became inseparably united to the office of Emperor; in the scrupulous regard paid to the auspices through which this Power was believed to communicate its will; in the ominous interpretation put on all appearances of departure from the ordinary course of Nature; and in the reference to the Sibylline books in all questions of difficulty. This impersonal Power is to the Romans both the object of awe and the source of their confidence. They seem never to distrust the steadfastness of its favour. They rather feel themselves its willing instruments, co-operating with it, blindly sometimes and sometimes remissly, and for every failure of intelligence or vigilance, punished by temporal calamities.

The word by which Virgil recognises the agency of this impersonal, or perhaps we should rather say undefined, Power, is 'Fatum,' or more often in the plural, 'Fata.' It is by the 'Fates' that the action is set in motion and directed to its issue. The human and even the divine actors in the story are instruments in their hands; some more, some less conscious of the part they are performing. Even Jupiter is represented rather as cognisant of the Fates than as their author. Sometimes indeed they are spoken of as 'Fata Iovis;' and to the assurance given by him to Venus 'manent immota tuorum Fata tibi,' he adds the words 'neque me sententia vertit[1].' But again, while his will is suspended in a great crisis of the action, their operation is persistent and inevitable:—

> Rex Iuppiter omnibus idem:
> Fata viam invenient[2].

The original relation between this impersonal agency and the

---

[1] 'The destinies of thy descendants remain unchanged, nor does my purpose make me waver.'

[2] 'King Jove is impartial to all: the Fates will find their own way.' x. 112–3.

deliberate purpose of Jupiter is left undefined. But there is no collision between them. While the prayers of men are addressed to a conscious personal being, 'Iuppiter omnipotens,' the sovereignty of an impersonal Power over the fortunes of nations is acknowledged, as in the line—

> Fortuna omnipotens et ineluctabile fatum [1].

Every reader of the Aeneid must feel the predominance of this idea in the poem, and the constantly recurring and even monotonous expression of it. In the first three books, for instance, the word 'Fatum' or 'Fata' occurs more than forty times. Aeneas starts on his wanderings 'fato profugus.' Juno desires to secure the empire of the world to Carthage 'Si qua fata sinant.' She struggles against the conviction of her powerlessness to prevent the Trojan settlement in Italy, 'Quippe vetor fatis.' Aeneas comforts his companions by the announcement of the peaceful settlements awaiting them,—

> sedes ubi fata quietas
> Ostendunt.

Venus consoles herself for the destruction of Troy by the thought of the destiny awaiting Aeneas, 'fatis contraria fata rependens.' Jupiter reassures her after the storm with the words 'manent immota tuorum Fata tibi;' and he reveals to her one page in their secret volume,—'fatorum arcana movebo.' Mercury is sent to prepare the reception of Aeneas in Carthage,

> ne fati nescia Dido
> Finibus arceret.

Aeneas describes himself as starting from Troy 'data fata secutus.' A hundred more instances might be given of the dominating influence of this idea in the poem. It is the 'common-place' of the Virgilian epic. While it adds impressiveness to the historical significance of the poem, it detracts largely from the personal interest by the limits which it imposes on the

---

[1] 'All-powerful fortune and fate from which there is no escape.'

free agency of the divine and human actors playing their part in it.

The same idea is often expressed by Tacitus, but it does not in him dominate so absolutely over human will, nor is it asserted with the same firmness of conviction.   His conception of the regulating power over all human, or at least over all national existence, seems to waver between this idea of some unknown power steadily working out its purpose, of an element in human affairs baffling all calculation—the παράλογος of Thucydides and the 'Fortuna saevo laeta negotio' of Horace—and of the gods generally as personal avengers of crime, and sometimes as the kind protectors of the State.   Thus in the Germania[1] the earliest foreboding of the danger which threatened and ultimately overthrew the fabric of the Empire is indicated in the words 'urgentibus imperii fatis:' in the Agricola the result of the invasion of Britain under Claudius is summed up in the words 'domitae gentes, capti reges, et monstratus fatis Vespasianus[2]:' in the Histories the grounds of confidence on the part of the Vespasians in taking arms against the Vitellians are summed up in the words 'dux Mucianus et Vespasiani nomen ac nihil arduum fatis[3].'   But elsewhere he speaks of 'ludibria rerum humanarum[4],' in language reminding us of Lucretius, and, in almost the very words of Horace, of 'instabilis fortunae summaque et ima miscentis[5].'   Like Horace, he seems to acknowledge the supremacy of chance or an ironical spirit over individual fortunes, and, like Virgil, that of Fate over the national destiny.   But in the Annals, his latest work, he seems to

---

[1] 'As the doom of the empire was pressing on to its accomplishment.' i. 33.

[2] 'Nations were subdued, kings were taken prisoners, and Vespasian made known to the fates.'   Agric. 13.

[3] 'The leadership of Mucianus, the name of Vespasian, and the fact that nothing was too difficult for the fates to accomplish.'   Hist. ii. 82.

[4] 'The irony of human affairs.'   Ann. iii. 18 ; cf. the lines of Lucretius. v. 1233-5 :—

        Usque adeo res humanas vis abdita quaedam
        Opterit et pulchros fascis saevasque secures
        Proculcare ac ludibrio sibi habere videtur.

[5] 'The instability of fortune, which confounds the highest with the lowest.'   Hist. iv. 47 ; Hor. Od. i. 34. 12.

incline more to the belief in the personal agency of the gods, and especially in their agency as the avengers of guilt. Thus he opens the passage of the deepest tragic gloom in all his sombre record with the words, 'Noctem sideribus illustrem quasi convincendum ad scelus dii praebuere[1].' So too he speaks of appealing to the 'avenging gods[2];' and of the 'fear of the wrath of heaven[3].' Occasionally indeed he speaks of 'the kindness of the gods[4],' but more often of their wrath or their indifference. Thus he attributes the ascendency of Sejanus not to any superior ability on his own part, but to 'the wrath of the gods against the Roman commonwealth[5];' and, in recounting a number of omens which followed on the murder of Agrippina, he makes the sarcastic comment, 'quae adeo sine cura deum eveniebant, ut multos post annos Nero imperium et scelera continuaverit[6].' In a writer like Tacitus it is impossible to distinguish with certainty between the pure expression of his convictions and the rhetorical and poetical colouring of his style. Yet both the frequency with which such passages recur, and the earnestness of their tone even when they seem most ironical, leave no doubt that, like Thucydides, he was not indifferent to these questions, although 'perplexed in the extreme' by the apparent absence, or at least uncertainty, of any steadfast moral order in the award of happiness and calamity to men.

The 'Fatum' or 'Fata' of Virgil can scarcely be said to act with the aim of establishing right in the world, or of punishing wrong. Their action is purely political, neither ethical, though its ultimate tendency is beneficent, nor personal. Yet in the prominence which is given to this determining element in national affairs Virgil is expressing the strongest and most abiding belief of the Roman people, just as the Greek poets and historians of the fifth century B. C., in the prominence they

---

[1] ' A night bright with stars, as if for the purpose of proving the crime, was granted by the gods.' Ann. xiv. 5.

[2] Ann. iv. 28.     [3] Ib. i. 30.     [4] Ib. xii. 43.     [5] Ib. iv. 1.

[6] ' All which events happened with such entire indifference on the part of the gods, that Nero continued his career of empire and crime for many years afterwards.' Ann. xiv. 12.

give to the element of uncertainty in the world,—the irony in human affairs, or the Nemesis of the gods excited against great prosperity even when not misused or gained by crime,—expressed the dominant idea in the minds of their contemporaries. Mr. Grote traces the origin of this last idea to the experience of the rapid vicissitudes from one extreme of fortune to the other, brought about by the great prosperity of the Greek states on the one hand and their incessant wars and political feuds on the other. The origin of the other idea is to be found in the almost unbroken success of Rome in all her enterprises, from the burning of the city by the Gauls till the full establishment of empire. There is no history in which chance plays so small a part, and in which so little is episodical. The 'good fortune of the Roman people' will be found to be explained either by the traditional policy of never making a new enemy until they had well disposed of the old, or by the magnanimity (as compared at least with the policy of other States [1]) by which they converted the nations successively conquered by them into fellow-citizens or obedient allies, or by the indomitable resolution which never knew to yield to defeat. No important event in their history is isolated; each serves as a link in the chain which connects their past with their future. The unvarying result of their national discipline and policy, and of the force accumulated through centuries before they became corrupted by the gains of conquest, might well appear to a race, gifted with little speculative capacity, to be determined and accomplished by an Omnipotent Power behind them.

This idea determines the general conduct of the action in the Aeneid. The actors in the story either oppose the irresistible tendency of things and suffer defeat or perish in their resistance; or, with gradually increasing knowledge, they co-operate with and become the instruments of this tendency. And as it is by faith in the divine assistance and guidance that

---

[1] Cf. Tac. Ann. xi. 24: 'Quid aliud exitio Lacedaemoniis et Atheniensibus fuit, quamquam armis pollerent, nisi quod victos pro alienigenis arcebant?' etc.

the latter are able to act their part successfully, the religious motives of the representation assume a prominence at least equal to that of its national and political motives. Thus the object of all the hero's wanderings is not only to found a city, but to introduce a new worship into Italy—'inferretque deos Latio.' When Hector appears to Aeneas in a vision he commits into his care the sacred symbols and images of Troy with the words

> Sacra suosque tibi commendat Troia Penates,
> Hos cape *fatorum comites* [1].

Aeneas is represented as starting on his enterprise

> Cum sociis gnatoque, *Penatibus et magnis Dis* [2];

as his descendant is represented in the enterprise which is crowned with the victory of Actium [3]. Finally, in the treaty with Latinus, while the secular and imperial power is left with the Italians, the religious predominance is claimed for Aeneas,—

> Sacra deosque dabo; socer arma Latinus habeto,
> Imperium sollemne socer [4].

The influence of the religious idea of the poem is seen also in the leading characteristic of the hero—'insignem pietate virum.' His piety appears in the faith which he has in his mission, and in the trust which he has in divine guidance. Prayer is his first resource in all emergencies; sacrifice and thanksgiving are the accompaniments of all his escapes from danger and difficulty. This characteristic deprives the representation of Aeneas of the interest springing from energetic resource or spontaneous feeling. But as much as the character loses in human interest, it gains in the impression produced

---

[1] 'Her sacred emblems and her gods Troy commits to thy care—take these as the companions of thy fates.'

[2] 'With his comrades and his son, the Penates and the great gods.'

[3] Aen. viii. 679.

[4] 'The rites of religion and the new Gods shall come from me—let the power of arms be with my father-in-law Latinus—let him keep his established rule.' Aen. xii. 192–3.

of a fitting instrument to carry out the purpose of a Power working secretly for a distant end.

The effect of the same idea is apparent in the way in which the action is furthered by special revelations, visions, prophecies, omens, and the like.  These intimations of the future are, for the most part, altogether of an unpoetical and unimaginative character.  The omens by which the Fates make their will known, such as the omen of the cakes and of the white sow with her litter, are, like those that occur so often in the pages of Livy, of an essentially prosaic type: not like those in Homer, striking sights or sounds acting on the imagination with the force of divine warning.  Occasionally Virgil's own invention, or perhaps the guidance of some Greek predecessor, suggests signs of a less trivial significance—such as that of the meteor or line of light marking out the way from the burning city to Mount Ida—

> Illam, summa super labentem culmina tecti,
> Cernimus Idaea claram se condere silva,
> Signantemque vias[1];

but for the most part the formal, superstitious, prosaic element in the Roman religion—the same element which made their generals before some decisive battle allow themselves to draw their auguries from the mode in which chickens ate their food,— is present in the religious guidance of the action.  The Roman belief in the supernatural was arrested and stunted at a primitive stage of religious development.  So far from elevating the thought and enlarging the imagination, that belief tended to repress all speculation, lofty contemplation, and poetry.  Even Virgil's idealising art fails to conceal the triviality of the media through which the invisible Power made its will and purpose manifest.

The mythological machinery of the poem also, although borrowed from the repertory of Homer, yet moves in obedience to this silent, impersonal, uncapricious Power.  Juno endea-

---

[1] ' We mark it gliding above the topmost roof of the house, hide itself in a bright stream in the forest of Ida, marking out the way.'  Aen. ii. 695-7.

vours to strive against it, till forced to confess her impotence. Venus by her intrigues serves to further its purposes. Yet both these Olympian divinities are but puppets 'in some unknown Power's employ,' which makes for its own end alike through their furtherance and antagonism. The gods who take part in the action are of Greek invention, but the Power which even they are obliged to obey, if not Roman in original conception, is yet essentially Roman in significance.

This thought of an unseen Power, working by means of omens and miracles on the mind of the hero of the poem, with the distant aim of establishing universal empire in the hands of a people, obedient to divine will and observant of all religious ceremonies, may be said to be the theological or speculative idea of the poem. It is the doctrine of predestination in its hardest form. It is a thought much inferior both in intellectual subtlety and in ethical value to that of the Fate of Greek tragedy in conflict with human will. Yet there is a kind of material force and greatness in Virgil's conception, and a consistency not with ideal truth but with visible facts. The ideal truth of Sophocles—the idea of final purification and reconcilement of a noble human nature with the divine nature—is not manifest in the world: it is only in harmony with the best hopes and aspirations of men. Virgil's idea was the shadow of the great fact apparent in his age,—the vast, inevitable, omnipotent, unsympathetic power of the Roman empire.

But there is another personal and humane religious element, not so prominent and not so influential on the action, but pervading the poem like an atmosphere, purifying it, and making it luminous with the light of a higher region. This is the element of religious faith or hope, personal to Virgil and yet catholic in its significance, and in harmony with the convictions of religious men of all times. The rigid, formal, and narrow conceptions of the Roman religion came into collision both with the belief in gods of like passions with men, revealed in the art and poetry of the Greeks, and with the development

of ethical feeling and especially of the sentiment of humanity
fostered by Greek philosophy.　Virgil's temperament, patriotic,
imaginative, and humane, was in accord with all these modes
of religious conception.　If national destiny and some portions
of the destiny of individuals are shaped by an inflexible
power—

> Desine fata deum flecti sperare precando[1],—

yet the personal agency of Beings, in immediate relation with
man, who are not only 'mindful of the righteous and un-
righteous[2],' but who also 'pios respectant,' is devoutly acknowledged—

> Di tibi, si qua pios respectant numina, si quid
> Usquam iustitia est et mens sibi conscia recti,
> Praemia digna ferant[3].

Their relation to man is expressed by the same word, *pietas*,
which expresses man's relation to them—

> Iuppiter omnipotens, si nondum exosus ad unum
> Troianos, si quid pietas antiqua labores
> Respicit humanos[4].

They are, like the gods of Tacitus, avengers of wrong as well
as rewarders of righteousness : but their avenging wrath against
the strong springs from their mercy to the weak—

> Di, si qua est caelo pietas, quae talia curet,
> Persolvant grates dignas et praemia reddant
> Debita, qui nati coram me cernere letum
> Fecisti et patrios foedasti funere voltus[5].

This close personal relation between men and an invisible

---

[1] 'Cease to hope that the determinations of the Gods can be turned aside
by prayer.'　　　　　　　　　　　　　　　　　　　　[2] i. 543.

[3] 'May the gods, if any Powers regard the merciful, if righteousness and
a pure conscience avail aught anywhere, bring to thee a worthy recompense.'
i. 603-5.

[4] 'Almighty Jove, if thou hast not yet utterly hated the Trojans to the
last man, if thy mercy as of old still regards human troubles.' v. 687-9.

[5] 'May the gods, if there is any pity in heaven to take heed of such
things, thank thee as thou deservest and make due recompense to thee who
hast made me to behold my son slain before my face, and hast stained a
father's countenance with the pollution of death.' ii. 536-9.

Being or Beings, like to man in feelings and moral attributes, but infinitely greater in power and knowledge, exists in the Aeneid side by side with the doctrine of the omnipotence of Fate, crushing, if necessary, human wishes and human happiness under its iron determinations.  But in the final award of happiness or misery after death, revealed in the sixth book, the agency of Fate gives place to that of a moral dispensation awarding to men their portions according to their actions.  The way in which Virgil indicates his belief in the spiritual life after death is analogous to, as well as suggested by, the myths in the Gorgias and in the tenth book of the Republic of Plato. While there is a certain vagueness and uncertainty in his view of the condition in which the souls of ordinary men pass the thousand years of purification before drinking of the waters of Lethe and entering again on a mortal life, the class of sinners to whom eternal punishment is awarded, and that of holy men who dwell for ever in Elysium, are indicated with great definiteness and beauty.  In the first class are those whom the old Roman world regarded as impious or unnatural,—those who have violated the primal sanctities of life, who have dealt treacherously with a client or the master of their household, who have risen in rebellion against their country, who have sacrificed their human affections and their duty as citizens to their greed of grain—

> Hic, quibus invisi fratres, dum vita manebat,
> Pulsatusve parens et fraus innexa clienti ;
> Aut qui divitiis soli incubuere repertis,
> Nec partem posuere suis, quae maxima turba est ;
> Quique ob adulterium caesi, quique arma secuti
> Impia, nec veriti dominorum fallere dextras,
> Inclusi poenam expectant . . . .
>     *      *      *      *      *
> Vendidit hic auro patriam, dominumque potentem
> Imposuit : fixit leges pretio atque refixit :
> Hic thalamum invasit natae vetitosque hymenaeos :
> Ausi omnes immane nefas ausoque potiti[1].

---

[1] 'Here they by whom their brethren were hated, while life was with them, or a father struck, or a client dealt with treacherously, or who brooded

In the other class are those who have died in battle for their
native land, who have lived pure and holy lives as priests or
poets, who have served mankind by great discoveries, or have
left memorials of themselves in good deeds done to their
fellow-men—

> Hic manus, ob patriam pugnando volnera passi,
> Quique sacerdotes casti, dum vita manebat,
> Quique pii vates et Phoebo digna locuti,
> Inventas aut qui vitam excoluere per artes,
> Quique sui memores alios fecere merendo[1].

## III.

The imperial and the religious ideas of Rome, as embodied
in the Aeneid, find their fullest realisation in the position
assigned to Augustus. The pride of empire, the loyalty to the
State, the religious trust, which in the age of Ennius attached
themselves to the 'Respublica Romana,' found, in the age of
Virgil, a new centre of attraction in the person of the Emperor.
A poem, which should express the dominant idea and sentiment of that age, could not fail to bring into prominence the
change through which the government not of Rome only but
of the whole civilised world was then passing. The relations
of the great poets of the time to the men at the head of affairs
made them the fittest exponents of this new tendency. They
used their art with the view of giving to public sentiment a
permanent direction in favour of the new order of things. The
political object of glorifying the personal rule of Augustus and

---

alone over some discovered treasure and assigned no share to their kindred
—and they are the greatest multitude—and they who were put to death as
adulterers, and they who followed to war an unholy standard, and they who
feared not to be false to the fealty they owed their lords, imprisoned await
punishment . . . Here is one who sold his country for gold, and made it
subject to a powerful master; another made and unmade laws for a bribe;
another violated a daughter's bed in forbidden wedlock—all men who dared
some monstrous deed of sin, and enjoyed its fruits.'  vi. 608-14, 621-4.

[1] 'Here a company, who received wounds fighting for their country, and
they who were pure priests, while life was with them, and they who were
holy bards and who spoke in strains worthy of Phoebus, or they who improved life by their discoveries, and who by their good deeds made others
keep them in memory.'  vi. 660-4.

of surrounding it with the halo of a divine sanction associated itself with the artistic, the patriotic, and the religious objects of Virgil. And although the excess of eulogy and some modes of its manifestation offend the modern, as they would have offended a more ancient sentiment of personal dignity, there is no reason to question the disinterested sincerity of Virgil's panegyric. The permanence of the change introduced by Augustus attests the fact that his policy not only kindled the enthusiasm of the moment, but met the most deeply-felt needs of the world. And though his personal qualities and the great things accomplished by him do not touch the imagination or awaken the sentiment of admiration in modern times, like those of his immediate predecessor in power, yet he was pre-eminently the man suited to his age, as an age of restoration and re-organisation, and he was pre-eminently a Roman of the Romans. The great C. Julius, in his genius and qualities, 'towers' not only above his own nation but, 'like Hannibal, above all nations.' The perfect success of Augustus was due to the fact not only that he was the man wanted by his epoch, but that he was the complete embodiment of the great practical talents and character of Rome. He not only monopolised in his own person all the chief functions, but in his administration he displayed all the best and most varied capacities of the Roman magistracy. In his government and in his legislation he exercised the influence formerly exercised by Censor and Chief of the Senate, by Consul and Proconsul, by Praetor and Aedile. To the aptitudes for these various duties he added those that fitted him at least to fill the place of 'Imperator' at the head of the Roman armies, and to give new importance and efficacy to the office of Pontifex Maximus. He possessed also in a remarkable degree the personal qualities of industry, vigilance, practical sagacity, authority, dignity, and urbanity, which are of most importance in the government of men. If his character falls below both the ancient and the modern ideal of heroism, it is thoroughly conformable to a Roman ideal of practical power and usefulness. He is the representative man of the brighter side of Roman imperialism, as Tiberius (till his final retirement from Rome),—in his strength of body and mind, his military and administrative capacity, his unrelieved application to business[1], his unsympathetic impartiality, his suspicious and ruthless policy in suppressing opposition, his callous indifference to suffering,—is of its more sombre side. It is a great enhancement of the representative character of Virgil's national epic, that it is associated with the name and acts of one who was not only the founder, but was the most typical embodiment of the Roman empire.

Although the choice of the subject of the Aeneid was determined, in a great measure, by its adaptability to the personal and political object of Virgil, no attempt is made to exhibit either the character or the actions of Aeneas as symbolical of those of Augustus. Still less are we to look for any modern parallels to the other personages of the poem, such as Turnus or Dido, Latinus or Lavinia, Drances or Achates. Yet the position assigned to Aeneas, as a fatherly ruler over his people, their chief in battle, their law-giver in peace, and their high-priest in all spiritual relations, may have been intended as a kind of symbol of the new monarchy. The Roman imagination acknowledged two ideals of a ruler of men,—the ideal of a Romulus and that of a Numa. In Aeneas both are combined with the characteristics of a new ideal which rather anticipated a future, than reproduced any older type of character. Augustus too might be regarded as at once the Romulus and the Numa of the new empire; and thus the parts played by Aeneas, as chief in battle and legislator in peace[2], might be regarded as a kind of foreshadowing of those which were afterwards played by Augustus on the real stage of human

---

[1] Cf. At Tiberius, nihil intermissa rerum cura, negotia pro solatiis accipiens. Tac. Ann. iv. 13.

[2] iii. 132-7 :—

Ergo avidus muros optatae molior urbis
Pergameamque voco, et laetam cognomine gentem
Hortor amare focos, arcemque attollere tectis,—
*     *     *     *     *
Iura domosque dabam.

affairs. But it would be no compliment either to the intellectual power of Augustus or to the discernment of Virgil, to suppose that the personal attributes of Aeneas were intended to have any resemblance to the strong and self-reliant character of the Emperor. The relation to Aeneas adds to the personal glory of Augustus by the ancestral distinction thus conferred upon him,—a distinction at all times highly prized among the Romans, and especially prized by the Caesars as helping to reconcile a proud aristocracy to their ascendency. In the immediate successors of Augustus, the obscurity of the Octavii and Atii was forgotten in the combined lustre of the Julian and Claudian families. And on one of those occasions, in which the sentiment of family pride was most powerfully appealed to,—the funeral of Drusus, son of Tiberius,—we read in Tacitus—'funus imaginum pompa maxime inlustre fuit, cum origo Iuliae gentis Aeneas omnesque Albanorum reges, et conditor urbis Romulus, post Sabina nobilitas, Attus Clausus, ceteraeque Claudiorum effigies, longo ordine spectarentur[1].' In thus throwing the halo both of a remote antiquity and of a divine ancestry around Augustus, Virgil helped to recommend his rule to the sentiment of his countrymen.

In seeking to enhance the greatness of a living ruler by associating him with the actions of a remote legendary ancestor, the panegyric of Virgil does not transcend the limits which Pindar allows himself in evoking the mythical glories of the past in honour of his patrons. But Virgil seeks to establish a closer connexion between the past and the present, than that established by Pindar. The connexion between the living man, who wins a victory in the games, and his heroic ancestor, is adduced as a proof of the inheritance by the descendant of the personal qualities which first gave distinction to his race. But the connexion between Aeneas and Augustus

---

[1] 'The funeral was most remarkable for the display of ancestral images, as the founder of the Julian house, Aeneas and all the Alban kings, and Romulus founder of the city, and after them the Sabine lords, Attus Clausus, and the other images of the Claudii, in a long line passed before the eyes of the spectators.' Ann. iv. 9.

is the connexion between means and end.  The actions of
Aeneas are not held up as a mere example which his descendant might emulate : they are the first links in the long
chain of events which reached from the siege of Troy to the
victory of Actium and the establishment of the empire.  The
distant vision of the glory awaiting the greatest of his descendants is, more than any immediate or personal end, the
motive which animates both the divine and human actors in
the enterprise.  It is after a vivid picture of the martial and
peaceful glories of the Augustan reign that the stirring appeal
is made—

> Et dubitamus adhuc virtutem extendere factis,
> Aut metus Ausonia prohibet consistere terra[1]?

The means through which the vision of this distant future
is revealed, are the voice of Jove himself in unfolding the
volume of the fates to Venus, that of the beatified shade of
Anchises in exhibiting the spectacle of his unborn descendants
to Aeneas, and the art of Vulcan in framing the 'fabric of the
shield surpassing all description.'

The glory attributed to Augustus in the shield of Aeneas
is that of a great warrior and conqueror, the champion, not,
like C. Julius, of the popular against the aristocratic party in
the State, of the Provinces against the Senate, but of the nation
against its old enemies, the monarchies of the East.  He
appears as celebrating a mighty triumph, and dedicating three
hundred temples to the gods of Italy in thankful acknowledgment of his victory.  The glory announced in the prophecy of Jupiter is that of the establishment by Augustus
of an Empire of Peace, as the completion of his warlike
triumph—

> Aspera tum positis mitescent saecula bellis :
> Cana Fides et Vesta, Remo cum fratre Quirinus
> Iura dabunt[2].

---

[1] 'And do we still hesitate to find by our deeds a wider field for our valour,
or does fear hinder us from establishing ourselves on Ausonian soil?' vi. 807–8.

[2] 'Then the ages of cruel strife will become gentle, and war be laid aside :
hoary faith, and Vesta, Quirinus with his brother Remus, shall give laws.'
i. 291–3.

And in the revelation of Anchises, Augustus is spoken of as—

> Augustus Caesar, Divi genus : aurea condet
> Saecula qui rursus Latio, regnata per arva
> Saturno quondam [1].

He is there proclaimed to be greater in the extent of his conquests and civilising labours than Hercules and Bacchus. And, though less prominently than in the Invocation to the Georgics, divine honours and the function of answering prayer are promised to him by the mouth of Jupiter—

> Hunc tu olim caelo, spoliis Orientis onustum,
> Accipies secura : vocabitur hic quoque votis [2].

The personal figure of the Emperor is thus encompassed with the halo of military glory, of beneficent action on the world, of a divine sanction, and of an ultimate heritage of divine honours.

The Aeneid considered as a representative work of genius is thus seen to be the expression or embodiment of an idea of powerful meaning for the age in which the poem was written, for the centuries immediately succeeding that age, and, through the action of historical associations, for all times. As the great poem of Dante gained both immediate and permanent attention by the human interest which it imparted to the spiritual idea on which mediaeval Europe based its life; as the inspiration of Milton's great Epic was drawn from his passionate sympathy with the intensest form of religious and political life in his age; so the quality of Virgil's genius which secured for him the most immediate and the most lasting consideration was his sympathetic comprehension of the imperial idea of Rome in its secular, religious, and personal significance. This idea he has ennobled with the associations of a divine origin and of a divine sanction; of a remote antiquity and an unbroken con-

---

[1] 'Augustus Caesar, of descent from a god : who shall establish again the golden age of Latium over fields where Saturn once reigned.' vi. 793–5.

[2] 'Him hereafter, laden with the spoils of the East, thou shalt welcome in heaven and feel no fear longer ; he too will be invoked with prayers.' i. 289–90.

tinuity of great deeds and great men; of the pomp and pride
of war, and of the majesty of government: and he has softened
and humanised the impression thus produced by the thought
of peace, law, and order given to the world.    In his stately
diction we are reminded only of the power, glory, majesty, and
civilising influence with which the idea of Rome is encompassed.    There is nothing to obtrude the thought of the spirit,
in which life, freedom, and individuality were crushed out of
the world.    And this idea, of which Virgil's poem is the
glorified representation, was one actually realised, one which
influenced the lives of generations of men, and which was an
important element in moulding the whole subsequent history
of the world.    Yet the idea is one more adapted to be the
inspiring influence of a great historical work, like the national
history of Livy, or 'The Decline and Fall of the Roman
Empire,' than of a great poem, which must satisfy the human
and moral sympathies of men as well as their sense of power.
Material greatness and civilisation, and the qualities of mind
and character through which these effects are produced,
exercise a great spell over the imagination and the masculine
sympathies of the world.    But the highest art does more than
this—it enlarges man's sense of a spiritual life, it purifies his
notions of happiness, it deepens his conviction of a righteous
government of the world.    Through the imagination it speaks
to the soul.    The idea of imperial Rome is rather that of the
enemy than of the promoter of the spiritual life or of individual
happiness: it impresses on the mind the thought of a vast
and orderly, but not of a moral and humane government.
The idea of the Roman Republic, as it shines through the
rude fragments of the Annals of Ennius in such utterances as
these—

> Moribus antiquis stat res Romana virisque[1],—

is suggestive of a nobler energy of character, of more abundant
public and private virtue, than the idea pervading and animating

---

[1] 'By the manners of the olden time and its men the Roman State stands
firm.'

the polished verse of the Aeneid.  The thought of the Rome
of Ennius is associated in our minds with the free political life
of the Forum and the Campus Martius, and with the grave
deliberations of the Senate, as well as with the exercise of
military force and administrative sovereignty.  The idea of
Italy pervading the Georgics has everything to attract and
nothing to repel our sympathies : and thus notwithstanding the
inferior opportunities for awakening human · interest which
necessarily attach to a didactic when compared with an epic
poem, the charm exercised by that poem is more unmixed and
unchanging than that of the poem which evokes the proud
memories of the Capitol.  In the Aeneid, Virgil is really the
panegyrist of despotism under the delusive disguise of paternal
government.  In so far as there is any conflict between right
and wrong in the Aeneid, the wrong appears to be the 'victrix
causa' 'which pleases the gods.'  The religious idea of the
Fates is invested with none of the ethical mystery with which
the analogous idea in Greek poetry is invested.  They act in
a hard, plain, arbitrary way, irrespective of right and wrong,
regardless of personal happiness or suffering.  The actors in
the poem who move our sympathies are those who perish in
blind resistance to, or blind compliance with, their decrees—
Dido, Pallas, Turnus, and Lausus.  The opposition between
natural human feeling and the 'divom inclementia' is reverently
accepted and acquiesced in by Virgil in the person of his hero.

The conclusion at which we arrive as to the value of the
Aeneid as an epic poem representative of the Roman Empire,
is that Virgil has given a true, adequate, and noble expression
to an idea which actually has exercised a greater spell over the
imagination and a greater influence over the daily lives of men,
than any other which owed its origin to their secular interests :
but that this idea, regarded from its political, religious, and
personal side, is one which does not touch the heart, or
enlighten the conscience : and this is an important drawback
to the claim which the Aeneid may have to the highest rank as
a work of art.

# CHAPTER XI.

## The Aeneid as an Epic Poem of Human Life.

### I.

THE national, religious, and political ideas which form the central interest of the poem have been considered in the previous chapter. We have seen how Virgil was moved by an impulse similar to that which acted on Ennius in a ruder age, and in what way he strove to express the meaning which the idea of Rome has for all times, and to find an adequate symbol of the dominant sentiment of his own time. It remains to consider how far the poem sustains by its command over our sympathies the interest thus established in its favour; and to ascertain what value the Aeneid, as a poem of action, unfolding a spectacle of human life, manners, character, and passion, possessed for the Romans and still possesses for ourselves.

The action of the poem, apart from its bearing on the destinies of the world, has a grandeur and dignity of its own. It is enacted on a great theatre, developes itself by incidents giving free play to the highest modes of human energy and passion, and through the agency of personages already renowned in legend and poetry. In that mythical age which the poet recalls to life no spectacle could be imagined more deserving to fix the attention of the world than the fall of Troy, the building of Carthage, and the first rude settlement on the hills of Rome. Whatever else may be said of the personages of the story, they are conceived of as playing no common part in human affairs. In following their fortunes we breathe the air of that high poetic region which forms the undetermined border-land between mythology and history. We look back on the ruined state of the greatest city of legendary times, and we mark the first beginnings of the two Imperial cities which in historical times disputed the empire of the world. The poem evokes the associations, ancient and recent, attaching to the various scenes through which the action passes,—Troy, Carthage, Sicily, the shores of Latium, the Tiber, and the hills on which Rome was built. The vagueness of the time in which the action is laid enables the poet to connect together, in a most critical position of human affairs, the fortunes of the chief powers of Asia, Africa, and Europe. The spheres of man's activity in which the action moves—war and sea-adventure in search of undiscovered lands—give the fullest scope to energetic representation. In his conception of the voyage of Aeneas and of a great war determining the issue of his enterprise, Virgil followed the greatest epic examples, and found a subject to which he could impart the interest of adventurous incident and heroic achievement. In his conception of the part played in the action by the passion of love, he introduced a more familiar and modern phase of life which the examples of the Greek tragedians and of the Alexandrine epic had proved to be capable of idealising treatment.

The actors moreover who play their part in these critical events are not 'common or mean.' The crisis is conceived of as one so momentous, from the issues involved in it, as to call forth the passions and the energies of the old Olympian Powers. But even the human personages of the story appear with a prestige of glory and sanctity, and yet are sufficiently unfamiliar to excite new expectations. Aeneas, as the son of a mightier goddess[1], is distinguished in the Iliad by the honours of a higher lineage than Achilles. He is brave in war, the comrade of Hector, a hero deemed worthy to encounter Achilles himself as well as Diomede in battle. He is especially dear to the gods, and is marked out by prophecy as destined to bear, and transmit to his descendants, the rule over the remnant of the Trojans. To Anchises attaches the sanctity of one enjoying a closer communion with the immortals, of one at once

---

[1] Il. xx. 105.

favoured and afflicted above others, and elevated, like Oedipus, out of weakness and suffering here, into honour and influence beyond the grave. Iulus receives a reflected glory from the transcendent greatness of the Julian house. Dido or Elissa was a name famous in Phoenician legend, and associated with the ancient renown of Tyre. Evander is illustrious from his Arcadian origin, from his relation to Hercules, from the fame of his mother as one of the Italian Camenae. Even the mere ethnical names of Latinus and Turnus receive individuality by being introduced in the line of old Italian dynasties, and in direct connexion with Faunus, Picus, and other beings of the native mythology.

It may therefore be said that in the choice of the time and the scenes in which his action is laid, in the character of the action itself, and in the eminence of the personages taking part in it, Virgil fulfils all the conditions of his art which reflexion on the models of the past and on the circumstances in life most capable of interesting the imagination could teach him. The care with which he prepared himself for his task is as remarkable as the judgment with which he conceived its main conditions. The conduct of his story shows the most intimate familiarity with the incidents and adventures contained in the Iliad and Odyssey, in the Cyclic poems and the dramas founded on them, in the Homeric hymns and the Alexandrine epic. It shows how Virgil so combines and varies the details thus suggested, as to recall many features of the Homeric age, and at the same time to produce the impression of something new in literary art. The revived image of that age must have affected the contemporaries of the poet in a manner different from its effect on us. To us both the Iliad and the Aeneid are ancient and unfamiliar: the one comes before us as an original picture of manners, the other as a copy taken in a long subsequent age. But to a Roman of the time of Augustus the life of the Homeric age must have appeared almost as remote as it does to us. The direct imitations of Homer in the Aeneid might produce on his mind the same mixed impression of novelty and familiarity which is produced on a modern reader by the reproduction and recasting of the doctrines, incidents, and language of the Bible in the two epic poems of Milton. The fascination of this world of supernatural agency and personal adventure, brought home to him for the first time in the most elevated tones of his own language, may have charmed the Roman reader in the same way as the revival of mediaeval romance in the literary languages of modern Europe charmed the readers of the latter part of the eighteenth and the first part of the nineteenth centuries. And if such were the first impressions produced by the poem, a closer examination of it must have shown that the imagination of Virgil had out of ancient materials built up something new in the world. If his representation of the heroic age wants the vivid truth and *naïveté* of Homer's representation, yet it is impressive with the dignity of antique associations, and rich with the colouring of his own human sensibilities.

But the Aeneid not only revives the romance of the Greek heroic age: it creates the romance of 'that Italy for which Camilla the virgin, Euryalus, and Turnus and Nisus died of wounds.' It bestows the colour and warmth of human life on dim traditions, on vague names, on the memories of early warfare clinging to ancient towns, and on the origins of immemorial customs and ceremonies. The task of giving poetic life to the dry prose of Cato, to the dust of antiquarian learning, and to the rigid formalism of the old Roman ceremonial must have taxed the poet's powers more than that of reawakening the interest in the old Homeric life. Virgil accomplishes this result through his power of living at the same time in the past and in the present; of feeling powerfully the associations of a remote antiquity, and the immediate action of all that was most impressive to thought and imagination in the age in which he lived.

The earlier works of Virgil had proved his strength in descriptive and didactic poetry, and in the expression of personal feeling, of national sentiment, and of ethical contemplation;

but they had given no indication of epic, and little of dramatic genius. Although the episode of the 'Pastor Aristaeus' is a specimen of succinct, animated, and pathetic narrative, it must be remembered that this was a late addition to the Georgics, and was probably written after considerable way had been made in the composition of the Aeneid. An epic poet, over and above his purely poetic susceptibility, must possess the art and faculty of a prose historian. Homer has in an unequalled degree the clearness, vividness, and movement in telling his story, which characterise such writers as Herodotus. The account given of Virgil's mode of composition proves that he took great pains both with the plan and the execution of his narrative. He is said to have arranged the first draught of his story in prose, and then to have worked on the various parts of it as they interested him at the time of composition. There are clear indications that the books were not written in the order in which they stand; and a few inconsistencies of statement between the earlier and later books were left uncorrected at the time of the author's death. The poem, in the careful arrangement of its materials, bears the stamp of the manner in which it was composed. Like that of every other great Roman, the genius of Virgil was thoroughly orderly and systematic. But along with the power of order Virgil had what many Roman writers want, the power of variety. The narrative of the Aeneid is full of movement, succinct or ample according to the prominence intended to be given to its different parts. The various streams of action are kept separate, yet not too far apart to cause any confusion or forgetfulness when the time comes to unite them. There is at once weight and energy in the movement of the main current: it neither hurries nor flags, but advances for the most part steadily, 'quadam intentione gravitatis.' If it wants the buoyancy and vivacity of the narrative of Herodotus, it shows the concentrated energy which distinguishes the works of the great Roman historians. It brings before us rather a series of grave events, bearing on a great issue and following an inevitable course, than the vicissitudes of individual fortunes and the play of human passions and impulses: and in this it is in accordance both with the actual history of Rome, and with the record of it contained in literature.

Virgil cannot be said to have failed either in the conception of his subject, in the collection and preparation of his materials, or in the art and faculty demanded for impressive narrative. Yet all feel that the Aeneid is much inferior to the Homeric poems in natural human interest, as it is much inferior in reflective interest to the greatest extant dramas of Aeschylus and Sophocles. The poem, as a whole, produces the impression rather of careful construction than of organic growth. The reflexion employed on it is rather that of a critic applying artistic principles to impart unity to many heterogeneous materials, than that of an imaginative thinker, seeing his story unfold itself before him in the light of some great intuition into the secret meanings of life.

His inferiority to Homer in the power of making his story at once vividly real and nobly ideal arises partly from an inferiority in his own temper, and partly from the inferior adaptability of the life of his own age to imaginative treatment. There is no trace in Virgil of that keen enjoyment of personal adventure and bodily activity which is present in every page of the Homeric poems. Virgil's materials are gathered from study and reflexion, not from strong and many-sided contact with life. Though he writes of 'arma virumque' with a Roman sense of the duty of disregarding danger and death, he has none of the 'delight of battle' which animates the Iliad and the poetical and prose romances of Scott. Neither does he make us feel that elevation of spirit in the presence of the danger of the sea, which the author of the Odyssey among ancient, and Byron among modern poets, communicate to their readers.

But the vast difference in manners, feelings, and modes of thought, between an early and a late age—between the spring and the autumn of ancient civilisation—presented still more insuperable obstacles to Virgil in his attempt to accomplish the work of Homer. In the first period imagination is the ruling faculty of life, the great impeller to action and discovery, the chief prompter both of hope and fear : and thus the movement and impulses of such an age readily yield themselves to imaginative treatment. Poets and dramatists of a later time who desire to represent life in its most energetic phase endeavour to reproduce some image of this early time by a constructive act of imagination. A dramatist may take the mere outline of some ancient legend and fill it with modern thought and sentiment. He is not called on for that realistic reproduction of manners and usages which an epic poet is expected to exhibit on his larger canvas. The difficulty which the latter has to meet is that of verifying by anything in his own experience the impression which he forms from the study of ancient art and records. Homer alone, by living the imaginative life of an earlier time, was able to represent that life in its truth, its fulness of being, its vivid sense of pleasure and pain. The age mirrored in the Homeric poems is the true age of romance and personal enterprise, when the individual acquires ascendency through his own qualities of strength, beauty, courage, force of mind, natural eloquence; when the world is regarded as the scene of supernatural agencies manifesting themselves in visible shape ; when men live more in the open air than in houses and cities, and have to procure subsistence, comfort, and security by energy of body and the inventive resources of their minds ; and when their hearts are alive to every natural emotion, not deadened by routine or enervated by excess of pleasure. Hence it is that all Homer's accounts of war and battles, of sea-adventure, of debates in the council of chiefs or in the assemblies of the people, of games and contests of strength, are so full of living interest. Hence too comes the vivacity with which all the details of procuring food, the enjoyment of eating and drinking and sinking to sleep, the arming or clothing of heroes, the management of a ship at sea, the ordinary occupations of the hunter or the herdsman are described. To the same cause is due the truth and appropriateness of all the descriptions from Nature,—of the dawn and sunrise, of storms, of the gathering of clouds, of the constellations, of the stillness of night, of the habits of wild animals, of the more violent forces of the elements, of the omens which suddenly appear to men engaged in battle or assembled in council in the open air and awaiting a sign for their guidance.

An image of this Homeric life Virgil has to reproduce from the midst of a state of society utterly unlike it. The Augustan Age was pre-eminently an age of order and material civilisation, in which great results were produced, not by individual force, but by masses and combinations of men directed by political sagacity and secret council; in which the life of the richer class was passed in great cities and luxurious villas; in which the comforts of life were abundantly supplied through the organisation of commerce and the ministrations of a multitude of slaves [1]; in which the outward world was enjoyed as a beautiful spectacle rather than as a field of active exertion and personal adventure; in which the belief in the supernatural was fixed in imposing outward symbols, but was no longer a fresh source of wonder and expectation; an age too, in which the natural emotions of the heart and imagination were becoming deadened by satiety and the 'strenua inertia' of luxurious living.

The art of Virgil is thus powerless to produce a true image of the life and manners of the Homeric age. Yet he does surround the actors in his story with an environment of religious belief and observances, of political and social life, of material civilisation, of martial movement and sea-adventure, formed partly out of his poetical and antiquarian studies, partly out of the familiar spectacle of his own age, partly out of his personal sympathies and convictions. And this representation, though

---

[1] For an instance of the number of slaves in a single household in the reign of Nero compare the speech of C. Cassius in Tac. Ann. xiv. 43: 'Quem numerus servorum tuebitur, cum Pedanium Secundum quadringenti non protexerint?' The simplicity of the old Roman life which Virgil idealises in the Georgics, as compared with the luxurious indulgence of the later Republic and the Empire, was in a great measure due to the comparative rarity of slavery in the earlier ages of Roman history.

it necessarily wants the vital freshness and vigour of Homer's representation, has a peculiar dignity and charm of its own. It must be accepted as an artistic compromise, and not as the idealised picture of any life that has ever been realised in the world. It is one of the earliest and most interesting products of that kind of imagination which has in modern times created the literature of romance[1]. The work in English poetry which comes most near to the Aeneid in the union of modern ethical and political feeling with the spectacle of the martial life and the ideas of the supernatural belonging to a much earlier time, is 'The Faery Queen[2]:' though the allegorical meaning of that poem is as different as possible from the solid basis of fact —the marvellous career of Rome—on which the Aeneid is founded. Virgil produces much more than Spenser the illusion of a kind of life not absolutely withdrawn from mundane experience. The scenes through which he guides the personages of his story are the familiar places of central Italy, of Sicily, of the Greek islands, of the shores of Africa. These personages are engaged in important transactions, such as make up the actual history of early nations,—wars, alliances, intermarriages, and the like. Even the supernatural element in the poem produces the illusion, if not of conformity with the belief of men in the age in which the poem was written, yet of conformity with that stage in the whole growth and decomposition of ancient beliefs which, through the works of art and poetry, has made the deepest impression on the world. Thus if Virgil's representation of scenes, persons, incidents, modes of life, supernatural belief, etc. wants both the freshness and *naïveté* of Homer and the ideality and exuberance of fancy characteristic of

---

[1] Cf. 'Virgil's Aeneis war der früheste Versuch in dieser künstlichen oder phantastischen Fassung des Epos, das erste romantische Heldengedicht, und machte den Uebergang zu den gleich zwitterhaften Epen der modernen Zeit.' Bernhardy, Gründriss der Römischen Litteratur.

[2] It is probably too early to institute a comparison between the epic of Virgil and any recent work of imagination, but not too early to indicate adherence to those critics who find a parallel not in art and genius only, but in the simplicity and sincerity of nature revealed in their works, between the author of the Aeneid and the author of the 'Idylls of the King.'

Spenser, it is yet a solid creation of the classical mind, exercised for the first time on a great scale in bodying forth an imaginary foretime, peopling it with the personages of earlier art or of the poet's fancy, and filling up the outlines of tradition with the sentiment, the interests, and the ideas of the age in which the poem was written.

In addition to his great knowledge of antiquity and his gift of living in the creations of earlier art and poetry, Virgil possessed in his own imaginative constitution elements of power which enabled him to give solidity and beauty to the world of his invention. Among these elements of power his feeling of religious awe, his sense of majesty investing the forms of government, his veneration for antiquity, his susceptibility to the associations attaching to particular places, are conspicuous. His sympathy with the primary human affections suggests to him the details of many pathetic situations. He has a Roman admiration for courage, endurance, and magnanimous bearing. His refined perceptions, perfected by a life of studious culture and by familiarity with the social life of men inheriting the traditions of a great governing class, enable him to make the various actors on his stage play their parts with grace and dignity.

By some of these sources of imaginative power Ennius also was moved in the composition of his epic. In that which is Virgil's strength, sympathy with the primary human affections, it would have been impossible for any poet who came after them to have surpassed Homer, Sophocles, or Lucretius. But in Homer this sympathy is combined with a sterner, in Sophocles with a severer mood. In Lucretius the feeling is identified with the general melancholy of his thought. The feeling of humanity in Virgil is as original and pervading as the feeling with which Nature affects him. From all these elements of inspiration, his imagination is able to body forth the world of his creation in the remote border-land of history and mythology, and to impart to it not only solidity and self-consistency, but also grandeur of outline and beauty of detail.

## II.

The first general impression produced by reading the Aeneid immediately after reading the Iliad, is that the supernatural 'machinery,' consisting in a great degree of the agency of the Olympian gods in hindering or furthering the catastrophe, is the most imitative and conventional element in the poem. But a closer examination of its whole texture brings to light beneath the more conspicuous figures of the Homeric mythology, the presence of other modes of religious belief, feeling, and practice. And even the parts assigned to the greater deities have been recast for the purposes of Virgil's epic. If these deities have lost much in vivacity and energy, they have gained in dignity of demeanour. The two most active amongst them are indeed as little scrupulous in the means they employ to attain their ends, as they show themselves in the Iliad. They are as regardless of individual happiness as they appear in some of the dramas of Euripides. And we cannot attribute to Virgil, what has been attributed to Euripides, the intention of bringing the objects of popular belief into disrepute [1]. He seems to feel that they are above man's questioning; that it is for him ' parere quietum ; ' and that it is well with him if through long suffering he at last obtains reconciliation with them. But the Venus and Juno of the Aeneid are at least exempt from some of the lower appetites and more ferocious passions with which they are animated in the Iliad. They have learned the tact and dissimulation of the life of an Imperial society. They are actuated by political rather than by personal passions. They move with a certain Roman state and dignity of bearing —

> pedes vestis defluxit ad imos
> Et vera incessu patuit dea.
> \*       \*       \*       \*       \*
> Ast ego, quae Divom incedo regina [2].

---

[1] This intention was well brought out in an article in Fraser's Magazine, which has since been republished by Mr. Froude in his 'Short Studies on Great Subjects.'

[2] 'Her robe flowed down to her feet, and she was revealed by her movement as indeed a goddess.' 'But I who move in state as the queen of the gods.'

The action of Juno in the Aeneid reminds us of the leading part taken by women in the political intrigues of the later Republic and early Empire; as by the βοῶπις of Cicero's Letters, and the younger Agrippina in the pages of Tacitus. The 'mother of the Aeneadae' combines a subtlety of device and persistence of purpose with the charm which befits the ancestress of a family in which personal beauty, as is attested by many extant statues, was as conspicuous as force of intellect and of character. The Jove of the Aeneid, though he appears without the outward signs of majesty which inspired the conception of the Pheidian Zeus, and though the part he plays in controlling the action appears somewhat tame, yet sometimes gives utterance to thoughts which recall the grave and steadfast attributes which the Romans reverenced under the title of ' Iuppiter Stator,'—

> Stat sua cuique dies; breve et inreparabile tempus
> Omnibus est vitae; sed famam extendere factis
> Hoc virtutis opus [1].

Neptune comes forth to calm the storm raised by Aeolus nòt with the earth-shaking might with which he passed from the heights of Samothrace to Aegae, nor in the radiant splendour in which he sped over the waves towards the ships of the Achaeans, but with the calm and calming aspect made familiar in the plastic art of a later time—

> alto
> Prospiciens summa placidum caput extulit unda [2].

Apollo is introduced taking part in the battle of Actium with something of the proud bearing which the greatest of his statues perpetuates—

> Actius, haec cernens, arcum intendebat Apollo
> Desuper [3].

---

[1] 'To each man his own day is appointed: brief and irrecoverable is the time of life to all; but to spread one's name widely by achievements, this is the work of valour.'   Aen. x. 467–9.

[2] 'Looking forth from the deep he raised his calm head from the surface of the wave.'   Cf. Weidner's Commentary on the First Two Books of the Aeneid.

[3] 'Apollo of Actium, marking this, was bending his bow from above.'

And as an augury of this late help afforded to his descendant, he appears in the action of the poem as guiding the hand, and encouraging the spirit of the mythical ancestor of the Julii in his first initiation into battle—

> Macte nova virtute, puer : sic itur ad astra,
> Dis genite, et geniture deos : iure omnia bella
> Gente sub Assaraci fato ventura resident :
> Nec te Troia capit [1].

Sympathy with the pure and heroic nature and the untimely death of Camilla introduces Diana to tell her early story and to express pity for her fate.  Mars appears only once aiding his own people against the foreign enemy [2].  Mercury and Iris perform the customary part of messengers between heaven and earth.  The Italian mythology contributes some of the few beings endowed with human personality which it produced.  The creation of Egeria, of the Nymph Marica, and of the goddess Juturna was due to the same sentiment, associated with lakes, rivers, and brooks, which gave birth to the Naiads and River-gods of Greek mythology.  Of these Juturna alone, as the sister of the Italian hero of the poem, bears any part in the action ; and as appearing in that personal human shape in which Greek imagination embodied its conception of deity, but from which Latin reverence for the most part shrank, she is represented as enjoying that doubtful title to distinction which made the innumerable heroines of the Greek mythology a ' theme of song to men '—

> Extemplo Turni sic est adfata sororem,
> Diva deam, stagnis quae fluminibusque sonoris
> Praesidet : hunc illi rex aetheris altus honorem
> Iuppiter erepta pro virginitate sacravit [3].

---

[1] ' Speed well, O boy, in thy young valour; such is the way to the stars, thou child of the gods and sire of gods to be: rightly shall all the wars that are destined to be, cease under the sway of the line of Assaracus: nor is Troy wide enough to hold thee.' Aen. ix. 641-4.

[2] ix. 717.

[3] ' Forthwith she thus addressed the sister of Turnus, she a goddess, her a goddess of the meres and sounding rivers; such the hallowed office that

Of the other powers of the Italian mythology Faunus is introduced[1] in accordance with the national conception of an undefined invisible agency guiding the conduct of men by means of
omens and oracles.    And in accordance with the euhemerism
which suited the prosaic bent of the Latin mind, the native
deities Saturnus, Janus, and Picus appear as a line of kings, who
lived and reigned in Latium before assuming their place in the
ranks of the gods.

The ordinary modes in which the divine personages of Virgil's
story take part in the action are suggested by incidents in the
Homeric poems or Hymns, and, apparently in some instances,
by the parts assigned to them in the dramas of Euripides.   Thus
the office performed by Venus in telling the story of Dido
previous to the landing of Aeneas on the shores of Africa, and
by Diana in telling the romantic incidents of Camilla's childhood,
may have been suggested by the prologues to the Hippolytus,
the Bacchae, and the Alcestis.    But other manifestations of
supernatural agency, and those not the least impressive, are due
to Virgil's own invention, and are inspired by that sense of awe
with which the thought of the invisible world affects his imagination.    Juvenal, when contrasting the comfort which enabled
Virgil to do justice to his genius with the poverty of the poets of
his own time, selects as an instance of his imaginative power the
passage in the Seventh Book of the Aeneid which describes the
terror inspired by Allecto.    And certainly the whole description
of the appearance of the Fury on earth, from the time when she
enters the palace of Latinus till she disappears among the woods
which add to the gloom of the black torrent of Amsanctus, is
full of energy.    So too is the brief description of Juno completing the work of her agent—one of many passages of which
the solemn effect is enhanced by the use of the language of
Ennius—

Jove, high king of Heaven, bestowed on her as the price of her love.' Aen. xii.
138–41.    This passage, with its monotonous and rhyming endings—sororem
—sonoris—honorem,—is probably one of those which Virgil would have
altered had he lived to give the ' limae labor' to his work.
    [1] vii. 81, etc.

Tum regina deum caelo delapsa morantis
Impulit ipsa manu portas, et cardine verso
Belli ferratos rumpit Saturnia postes[1].

Another passage in which the appearance of the Olympian
deities produces the impression of awe and sublimity is that
in which Venus reveals herself to her son in her divine proportions—

confessa deam, qualisque videri
Caelicolis et quanta solet[2]—

and, by removing the mist intervening between his mortal
sight and the reality of things, displays the forms of Neptune,
Juno, Jove himself, and Pallas engaged in the overthrow of
Troy,—

Apparent dirae facies inimicaque Troiae
Numina magna deum[3].

But there are traces in the Aeneid of another religious belief
and practice more primitive and more widely spread than the
worship of the Olympian gods, or of the impersonal abstractions
of Italian theology. The religious fancies which originally united
each city, each tribe, and each family into one community[4], had
been transmitted in popular beliefs and in ceremonial observances
from a time long antecedent to the establishment of the Olympian
dynasty of gods. This brighter creation of the imagination did
not banish the secret awe inspired by the older spiritual conceptions. Invisible Powers were supposed to haunt certain places,
to protect each city with their unseen presence or under some
visible symbol, and to make their abode at each family hearth,
uniting all the kindred of the house in a common worship.

These survivals of primitive thought appear in many striking
passages in the Aeneid. The idea of a secret indwelling Power,

---

[1] 'Then the queen of the Gods gliding from Heaven, with her own hand
pushed the lingering gates, and, as the hinge moved, she, with the might of
Saturn's daughter, bursts open the iron-fastened doors of War.'  vii. 620-2.

[2] 'In her true semblance as a Goddess, in form and size as she is wont to
appear to the dwellers in Heaven.'

[3] 'The awful forms become visible and the mighty majesty of the Gods
hostile to Troy.'

[4] Cp. De Coulanges, La Cité Antique.

identified with the continued existence and fortunes of cities, imparts sublimity to that passage in Book VIII. in which the Roman feeling of the sanctity of the Capitol obtains its grandest expression—

> Iam tum religio pavidos terrebat agrestis
> Dira loci; iam tum silvam saxumque tremebant.
> Hoc nemus, hunc, inquit, frondoso vertice collem,
> Quis deus incertum est, habitat deus: Arcades ipsum
> Credunt se vidisse Iovem, cum saepe nigrantem
> Aegida concuteret dextra nimbosque cieret [1].

This belief imparts dignity to what from a merely human point of view seems grotesque rather than sublime, the reception by the Trojans of the 'fatalis machina feta armis' within their walls. The fatal error is committed under the conviction that the protection enjoyed under the old Palladium would be renewed under this new symbol. The construction of the unwieldy mass is attributed to Calchas, acting from the motive expressed in the lines—

> Ne recipi portis aut duci in moenia possit,
> Neu populum antiqua sub religione tueri [2].

This same belief of the dependence of cities on their indwelling deities pervades the whole description of the destruction of Troy. Thus the despair produced by the first discovery of the presence of the enemy within the town obtains utterance in the words—

> Excessere omnis adytis arisque relictis
> Di, quibus imperium hoc steterat [3].

When Panthus the priest of Apollo appears on the scene, it is said of him—

[1] 'Even then the dread solemnity of the spot awed the frightened peasants : even then they trembled before the wood and rock. This grove, he says, this hill with leafy summit, some God—what God we know not—inhabits : the Arcadians believe that they have beheld even Jove himself, when ofttimes he shook the blackening aegis in his right hand, and summoned the storm clouds.' viii. 349–54.
[2] 'That it may not be able to be received within the gates or drawn within the walls, nor to guard the people beneath its ancient sanctity.' ii. 187–8.
[3] 'Quitting shrines and altars, all the Gods by whom this empire stood fast, have departed.' ii. 351–2.

> Sacra manu victosque deos parvumque nepotem
> Ipse trahit[1].

A kind of mystic glory from the companionship of these 'defeated gods,' for whom he was seeking a new local habitation, invests the adventurous wanderings of Aeneas. The preservation and re-establishment of these gods is the pledge of the revival, under a new form and in a strange land, of the ancient empire of Troy, and of her ultimate triumph over her enemy.

But still more ancient than the belief in local deities indwelling in the sites of cities was the worship of the dead, the belief in their reappearance on earth, and of their continued interest in human affairs. It is in Virgil, a poet of the most enlightened period of antiquity, that we find the clearest indications of the earliest form of this belief and of the ceremonies to which it first gave birth—

> Inferimus tepido spumantia cymbia lacte,
> Sanguinis et sacri pateras, *animamque sepulchro*
> *Condimus*, et magna supremum voce ciemus[2].

The doctrine of the continued existence of the dead, the most ancient and the most enduring of all supernatural beliefs, affects Virgil through the strength both of his human affection and of his religious awe. Both of these feelings are wonderfully blended in that passage in which the ghost of Hector appears to Aeneas, and entrusts to him the sacred emblems and gods of the doomed city. How deep on the one hand is the feeling of old affection mingled with awful solemnity which inspires the address of Aeneas to his ancient comrade—

> O lux Dardaniae! spes o fidissima Teucrum!
> Quae tantae tenuere morae? quibus Hector ab oris
> Expectate venis? ut te post multa tuorum
> Funera, post varios hominumque urbisque labores,

---

[1] 'With his own hand he bears the sacred emblems and the defeated Gods and drags his little grandson.' ii. 320-1.

[2] 'We bear bowls foaming with warm milk, and saucers of sacred blood, and lay his spirit to rest in the tomb, and call him for the last time with a loud voice.' Aen. iii. 66-8. The passage is referred to by M. de Coulanges in one of the early chapters of 'La Cité Antique.'

Defessi aspicimus : quae caussa indigna serenos
Foedavit voltus, aut cur haec volnera cerno[1]?

And how pure appears the love of country still moving the august shade in the world below, in the lines which follow—

Ille nihil, nec me quaerentem vana moratur,
Sed graviter gemitus imo de pectore ducens,
' Heu fuge, nate dea, teque his,' ait, ' eripe flammis:
Hostis habet muros : ruit alto a culmine Troia :
Sat patriae Priamoque datum : si Pergama dextra
Defendi possent, etiam hac defensa fuissent.
Sacra suosque tibi commendat Troia Penates :
Hos cape fatorum comites, his moenia quaere,
Magna pererrato statues quae denique ponto[2].'

Under the influence of the same feelings of affection and reverence, Andromache is introduced bringing annual offerings to the empty tomb and altars consecrated to the Manes of her first husband—

Sollemnis cum forte dapes, et tristia dona
Ante urbem in luco falsi Simoentis ad undam,
Libabat cineri Andromache manisque vocabat
Hectoreum ad tumulum, viridi quem caespite inanem
Et geminas, caussam lacrimis, sacraverat aras[3].

Similar honours are paid by Dido to the spirit of Sychaeus—

---

[1] 'O light of the Dardan land, most trusted hope of the Trojans, why hast thou tarried so long ? from what shores, Hector, dost thou, the object of much longing, come ? how, after many deaths of thy kinsmen, after manifold shocks to the city and to those who dwell within it, do we, in our utter weariness, behold thee ? what cruel cause hath marred thy calm aspect, or why do I behold these wounds ? ' ii. 281–6.

[2] 'He makes no reply, nor detains me by answer to my idle questions, but with a deep groan from the bottom of his breast, " Ah fly," he says, " Goddess-born, and wrest thyself away from these flames : the enemy holds the walls ; Troy falls in ruins from its lofty summit ; enough has been granted to my country and to Priam ; could Pergama have been defended by any single hand even by this it should have been defended. Troy commits to thee her sacred emblems and household Gods : take them as companions of thy destinies, seek a fortress for them, which thou shalt raise of mighty size after thy wide wanderings over the deep are over."'

[3] 'At a time when Andromache, in a grove in front of the city by the stream of Simoeis—not the true Simoeis—happened to be bringing the yearly offering of food, a melancholy gift to the dead, and to be calling his Manes to the tomb of Hector—the empty mound of green turf which she had hallowed with the two altars, which gave food for her tears.' iii. 301–5.

Praeterea fuit in tectis de marmore templum
Coniugis antiqui, miro quod honore colebat,
Velleribus niveis et festa fronde revinctum[1].

The long account of the 'Games' in Book V., which, from a Roman point of view, might be regarded as a needless excrescence on the poem, is justified by the consideration that they are celebrated in honour of the Manes of Anchises.

The whole of the Sixth Book—the master-piece of Virgil's creative invention—is inspired by the feeling of the greater spiritual life which awaits man beyond the grave. The conceptions and composition of that Book entitle Virgil to take his place with Aeschylus, Sophocles, and Plato among the four great religious teachers,—the 'pii vates' who, in transmitting, have illumined the spiritual intuitions of antiquity.

The sense of devout awe is the chief mark of distinction between the 'Inferno' of Virgil and that of Homer, the conception of which is due to the suggestive force of natural curiosity and natural affection. The dead do not appear to Virgil merely as the shadowy inhabitants of an unsubstantial world,—νεκύων ἀμενηνὰ κάρηνα,—but as partakers in a more august and righteous dispensation than that under which mortals live. The spirit of Virgil is on this subject more in harmony with that of Aeschylus than of Homer, but his thoughts of the dead are happier and of a less austere majesty than those expressed in the Choëphoroe. The whole humanising and moralising influence of Greek philosophy, and especially of the Platonic teaching, combines in Virgil's representation with the primitive fancies of early times and the popular beliefs and practices transmitted from those times to his own age. But just as he fails to form a consistent conception of the action of the powers of Heaven out of the various beliefs, primitive, artistic, national, and philosophical, which he endeavours to reconcile, so he has failed to produce a consistent picture of the spiritual life out of the various popular,

---

[1] 'Besides there was within the palace a marble chapel in memory of her former lord, which she cherished with marvellous reverence, wreathing it with snow-white fillets and festal leaves.' iv. 457–9.

mystical, and philosophical modes of thought which he strove to combine into a single representation.   Perhaps if he had lived longer and been able to carry further the 'potiora studia' on which he was engaged simultaneously with the composition of the Aeneid, he might have effected a more specious reconcilement of what now appear irreconcileable factors of belief.   Or, perhaps, in the thought which induces him to dismiss Aeneas and the Sibyl by the gate through which

> falsa ad caelum mittunt insomnia Manes[1]—

we may recognise a trace, not certainly of Epicurean unbelief, but of that sad and subtle irony with which the spirit of man inwardly acknowledges that it is baffled in its highest quest. The august spectacle which is unfolded before Aeneas,—that, too, like the vision of Er the son of Armenius, is but a $\mu \hat{v} \theta os$,— a symbol of a state of being, which the human imagination, illuminated by conscience and affection, shadows forth as an object of hope, but which it cannot grasp as a reality.   In the grandeur of moral belief which inspires Virgil's shadowy representation, in his recognition of the everlasting distinction between a life of righteousness and of unrighteousness, of purity and of impurity, he but reproduces the profoundest ethical intuitions of Plato.   But in the indication of that trust in a final reunion which has comforted innumerable human hearts—

> coniunx ubi pristinus illi
> Respondet curis aequatque Sychaeus amorem [2]—

the Roman poet is moved by the tender affection of his own nature, and follows the light of his own intuition.

Ancient commentators have drawn attention to the large place which the account of religious ceremonies occupies in the Aeneid, and to the exact acquaintance which Virgil shows with the minutiae of Pontifical and Augural lore.   It is in keeping with the character of Aeneas as the hero of a religious epic, that

---

[1] 'The Manes send unreal dreams to the world above.'
[2] 'Where her former husband Sychaeus sympathises with all her sorrows and loves her with a love equal to her own.'

the commencement and completion of every enterprise are accompanied with sacrifices and other ceremonial observances. M. Gaston Boissier [1], following Macrobius, has pointed out the special propriety of the offerings made to different gods, of the peculiar use of such epithets as 'eximios' applied to the bulls selected for sacrifice, of the ritual application of the words 'porricio [2]' and 'porrigo,' and of the words addressed to Aeneas by the River-Nymphs [3],—'Aenea, vigila,'—which would recall to Roman ears those with which the commander of the Roman armies, on the outbreak of war, shook the shields and sacred symbols of Mars.   Other passages would remind the readers of Virgil of the ceremonial observances with which they were familiar, as for instance that in which Helenus prescribes to Aeneas the peculiarly Roman practice of veiling the head in worship and sacrifice—

> Quin, ubi transmissae steterint trans aequora classes,
> Et positis aris iam vota in litore solves,
> Purpureo velare comas adopertus amictu ;
> Nequa inter sanctos ignis in honore deorum
> Hostilis facies occurrat et omina turbet [4].

There are traces also of a worship, which from its wider diffusion, and its late survival, seems to belong to a remoter antiquity than the peculiar ceremonial of Rome,—as in the prayer offered to the god of Soracte—

> Summe deum, sancti custos Soractis, Apollo,
> Quem primi colimus, cui pineus ardor acervo

---

[1] Cp. 'Un Poëte Théologien,' in the Revue des Deux Mondes.
[2] Cf. Aen. v. 236 :—
> Vobis laetus ego hoc candentem in litore taurum
> Constituam ante aras, voti reus, extaque salsos
> Porriciam in fluctus, et vina liquentia fundam.
viii. 273 :—
> Quare agite, O iuvenes ! tantarum in munere laudum
> Cingite fronde comas et pocula porgite dextris.
[3] Created out of his ships.
[4] 'Nay when thy fleet, after crossing the seas, shall have come to anchor, and, after raising altars, thou shalt pay thy vows upon the shore, then veil thy head with a purple robe, lest, while the consecrated fires are burning in the worship of the Gods, the face of some enemy may meet thee, and confound the omens.'   iii. 403–7.

Pascitur, et medium freti pietate per ignem
Cultores multa premimus vestigia pruna [1].

The desire to infuse a new power into the religious observance, belief, and life of his countrymen thus appears to have
acted as a strong suggestive force to Virgil's imagination.  This
is apparent in the importance which he attaches to the offices
of Priest or Augur, to the dress, ornaments, or procedure of the
chief person taking part in prayer or sacrifice, to the ceremonies
accompanying every important action, to the sacred associations
attaching to particular places.  Amid all the changes of the
world, Virgil seems to cling to the traditions of the religious
and spiritual life,—as Lucretius holds to the belief in the laws
of Nature,—as the surest ground of human trust.  He has no
thought of superseding old beliefs or practices by any new

Vana superstitio veterumque ignara deorum [2],

but rather strives to reconcile the old faith with the more
enlightened convictions and humaner sentiments of men.  His
religious belief, like his other speculative convictions, was composite and undefined; yet it embraced what was purest and
most vital in all the religions of antiquity, and, in its deepest
intuitions, it seems to look forward to some aspects of the
belief which became dominant in Rome four centuries later.


## III.

While the various religious elements in Virgil's nature find
ample scope in the representation of the Aeneid, his apathy in
regard to active political life is seen in the tameness of his
reproduction of that aspect of human affairs.  In the Homeric
βουλή and ἀγορά we recognise not only the germs of the future

---

[1] 'Highest of Gods, Apollo, guardian of holy Soracte, in whose worship
we are foremost, in whose honour the heaped-up pinewood blazes, while we,
thy worshippers, with pious trust, even through the midst of the flame
plant our steps deep in the embers.'  xi. 785–8.  Cp. the Beltane fires which
are said to be still kept up among remote Celtic populations, and which
seem to be a survival of a primitive Sun-worship.

[2] 'Idle superstition, which knows not the ancient Gods.'

political development of the Greeks, but the germs out of which
all free political life unfolds itself.   To the form of government
exhibited in the Aeneid, the words which Tacitus uses of a
mixed constitution might be more justly applied,—'it is one
more easily praised than realised, or if ever it is realised, it is
incapable of permanence[1].'   And even if the Virgilian idea
could be realised in some happy moment of human affairs, it
does not contain within itself the capacity of any further development.   The difficulties of the problem of government are
solved in Virgil by the picture which he draws of passive and
loyal submission on the part of nobles and people to a wise,
beneficent, and disinterested ruler and legislator[2].   The idea of
the ruler in the Aeneid is the same as that of the 'Father.'   It
is under such a rule, exercised from Rome as its centre, that the
unchanging future of the world is anticipated—

> Dum domus Aeneae Capitoli immobile saxum
> Accolet, imperiumque Pater Romanus habebit[3].

The case of Mezentius does indeed show that Virgil recognised
the ultimate right of rebellion when the paternal king passed
into the tyrannical oppressor ; but such an instance affords no
scope for representing the manifestation of political passions
and virtues.   The free play of conflicting forces in a community
has no attraction for Virgil's imagination.   He suggests no
thought either of the popular liberty realised in the best days
of the Roman commonwealth, or of the sagacity and steadfast
traditions of the Roman Senate.   The only trace of discussion
and opposition appears in the debate within the court of Latinus.

---

[1] Ann. iv. 33.

[2] It is true, as Gibbon remarks in his Dissertation on the Sixth Book of
the Aeneid, that the expression 'dare iura' is only once applied to Aeneas
—but it is the regular expression used of a ruler of a settled community, as
for instance of Dido.   It is applied at the end of the Georgics to Augustus,
'per populos dat iura.'

[3] 'While the house of Aeneas shall dwell by the steadfast rock of the
Capitol, and the fatherly sway of a Roman shall endure.'   Cp. the applica-
tion of 'pater' as an epithet of Aeneas, and Horace's line in reference to
Augustus—

> Hic ames dici pater atque princeps.

But the antagonism between Drances and Turnus is one of personal rivalry, not of political difference; and the only limit to the sovereignty of Latinus lies in his own weakness of will and in the opposition of his household.

But besides the ideals of popular freedom and senatorian dignity which were realised in the Republic, the Roman mind was impressed by another political ideal, the 'Majesty of the State.' The one political force that remained unchanged, amid the various changes of the Roman constitution from the time of the kings to the time of the emperors, was the power of the executive. And this power depended not on material force, but on the sentiment with which the magistrate was regarded as the embodiment for the time being of that attribute in the State which commanded the reverence of the people. The greatest political offence which a Roman could commit under the Republic was a violation of the 'majesty of the Commonwealth;' under the Empire 'of the majesty of the Emperor.' The sentiment out of which this idea arose was felt by Virgil in all its strength. Thus although the actual government of Latinus is exhibited as a model neither of wisdom nor of strength, it is invested with all the outward semblance of powerful and ancient sovereignty—

> Tectum augustum, ingens, centum sublime columnis,
> Urbe fuit summa, Laurentis regia Pici,
> Horrendum silvis et religione parentum.
> Hic sceptra accipere et primos attollere fasces
> Regibus omen erat; hoc illis curia templum,
> Hae sacris sedes epulis; hic, ariete caeso,
> Perpetuis soliti patres considere mensis[1].

The spectacle of the fall of Troy acquires new grandeur from the representation of Troy, not, as it appears in Homer, as a

---

[1] 'A palace, august, vast, propped on one hundred columns, stood in the highest place of the city, the royal abode of Laurentian Picus, inspiring awe from the gloom of woods and old ancestral reverence. Here it was held auspicious for kings to receive the sceptre and first to lift up the fasces: this temple was their senate-house, this the hall of their sacred banquets; here after sacrifice of a ram the fathers used to take their seats at the long unbroken tables.' vii. 170-6.

city with many allies, but as the centre of a wide and long-established empire—

> Postquam res Asiae Priamique evertere gentem
> Inmeritam visum Superis, ceciditque superbum
> Ilium et omnis humo fumat Neptunia Troia [1].

> Urbs antiqua ruit, multos dominata per annos [2].

> Haec finis Priami fatorum; hic exitus illum
> Sorte tulit, Troiam incensam et prolapsa videntem
> Pergama, tot quondam populis terrisque superbum
> Regnatorem Asiae [3].

The tragic splendour of Dido's death is enhanced by her proud sense of a high destiny fulfilled and of queenly rule exercised over a great people—

> Vixi, et, quem dederat cursum Fortuna, peregi:
> Et nunc magna mei sub terras ibit imago.
> Urbem praeclaram statui, mea moenia vidi [4].

Thus although the necessities of his position and his own 'inscitia reipublicae' prevented Virgil, in his representation, from appealing to the generous political emotions of a free people, he was able not only to gratify the pride of empire felt by his countrymen, but to sustain among them the sense of imaginative reverence with which the sovereignty of the State over its individual members deserves to be regarded.

But there is another class of political facts which interest the mind as much as those which arise out of the play of conflicting forces within a free commonwealth,—viz. the relations of independent powers with one another. And of this class of facts both Homer and Virgil make use in their representations. In

---

[1] 'After the Powers on high determined to overthrow the empire of Asia and the nation of Priam that deserved no such fate, and proud Ilium fell, and Troy built by Neptune is reduced utterly to ashes.'  iii. 1–3.

[2] 'An ancient city, that held empire through many years, is falling in ruins.'  ii. 363.

[3] 'Such was the final doom of Priam; this the end allotted to him, while he saw Troy on fire and its citadel in ruins,—Troy that formerly held proud sway in Asia over so many peoples and lands.'  ii. 554–7.

[4] 'I have lived, and finished the course that fortune gave me; and now my shade shall pass in majesty beneath the earth; I have founded a famous city, I have seen my own walls arise.'  iv. 653–5.

Homer we see the spectacle, never realised in actual Grecian history at least till the days of Alexander, of the many independent Greek powers united under one leader in a common enterprise, and of the various powers of the western shores of Asia combined in defence of their leading State. The antagonism between the Greeks and Trojans is, in point of general conception, more like the hostile inter-relations of nations in modern times, than like the wars of city against city, with which the pages of later Greek history are filled[1]. The union of the Italian tribes and cities under the command of Turnus, and that of Trojans, Arcadians, and Etrurians—all foreigners recently settled in Italy—under Aeneas, may be compared to the union of independent Greek powers under Agamemnon, and that of 'the allies summoned from afar,' who, while following their own princes, yet submitted to the command of Hector. Yet in Virgil's conception of the great powers of the world, and even of cities most remote from one another, as having an intimate knowledge of each other's fortunes,—in the idea of what in modern times would be called a 'foreign policy' and 'the balance of power,' which dictates the mission of Turnus to Diomede, and the appeal of Aeneas to the Etrurians to take part with him in averting the establishment by the Rutulians of a sovereignty over the whole of Italy,—we meet with a condition of international relations and policy, which, if based on the experience of any period of ancient history, might have been suggested by the memory of the time when Hannibal's great scheme of combining the fresh vigour of the western barbarians, the smouldering elements of resistance in Italy, and the military power and prestige of the old monarchies of Macedonia and Syria, was defeated not more by the irresolution and disunion among those powers, than by the traditional policy through which Rome had made her dependent allies feel that her interest

---

[1] The Peloponnesian war, which united the Dorian and oligarchical States of Greece under the lead of Sparta against Athens and her allies, admits, as is indicated by Thucydides in his Introduction, of the best parallel to the Trojan war, as represented by Homer.

was identified with their own.  But this aspect of the world, though an anachronism from the point of view either of the time when the poem was written, or of that in which the events represented are supposed to happen, enhances the dignity of the action, by exhibiting the enterprise of Aeneas as a spectacle attracting the attention and involving the destinies of the great nations of the world.

The state of material civilisation exhibited in the Aeneid must be regarded also as a poetical compromise between the simplicity and rude vigour of primitive civilisation and the splendour and refinement of the age in which the poem was written.  Thus Acestes, the friendly king and Sicilian host of Aeneas, welcomes him on his return from Carthage in the rough dress of some primitive hunter—

> Horridus in iaculis et pelle Libystidis ursae[1].

Evander receives him beneath his humble roof,

> stratisque locavit
> Effultum foliis et pelle Libystidis ursae[2].

The Arcadian prince is roused in the morning by the song of birds under the eaves, and proceeds to visit his guest accompanied by two watchdogs which lay before his door.  On the other hand the description, in the account of the building of Carthage, of the foundation of the great theatre—

> hic lata theatris
> Fundamenta petunt alii, immanisque columnas
> Rupibus excidunt, scaenis decora alta futuris[3];

the picture of the great Temple of Juno—

> Aerea cui gradibus surgebant limina nexaeque
> Aere trabes, foribus cardo stridebat aenis[4];

of the rich frescoes and bas-reliefs adorning it—

[1] 'In rough guise, armed with javelins and wearing the skin of a Libyan bear.'
[2] 'And seated him on a couch of leaves and the skin of a Libyan bear.'
[3] 'Here others lay the broad foundations for theatres, and hew out from the rocks huge columns, the high ornaments of a future stage.'  i. 427-9.
[4] 'Bronze was the threshold with its rising steps, bronze-bound the posts, of bronze the doors with their grating hinges.'  i. 448-9.

Artificumque manus inter se operumque labores
Miratur, videt Iliacas ex ordine pugnas
Bellaque iam fama totum volgata per orbem[1];

of the great dome under which the throne of Dido is placed—

media testudine templi, etc.;

the description of the Temple of Apollo at Cumae,—the account of the banquet in the palace of Dido with its blaze of 'festal light'—

dependent lychni laquearibus aureis
Incensi, et noctem flammis funalia vincunt[2],

(a picture partly indeed, like that in Lucretius—

Si non aurea sunt iuvenum simulacra per aedes, etc.,

suggested by the imaginative description of the banquet in the Palace of Alcinous)—appear to owe their existence to the impression produced on the mind of Virgil by some of the great architectural works of the Augustan Age—such as the Theatre of Marcellus, the Pantheon, the Temple of the Palatine Apollo, and by the spectacle of profuse luxury which the houses and banquets of the richer classes at Rome exhibited.

The class from which the personages of the Aeneid are taken is almost exclusively that of those most elevated in dignity and influence. Virgil does not attempt to bring before us the rich variety of social grades, which adds vivacity and verisimilitude to the spectacle of life and manners presented by Homer, Chaucer, and Shakspeare. It does not enter into Virgil's conception of epic art to introduce types of the class to which Thersites, Irus, Eumaeus, Phemius, and Eurycleia belong. If he makes any exception to his general practice of limiting his representation to the class of royal and noble

---

[1] 'And marvels at the skill of the artists working together and the toil with which their works are done, he sees the whole series of the battles fought at Troy and the war whose fame was already noised through all the world.' i. 455-7.

[2] 'Burning lamps hang from the roof of fretted gold, and torches with their blaze banish the night.'

personages, it is in the glimpse which he affords of devoted loyalty in the person of Palinurus and of affection and grief in that of the bereaved mother of Euryalus. Where, after the example of Homer, he introduces various figures belonging to the same class, he fails to distinguish them from one another by any individual trait of character or manners. Thus Dido has her suitors as well as Penelope; but the former produce no life-like impression of any kind, like that produced by the careless levity and gay insolence of Antinous and Eurymachus.

As a painter of manners Virgil adopts the stately and conventional methods of Greek tragedy rather than the vivid realism of Homer. The intercourse of his chief personages with one another is conducted with the dignity and courtesy of the most refined times. Homer's personages indeed act for the most part with a natural dignity and courtesy of bearing,—proceeding from the commanding character which he attributes to them, as well as from the lively social grace of their Greek origin,—which can neither be surpassed nor equalled by any conventional refinement. But these social virtues can be rapidly exchanged for vehemence of passion and angry recrimination. In the manners of Virgil's personages we recognise the influence of refined traditions, and of the habits of a dignified society. His personages show not only courtesy but studied consideration for each other. Thus while Latinus addresses Turnus in words of courteous acknowledgment—of which the original suggestion may be traced to a tragedy of Attius—

> O praestans animi iuvenis! quantum ipse feroci
> Virtute exsuperas, tanto me impensius aequum est
> Consulere, atque omnis metuentem expendere casus [1];

Turnus replies to him in the terms of respect which are due to his age and position—

---

[1] 'Youth of surpassing spirit, the higher thou risest in thy towering courage, the more fit is it that I take earnest counsel and weigh anxiously every chance.' xii. 19–21.

> Quam pro me curam geris, hanc precor, optime, pro me
> Deponas letumque sinas pro laude pacisci.
> Et nos tela, pater [1], etc.

The element of self-command amid the deepest movements of feeling and passion enhances the stately dignity of manners represented in the poem. Thus in the greatest sorrow of Evander, when he is recalling with fond pride the youthful promise of Pallas—

> Tu quoque nunc stares immanis truncus in armis,
> Esset par aetas et idem si robur ab annis,
> Turne [2],—

he remembers that he is detaining the Trojans, who had come to pay the funeral honours to his son—

> sed infelix Teucros quid demoror armis?
> Vadite et haec memores regi mandata referte [3].

The queenly courtesy of Dido springs from deeper elements in human nature than conformity to the standard of demeanour imposed by elevated rank—

> Solvite corde metum, Teucri, secludite curas.
> Res dura et regni novitas me talia cogunt
> Moliri et late finis custode tueri.
> Quis genus Aeneadum, quis Troiae nesciat urbem
> Virtutesque virosque, aut tanti incendia belli?
> Non obtunsa adeo gestamus pectora Poeni,
> Nec tam aversus equos Tyria Sol iungit ab urbe [4], etc.

The sea adventures of the Aeneid seem to be suggested

---

[1] 'The care thou hast for my sake, I pray thee, Sire, for my sake to lay aside, and allow me to hazard my life for the prize of honour. I too,' etc.

[2] 'Thou too, O Turnus, would'st now be standing a huge trunk with thy arms upon thee, were but thy age equal to his and the strength derived from years the same.' xi. 173-4.

[3] 'But why, in my misfortune, am I detaining the Trojans from deeds of arms—go, and mindful bear these commands to your king.' i. 561, etc.

[4] 'Banish fear from your hearts, ye Trojans, lay aside your cares, our hard lot and my new rule force me to take such anxious measures, and to guard my realm on all its wide frontiers. Who cannot have heard of them who follow Aeneas and of the city Troy, its men and manful prowess, or the fires that raged in that mighty war? Not so dull are the hearts of us the people of Phoenicia, nor is it so far away from our Tyrian city that the Sun yokes his horses.'

rather by the experience of travellers in the Augustan Age,
than by the spirit of wonder and buoyant resistance with which
Odysseus and his companions encounter the perils of unex-
plored seas and coasts.　The fabulous portents of legendary
times appear in the shape of the Harpies, the Cyclops, the
sea-monster Scylla, etc., but they do not produce that sense of
novelty and vivid life which the same or similar representations
produce in the Odyssey.　The description of the Harpies is
grotesque rather than imaginative.　There is a touch of pathos
in the introduction of the Cyclops—

> Lanigerae comitantur oves : ea sola voluptas
> Solamenque mali [1],

reminding us of the κριὲ πέπον, etc. of the Odyssey; and the
picture of his assembled brethren—

> Cernimus adstantis nequiquam lumine torvo
> Aetnaeos fratres, caelo capita alta ferentis,
> Concilium horrendum [2]—

is conceived with a kind of grim power, showing that the
imagination of Virgil does not merely reproduce, but endows
with a new life the figures which he borrows most closely from
his original.　But the life-like realism, the combined humour
and terror of Homer's representation, are altogether absent from
the Aeneid.　These marvellous creations appear natural in the
Odyssey, and in keeping with the imaginative impulses and
the adventurous spirit of the ages of maritime discovery : but
they stand in no real relation to the feelings and beliefs with
which men encountered the occasional dangers and the frequent
discomforts of the Adriatic or the Aegean in the Augustan Age.

In his conception of these real dangers of the sea, which
have to be met in the most advanced as well as the most
primitive times, Virgil's inferiority to Homer, both in general
effect and in lifelike detail, is very marked.　The wonderful

---

[1] 'His woolly sheep follow him; this is his sole joy and solace of his
suffering.' iii. 660-1.
[2] 'We see standing by him, all of no avail, the stern-eyed brothers dwelling
on Etna, bearing their heads high in air, a grim assembly.' iii. 677-9.

realism of the sea adventures in the fifth Book of the Odyssey
produces on the mind the impression that the poet is recalling
either a peril that he himself had encountered, or one that he
had heard vividly related by some one who had thus escaped
'from the issue of death:' and that there was in the poet too
the genuine delight in danger, the spirit

> 'That ever with a frolic welcome took
> The thunder and the sunshine,'

which has been attributed to the companions of his hero's
wanderings.

Odysseus, like Aeneas, feels his limbs and heart give way
before the sudden outburst of the storm; but, though swept
from the raft and overwhelmed for a time under the waves, he
never loses his presence of mind or his courage—

> ἀλλ' οὐδ' ὣς σχεδίης ἐπελήθετο τειρόμενός περ,
> ἀλλὰ μεθορμηθεὶς ἐνὶ κύμασιν ἐλλάβετ' αὐτῆς,
> ἐν μέσσῃ δὲ καθῖζε τέλος θανάτου ἀλεείνων [1].

The poet of the Odyssey may have encountered such storms
as are described in the passage here referred to, and we cannot
doubt that in such case he bore his part bravely, 'redeeming
his own life and securing the safe return of his comrades.' If
Virgil in some unadventurous voyaging ever happened to be
'caught in a storm in the open Aegean,' it probably was in the
position of a helpless sufferer that he contemplated the wild
commotion of the elements.

On the other hand he shows a keen enjoyment of the pleasure of sailing past famous and beautiful scenes with a fair wind
and in smooth water—

> Linquimus Ortygiae portus pelagoque volamus
> Bacchatamque iugis Naxon, viridemque Donysam,
> Olearon, niveamque Paron, sparsasque per aequor
> Cycladas, et crebris legimus freta consita terris.
> Nauticus exoritur vario certamine clamor [2].

[1] 'But not even thus though hard-bestead did he forget the raft, but springing after it laid hold of it among the waves, and sat down in the middle,
thus escaping the issue of death.'

[2] 'We leave the harbours of Ortygia and scud over the open sea, and

The first sight of land from the sea is vividly brought before the eye in such passages as these—

> Quarto terra die primum se attollere tandem
> Visa, aperire procul montis, ac volvere fumum [1].

> Iamque rubescebat stellis Aurora fugatis,
> Cum procul obscuros collis humilemque videmus
> Italiam [2].

> Crebrescunt optatae aurae, portusque patescit
> Iam propior, templumque apparet in arce Minervae [3].

The disappearance of the shores left behind, and the opening up of new scenes in the rapid onward voyage, leave on the mind a fresh feeling of novelty and life in such passages as—

> Protinus aerias Phaeacum abscondimus arces,
> Litoraque Epiri legimus, portuque subimus
> Chaonio, et celsam Buthroti accedimus urbem [4];

and in this in which the historic associations of famous cities are evoked—

> Apparet Camarina procul, campique Geloi,
> Immanisque Gela, fluvii cognomine dicta.
> Arduus inde Acragas ostentat maxima longe
> Moenia, magnanimum quondam generator equorum [5], etc.

These and similar passages—such as that describing the moonlight sail past the enchanted shores of Circe—remind us of the great change which had come over the world between the age

skirt the coasts of Naxos, on whose ridges the companies of Bacchus revel, and green Donysa, Olearos, and snow-white Paros, and the Cyclades spread over the sea, and the narrow waters studded with frequent isles. The mariner's cheer arises with varying rivalry.' iii. 124-8.

[1] 'On the fourth day for the first time the land at length appeared to rise up, to open up the view of its distant mountains, and to send its rolling smoke on high.' iii. 205-6.

[2] 'And now the stars had disappeared, and in the first blush of dawn we see far off the dim outline of the hills and the low land of Italy.' iii. 521-3.

[3] 'The longed-for breezes blow stronger, and the harbour now nearer opens up, and the temple of Minerva comes into sight on the cliff.' iii. 530-1.

[4] 'Soon we leave out of sight the airy heights of the Phaeacians, and skirt the shores of Epirus and draw near the Chaonian harbour, and approach the lofty city of Buthrotum.' iii. 291-3.

[5] 'Camarina comes into sight far away, and the plains of the Gela, and vast Gela called from the name of the river—after that high Acragas shows its mighty walls afar—in old days the breeder of high-mettled steeds.' iii. 701-4.

of the Odyssey and that of the Aeneid. The one poem is pervaded by the eager curiosity of the youthful prime of the world, attracting the most daring and energetic spirits to the discovery and peopling of new lands; the other by that more languid curiosity, awakened by the associations of the past,—by the longing for some change to break the routine of a too easy life,—and by the refined enjoyment of beauty, urging men to encounter some danger and more discomfort for the sake of visiting scenes famous in history, rich in natural charms, or in works of art, the inheritance from more creative times.

In his scenes of battle, Virgil is as inferior to the poet of the Iliad as he is to the poet of the Odyssey in those of sea adventure. In the details of single fights, in the account of the wounds inflicted on one another by the combatants, in the enumeration of the obscurer warriors who fall before the champions of either side—

> his addit Amastrum
> Hippotaden, sequiturque incumbens eminus hasta
> Tereaque Harpalycumque et Demophoönta Chromimque [1],

he follows closely in the footsteps of Homer. He is, however, more sparing of these details, so as to avoid the monotony of Homer's battle-fields and single combats. The Iliad was originally addressed to a people of warriors—

> οἷσιν ἄρα Ζεὺς
> ἐκ νεότητος ἔδωκε καὶ ἐς γῆρας τολυπεύειν
> ἀργαλέους πολέμους, ὄφρα φθιόμεσθα ἕκαστος [2].

And although through the mouth of the wisest of his heroes, Homer expresses some sense of weariness of the

> 'war and broils, which make
> Life one perpetual fight'—
> αἶψα τε φυλόπιδος πέλεται κόρος ἀνθρώποισι—

---

[1] 'To these he adds Amaster son of Hippotas, and follows plying them with his hurled spear Tereus and Harpalycus and Demophoon and Chromis.' Aen. xi. 673-5.
[2] 'To whom Zeus gave from youth even to old age the grievous task of war, till we each should die.' Il. xiv. 85-7. The fascination which the poem has even for modern readers is due, in no slight degree, to the spell which some aspects of war exercise over the imagination in all times.

yet all accepted this life as their destiny; and those who first
listened to the song of the poet would feel no satiety in the
details of battle and records of martial prowess, glorifying
perhaps the reputed ancestors of those chiefs whom they themselves followed to the field or to the storming of cities. To
Virgil's readers, the record of such a time as that described
in the Iliad would come like echoes from an alien world. In
so far as the Romans of the Augustan Age had any vital passion corresponding to the interest with which Homer's Greeks
must have witnessed in imagination the spectacle of wounds
and death in battle, it was in the basest form which the lust
of blood has ever assumed among civilised men,—the passion
for the gladiatorial shows. It is clear that Virgil himself,
though he can feel and inspire the fire of battle at some critical
moment—

> ingeminant hastis et Troes et ipse
> Fulmineus Mnestheus [1];

though he can express a Roman contempt for death,—

> Est hic, est animus lucis contemptor [2],

and can sympathise with the energetic daring of his Italian
heroes and heroine,—Turnus, Lausus, Pallas [3], and Camilla,—
yet shares the sentiment with which his hero looks forward to
peace as the crown of his labours, and regards the wars which
he was compelled to wage as a hated task imposed on him by
the Fates—

> Nos alias hinc ad lacrimas, eadem horrida bella,
> Fata vocant [4].

Yet even in the incidents of his battle-pieces Virgil does not
follow Homer slavishly. The warlike action of the poem is not

---

[1] 'They ply their spears with redoubled force, both the Trojans and
Mnestheus himself with the flash of lightning.'
[2] 'There is here, here a spirit that recks not of life.'
[3] Cf. viii. 510 :—
> .ni, mixtus matre Sabella,
> Hinc partem patriae traheret.
[4] 'Us the fates summon hence to other scenes of woe, to the same grim
wars.' xi. 96-7. Cf. the epithet 'lacrimabile,' which he applies to war.

a mere succession of single combats, or a confused *mêlée* of battle, surging 'this way and that,' between the rampart that guards the ships and the walls of the city. It is said that the greatest soldier of modern times, in the enforced leisure of his last years, condescended to express a criticism, not indeed a favourable one, on Virgil's skill as a tactician; and it is an element of novelty in the representation of the Aeneid that it suggests at least some image of the combined operations of modern warfare. But it is in the play which Virgil gives to the other human emotions of his personages, tempering and counteracting the blind rage of battle, that the poet of a more advanced era most conspicuously appears. The ancient world at its best, whether we judge of it from the representations of its poets, or the recorded acts of its greatest men and most powerful and enlightened States, did not rise to that height of chivalrous generosity which scorns to take an enemy at a disadvantage, or to wipe away the memory of defeat or disaster by a cruel revenge. Achilles in his treatment of Hector, Caesar in his treatment of Vercingetorix, the Spartans in dealing with Plataeae, the Syracusans with the remnant of the defeated Athenians, the Athenians themselves with the helpless defenders of Melos, the Romans with the Samnites who spared their lives at the Caudine Forks,—all alike fall below the standard of nobleness which men of temper inferior to that of the great men and nations of antiquity often reached in mediaeval times. Those who appear to come nearest this standard in ancient times,—who could at least honour courage in an enemy or refuse to press too heavily upon him in his defeat,—are the Carthaginian Hannibal and his not unworthy conqueror. Virgil cannot be said, in this respect, to rise altogether superior to the spirit of the old Greek and Roman world. In the Aeneid it is thought no shame, but rather a glory, for soldiers to slay defenceless or wounded men in battle or in the dim confusion of a night foray. Yet the sentiments of his warriors engaged in battle are more tempered with humanity than those of the heroes of the Iliad. There is no word of throwing the bodies of the slain to dogs and vultures. There is no such deadly struggle over the bodies of Lausus or Pallas as over that of Patroclus. Turnus and Aeneas alike act on the principle expressed in the request of the dying champion of Italy,—

> Ulterius ne tende odiis [1].

Not only is the warlike passion less cruel in the Aeneid, but the feeling of the sanctity which invests the dead is stronger. The only passage in the Aeneid which might have exposed Virgil to the reproach of Lucretius, as forgetting in the supposed interests of religion the certain claims of humanity, is that in which Aeneas, following the example of Achilles, sets aside the captive youths for immolation to the Manes of Pallas.

But the chief source of interest in the Virgilian battle-pieces is the pathetic sympathy awakened for the untimely death of some of the nobler personages of the story. The tender compassion called forth by the blight which fell in his own time upon the earliest of the 'breves et infaustos populi Romani amores [2],' and reappeared again in the deaths of Drusus and Germanicus—that compassion which dictates the words

> si qua fata aspera rumpas
> Tu Marcellus eris [3],

appears in his description of the fates of Pallas and Lausus, of Euryalus and Camilla. The reverence for the purest of human affections which shines through the lines

> Transiit et parmam mucro levia arma minacis,
> Et tunicam, molli mater quam neverat auro [4],

and

> At vero, ut voltum vidit morientis et ora,
> Ora modis Anchisiades pallentia miris,
> Ingemuit miserans graviter dextramque tetendit,
> Et mentem patriae subiit pietatis imago [5],

---

[1] 'Press not further in thy hate.'

[2] 'The short-lived and ill-starred loves of the Roman people.'

[3] 'If in any way thou canst break the cruel bonds of fate, thou too shalt be a Marcellus.'

[4] 'And the sword-point pierced through the shield, slight defence in his menacing onset, and the tunic which his mother had interlaced with threads of gold.' x. 817-8.

[5] 'But then, when he beheld the look and face of the dying youth, he,

may be discerned also in some of the minor incidents of the poem, as in these lines—

> Vos etiam, gemini, Rutulis cecidistis in arvis,
> Daucia, Laride Thymberque, simillima proles,
> Indiscreta suis gratusque parentibus error [1].

The emotions awakened by the deaths of Mezentius and of Turnus are of a sterner character. So too the poet's compassion for the heroine of his later books, Camilla, falling by the hand of an ignoble antagonist, is mixed with a sense of scornful satisfaction at the retribution which immediately followed—

> Extemplo teli stridorem aurasque sonantis
> Audiit una Arruns haesitque in corpore ferrum.
> Illum expirantem socii atque extrema gementem
> Obliti ignoto camporum in pulvere linquunt;
> Opis ad aetherium pinnis aufertur Olympum [2].

Virgil's susceptibility to local associations and to impressions of a remote antiquity must also be taken into account as supplying materials and stimulus to his inventive faculty. No poet so often appeals to the imaginative interest attaching to the earlier condition of places or things of old renown or famous in the later history of the world. Thus the building of Carthage, the first view of the Tiber—

> Hunc inter fluvio Tiberinus amoeno
> Verticibus rapidis et multa flavus harena
> In mare prorumpit [3]—

the gathering of the Italian races from 'mountainous Praeneste, from the tilled lands around Gabii, from the banks of the cool

---

the son of Anchises, that face so wondrous pale, he uttered a deep groan in his pity, and held out his hand, and the thought of all his love for his father came over his mind.' x. 821–4.

[1] 'Ye too fell in the Rutulian fields, Larides and Thymber, twin sons of Daucis, most like to one another, indistinguishable to your own family, and a most pleasing cause of confusion to your parents.' x. 390–2.

[2] 'Immediately the whiz of the arrow and the sound of the air were heard by Arruns at the same moment as the iron fixed in his body. Expiring and uttering his last groan, forgotten by his comrades, he is left on the unheeded dust of the plain; while Opis flies aloft to high Olympus.' xi. 863–7.

[3] 'Between it Tiberinus with his fair stream, in rapid eddies and yellow with much sand bursts forth into the sea.'

Anio, and the rivulets sparkling among the Hernican hills,'—
the contrast between the primitive pastoral aspect of the Tarpeian Rock and the Capitol, of the site of the Forum and
the Carinae, and the familiar spectacle of outward magnificence
which they presented in the Augustan Age,—are brought before
the mind with a more stimulating power than the experiences
of storm or battle through which the hero of the poem is conducted. The local associations of Mount Eryx, of the lake of
Avernus, of the fountain Albunea, of the valley of Amsanctus,
of the Arician grove, of the site of Ardea, are evoked with impressive effect. The names of the promontories Palinurum,
Misenum, and Caieta are invested with an interest derived from
their connexion with the imaginary incidents and personages
of the poem. The ritual observances and the legend connected
with the Ara Maxima suggest the description of ceremonies and
the narrative of events in the earlier half of Book viii.; and the
custom—so ancient that its original meaning was forgotten—of
opening the gateway of Janus Quirinus on the rare occasions
when a state of war arose out of a state of unbroken peace,
is traced back to a time antecedent to the existence either of
Rome or Alba—

> Mos erat Hesperio in Latio, quem protinus urbes
> Albanae coluere sacrum, nunc maxima rerum
> Roma colit, etc.
> \*       \*       \*       \*       \*
> Ipse Quirinali trabea cinctuque Gabino
> Insignis reserat stridentia limina Consul ;
> Ipse vocat pugnas, sequitur tum cetera pubes,
> Aereaque adsensu conspirant cornua rauco [1].

Perhaps the most original and not the least impressive of
those personages whom Virgil introduces into his composite
representation—the Sibyl—is conceived under the strong sense

---

[1] 'There was a custom in Hesperian Latium which from that time onward
the Alban cities observed, and now Rome, mistress of the world, observes.
. . . With his own hand, arrayed in the robe of state of Quirinus, his toga
girt with the Gabian girding, the Consul unbars the creaking gates : with
his own voice he calls for battle; the rest of the warlike youth echo him,
and the brazen horns combine with their hoarse accompaniment.' vii.601-15.

of the mystery and sanctity which invested the oracles of the Sibylline books.

The personal and national susceptibilities of Virgil's imagination and the circumstances of the age in which he lived are thus seen largely to modify that representation of life and manners of which the main outlines are suggested by the Homeric poems, and of which many of the details are derived from the Cyclic poems, from the Greek tragedies founded on the events which followed on the death of Hector, and from the Italian traditions and aetiological myths which Cato had preserved in his 'Origines,' and Varro and other writers in their works on antiquities. Virgil's power as an epic poet does not consist in original invention of incident or action, but in combining diverse elements into a homogeneous whole, and in imparting poetic life to old materials, many of them not originally conceived in a poetic spirit. The interest which he thus imparts to his narrative is different from, and inferior to, that attaching to the original representation in the Homeric poems. Had Virgil's representation been as faithfully drawn from the life as that of Homer, it still would have been less interesting, from the fact that ancient Romans are less interesting in their individuality than the Greeks of the great ages of Greek life, and from the fact also that the manners of an advanced age do not affect the imagination in the way in which those of a nation's youth affect it. Not only was Virgil's own genius much less creative than that of Homer, his materials possessed much less plasticity. There is no need of any act of reconstructive criticism to enable us to feel the immediate power of the Iliad and the Odyssey. To do justice to the power of the Aeneid we must endeavour to realise in imagination the state of mind of those who received the poem in all the novelty of its first impression,—at once 'rich with the spoils of time,' and 'pregnant with celestial fire.'

## IV.

The most important element in the Aeneid, regarded as a poem of heroic action, remains still to be considered, viz. the conception and delineation of individual character. The greatest of epic poets in ancient times was also endowed with the most versatile dramatic faculty. And this faculty was displayed not only in the conception of a great variety of noble types of character, but also in the modes in which these conceptions were embodied. The Greek language is greatly superior to the Latin in its adaptability to natural dialogue. In this respect Cicero's inferiority to Plato is as marked as Virgil's inferiority to Homer. The language of Homer and the language of Plato are equally fitted for the expression of the greatest thoughts and feelings, and for the common intercourse of men with one another. Neither that of Virgil nor of Cicero adapts itself easily to the lively play of emotion or to the rapid interchange of thought. The characters of Homer, like the characters of Shakspeare, reveal themselves in their complete individuality, as they act and re-act on one another in many changing moods of passion and affection. The personages of Virgil are revealed by the poet, partly in his account of what they do, and partly through the medium of set speeches expressive of some particular attitude of mind. Virgil's imagination is the imagination of the orator rather than of the dramatist. It is not a complete and complex man, liable to various moods, and standing in various relations to other men, but it is some powerful movement of the θυμός in man, that the oratorical imagination is best fitted to express. Milton also, like Virgil, reveals the characters of his personages with the imaginative power of an orator rather than with that of a dramatist. But he possesses another resource in the analytical power with which he makes his chief personage reveal his inmost nature and most secret motives in truthful communing with himself. It is through the soliloquies in the 'Paradise Lost' that we can best realise the whole conception of Satan, in his ruined magnificence, and in his lost but not forgotten capacity of happiness and nobleness. The soliloquies of these personages perform for the epic poet the part performed by the elaborate introspection and discussion of motives in modern prose fiction. Homer also avails himself frequently of the soliloquy, as he does of natural dialogue and more formal oratory. In the Aeneid the chief personage is often introduced, like the heroes of the Iliad and Odyssey,

> 'This way and that dividing the swift mind;'

but the process generally ends in the adoption, without any weighing of conflicting duties or probabilities, of the obvious course indicated by some supernatural sign. The soliloquies of Dido are to be regarded rather as passionate outbursts of prayer to some unknown avenging power than as communings with her own heart. The single soliloquy, if it may be called such, which brings the speaker nearer to us in knowledge and sympathy, is the proud and stately address in which Mezentius seems to make the horse, which had borne him victorious through every former war, a partaker of his sorrow and his forebodings—

> Rhaebe, diu, res si qua diu mortalibus ulla est,
> Viximus [1], etc.

But not only are the media through which Virgil brings his personages before us less varied and flexible than those of Homer, but the characters themselves are more tamely conceived, and less capable of awakening human interest. And this is especially true of the character of Aeneas as contrasted with those of Achilles and of Odysseus. The general conception of Aeneas is indeed in keeping with the religious idea of the Aeneid. He is intended to be an embodiment of the courage of an ancient hero, the justice of a paternal ruler, the mild humanity of a cultivated man living in an age of advanced civilisation, the saintliness of the founder of a new

---

[1] 'Rhaebus, we have lived long, if aught is long to mortals,' etc. Aen. x. 861, etc.

religion of peace and pure observance, the affection for
parent and child, which was one of the strongest instincts in
the Italian race.  A life-like impersonation of such an ideal
would have commanded the reverence of all future times.  Yet
at no time has the character of Aeneas excited any strong
human interest.  No later poet or moralist set it up, as Horace
sets up the characters of Achilles and of Ulysses, as a subject
of ethical contemplation.  Ovid in the deepest gloom of his
exile retains enough of his old levity to jest at his single lapse
from saintly perfection—

> Et tamen ille tuae felix Aeneidos auctor
> Contulit in Tyrios arma virumque toros[1].

As compared with the hero of the Odyssey, Aeneas is altogether
wanting in energy, spontaneity, intellectual resource, and insight.  The single quality in which he is strong is endurance.
The principle which enables him to fulfil his mission is expressed in the line—

> Quidquid erit, superanda omnis fortuna ferendo est[2].

His courage in battle springs from his confidence in his
destiny—

> Tum socios maestique metum solatur Iuli
> Fata docens[3].

One of the few touches of nature which redeem his character
from tameness is the momentary feeling of the rage of battle
roused by the resistance of Lausus—

> saevae iamque altius irae
> Dardanio surgunt ductori[4].

The occasion in which he seems most worthy of his place as
a leader of men is after the death of Mezentius, where the self-
restraint of his address contrasts favourably with the intemperate
ardour expressed in some of the speeches of Turnus—

---

[1] Trist. ii. 533–4.
[2] 'Whate'er it be, every fortune must be conquered by endurance.'
[3] 'Then he cheers his comrades and soothes the fears of sad Iulus, telling
them of their destinies.'
[4] 'And now higher rises the fierce rage of the Trojan leader.'

Maxima res effecta, viri: timor omnis abesto[1].

He appears as a passive recipient both of the devotion and of the reproaches of Dido. He undergoes no passionate struggle in resigning her. The courtesy and kindliness of his nature elicit no warmer expression of regret than the words—

> nec me meminisse pigebit Elissae,
> Dum memor ipse mei, dum spiritus hos regit artus[2].

The only exercise of thought required of him is the right interpretation of an omen, or the recollection of some dubious prediction at some critical moment. Even the strength of affection which he feels and which he awakens in the hearts of his father and son does not move us in the way in which we are touched by the feelings which unite Odysseus to Penelope and Telemachus, to Laertes and the mother who meets him in the shades, and tells him that she had 'died neither by the painless arrows of Artemis nor by wasting disease '—

> ἀλλά με σός τε πόθος σά τε μήδεα, φαίδιμ' Ὀδυσσεῦ,
> σή τ' ἀγανοφροσύνη μελιηδέα θυμὸν ἀπηύρα[3].

The failure of Aeneas to excite a lively personal interest is not to be attributed solely to a failure of power in the poet's imagination. In the part he plays he is conceived of as one chosen by the supreme purpose of the gods, as an instrument of their will, and thus necessarily unmoved by ordinary human

---

[1] 'A great deed has been done, my warriors,—let all fear be banished.' This contrast was suggested by Mr. Nettleship's interpretation of the character of Turnus ('Suggestions,' etc., pp. 15 *et seq*.). As will appear later, I am inclined to think that he insists too exclusively on the 'violentia,' which is undoubtedly a strong element in the character of the Italian hero. The antagonism of Turnus to Aeneas, as of the Italians to the Trojans, he justly regards as an instance of the strife of passion with law. If the Greek drama suggested the ethical aspect of this strife, a comparison with Horace, Ode iii. 4, of which Ode the leading idea is the superiority of the ' vis temperata ',over the ' vis consili expers,' as illustrated in the wars of the Olympian Gods with the Titans, and in the triumph of Augustus over the elements of disorder opposing him, suggests that the political inspiration of the idea came from ' the stately mansion on the Esquiline '—
'Molem propinquam nubibus arduis.'
[2] 'Nor shall it irk me to remember Elissa, while I can remember my own self, while breath animates my frame.'
[3] ' But my longing for thee, the thought of all thy cares, noble Odysseus, and of all thy gentleness bereft me of sweet life.'

impulses. In the words of M. de Coulanges, 'Sa vertu doit
être une froide et haute impersonnalité, qui fasse de lui, non un
homme, mais un instrument des dieux[1].' The strength required
in such an instrument is the strength of faith, submission,
patience, and endurance; and it is with this strength that
Aeneas encounters the many dangers and vicissitudes to which
he is exposed, and withdraws from the allurements of ease and
pleasure. The very virtues of his character act as a check
rather than as a stimulus to those natural impulses out of
which the most living impersonations are formed. To compare great things in art with what are not so great, the
impression produced by the superiority of Aeneas to ordinary
passion is like the impression produced by the superior tolerance
and enlightenment of some of Scott's heroes, when contrasted
with the more animated impulses and ruder fanaticism of the
other personages in his story. That he is, on the one hand,
the passive receptacle of Divine guidance, and, on the other,
the impersonation of a modern ideal of humanity, playing a
part in a rude and turbulent time, are the two main causes of
the tame and colourless character of the protagonist of the
Aeneid. And as loyalty to a leader is the sole form of political,
as distinct from patriotic virtue which Virgil acknowledges, the
other Trojan chiefs—the faithful Achates, the speaker Idome-
neus, the more martial figures of Mnestheus and Serestus—
do little more than play the part of the ἄγγελος or of the κωφὰ
πρόσωπα in a Greek tragedy. The interest awakened by
Anchises arises solely from the halo of sacred associations
investing him. Iulus, as the eponymous ancestor of the Iulii,
seems to be a favourite of the author; yet he fails to interest us
as a youth of high spirit and promise. Telemachus we know
and sympathise with in his rising rebellion against the insolence
of the suitors—

> νῦν δ' ὅτε δὴ μέγας εἰμί, καὶ ἄλλων μῦθον ἀκούων
> πυνθάνομαι, καὶ δή μοι ἀέξεται ἔνδοθι θυμός[2],

[1] La Cité Antique.
[2] 'And now that I am a man, and know it from the lips of others, and
feel my spirit wax strong within me.'

in his longing for the return of his father to redress his wrongs, in his kindly hospitality, and sense of the outraged honour of his house—

νεμεσσήθη δ' ἐνὶ θυμῷ
ξεῖνον δηθὰ θύρῃσιν ἐφεστάμεν[1].

That Iulus fails to awaken a similar interest, that we do not share his ardour in the chase or the glow of pride with which he lays his first enemy low, is due to the fact that the poet's imagination fails in the vital realisation of his conception.

Most of the minor characters who appear in the Aeneid require no analysis. Creusa, Anna, and Andromache are vague impersonations of womanly tenderness and fidelity of affection. Lavinia, the shadowy Helen of the story, appears only for a moment, and though she is described by images suggestive of beauty and of a delicate nurture—

mixta rubent ubi lilia multa
Alba rosa[2],

we are left without the knowledge by which to measure the extent of the wrong done to her and Turnus by the enforced severance of their affections. Amata exhibits the blind animal rage of a mother whose affections have been outraged, but her figure wants the firm outlines and substance of the Hecuba of the Iliad. The prophetic office of Helenus enables him to advance the action of the story by preparing the mind of Aeneas for his immediate future: the jealous interference of Iarbas accelerates the doom of Dido: Acestes performs the part of a kindly host to the Trojans in Sicily. But of any individual traits of character they exhibit no trace whatever. Drances serves as a vehicle of impassioned oratory, and as a kind of foil to the generous impulsiveness of Turnus,—just as the timid craft of Arruns is a foil to the splendid rashness of Camilla;—and perhaps he is not much less real to our imaginations than Polydamus, who is the only personage of the Iliad that we think of rather as the embodiment of an abstract

---

[1] 'And his spirit was wroth that the stranger tarried long at the door.'
[2] 'Where the white lilies blush with the mingling of many roses.'

quality,—moderation,—than as a living man. But in the delineation of Drances there is no sign of that power which, by
a few graphic strokes of description and the force of dramatic
insight, has made Thersites stand forth for all times as the type
of an envious and ignoble demagogue. Though there is more
effort of thought in the delineation of Latinus as swayed to and
fro by his religious sense of duty and the influence of others,
and though there is true pathos in the words with which he
allows the declaration of war to be made—

> Nam mihi parta quies, omnisque in limine portus:
> Funere felici spolior [1] ;—

yet he does not live before us as Priam lives in the scene with
Helen on the walls of the town, and he has no power to move
our hearts with the awful compassion which the grief of Priam
awakens in the last books of the Iliad. Perhaps the most
impressive of the secondary personages in the Aeneid is
Evander, as he appears in the dignity of his simple state in
the eighth Book, and in the dignity of his great sorrow in the
eleventh. Pallas and Lausus, Nisus and Euryalus, afford occasions for pathetic situations, rather than perform any part
affording scope for the display of character. The romantic
career of Camilla interests us; and she has the further attraction
to modern readers of reminding them of a martial heroine of
actual history: but we scarcely recognise in the vivid delineation
of her deeds those complex elements which in their union form
a whole character for our imaginations, whether in the representations of literature or in our experience of life.

The chief personal interest of the story is centred in those
whose fortunes and action bring them into antagonism with the
decrees of Fate, and who perish in consequence,—in Turnus,
Mezentius, and Dido. Patriotism, courage, and passion are
exhibited in a fatal but not ignoble struggle with the purposes
and chosen instruments of Omnipotence. The tragic interest
of this antagonism stimulates the imagination of the poet to a

---

[1] 'For my rest is assured, my haven is close at hand—it is of happy
funeral rites that I am bereft.'

more energetic delineation of character. And in the representation of this struggle it is quite true, as has been well shown by Mr. Nettleship, that Virgil's own sympathies go with the 'victrix causa' which 'pleased the gods,' not with the 'victa' which pleases our modern sensibilities. He professes not to question but

'To justify the ways of God to men.'

The death of Mezentius satisfies poetical as well as political justice. Turnus brings his doom upon himself by the intemperate vehemence and self-confidence with which he asserts his personal claims. Though Aeneas and Dido are both represented as 'forgetful of their better name,' yet, as happens in real life more generally than in fiction, it is the woman only who suffers the penalty of this forgetfulness. Yet though in all these cases the doom of the sufferers is brought about in part through their own fault, Virgil does not, as an inferior artist might do, endeavour to augment the sympathy with his chief personage, by an unworthy detraction from his antagonist. No scorn of treachery or cowardice, no indignation against cruelty, mingles with the feeling of admiration which the general bearing of Turnus excites. The basis of his character seems to be a generous vehemence and proud independence of spirit. If Aeneas typifies the civilising mission of Rome and is to be regarded as an embodiment of the qualities which enabled her to give law to the world, Turnus typifies the brave but not internecine resistance offered to her by the other races of Italy, and is an embodiment of their high and martial spirit—of that 'Itala virtus' which, when tempered by Roman discipline, gave Rome the strength to fulfil her mission. The cause which moves Turnus to resist the Trojans is no unworthy one, either on patriotic grounds or on grounds personal to himself. If the Greeks were justified in making war against the Trojans on account of Helen, the Italians may be justified in making war against the same people on account of Lavinia. His appeals to his countrymen are addressed to the most elemental of patriotic impulses—

> nunc coniugis esto
> Quisque suae tectique memor : nunc magna referto
> Facta, patrum laudes [1].

He slays his enemy in fair battle, and though he shows exultation in his victory, yet he does not sully it by any ferocity of act
or demeanour—

> qualem meruit Pallanta remitto,
> Quisquis honos tumuli, quidquid solamen humandi est
> Largior [2].

After his hopes of success are shaken by the first defeat of the
Latins, and by the failure of the mission to Diomede, and when
the timidity of Latinus and the envy of Drances urge the
abandonment of the struggle, he still retains a proud confidence in his Italian allies—

> Non erit auxilio nobis Aetolus et Arpi,
> At Messapus erit, felixque Tolumnius [3], etc.

He is ready, like an earlier Decius, to devote his life in single
combat against the new Achilles, armed with the armour of
Vulcan—

> vobis animam hanc soceroque Latino
> Turnus ego, haut ulli veterum virtute secundus,
> Devovi : ' Solum Aeneas vocat.' Et vocet oro :
> Nec Drances potius, sive est haec ira deorum,
> Morte luat, sive est virtus et gloria, tollat [4].

He sees 'the inspiring hopes of triumph disappear, but the
austerer glory of suffering remains, and with a firm heart he
accepts that gift of a severe fate [5] '—

---

[1] ' Now be each mindful of wife and home : recall now the mighty deeds,
your fathers' renown.'

[2] ' I give back Pallas even as was due to him ; whatever respect there is
to a tomb, whatever comfort in burial, I freely bestow.' Cp. the contrast :—
ἦ ῥα καὶ Ἕκτορα δῖον ἀεικέα μήδετο ἔργα.

[3] ' The Aetolian and Arpi will not aid us, but Messapus will and fortunate
Tolumnius.'

[4] ' For you and my father-in-law Latinus, I, Turnus, second to none of
the men of old in valour, have devoted this my life : " me only Aeneas chal-
lenges "—ay, let him challenge me ; nor let Drances rather, if this is the
anger of Heaven, pay the penalty by his death, or if it is a call to valour
and glory, let the valour and glory be his.' Aen. xi. 440, etc.

[5] Napier's Peninsular War, Death of Sir John Moore.

Usque adeone mori miserum est ?  Vos o mihi Manes
Este boni, quoniam Superis aversa voluntas :
Sancta ad vos anima atque istius inscia culpae
Descendam, magnorum haut unquam indignus avorum[1].

In the final encounter he yields, not to the terror inspired by
his earthly antagonist, but to his consciousness of the hostility
of Heaven—

di me terrent et Iuppiter hostis[2].

His last wish is that the old age of his father, Daunus, should
not be deprived of the consolation of his funeral honours.
Although the headlong vehemence of his own nature, no less
than his opposition to the beneficent purposes of Omnipotence,
seems to justify his fate, yet, as in the Ajax of Sophocles, the
αὐθαδία in Turnus is rather the flaw in an essentially heroic
temper, than his dominant characteristic.   The poet's sympathy
with the high spirit of youth, as manifested in love and war, and
his pride in the strong metal out of which the Italian race was
made, have led him, perhaps involuntarily, to an embodiment of
those chivalrous qualities, which affect the modern imagination
with more powerful sympathy than the qualities of a temperate
will and obedience to duty which he has striven to embody in
the representation of Aeneas.

The vigorous sketch of Mezentius, as he appears in Book x.,
has received from some critics more admiration than the sustained delineation of Turnus through all the vicissitudes of
feeling and fortune through which he passes.   Chateaubriand
says, that this figure is the only one in the Aeneid that is
'fièrement dessinée.'   Landor describes him as 'the hero
transcendently above all others in the Aeneid.'   And there is
certainly a vague grandeur of outline in this conception of the
'contemptor divom' and oppressor of his people, who is 'not
only the most passionate in his grief for Lausus, but likewise

---

[1] 'Is death then so sad a doom?   Be ye merciful to me, spirits of the
dead, since the favour of the Powers above is turned from me ; a spirit,
pure and untainted by that shame, I shall pass to you, never dishonouring
my mighty ancestors.'   Aen. xii. 644–8.
[2] 'It is the Gods that terrify me, and the enmity of Jove.'

gives way to manly sorrow for the mute companion of his
warfare,' indicative of a bolder invention than that which is
usually ascribed to Virgil.　It is remarkable that poets whose
spirit is most purely religious,—both in the strength of conviction and the limitation of sympathy produced by the religious spirit—Aeschylus, Virgil, and Milton—seem to be
moved to their most energetic creativeness by the idea of
antagonism to the supreme will on the part of a human, or
superhuman but limited will : and that they cannot help raising
in their readers a glow of admiration as well as a sense of
awe in their embodiment of this clash between finite and
infinite power.　The sketch of Mezentius cannot indeed be
compared with two of the most daring conceptions and perfected creations of human genius,—the Prometheus of Aeschylus
and the Satan of Milton,—yet, if it does not enlist our ethical
sympathies like the former of these, like the second it receives
the tribute of that involuntary admiration, which is given to
courage, even when allied with moral evil, so long as it is not
absolutely divorced from the capability of sympathetic and
elevated emotion.

In the part which Dido plays in the poem, Virgil finds a
source of interest in which he had not been anticipated by
Homer.　And although the passion of love, unreturned or
betrayed, had supplied a motive to the later Greek tragedy
and to the Alexandrine epic, it was still not impossible for a
new poet to represent this phase of modern life with more
power and pathos than any of his predecessors.　It was comparatively easy to produce a more noble and vital impersonation than the Medea of Apollonius.　But the Dido of
Virgil may compare favourably with the creations of greater
masters,—with the Deianeira of Sophocles, with the Phaedra
and the Medea of Euripides.　And Virgil's conception is at
once more impassioned than that of Sophocles, and nobler
and more womanly than those of Euripides.　Her character,
as it is represented before the disturbing influence of this new
passion produced by supernatural artifice, is that of a brave

and loyal, a great and queenly, a pure, trusting, and compassionate nature. The most tragic element in the development of her love for Aeneas is the struggle which it involves with her high-strung sense of fidelity to the dead—

> Ille meos primus qui me sibi iunxit amores
> Abstulit : ille habeat secum servetque sepulchro[1].

The first feeling awakened in her mind by Aeneas is compassion for his sufferings, and the desire to make the Trojans sharers in the fortune which had attended her own enterprise. When by the unsuspected agency of the two goddesses she has been possessed by the fatal passion, it is to no ignoble influence that she succumbs. It is the greatness and renown of one whom she recognises as of the race of the gods, which exercise a spell over her imagination—

> Multa viri virtus animo, multusque recursat
> Gentis honos ; haerent infixi pectore voltus
> Verbaque, nec placidam membris dat cura quietem[2].

No weakness, no unwomanly ferocity mingles with the reproaches which she utters on first awakening to the betrayal of her trust. A feeling of magnanimous scorn makes her rise in rebellion against the plea that her desertion was the result of divine interposition—

> Scilicet is Superis labor est ! ea cura quietos
> Sollicitat[3] ;

and a lofty pathos animates her trust in a righteous retribution, the knowledge of which will comfort her among the dead—

> Spero equidem mediis, si quid pia numina possunt,
> Supplicia hausurum scopulis et nomine Dido
> Saepe vocaturum. Sequar atris ignibus absens,
> Et, cum frigida mors anima seduxerit artus,

---

[1] 'He who first won my love has taken it with him : let him keep it and treasure it in his tomb.'
[2] 'Often his own heroic spirit, often the glory of his race, recur to her mind: his looks remain deep-printed in her heart, and his words, nor does her passion allow her to rest.'
[3] 'That forsooth is the task of the Powers above ; this trouble vexes their tranquil state.'

> Omnibus umbra locis adero :—dabis,. improbe, poenas :
> Audiam, et haec Manes veniet mihi fama sub imos [1].

The awe inspired by supernatural portents, by restless visions in the night, by the memory of ancient prophecies, by the voice of her former husband summoning her from the chapel consecrated to his Manes, confirms her in her resolution to die. Her passion goes on deepening in alternations of indignation and recurring tenderness. It reaches its sublimest elevation in the prayer for vengeance, answered long afterwards in the alarm and desolation inflicted upon Italy by the greatest of the sons of Carthage—

> Exoriare aliquis nostris ex ossibus ultor,
> Qui face Dardanios ferroque sequare colonos,
> Nunc, olim, quocunque dabunt se tempore vires [2].

In her last moments she finds consolation in the great memories of her life—

> Urbem praeclaram statui : mea moenia vidi :
> Ulta virum, poenas inimico a fratre recepi :
> Felix, heu ! nimium felix, si litora tantum
> Nunquam Dardaniae tetigissent nostra carinae [3].

Her latest prayer is that, even though no outward retribution overtake her betrayer, yet the bitterness of his own heart may be her avenger—

> 　　　　　　moriemur inultae,
> Sed moriamur, ait : sic, sic iuvat ire sub umbras.
> Hauriat hunc oculis ignem crudelis ab alto
> Dardanus, et secum nostrae ferat omina mortis [4].

---

[1] ' I trust indeed, if the pitiful Gods avail aught, that among the rocks in mid sea thou shalt drink deep of the cup of retribution, and often call on Dido by name; I, from far away, will follow thee with baleful fires, and when chill death has separated my spirit from my frame, my shade will haunt thee everywhere ; heartless, thou shalt suffer for thy crime : I shall hear of it, and this tale will reach me among the spirits below.'

[2] ' Arise thou, some avenger, out of my bones, who with brand and sword mayest chase the settlers from Troy, now, hereafter, whensoever there shall be strength to bring thee forth.'

[3] ' I have built a famous city : I have seen my own walls arise : avenging my husband, I exacted retribution from an unkind brother ; fortunate, alas ! too fortunate, had not the Trojan keels ever touched our shore.'

[4] ' I shall die unavenged,' she says, ' still let me die—it is thus, thus, I fain would pass to the shades : may the cruel Trojan drink in with his eyes

Once more she appears among the Shades, and maintains her lofty bearing there as in the world above.  No sympathy with his hero makes the poet here forget what was due to her.  She listens in scornful silence to the tearful protestations of her 'false friend [1],' and passes on without any sign of forgiveness or reconciliation—

> Tandem corripuit sese atque inimica refugit
> In nemus umbriferum, coniunx ubi pristinus illi
> Respondet curis aequatque Sychaeus amorem [2].

## V.

That the passion of Dido is powerfully conceived and delineated, that it satisfies modern feeling more legitimately than the representation of the unhallowed impulses of Phaedra, or of the cruel and treacherous rancour of Medea, will scarcely be questioned.  Yet perhaps it is doing no injustice to the genius of Virgil to say that his power in dealing with human life consists generally in conceiving some state of feeling, some pathetic or passionate situation, rather than in the creation and sustained development of living characters.  How the great impersonations of poetry and prose fiction, which are more real to our imaginations than the personages of history or those whom we know in life, come into being, is a question which probably their authors themselves could not answer.  Though reflexion on human nature and deliberate intention to exemplify some law of life may precede the creative act which gives them being, and though continued reflexion may be needed to sustain

the sight of this fire from the deep, and carry along with him the omen of my death.'

[1]      'Still fly, plunge deeper in the bowering wood,
       Averse, as Dido did with gesture stern
       From her false friend's approach in Hades, turn,
    Wave us away, and keep thy solitude.'
                    The Scholar Gipsy, by Matthew Arnold.

[2] 'At length she started away and fled unforgiving into the shades of the forest, where her former husband, Sychaeus, feels with all her sorrows and loves her with a love equal to her own.'

them in a consistent course, yet no mere analytic insight into the springs of action can explain the process by which a great artist works. The beings of his imagination seem to acquire an existence independent of the experience and of the deliberate intentions of their author, and to inform this experience and mould these intentions as much as they are informed and moulded by them. Virgil's imagination in the creation of Dido seems to be possessed in this way. She grows more and more real as her passion deepens. Virgil's intention in this representation may have been to show the tragic infatuation of a woman's love—

furens quid femina possit :

but his sympathetic insight into this passion—an insight already shown in the Eclogues—stimulates the forces of his imagination to a nobler as well as a more vital creation than in any other of his impersonations. Dido ranks for all times as one of the great heroines of poetry. So long as she appears on the scene the interest in the exhibition of her nature overpowers all other interests. But this is not the case with Virgil's other personages. We are more interested in what they say and in what happens to them than in what they are. In other words, it is by his oratorical and descriptive, rather than by his dramatic faculty, that he secures the attention of his readers. As oratory was one of the most important powers in ancient life, so it became a prominent element in ancient epic and dramatic poetry,—in Homer, Ennius, and Virgil, as well as in Sophocles, Euripides, and the Roman tragedians. The oratory of the Aeneid shows nothing of the speculative power—of the application of great ideas to life—which gives the profoundest value not only to many speeches in Sophocles, but also to some of those in the Iliad, and notably to such as proceed from the mouth of Odysseus. It cannot equal the vivid naturalness of the speeches of Nestor, nor the impassioned grandeur of those of Achilles. Neither is it characterised by the subtle psychological analysis which is the most interesting quality in the rhetoric of Euripides. On the other hand, it is not disfigured by the forensic special pleading and word-fencing which is an occasional flaw in the dramatic art of Sophocles, and a pervading mannerism in that of the younger poet. The impression of grave political deliberation is left on the mind by some of the fragments of Ennius more effectually than by anything uttered in the councils of gods or men in the Aeneid. But it is in the greatest of modern epics that the full force of intellect and feeling animating grave councils of state is most grandly idealised. The speeches in Virgil, though they want the intellectual power and the majestic largeness of utterance of those in Milton, are, like his, stately and dignified in expression; they are disfigured by no rhetorical artifice of fine-spun argument or exaggerated emphasis; they are rapid with the vehemence of scorn and indignation, fervid with martial pride and enthusiasm, or, occasionally, weighty with the power of controlled emotion. They have the ring of Roman oratory, as it is heard in the animated declamation of Livy, and sometimes seem to anticipate the reserved force and 'imperial brevity' of Tacitus. They give a true voice to 'the high, magnanimous Roman mood,' and to the fervour of spirit with which that mood was associated. And this effect is sometimes increased by the use which the polished poet of the Augustan Age makes of the grave, ardent, but unformed utterances—'rudes et inconditae voces'—of the epic and tragic poets of the Republic.

The descriptive faculty of Virgil is quite unlike that of Homer, but yet it has great excellences of its own. In the Iliad and Odyssey man appears 'vigorous and elastic such as poetry saw him first, such as poetry would ever see him[1];' and the outward world is described in the clear forms and the animated movement which impress themselves immediately on the sense and mind of men thus happily organised. Virgil too presents to us the varied spectacle of human life and of the outward world under many impressive aspects. But these aspects of things do not affect the mind with the immediate

[1] Landor's Pentameron.

impulse which the natural man receives from them, and of which he retains the vivid picture in his mind. As in his pastoral poems and in the Georgics Virgil seems to abstract from the general aspect of things the characteristic sentiment which Nature inspires in particular places and at particular times, and to see the scene which he describes under the influence of that sentiment, so in the Aeneid various human 'situations' are conceived under the influence of some sense of awe or wonder, of beauty or pathos, of local or antique association; and the whole description is so presented as to bring this central interest into prominent relief. The thought of the whole situation, not the sequence of events in time or causal connexion, is what determines the grouping and subordination of details.

Thus in the description of the storm in Book i., the dominant feeling by the light of which the circumstances are to be realised is that of sudden and overwhelming power in the elements and of man's impotence to contend against them. In the description of the harbour in which the ships of Aeneas find refuge we feel the sense of calm and peace after storm and danger. In the interview between Venus and her son the impression left on the mind is that of a mysterious supernatural grace enhancing the charm of human beauty, such as is produced by the pictorial representations of religious art. We seem to look on the rising towers and dwellings of Carthage with that joyful sense of wonder and novelty with which the thought of the beginning of great enterprises, or of the discovery of unknown lands, and the first view of ancient and famous cities, such as Rome or Venice, appeal to the imagination. In the second Book the effect of the whole representation is enhanced by the sentiment of awe and mystery with which night, and darkness, and the intermittent flashes of light which break the darkness, impress the mind. Thus as a prelude to the terrible and tragical scenes afterwards represented, the apparition of Hector comes before Aeneas in the deepest stillness of the night—

> Tempus erat quo prima quies mortalibus aegris
> Incipit [1].

Then follow the confused sights and sounds of battle, like those of the νυκτομαχία in the seventh Book of Thucydides and of that in the Vitellian war of Tacitus,—the spectacle revealed by the light of the burning city—

> Sigaea igni freta lata relucent [2];

the vivid gleams in which the death of Priam, the cowering figure of Helen, the majestic forms of the Olympian gods taking part in the work of destruction, are for a moment disclosed out of the surrounding darkness, the alarm and bewilderment of the escape from the house of Anchises and of the vain attempt of Aeneas to recover the lost Creusa—

> Horror ubique, animos simul ipsa silentia terrent [3].

The third Book is pervaded by the feeling of the sea,—not as in the Odyssey of its buoyant and inexhaustible life, nor yet of the dread which it inspired in the earliest mariners,—but in that more modern mood in which it unfolds to the traveller the animated spectacle of islands and coasts famous for their beauty or their historic and legendary associations. In the fifth Book, as is pointed out by Chateaubriand, the effect of the limitless and monotonous prospect of the open sea in producing a sense of weariness and melancholy, such as that expressed in 'The Lotus-eaters'—

>                   ' but evermore
> Most weary seem'd the sea, weary the oar,
> Weary the wandering fields of barren foam,'

is profoundly felt in the passage—

> At procul in sola secretae Troades acta
> Amissum Anchisen flebant cunctaeque profundum
> Pontum adspectabant flentes ; ' heu tot vada fessis
> Et tantum superesse maris,' vox omnibus una [4].

---

[1] ' It was when their first sleep begins to weary mortals.'
[2] ' The broad waters of Sigaeum reflect the fire.'
[3] ' There is dread on every side, while the very silence awes the mind.'
[4] ' But some way off in a lonely bay the Trojan women apart were

It was seen how the sense of supernatural awe adds to the tragic grandeur of the despair and death of Dido, as in the lines, which bear some trace of a vivid passage in Ennius—

> agit ipse furentem
> In somnis ferus Aeneas : semperque relinqui
> Sola sibi, semper longam incomitata videtur
> Ire viam, et Tyrios deserta quaerere terra[1].

Thus too the mind is prepared for the spectacle revealed in the Descent into Hell by the awful sublimity of the Invocation—

> Di quibus imperium est animarum umbraeque silentes[2].

The description of the funeral rites of Pallas produces that complex impression of sadness and solemnity mixed with proud memories and thoughts of the pomp and circumstance of war which affects men in the present day, when witnessing the spectacle of the funeral of some great soldier who has died full of years and honour—

> Post bellator equus positis insignibus Aethon
> It lacrimans guttisque umectat grandibus ora.
> Hastam alii galeamque ferunt, nam cetera Turnus
> Victor habet.　Tum moesta phalanx Teucrique sequuntur
> Tyrrhenique omnes et versis Arcades armis[3].

In the employment of illustrative imagery Virgil is much more sparing than Homer.　The varied forces of Nature and of animal life supplied materials to the Greek poet by which to enhance the poetical sense of the situation which he de-

---

weeping for their lost Anchises, and as they wept were gazing on the deep— "Ah, to think that so many dangerous waters, so vast an expanse of sea remained still for them, the weary ones!" was the cry of all.'

[1] 'In her dreams Aeneas himself fiercely drives her before him in her frenzy; and she seems ever to be left all alone, ever to be going uncompanioned on a long road, and to be searching for her Tyrians on a desert land.'

[2] 'Powers whose empire is over the spirits of the dead, and ye silent shades.'

[3] 'Behind his war-horse Aethon, with all his trappings laid aside, goes weeping, wetting his face with great drops.　Others bear his spear and shield—the rest of his armour Turnus keeps—then follow in mournful array the Trojans, and all the Tyrrhenian host, and the Arcadians with arms reversed.'

scribes ; and all these forces are apprehended by him with
a vivid feeling of wonder, and presented to the imagination
with a truthful observation of outward signs, and with a sympathetic insight into their innermost nature.   Virgil is not only
more sparing in the use of these figures ; he is also tamer and
less inventive in their application.   In those drawn from the
life of wild animals he, for the most part, reproduces the
Homeric imagery, though we note as one touch of realism in
them that the wolf, familiar to Italy, frequently takes the place
of the lion, which was probably still an object of terror in
Western Asia at the time when Homer lived.   Another class
of images reproduced from Homer is that of those in which
a mortal is compared to an immortal, as at i. 498—

> Qualis in Eurotae ripis, aut per iuga Cynthi,
> Exercet Diana choros, etc.,

though in this some variations are introduced from a simile in
Apollonius.   Another passage of the same kind is immediately
derived from the Alexandrine poet—

> Qualis, ubi hibernam Lyciam Xanthique fluenta[1], etc.

There is, however, another class of 'similes' used by Virgil
in his epic, after the example of the Alexandrines, which can
scarcely be said to fulfil the function of a poetical analogy, but
merely to give a realistic outward symbol of some movement of
the mind or passions, without any imaginative enhancement of
the situation.   Such, for instance, is the comparison at vii.
377, etc. of the mind of Amata to a top whipped by boys round
an empty court,—a comparison suggested by a passage in
Callimachus[2]; and that again at viii. 22, etc. of the variations
of purpose in the mind of Aeneas, produced by the surging sea
of cares besetting him, to the variations of light reflected from
the water in a copper cauldron,—a comparison directly imitated
from Apollonius (iii. 754, etc.).   There are others again of

---

[1] iv. 143, etc.  Referred to in the 'Parallel Passages' in Dr. Kennedy's
notes.
[2] Referred to by M. Benoist.

what may be called a somewhat conventional cast, which acquire individuality from the colour of local associations, such as the introduction (at xii. 715) of two bulls battling together (as they are also described in the Georgics)—

ingenti Sila, summove Taburno;

the comparison (at xii. 701 etc.) of Aeneas, towering in all his warlike power, to Athos or Eryx—

aut ipse, coruscis<br>
Cum fremit ilicibus, quantus, gaudetque nivali<br>
Vertice se attollens, pater Appenninus ad auras[1];

and that at ix. 680, etc., in which the two sons of Alcanor are likened to two tall oaks growing—

Sive Padi ripis Athesim seu propter amoenum[2].

But there are other comparisons in Virgil indicative of more original invention, observation, and reflexion, which serve the true purpose of imaginative analogies, viz. that of exalting the peculiar sentiment with which the poet desires the situation he is describing to be regarded. In the perception of these analogies it is not merely intellectual curiosity that is gratified by the apprehension of the τοῦτο ἐκεῖνο in the phenomena; but the imagination is enlarged by the recognition of analogous forces operating in different spheres, which separately are capable of producing a vivid and noble emotion. As an instance of this perception of the analogy between great forces in different spheres, the one of human, the other of natural activity, we may take the comparison of the Italian host advancing in orderly march after its tumultuous gathering from many quarters, to the movement of mighty rivers when their component waters have found their appointed bed—

Ceu septem surgens sedatis amnibus altus<br>
Per tacitum Ganges, aut pingui flumine Nilus<br>
Cum refluit campis et iam se condidit alveo[3].

[1] 'Or with the grandeur of father Appenninus himself, when he makes his waving ilexes heard aloud, and is glad as he towers with snowy summit to the sky.'

[2] 'Either on the banks of the Po, or by the fair Adige.'

[3] 'As Ganges swelling high in silence with its seven calm streams, or the

Others again show the vivid interest mixed with poetical wonder which animated Virgil's power of observation in his Georgics— as for instance that at i. 430 of the busy workers in Carthage to bees in early summer toiling among the flowery fields—an image ennobled also by Milton, who characteristically describes the bees as 'conferring their state-affairs,' while it is not to their political, but to their industrial, martial, and social or domestic aptitudes,

> (cum gentis adultos
> Educunt fetus)

that Virgil draws attention.   Of the same class is the comparison at iv. 404, etc., of the Trojans preparing to leave the shores of Carthage to the movement of ants engaged in gathering together some heap of corn for their winter's store—

> It nigrum campis agmen, etc.

Others again are suggested by his subtle and sympathetic discernment of the conditions of inward feeling; as the comparison at iv. 70, etc. of Dido to the hind, which, unsuspecting of danger, has received a mortal wound from a hand ignorant of the harm which it has inflicted—

> haeret lateri letalis harundo.

The awe and mystery of the unseen world suggest the comparison of the crowd of shades pressing round Charon's boat to innumerable leaves falling in the woods, or to flocks of birds driven across the sea by the first cold of autumn—

> Quam multa in silvis autumni frigore primo
> Lapsa cadunt folia, aut ad terram gurgite ab alto
> Quam multae glomerantur aves, ubi frigidus annus
> Trans pontum fugat et terris inmittit apricis[1].

The point of comparison in this simile is not merely the obvious

---

Nile when with its fertilising flood it ebbs from the plains, and has already subsided within its channel.'   ix. 30–2.

[1] 'As many as the leaves that fall in the woods at the first cold touch of autumn, or as many as the birds which are gathered to the land from the deep, when the chill of the year banishes them beyond the sea, and wafts them into sunny lands.'   vi. 309–312.

one of the number of leaves falling or birds flying across the sea
in autumn, but rather the inner likeness between the passive
helplessness with which the leaves have yielded to the chill
touch of the year, and that with which the shades—νεκύων
ἀμενηνὰ κάρηνα—have yielded to the chill touch of death. Nor
perhaps is it pressing the language of Virgil too far to suppose
that in the words 'terris inmittit apricis' he means to leave on
the mind a feeling of some happier possibilities in death than
the certainty of 'cold obstruction.' One of the most characteristically Virgilian similes—that at vi. 453—

> qualem primo qui surgere mense
> Aut videt, aut vidisse putat per nubila Lunam—

is almost a translation of the lines of Apollonius (iv. 1447)—

> τὼς ἰδέειν, ὥς τίς τε νέῳ ἐνὶ ἤματι μήνην
> ἢ ἴδεν, ἢ ἐδόκησεν ἐπαχλύουσαν ἰδέσθαι [1],—

but the whole poetical power of the passage consists in the
application of the image to the sudden recognition by Aeneas
of the pale and shadowy form of his forsaken love, dimly discerned through the gloom of the lower world. Other images
are suggested by the poet's delicate sense of grace in flower or
plant, combined with his tender compassion for the beauty of
youth perishing prematurely. Such are those which enable us
more vividly to realise the pathos of the death of Euryalus and
of the burial of Pallas. Yet though these images are characteristically Virgilian, they also bear unmistakeable traces of
imitation. The lines—

> Purpureus veluti cum flos succisus aratro
> Languescit moriens, lassove papavera collo
> Demisere caput, pluvia cum forte gravantur [2];

and again—

---

[1] 'Like the moon when one sees it early in the month, or fancies he has
seen it rise through mists.'
'So to see, as when one sees or fancies he has seen the dim moon in the
early dawn.'
[2] 'As when a purple flower cut down by the plough pines and dies, or as
poppies droop their head wearily, when weighed down by the rain.'

Qualem, virgineo demessum pollice, florem,
Seu mollis violae, seu languentis hyacinthi,
Cui neque fulgor adhuc, nec dum sua forma recessit;
Non iam mater alit tellus, viresque ministrat[1]—

recall not only the thought and feeling of Homer—

μήκων δ' ὡς ἑτέρωσε κάρη βάλεν etc.,

but the cadences and most cherished illustrations of Catullus, in whose imagination the grace of trees and the bloom of flowers are ever associated with the grace and bloom of youth and youthful passion.

Had Virgil lived to devote three more years to the revisal of his work, there is no reason to suppose that he would have added anything to its substance.  Some inconsistencies of statement, as, for instance, that between iii. 256 and vii. 123, would have disappeared, and some difficulties would have been cleared up.  But the chief part of the 'limae labor' would have been employed in bringing the rhythm and diction of the poem to a more finished perfection than that which they exhibit at present.  The unfinished lines in the poem would certainly have been completed and more closely connected with the passages immediately succeeding them.  There is no indication that these lines were left purposely incomplete in order to give emphasis to some pause in the narrative.  Virgil was the last poet likely to avail himself of so inartistic an innovation to give variety to his cadences.  For the most part they appear to be weak props ('tibicines'[2]) used provisionally to fill up the gap between two passages, and indicating but not completing the thought that was to connect them.

What more of elegance, of compact structure, or of varied harmony Virgil might have imparted to his rhythm, it is impossible to determine.  We might conjecture that his aim

[1] 'Like a delicate violet, or a drooping hyacinth, when plucked by a maiden, from which the bloom and the beauty have not yet departed—but the earth does not now nourish it and supply its forces.'
[2] 'Ac ne quid impetum moraretur quaedam imperfecta transmisit, alia levissimis versibus veluti fulsit, quos per iocum pro tibicinibus interponi aiebat ad sustinendum opus, donec solidae columnae advenirent.' Donatus, quoted by Ribbeck in the Life prefixed to his smaller edition of Virgil.

would have been, as regards both expression and metrical effect, to act on the maxim 'ramos compesce fluentes,' than to give them ampler scope.   In a long narrative poem like the Aeneid that perfect smoothness and solidity of rhythmical execution which characterise the Georgics—in which poem the position and weight of each single word in each single line is an element contributing to the whole effect—is hardly to be expected.   A narrative poem demands a more easy, varied, and even careless movement than one of which the interest is contemplative, and which requires to be studied minutely line by line and paragraph by paragraph, before its full meaning is realised.   If the movement in the Aeneid appears in some place rougher, or less compact, or more languid than in others, this may be explained not only by the imperfect state in which the poem was left, but by the difficulty or impossibility of maintaining the same uniform level of elevation in so long a flight.   Yet it cannot be said that there is any loss of power, any trace of contentment with a lower ideal of perfection in the general structure of the verse of the Aeneid.   The full capacities of the Latin hexameter for purposes of animated or impressive narrative, of solemn or pathetic representation, of grave or impassioned oratory, of tender, dignified, or earnest appeal to the higher emotions of man, are realised in many passages of the poem.   Virgil's instrument fails, or, at least, is much inferior to Homer's, in aptitude for natural dialogue or for bringing familiar things in the freshness of immediate impression before the imagination.   The stateliness of movement appropriate to such utterances as

> Ast ego quae Divom incedo regina [1]

does not readily adapt itself to the description of the process of kindling a fire or preparing a meal—

> Ac primum silici scintillam excudit Achates,
> Suscepitque ignem foliis atque arida circum
> Nutrimenta dedit rapuitque in fomite flammam [2].

---

[1] 'But I the stately Queen of the Gods.'
[2] 'And first Achates struck a spark from a flint, and caught the light

To English readers the verse of the Aeneid may appear inferior
in majesty and fulness of volume to that of Milton in his passages of most sustained power ; but it is easier and less en-
cumbered and thus more adapted to express various conditions
of human life than the ordinary movement of the modern epic.
It flows in a more varied, weighty, and self-restrained stream
than the more homogeneous and overflowing current of Spenser's
verse. The Latin hexameter became for Virgil an exquisite and
powerful medium for communicating to others a knowledge of
his elevated moods and pensive meditativeness, and for calling
up before their minds that spectacle of a statelier life and a more
august order in the contemplation of which his spirit habitually
lived.

The last revision would also have removed from the poem
some redundancies, obscurities, and weakness of expression.
There is a greater tendency to use ' otiose ' epithets than in
the Georgics, and a minute criticism has taken note of the
number of times in which such words as 'ingens' and 'im-
manis' occur in the poem. Though the interpretation of the
meaning of the Aeneid as a whole is probably as certain as
that of any other great work of antiquity, yet there are passages
in it which still baffle commentators in deciding which of two or
three possible meanings was in the mind of the poet, or whether
he had himself finally resolved what turn he should give his
thought. As there are lines left incomplete, so there are lame
conclusions to lofty and impassioned utterances of feeling.
Such for instance is the prosaic and tautological conclusion of
the passage in which Lausus is brought on the scene—

dignus, patriis qui laetior esset
Imperiis et cui pater haud Mezentius esset [1].

But it is only a microscopic observation of the structure of
the poem that detects such blemishes as these. In the Aeneid

in some leaves, and cast dry sticks about them to feed them, and blew the
spark within the fuel into a flame.'

[1] 'Worthy to be happier in a father's command and to have another
father than Mezentius.'

Virgil's style appears as great in its power of reaching the secrets of the human spirit, as in the Georgics it proved itself to be in eliciting the deeper meaning of Nature. He combines nearly all the characteristic excellences of the great Latin writers. His language appears indeed inferior not only to that of Lucretius and Catullus but even to that of Ennius in reproducing the first vivid impressions of things upon the mind. The phrases of Virgil are generally coloured with the associations and steeped in the feeling of older thoughts and memories. Yet if he seems inferior in direct force of presentation, he unites the two most marked and generally dissociated characteristics of the masters of Latin style,—the exuberance and vivacity of those writers in whom impulse and imagination are strong, such as Cicero, Livy, and Lucretius,— the terseness and compactness of expression, arising either from intensity of perception or reflective condensation, of which the shorter poems of Catullus, the Odes and Epistles of Horace, the writings of Sallust, and the memorial inscriptions of the time of the Republic and of the Empire afford striking examples. Virgil's condensation of expression often resembles that of Tacitus, and seems to arise from the same cause, the restraint imposed by reflexion on the exuberance of a poetical imagination.    By its combination of opposite excellences the style of the Aeneid is at once an admirable vehicle of continuous or compressed narrative, of large or concentrated description, of fluent and impassioned, or composed and impressive oratory.    It possesses also the power, which distinguishes the older Latin writers, of stamping some grave or magnanimous lesson in imperishable characters on the mind—

> Tu ne cede malis sed contra audentior ito.
> Disce puer virtutem ex me verumque laborem,
> Fortunam ex aliis.
> Aude, hospes, contemnere opes et te quoque dignum
> Finge deo [1].

[1] 'Yield not thou to thy hardships, but advance more boldly against them.'

But Virgil is not only great as a Latin writer. The con-current testimony of the most refined minds of all times marks him out as one of the greatest masters of the language which touches the heart or moves the manlier sensibilities, who has ever lived. A mature and mellow truth of sentiment, a con-formity to the deeper experiences of life in every age, a fine humanity as well as a generous elevation of feeling, and some magical charm of music in his words, have enabled them to serve many minds in many ages as a symbol of some swelling thought or over-mastering emotion, the force and meaning of which they could scarcely define to themselves. A striking instance of this effect appears in the words in which Savonarola describes the impulse which forced him to abandon the career of worldly ambition, which his father pressed on him, in favour of the religious life. It was the voice of warning which he ever heard repeating to him the words—

Heu, fuge crudeles terras, fuge litus avarum [1].

And while his tenderness of feeling has made Virgil the familiar friend of one class of minds, his high magnanimous spirit has equally gained for him the admiration of another class. The words of no other poet, ancient or modern, have been so often heard in the great debates of the English Parliament, which more than any other deliberations among men have reproduced the dignified and masculine eloquence familiar to the Roman Senate. One of the greatest masters of expression among living English writers has pointed, as characteristic of the magic of Virgil's style, to ' his single words and phrases, his pathetic half-lines giving utterance, as the voice of Nature herself, to that pain and weariness yet hope of better things which is the experience of her children in every time [2].' It is in

'Learn from me, my child, to bear thee like a man and to strive strenu-ously, from others learn to be fortunate.'

' Have the courage, stranger, to despise riches, and mould thyself too to be a fit companion of the God.'

[1] 'Ah! fly that cruel land, fly that covetous coast.' Mentioned by Mr. Symonds in his History of the Renaissance in Italy.

[2] Grammar of Assent, by J. H. Newman, D.D.

the expression of this weariness and deep longing for rest, in making others feel his own sense of the painful toil and mystery of life and of the sadness of death, his sense too of vague yearning for some fuller and ampler being, that Virgil produces the most powerful effect by the use of the simplest words in their simplest application.

> 'O passi graviora—'
> 'Vobis parta quies—'
> 'Dis aliter visum—'
> 'Di, si qua est caelo pietas—'
> 'Heu vatum ignarae mentes—'
> 'Iam pridem invisus superis et inutilis annos
>   Demoror—'
> 'Si pereo hominum manibus periisse iuvabit—'
> 'Noctes atque dies patet atri ianua Ditis—'
> 'Nesciaque humanis precibus mansuescere corda—'
> 'Impositique rogis iuvenes ante ora parentum—'
> 'Quod te per caeli iucundum lumen et auras—'
> 'Tendebantque manus ripae ulterioris amore—'
> 'Securos latices et longa oblivia potant—[1]'

these and many other pregnant sayings affect the mind with a strange potency, of which perhaps no account can be given except that they make us feel, as scarcely any other words do, the burden of the mystery of life, and by their marvellous beauty, the reflexion, it may be, from some light dimly discerned or imagined[2] beyond the gloom, they make it seem more easy to be borne.

---

[1] To attempt to translate these 'pathetic half-lines' etc., apart from their context, would only be to spoil them, without conveying any sense of the feeling latent in them.

[2] Aut videt, aut vidisse putat.


**THE END.**